The Archaeology of Korea surveys Korean prehistory from the earliest paleolithic settlers, perhaps half a million years ago, through the formation of the Three Kingdoms and on to the creation of United Silla in AD 668, when the peninsula was largely united for the first time. The author treats the development of state-level societies and their relationship to polities in Japan and China, and the development of a Korean ethnic identity. Emphasizing the particular features of the region, the author dispels the notion that the culture and traditions of Korea are but pale imitations of those of its neighbors, China and Japan.

Sarah Nelson has specialized in Korean archaeology for twenty years. She draws on her own research and that of Korean colleagues; and while much of the material comes from the Republic of Korea, the north is considered as far as sources permit.

CAMBRIDGE WORLD ARCHAEOLOGY

THE ARCHAEOLOGY OF KOREA

BRIDGET AND RAYMOND ALLCHIN The Rise of Civilization in India and Pakistan
DAVID W. PHILLIPSON African Archaeology
CLIVE GAMBLE The Palaeolithic Settlement of Europe
ALASDAIR WHITTLE Neolithic Europe: a Survey
CHARLES HIGHAM The Archaeology of Mainland Southeast Asia

CAMBRIDGE WORLD ARCHAEOLOGY

THE ARCHAEOLOGY OF KOREA

SARAH MILLEDGE NELSON

Department of Anthropology
University of Denver

CAMBRIDGE
UNIVERSITY PRESS

Published by the Press Syndicate of the University of Cambridge
The Pitt Building, Trumpington Street, Cambridge CB2 1RP
40 West 20th Street, New York, NY 10011–4211, USA
10 Stamford Road, Oakleigh, Victoria 3166, Australia

First published 1993

Printed in Great Britain at the University Press, Cambridge

A catalogue record for this book is available from the British Library

Library of Congress cataloguing in publication data

Nelson, Sarah M., 1931–
The archaeology of Korea / Sarah Milledge Nelson.
    p.   cm. – (Cambridge world archaeology)
Includes bibliographical references and index.
ISBN 0 521 40443 6. – ISBN 0 521 40783 4 (pbk.)
1. Korea – Antiquities.   2. Korea – Civilization – To 935.
3. Archaeology – Korea.   I. Title.   II. Series.
DS903.N45   1993
951.9'01 – dc20   91–40202 CIP

ISBN 0 521 40443 6 hardback
ISBN 0 521 40783 4 paperback

wv

CONTENTS

ILLUSTRATIONS

TABLES

PREFACE AND ACKNOWLEDGMENTS

This book has been written in the hope of placing Korea on the map of world archaeology, from which it has been conspicuously absent. In that spirit it is offered to several publics: to professional archaeologists working in other regions, to armchair archaeologists interested in discoveries worldwide, to students needing a resource on Korea, to Asianists who are primarily historians or art historians. It is not a book for insiders, not a book directed at the small cadre of Koreanists with the background to gnaw over a few delicious bones, partly because too little has been published in Korean archaeology for this to be productive, but, more important, because it deserves a wider audience.

In 1970, when I first went to Korea, I discovered that very little was written about the archaeology in English or other western languages. Learning about the archaeology of Korea was not a task to be taken lightly. It required a reading knowledge of the language and its complex grammar, in both *han'gul*, the Korean alphabet, and *hanja*, Chinese characters. Beyond those barriers, the Korean language is more adapted to nuance than to straightforward declarative sentences. When reading Korean with various native Korean tutors, I would ask exactly where in the sentence it said such-and-such. "You have to catch between the lines," they told me. And sometimes even my tutors could not be sure they had caught it right.

Learning about the archaeology of Korea required help from many Korean archaeologists, who have been generous throughout the years with their knowledge and their publications. To all of them I owe a great debt.

My first trip, when I had exactly one year to create and carry out a dissertation project, I was very fortunate to meet and be assisted by the top echelon of Korean archaeologists: Dr. Kim Won-yong, the director of the National Museum in Seoul, and Dr. Sohn Pow-key of Yonsei University. I am very grateful that both took time out of their busy schedules to give me guidance. Pak Dong-won, Professor of Geography at Seoul National University, tutored me in Chinese characters, and equally importantly he introduced me to his classmate, Im Hyo-jai, an archaeologist at Seoul National University, with whom I devised a project. During that year I also met Choi Mong-lyong, Lim Byung-tae, Han Byong-sam and others who were all extremely helpful.

Circumstances did not permit my return to Korea until 1978, when I was invited by the Institute for Shipboard Education to be an interport lecturer on Korea for Semester-at-Sea. Disembarking in Pusan, I took a couple of weeks in

Korea to reestablish contacts and discuss the latest developments in Korean archaeology. My thanks to all those who helped, including Kim Jong-hak in Pusan, and to my colleagues previously mentioned who smoothed my path. In 1983, with a grant awarded by the Academy of Korean Studies, I spent another month researching in Korea, both in Seoul and around the peninsula visiting sites, museums and universities. Particularly helpful were Kim Dong-ho at Dong-A University, Yi Yung-jo at Chungbuk University, Han Byong-sam at Kyongju National Museum, and Chung Yong-hwa at Yongnan University in Taegu. The colleagues I always turned to were helpful as ever, especially Im Hyo-jai, Kim Won-yong and Sohn Pow-key. I met Hwang Yong-hoon at Kunghee University, and Professor Chung Yong-ho of Danguk University, in the company of Martha Sloan. I was introduced to Lee Yong-nam, a microbiologist with an avocational interest in archaeology, who facilitated my work as well. The Academy of Korean Studies awarded me a grant to have illustrations drawn for this book, so they have my double gratitude.

A grant from the International Cultural Society of Korea allowed me to spend another month in Korea in the fall of 1986. I was taken to important newly discovered sites by many of my old colleagues and aided in various ways by Kay Black, Kim Ju-hyung, Rose Lee and Levke Schlütter. Han Byong-sam, Han Churl-mo and Chi Kongil were very helpful at the National Museum, as were all the group at Seoul National University – both the museum and the department.

The Pacific Science Congress in Seoul in 1987 offered another opportunity to visit Korea, and I profited again from the aid of many helpful people: Kim Byong-mo, Yi Seon-bok, Bae Ki-dong, Lim Young-jin and Pak Soon-bal among others. I visited sites in Seoul with Gina Barnes, and in Kwangju with Fumiko Ikawa-Smith, where we toured the Juam Dam sites with Kim Hee-su. Laurel Kendall rescued me when my hotel was the target of a labor strike.

In 1989 Earthwatch and the Center for Field Research awarded me a grant for a month of fieldwork in Korea. With the help of a dozen volunteers and two students, Patty Conte and Leslie Johnson, I carried out a project on sites in three different regions. Lee In-suk was very helpful at Seoul National University, and Chung Yang-mo at the National Museum. Thanks also to Han Yong-hee at the Chinju Museum and An Jun-bae at Pusan Women's University. The unsung hero of the occasion was Choe Chong-pil, who assisted with everything from logistics and reservations for the group at *yogwans* to discussions of the methodology and interpretations of Korean archaeology, and brought his bright and eager students along to mingle with the volunteers. Inge and Gunter Rösch were marvelously hospitable and helpful. Thanks also to Choong-Soon Kim, who was also researching in Korea at the time.

Most recently I went to Korea in the summer of 1990. Once again, my thanks to Im Hyo-jai, Lee In-suk, Lee Yong-nam, Choe Chong-pil, Bae Ki-dong, Dominique Kassab and the Rösches, for making my stay pleasant and productive. Also, a special thanks to the library of the National Museum of Korea for facilitating my work there.

In the meantime I became interested in the connections between Korea and northern China. In 1981, 1982 and 1985 I led students and friends on tours of various archaeological sites of China, after beginning to study the Chinese language in 1981. In 1987, accompanied by Ardith Hunter, I toured the Dongbei region. Our interpreter, Mingming Shan, was invaluable. The Chinese archaeologists in Shenyang, Chaoyang, Changchun, Jilin and Harbin were extremely helpful and hospitable. I received a grant from the Committee on Scholarly Communication with The People's Republic of China (CSCPRC) to return to China for six weeks the following year. Most recently, I attended the International Circum-Bohai Archaeology Conference in Dalian with the assistance again of the CSCPRC. I profited not only from papers presented at the meeting, but also from the opportunity for long conversations with Song Nai Rhee and David Goodrich, as well as my "pen-pal" from Novosibirsk, Sergei Komissarov, and many Japanese and Chinese colleagues.

I must also extend thanks for many conversations about the book, and about archaeology in general, with Susan Kent, Linda Donley-Reid, Fumiko Ikawa-Smith, Nancy Price, Lothar von Falkenhausen, Anne Underhill, Peter Bleed, Bong Won Kang and too many others to mention every one. My husband, Harold S. Nelson, deserves thanks as well, for his company in some of my travels, for his photography, for his patience, and not least for my first acquaintance with Korea.

Thanks to Nancy Levesque, Janice Straley, Kathy Williams, Paul Moskoe and Christina Todd, who helped enter the various transformations of the manuscript into the computer; to Julie Hoff, Kristi Butterwick, Troy Sagrillo, Wa-jia Tang and Heather Shepard, who drew the figures and maps; to H.J. Kwon, who located sites on the maps; and to Michelle Bahe who helped check the bibliography and performed many other tedious chores. Finally, many thanks to Jessica Kuper, editor for archaeology at Cambridge University Press, for her patience and goodwill, and to Marigold Acland and Frances Brown for their care with the manuscript.

Naturally, no one is to be blamed for my stubbornness in preferring my own interpretations, and I personally lay claim to whatever errors lurk in the manuscript. As to my interpretations, I have tried to be consistent, and to have articulated my thoughts clearly enough to allow for fruitful discussion with any dissenters.

A few words may be needed about the transliteration of Korean words and names. For words and place names, I have used a modified form of the McCune-Reischauer system, omitting diacritical marks but using the English letters that best convey spoken Korean. I made this decision hoping it would make the book more accessible to non-Koreanists, since the results appear less intimidating, and words can be pronounced by English speakers in a reasonable approximation to the Korean. The official Korean transliteration is true to the Korean alphabet, but looks difficult in English – "Jeonra" for "Cholla," for example. An exception is made for spellings common in English, such as Seoul, and for personal names. In the bibliography, I have used whatever English transliteration each scholar seemed to prefer for his own name, judging from publications or tables of contents in English. This decision caused some problems – for example the same name can be written in English as Lee, Li, Rhee, Rhi or Yi and sometimes the same author has used several alternative spellings of his name. In those cases I selected the most common usage as the basic heading. The bibliography would have become impossibly unwieldy if the variant spelling had been noted in every instance, but wherever a name appears in a western language publication I have adhered to that spelling. The titles of papers written in Korean are given in translation only, with the notation that they are in Korean. To give non-Korean readers more access to the literature, names of journals are in the original language. I hope the bibliography will be a resource through which the interested reader can expand his/her knowledge beyond this book.

CHAPTER I

INTRODUCTION

Korean archaeology is important not only for understanding the unique sequences of prehistoric events in East Asia, but also for the light it can shed on cultural processes. This book attempts to place the archaeology of Korea in both these contexts, with an emphasis on the variability in the archaeological record and the multiple interpretations given to that variation. In the past decade excavations from the Korean earth have produced a variety of unexpected discoveries, which individually and in the aggregate require a rethinking of Korea's archaeological sequences as well as new understandings of the development of socio-political forms on the Korean peninsula. From paleolithic hand-axes to Silla tombs, from bronze daggers to polished jades, recent archaeological finds demand alternative interpretations of Korean prehistory. Korean archaeologists and a handful of foreign scholars have produced fruitful works, which are summarized and evaluated in this book.

Archaeology in Korea

Korean archaeological interpretations vary in both method and theory. Some are dependent on ancient documents, some on traditions, some on nationalistic pride, some on anthropological concepts. This book seeks to balance these viewpoints, and to present the discoveries based on the best evidence currently available. Probably no Korean archaeologist will agree with all my interpretations, but probably nothing I have written will be without some concurrence.

Several discussions of problems in Korean archaeology help to point up the difficulties and lead to solutions. Western perspectives have been voiced from several different traditions. I present here views from Germany, England, the United States and Italy before turning to the most recent and eloquent Korean statement of concerns and solutions.

Lothar von Falkenhausen (1987) considers four problems in Korean prehistory. First, the problem of the definition of territory. Although in the time period of this book there was no polity of Korea, peoples who might be considered Korean occupied a *Grossraum* (extraterritorial sphere of influence) stretching from the eastern border of the Mongols into central Japan. In speaking of prehistoric Korea, what territory do we mean? Second, Falkenhausen questions whether the inhabitants of this *Grossraum* belong to a single cultural entity. It is possible that dwellers in the Korean peninsula were ethnically heterogeneous. We know nothing of either language diversity or self-defined ethnic units. Third, it is necessary to consider whether the appearance of cultural elements from China and Manchuria came about all at once or at different times, and whether these elements arrived by diffusion or movement of peoples. He points out that "it is not enough to know when and from where single new cultural elements came to Korea" (Falkenhausen 1987:4). Finally, Falkenhausen mentions the liability of relying too heavily on the historic texts.

A different set of problems is highlighted by Gina Barnes (1983). She discusses the need to analyze the bases of power and the social structure, particularly of the Wonsamguk and Samguk periods, respectively prehistoric and historic times. The approach to these problems is complicated by the difficulties with periodization, including the lack of congruence between traditional dates and archaeology. Heterogeneity in material culture, she points out, is often interpreted as if it had only one cause (usually temporal change) rather than many, including regional differences and status differences.

Focusing on earlier time periods, Nelson (1983) emphasizes the problems of the over-use of typology, the lack of attention to variability, the need for intensive study of paleoenvironments, and the need to explicate the steps through which conclusions are reached. Maurizio Riotto (1989) is less analytical, but speaks in his preface of "the complex situation of Korean archaeology, where doubts are surely more numerous than certainties."

Kim Won-yong, in the keynote speech at the Sixth International Conference on Korean Studies, demonstrates that he is aware of these problems, and proposes some directions for the study of Korean culture. First, he attacks the question of what is traditional culture. Pointing out the flow of cultural forms and ideas, he defines traditional culture as "cultural materials that are transmitted and received communally within one society." He goes on to warn that, "If we are not careful, however, we can mistake the totality of its culture elements for pure racial originality or the culture complex that emerged with the race as an eternally unchanging entity" (Kim W.Y. 1987b:4). He suggests as a research plan that Korean cultural study should look for continuous elements that are the "root and stem." Kim also notes the "nationalistic inclination" (p. 8) of many scholars, taking North Korean scholars to task for admitting of no foreign influences on the peninsula, and some South Koreans for subjective views.

Since Korean archaeology is often interpreted through a historical lens, it is also useful to consider the differences between the writing of history in North and South Korea. North Korean historians present a strictly Marxist view, dividing the early societies into "primitive" and "ancient" types. Since the definition of ancient society includes slavery, it is necessary to find evidence of this in the early Korean states (Kang M.G. 1990).

Several serious discussions of methodology appeared in Korean journals in the 1980s, discussing classification (Son B.H. 1982), typology (Choi S.N. 1984), seriation (Lee H.J. 1983), chronology (Choi S.N. 1989a, Lee H.J. 1984) and

radiocarbon dating (Choi S.N. 1982a). These bring a more self-conscious application of various methods to Korean archaeology. Kim Won-yong acknowledges western contributions (1982d), but points with pride to the largely
indigenous development of Korean archaeology (1988).

Korean prehistory is frequently formulated in Korea as ethnicity in retrospect,
that is, perceiving the elucidation of the formation of the Korean people as the
chief purpose of archaeology. The whole Korean peninsula is populated with
Koreans, distinct in culture and language from any other group. Korea includes
no acknowledged minorities or remnant populations. What is it that makes
Koreans a distinct ethnic group? How was that ethnicity forged? Where did the
people come from? How much of the culture came with immigrants, and how
much grew on peninsular Korean soil? These questions are asked of archaeology,
but ethnicity as a concept is difficult to approach with archaeological data.
However, applying ethnic labels to archaeological sites is not uncommon,
especially in East Asia, where the dominance of the Chinese written tradition
seems to demand this response.

The concept of ethnicity is elusive enough when applied to living peoples.
How then shall we recognize ethnicity when only the material remnants of
cultural systems, impoverished through the ages in various natural and cultural
ways, are the major source of data? Archaeologists from opposite sides of the
globe have argued that ethnicity cannot be studied with archaeological data
(Mongait 1969:17, Rouse 1986:62) or that there are better questions to ask of the
data than the "genealogical affinity between two cultural units" (Binford
1968:8). And yet, when considering the archaeology of Korea, it is difficult to
avoid the question of ethnicity. Koreans consider the ethnicity of past
inhabitants of the Korean peninsula to be the most interesting and important
facet of archaeological explanations for several reasons. Rescuing the national
history from some colonialist interpretations of the Japanese can be a matter of
national pride (e.g. Sohn *et al.* 1987). In a population such as Korea which is now
homogeneous in physical type, in language and in culture, the ancestors of one
are believed to be the ancestors of all. And for a society which has not been
expansionist for over a millennium but on the contrary has been invaded virtually from all sides (with even a cultural invasion from America), the ethnicity of
their forebears, the formation of the Korean people distinct from all their
neighbors, is an important local concern.

Korea today is a peninsula with a unified culture and language, divided in half
by world political decisions which arose from exogenous concerns without
reference to the local situation. The peninsula was divided into north and south,
and influenced respectively by east and west. The formerly industrialized north –
now the People's Democratic Republic of Korea – with its water power and raw
materials, has been economically surpassed by the formerly agricultural south –
the Republic of Korea, *Taehan Minguk* – so that recently ROK has ceased to be
considered a developing nation and is now a member of the industrialized world.

Neither ethnicity nor environment will explain this phenomenon, although both will contribute to an understanding of the divided peninsula. Only a perspective that includes the effects of world politics and the world economy will allow a full understanding of the situation.

The same is true of prehistory, when the "world" of the Korean peninsula was much smaller, but included large parts of East Asia. As long as the Korean peninsula has been inhabited, even back to the Pleistocene, the inhabitants have participated in regional change and regional events. Ancient Korea cannot be understood apart from ancient East Asia. To use the archaeology of Korea simply to describe the development of the Korean people is to lose some of the richness of explanation which archaeology can provide. Striking relationships in artifact styles and behavioral and organizational patterns link prehistoric Korea to Manchuria and Siberia, as well as to China and Japan. This is not to say that Korean archaeology is merely derivative from its neighbors. Korea's prehistory reveals its own styles and patterns, its own development. Although there were diverse elements in its formation, Korean ethnicity has deep roots, having been firmly forged no later than AD 668, when United Silla created a political unity in the peninsula. This Koreanness may have been woven from several strands, but it was strongly woven, creating a Korean ethnicity which has tenaciously survived in spite of many centuries of Chinese cultural overlay and more recent Japanese conquest and western influences.

Western views of Korea

The splendors of the archaeology of Korea contrast sharply with western (especially American) stereotypes of the peninsula. The persistent undervaluing of this distinctive, ancient and artistic heritage stems from a number of historical causes. For most Americans, images of Korea were shaped by reports from the Korean War, and are generally negative: bleak, cold, impoverished. Of course, these were not the only impressions brought back. Even in the midst of the war the trained archaeological eye found traces of the past (MacCord 1958). Archaeological discoveries were made by Americans among the later troops, as well (Chase 1960, Bowen 1979), but these are rare exceptions. Soldiers are not necessarily accurate cultural reporters.

In addition to these recent impressions of Korea among the general public, even among scholars a widespread notion lingers that Korean culture is merely a pale imitation of China, or perhaps Japan, and is therefore of secondary importance. While it is true that there are traceable connections with both China and Japan, as noted above, styles, trade goods and people flowed both ways. Korea was sometimes the donor, although more often the recipient, of ideas, things and populations. The cultures that flourished in Korea before the introduction of Buddhism were organized in indigenous Korean ways, and produced some remarkable artifacts and social structures with their own unique characteristics.

Chinese artifacts in Korean sites stand out as distinct and intrusive items, contrasting sharply in form and ornamentation with analogous Korean artifacts. Korea is not and was not a mere off-shoot of China.

Nor is Korea a clone of Japan. Cultural similarities exist in the present, as in the past, but there are marked differences as well. Much that is common to the two is of Korean origin, or Chinese culture mediated by Korea. Western scholars have been too receptive to Japanese claims of influence on Korea, when the archaeological evidence strongly suggests that for much of the early days the reverse was the case. In the distant past with which this book is concerned, there was no polity of Korea, no unity of the Korean peninsula. But it is often unacknowledged that there was also no "Japan," and even though the Shang state in China existed in the second millennium BC, the boundaries of the polity (or polities) of early China were considerably less expansive than the China of today. The whole of East Asia was frequently in ferment, with competing groups elbowing and jostling each other, changing and being changed. Archaeology allows us a glimpse of these complex relationships, a hint of the richness of the past mosaic.

Perceiving Korean prehistory as an entity to be studied in its own right, and not as derivative, has another value. It contributes to an understanding of East Asia as a whole, and allows a more balanced reconstruction of prehistory and protohistory in this region than those based merely on Chinese and Japanese documents. The archaeology of Manchuria and Siberia, with important connections to Korea at various times, has also suffered from western preoccupation with China and Japan. The systematic interaction of East Asian cultures, and Korea's participation in the Chinese "Interaction Sphere" (Chang 1977), can only be appreciated by including Korea's archaeology on an equal basis.

The view of the prehistory of Korea presented in this volume is an outsider's view. The potential for increased objectivity inheres in this circumstance, for the author has no nationalistic stake in the interpretations. Both adherence to tradition and conclusions for the sake of national pride are thus minimized. On the other hand, no matter how familiar with the language and culture, the foreigner can never be an insider with shared cultural ideas, some of which may bear upon the prehistoric past. Both outsider and insider perspectives are useful, but they are likely to be different (Rowlands 1987:2).

Geographic limits

Geographically, present-day Korea is separated from the Asian continent by two rivers arising from Paektusan, the highest mountain in Korea, and zigzagging generally northeast and southwest to the coasts. With seas on its other three sides, the Korean boundaries appear to be almost as distinct as those of an island. This, however, is an illusion. Many other boundaries have divided ancient states; there is nothing "natural" about the Yalu and Tumen rivers as a boundary.

Furthermore, the territory within the peninsula did not have a uniform cultural pattern during most of the prehistoric past. However, the geographic integrity of the peninsula may have contributed to the development of a unique cultural and linguistic group, distinguishable from their neighbors on all sides. Since at various times in prehistory and protohistory cultures that can be identified as Korean spread beyond the boundaries of the present divided land, this volume does not rigidly follow the present borders, but also considers relevant much of Manchuria, especially the Liaodong peninsula, at various times in the past.

Korean physical anthropology, language and culture

Careful anthropological studies in many parts of the world have long ago demonstrated that there is no necessary connection between "race," language and culture (Boas 1940), but, as noted above, modern Korea exhibits a remarkable congruence among the three. The Korean language is a prime example of both the distinctiveness of the peninsula from nearby lands and the relative homogeneity within. The Korean language is a separate language which does not grade by dialects into any other known language. It is spoken as the primary language of the entire Korean population, and dialect differences are minor throughout the length of the peninsula (Lee K.M. 1977).

The Korean and Chinese languages are entirely different and unrelated, although the Korean vocabulary is enriched by Chinese loan words. Like English words from Greek and Latin roots, they are much used in scholarly discourse. Many of these Sino-Korean words have final consonants, possibly preserving ancient Chinese pronunciations to some extent, but some of the variation in pronunciation may also have arisen as assimilation to Korean pronunciation. The Korean and Japanese languages have comparable grammatical structures (Miller 1980), but vocabulary similarities appear to be largely based on identity of Chinese loan words in both languages, and less on common lexical items. The differentiation of the Korean and Japanese languages from a common Altaic stem is believed to have occurred about four thousand years ago (Lee K.M. 1977, Miller 1980). An original homeland in the steppes, followed by a move to a region south of the Altai mountains, is believed to antedate the fragmentation into separate languages (Miller 1986). Linguists place the Tungusic speakers in the Altaic family tree (Lee Y.J. 1982), accounting for the ease with which the bronze-using inhabitants of Korea are pigeonholed as Tungusics.

Koreans as a people can be distinguished as a physical type, different from the Japanese and Chinese. Physical comparison of many kinds, including blood types and fingerprints (Ohno 1970), show the Koreans to be related to their neighbors, but possessing their own distinctive patterns of gene frequencies. Human bones are rare in archaeological contexts and few of those that have been unearthed have been studied, allowing little to be said about the prehistoric population (Kwon 1990, 1986, Kim 1986a:21).

Distinctively Korean cultural patterns in the present are many. Ethnicity is often expressed most forcefully in traits such as food, clothing and shelter. Korean houses feature the *ondol* floor, a unique heating arrangement of flues conducting warm air from the cooking fire through pipes under the floors to heat the house. Possibly a relative of the heated *kang* bed of north China, the *ondol* floor differs in that it heats entire rooms rather than only the raised bed. Chairs were not traditionally used in Korea; it was more comfortable to sit on a cushion directly on the warm floor. Korean culinary practices also differ from those of China and Japan, both in regard to habitual modes of food preparation and the content of the basic meal. While most Asians eat rice as their basic staple, traditional Korean food runs to soups and stews as well, and lacks both the emphasis on raw sea products of Japan and the chopped dishes of China. Korean *kimchi* may have its counterparts elsewhere, but this vegetable dish is uniquely Korean, dating back to before the introduction of red peppers, when cockscomb flowers were used for spice and color. Traditional Korean clothing is also distinctive, featuring baggy trousers tied at the ankle, and shoes with upturned toes. These differences in the basics of food, clothing and shelter suggest a long cultural continuity, a common ethnicity formed in the distant past. In fact, the *ondol* floor, and jars suitably shaped to have contained a prehistoric ancestor of *kimchi*, occur in prehistoric sites, while traditional clothing and houses are represented in tomb murals of 1,500 years ago and older.

Shamanism, dominated by the female *mudang*, still has adherents in Korea, especially in the countryside where traditional values are best preserved. Kim Won-yong (1990) has pointed to shamanism as a basic trait of the traditional culture. The archaic language used in *kut*, the *mudang* rituals, along with paraphernalia that echoes the distant past, and the use of ancient percussion instruments, all suggest a long development distinct from Japan and China. The emphasis on dance, on rhythmic instruments, and on dangling attachments to the accouterments of the whirling *mudang*, combining noise, glitter and rhythm, hark back to earlier times.

Having made the point, however, that Korea should be seen as a distinct and separate culture not derived from China, it is necessary to reemphasize the need for viewing Korea within the larger perspective of East Asia. Korea was sufficiently isolated at times to develop its own ethnicity, and had enough contact at other times to effect profound changes in the social, economic and political structure. External pressures, from Manchuria, the Soviet Maritime region and eastern Siberia, in addition to Japan and China, must be taken into account along with internal development. In the attempt to explain the "acceptance" of cultural traits from outside in terms of the culture itself, the possibility of sheer force applied by a technologically dominant external culture, which has its own political and economic goals, cannot be overlooked.

Data sources

The data in this book largely derive from archaeological excavations and surveys. Archaeology in Korea is of relatively recent vintage, and excavations in its short history have been uneven in quality. Apart from an attempt by a certain Chong Chi-hae in 1748 to identify his ancestral tomb by means of digging into a mound (Kim W.Y. 1981:22), the first continued interest in Korea's antiquities was evinced by Japanese archaeologists, after the Japanese annexation of Korea in 1910. Tombs were the initial target of investigation, especially those around Kyongju, Pyongyang and Jian, centers of early Korean capitals. Spectacular finds of usually perishable artifacts including lacquerware, basketry, and cloth attracted worldwide attention. Some attention was paid to megalithic monuments ("dolmens"), which are denser in Korea than elsewhere in East Asia, and some neolithic sites were noted and collected. Perhaps fifty reports resulted from these surveys and excavations (Choi M.L. 1984b:13).

During World War II, archaeology in Korea languished, and since the division of the country at the 38th parallel at the end of World War II it has had separate histories in its two parts. The Korean War provided another setback to archaeological excavations, although at least one site was hastily excavated when exposed by military operations (MacCord 1958). Gradually, following the truce of 1953 when the peninsula was once again divided roughly in the middle, Koreans in both North and South have taken a keen interest in their own past. Archaeology has diverged between North and South, and even the publications look substantially different. In North Korea only *han'gul*, the Korean alphabet, is used (along with quotations from Kim Il-sung), while most archaeological reports in the south include a generous sprinkling of Sino-Korean words represented by Chinese characters.

Over a hundred Korean scholars are now trained in archaeology and various related disciplines, actively pursuing archaeological research in South Korea, in addition to unknown numbers of archaeologists active in the north. Several archaeology journals are being published, and site reports appear from all the major universities and museums as well as some smaller ones. Archaeological reports from the north have been difficult to obtain, and at one time were illegal to own in the Republic of Korea. With the movement toward reunification, however, information about North Korean archaeology has become available in the south (Im 1985b), and an entire bibliography of publications from the north has recently been published (Yi, Lee and Shin 1989).

Excavations with research designs are rare. Much more attention has been paid to the necessary preliminaries of constructing chronologies and typologies than to culture process (Nelson 1983). Systematic surveys have become standard procedures with the need for salvage archaeology at dam sites and for road and building construction, resulting in large numbers of newly discovered sites which must be assessed. Supporting independent environmental evidence is only beginning to be collected and studied by palynologists, paleobotanists, zoologists and geologists, but a great deal of important new evidence has been collected in the past decade.

Documentary sources relate to the protohistory of Korea rather than to prehistory. Purporting to apply to time periods as far back as the end of the Shang dynasty (1122 BC by traditional dating), these documents cannot be accepted uncritically, but neither can they be entirely discounted. Several kinds of texts, written variously in China, Korea and Japan, have pertinent passages, but these ancient writings may be suspect on many grounds. Errors may have crept in as a result of miscopying, editing or deliberate distortion. Some documents are only fragments of the original writings. To the Chinese, Korea was a distant place, inhabited by "barbarians" whose chief value lay in the tribute which might be extracted. No consistency is found in the documents with regard to the kind of information available either through time or within specific regions of Korea. Some of the Chinese documents describe battles in meticulous detail, and others itemize quaint customs. The geography is vague, and scholars disagree about the locations of named rivers or other features. Discussions of the Chinese documents themselves can be found in Gardiner (1969a) and Parker (1890), which also contain partial translations into English.

The Korean *Samguk Sagi* (History of the Three Kingdoms) and *Samguk Yusa* (Memorabilia of the Three Kingdoms) were written in their present form much later than the events they record, although it is thought that they are based on early documents no longer extant. Each of these documents views Korean history through its own distorting lens, either Confucian or Buddhist, presenting mythic founding legends and detailed historical events as equally credible. Japanese sources, more nearly contemporaneous with the Three Kingdoms, tend to ascribe a secondary status to Korea, a stance which may have arisen from motives other than historical accuracy. Some Korean history, especially from the Paekche Kingdom, may be among the sources for the *Nihon Shoki* and *Kojiki*, although with reinterpretations to fit the Japanese model (Hong 1988).

A large literature in several languages covers the exegesis of this body of material, some by scholars with knowledge of ancient as well as modern forms of the original languages, and contrary opinions have been voiced concerning nearly every point. I have noted differences of reading when relating the ancient writings to the archaeological record. The documents are used in this volume not for the purpose of reconstructing historical events, but as paleoethnographic material to be tested against archaeological evidence and occasionally to add detail and color to the dry recitation of archaeological finds.

Ethnographic analogy is used sparingly in this volume. The most useful analogies stem from Korea itself; Korean archaeologists frequently perceive continuities between present and past. Korea has not merely preserved some ancient lifeways and traditions, it has preserved many largely unmixed with exogenous traditions (Osgood 1954). Korea has tended to compartmentalize foreign cultures into separate realms and to maintain an ancient core of traditional norms and behavior relatively unchanged.

Archaeological analogy is also used, to some extent, as much to test the applicability of archaeological inferences from other regions as to supply hypotheses about prehistoric Korea. For example, Korea is in a continental position similar to that of western Europe. Since Korea was partly conquered by Han China as Britain was partly conquered by Rome, there may be lessons to learn from the similarities and differences. General explanations applied to western Europe should be equally applicable to Korea, especially when the explanatory device is related to the geographic position at the edge of the continent.

Korean archaeological sequences

The development of Korean culture can be seen both as a unique history of particular events in the past and as one example of systematic and general cultural processes. But because the specifics of Korean prehistory and protohistory are not generally known in the west, these details need to be presented and the framework of the specific historical sequence constructed before we can begin to understand the processes of these changes.

I have not used the traditional terms paleolithic, neolithic, bronze age and iron age as chapter headings, because these terms are used in Korea with little consistency. The typology of band, tribe, chiefdom and state has been applied to Korean archaeology, but in my opinion the Korean case is not illuminated by reference to this sequence of evolutionary steps. Pigeonholing, or worse, results when, like Cinderella's step-sisters, we must cut off their heels or toes to fit the case. All divisions into time periods are of course arbitrary, but I have chosen to divide the seamless archaeological record into chapters according to major changes in organization, as evident in the archaeological record itself.

After a chapter on the Korean environment, discussion of the archaeology begins with small groups of foragers whose remains pose questions of temporal placement, relationships with other groups in Asia, and the nature of their foraging way of life. Unanticipated recent finds of hand-axes, originally touted as dating from the Middle Pleistocene (but now disputed), have posed new questions while supplying the beginnings of some answers. Other newly excavated cave and open-air sites add new dimensions to an understanding of paleolithic Korea. A number of sites with microcores, microblades, ski-spall blades and the like probably represent a transitional period between the foragers and the early village settlements (Chapter 3).

A ceramic horizon with settled villages appears in Korea with various styles and dates around the peninsula. This manifestation seems to be related to the widespread appearance of simple pottery containers in Asia as early as 12,000 years ago, corresponding to the earliest radiocarbon date for this period. Many more dates cluster around 6000 BC. Although this development is often called "neolithic" in Korea, nothing is directly implied about the beginnings of agriculture in conjunction with the ceramics (Chapter 4).

Early in the second millennium BC (according to radiocarbon dates), a new ceramic horizon with plainer pottery can be recognized in sites along the south coast. Over the next thousand years, rice planting, bronze manufacturing, horseriding and differentiation into social classes began to appear in the Korean peninsula. Various kinds of burial markers are found, including dolmens and cairns, beneath which higher-ranking people were buried with grave goods which marked their special status (Chapter 5).

The introduction of iron coincides with the protohistoric period, for it was probably Korea's iron deposits that attracted Chinese trade and conquest. As a literate civilization, the Chinese recorded snippets of Korean history, geography and culture. Still earlier sources may occasionally refer to the Korean peninsula but some doubt remains whether references to Dong-hu or Dong-i, "eastern barbarians," meant Koreans at all times. However, by the time iron came into widespread use the description of groups on the Korean peninsula in historical documents is usually unambiguous. Trade interests, settlements of Han Chinese in Korea and the need to secure the northern frontier led to the conquest of northern Korea by the Han dynasty, which established direct rule of the conquered territory. Although disputed by North Koreans, the archaeological evidence leans strongly toward the presence of Han Chinese in the north. Southern Korea, however, was left to develop along its own lines, and to the north, just beyond the reach of the Han commandery, the Koguryo tribal league was gaining strength (Chapter 6).

By AD 313, when the Chinese Lelang colony was at last defeated by Koguryo and Chinese rule came to an end, three separate states had crystallized in Korea. Known as the Three Kingdoms, they were Silla in the southeast, Paekche in the southwest, and Koguryo in the north. The Kaya region, which never coalesced into a state, is included also. Each kingdom exhibited its own style. Shimmering golden crowns and jewelry are characteristic of Silla, while early Buddhist temples and statues that influenced the Yamato court of Japan are the best-known representations of Paekche culture. Large pyramidal stone tombs with painted murals have left pictorial documents of the lives of the Koguryan upper class. Shifting alliances among the kingdoms, both with each other and with polities in China and Japan, and intermittent warfare caused frequent changes in the boundaries between the kingdoms, if indeed the kingdoms had territorial limits. Ultimately Silla conquered both Paekche and Koguryo, uniting the peninsula for the first time in 668 (Chapter 7).

The book, then, follows a chronological path from foragers to the origin of the state. In the following chapter, the environmental setting is explored.

CHAPTER 2

ENVIRONMENT

The prehistoric and protohistoric sequences in Korea need to be framed by an understanding of the Korean peninsula in relation to its own unique geomorphology, biota and climate, as well as to the rest of East Asia. Korea cannot be subsumed under Japan or China geologically or geographically, any more than it can be archaeologically. As a large peninsula separated from the Asian continent by the broad and shallow Yellow Sea, it shares some continental traits in climate, flora and fauna with parts of China. Its long and sometimes sinuous coastline includes some microenvironments similar to those of the Japanese islands. But the majority of the peninsula is rugged and forested. In these regions where early peoples found subsistence and satisfied their other needs, Korea is more comparable to wooded eastern Manchuria and the Soviet Maritime region than it is to either China or Japan. This similarity is reflected in the presence of people Korean in culture and language living even now beyond the borders of the Korean state in these regions.

Korea extends like a thumb from the continental land mass (Fig. 2.1), pointing toward Kyushu, the southernmost major island of Japan. The present border of North Korea is joined to China for most of its continental border, with only 16 km of the northeast abutting on Siberia. The peninsula is irregular in shape. Some fancy that the shape of the country, with north at the top, resembles a rabbit facing west, with its ears in the northeast (Fig. 2.2). Asian maps were customarily oriented with east at the top, so Koreans perceive more appropriately the shape of a tiger, with its tail erect and its head on the south side. The irregularity of the coastline allows these fancies.

Geomorphology

Whether rabbit or tiger, the land mass of Korea covers 220,843 sq km, similar to that of England. It is approximately 1,000 km long, and at the "waist" is less than 200 km wide. Extending from approximately 34 degrees to 43 degrees North latitude, the peninsula falls entirely within the temperate zone, although broadleaved evergreen plants and bamboo grow in the south. Seoul city is close to the 38th parallel, at roughly the same latitude as Denver, Colorado and Athens, Greece.

Although surrounded on three sides by water, Korea is not far from foreign lands from any of its coasts. The shortest distance across the Yellow Sea to the

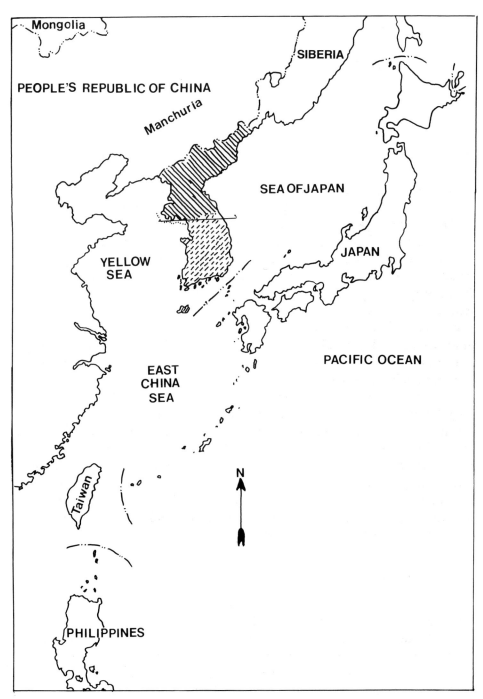

2.1 Korea in its East Asian setting.

2.2 Korea's mountains and rivers.

Shandong peninsula of China is less than 200 km, while the distance to Japanese territory across the Tsushima Strait is even less, and on clear days land is never out of sight when crossing by boat from southeastern Korea to Kyushu, Japan.

Geologically, Korea consists of a block of ancient Pre-Cambrian granite topped by later sediments and granitic intrusions, which is tilted down in the west toward the Yellow Sea. The crystalline schist system which forms the oldest rock of this block is exposed in only a few places. Most of the granite-gneiss hills which make up the present landscape are Archaeozoic rocks, known as the Younger Granite (Bartz 1972:8). Thick limestone beds have produced some large caves in central regions of South Korea and around Pyongyang. These caves tend to have fissures for openings, rather than featuring flat floors which would have been welcoming to human inhabitants, but a few caves were of appropriate shape and large enough to be occupied by human beings (Kim S.J. 1978).

The ancient granites contain metals, of which gold, copper, tin and iron were probably available at or near the surface for the early metal workers of Korea to exploit. Korea has been a major gold producer since antiquity. Extensive gold mines, especially in the north, made the country the biggest gold producer in the world in the first half of this century (Bartz 1972:89). Gold is still mined in the Chungchong provinces (Clare *et al.* 1969:17) and must have been easily available to the Silla Kingdom in the southeast, where sheet gold objects and gilded bronze artifacts have been found in great quantities in excavated tombs. Copper is found in the southeastern provinces and in Kyonggi Do, while one of the world's major tin belts runs down the middle of the Korean peninsula (deJesus 1977:36). Iron ore is still mined near Musan on the Tumen river, as well as in the southeast and in the hills of Kangwon Province. Tungsten, graphite and lead are also found in the north (Vreeland and Shinn 1976:40). Purple and green limestones and shales, as well as silicate crystals of various colors (especially amethyst and smoky topaz) were attractive for decorative uses. The soils are largely derived from granite and gneiss, being either light brown, acid, sandy soils or red-brown clays, with podzolic soils in the northern mountains (Kim S.J. 1978:30).

Unlike Japan, Korea has few volcanoes and little volcanic activity. Exceptions include the small island of Ullung Do in the East Sea (Sea of Japan), which is of volcanic origin, and the larger island of Cheju Do off the southwest coast, where Mt Halla raises its volcanic cone. In the peninsula proper, the only volcano is Mt Paektu in the far north – an extinct crater filled with a lake of great beauty where the gods were said to dwell, according to legend. Some basalt flows are found in the Kaema plateau, and in central Korea, dated to the Middle Pleistocene. Few sources of obsidian are found on the body of the peninsula, and no active volcanoes. In spite of this, hot springs occur in the southern part of the peninsula, especially near the submerging coasts.

Glacial activity is not evident in Korea, except in the highest mountains. Sheet glaciers did not exist. Mainly tilting and faulting, along with erosion, created the rugged peaks so characteristic of the Korean landscape. The mountain ranges are higher in the north and east, and plunge down almost directly into the Sea of Japan along most of the east coast. The mountains slope more gently toward the south and west, ending in numerous islands and islets in the Yellow Sea. The east coast has one major bend, corresponding to a fault in the Chugaryong valley, from Wonsan on the east coast to Seoul in the west. This fault creates the Seoul–Wonsan corridor as the major access to the northeast from the west coast.

An early missionary's comparison of Korean topography to "the sea [seen] from the top of a ship while a strong breeze raises the waves into an infinity of little mountains with varied forms" (Dallet 1954), remains an apt description of the overall configuration of the peninsula. Approximately 70 percent of the land surface is mountainous with steep slopes, even though the highest mountains are rarely more than 1,600 m above sea level, and the fraction of the land mass which is more than 100 m high comprises only about 5 percent of the peninsula (Bartz 1972). It is the steepness of the slopes, not the height of the mountains, that forms the characteristic Korean landscape of small basins in the midst of sharp peaks.

The major watershed range runs approximately north–south, trending northeast north of Wonsan, and southeast below it. The crest of the range is never far from the east coast, in places less than 20 km from the sea. Rivers arising from Korea's highest mountain, Paektu San, flow east and west to form the present international boundary. The northeast-trending mountains in the north are the Hamgyong and Pujollyong ranges, while the southeastern extension of the coastal range is known as the Taebaek mountains including the famous Diamond Mountains just north of the Demilitarized Zone. Although the range declines in altitude toward the south, the peaks remain rugged, forming a barrier between the valley of the Naktong river and the Sea of Japan. Even in the southwest, mountains may be difficult to cross. The Sobaek range in this region is impressive, rising to a height of nearly 2,000 m (6,238 ft) at Chiri San.

The shelf along the east coast is narrow, and the altitude changes from 1,000 m and more on the mountain tops to sea level in the space of only a few kilometers. Even the continental shelf is narrow along this coast, plunging abruptly into the Eastern Sea, whose average depth is 3,000 m. Sandy beaches with dune formation are found between rocky headlands. Lagoons form behind sandbars, where small fishing villages can still be found. Few bays or inlets make welcoming harbors, and those that exist have no easy access to the interior, because rivers to the east coast tend to be short and steep.

In contrast, the south and west coasts are dotted with over three thousand islands, about one-tenth of which are inhabited. Evidence of prehistoric human habitations can be found on many of these small bits of land. The coastline is so irregular on the west that the actual shoreline is five to ten times the straight line distance from one point to another (Bartz 1972).

The Yellow Sea is relatively shallow, having a maximum depth of 100 m. Ebbing and flowing into this confined area between China and Korea, the tidal fluctuations are great, with an average change from high to low tide of about 6 m, and a maximum difference of almost 10 m. The tides change quickly, and at low tide the exposed mud flats extend for 10 km or more, making navigation difficult (Bartz 1972).

The rivers of Korea are legion, beginning with small streams on virtually every rise. The rivers fail to provide relief from the difficult terrain, however, since they tend to follow the complex topography and remain relatively narrow and twisting throughout their lengths. Sand banks and islands form in the middle reaches of the larger rivers, but in many places they are constrained by steep hills on both sides. Six rivers are more than 400 km long. With the exception of the Tumen river, which marks the northern boundary with Russia and empties into the East Sea not far from Vladivostok, the major rivers run toward the west or south. The Yalu river (Amnok in Korean) flows southwestward to the Yellow Sea, forming the present boundary between Korea and China. In order, moving south down the west coast, are the Chongchon river, the Taedong river which flows by Pyongyang (the North Korean capital), the Imjin-Han river system where Seoul is located, and the Kum river flowing by Kongju. Present or former capitals of Korean states are all located on these rivers. The Yongsan is an important but smaller river in the southwest. The Naktong river, flowing generally toward the south to debouch near the southeast corner, makes four major zigzags along its course, turning abruptly to follow ancient faults. Former capitals of Silla (Kyongju) and a branch of Kaya (Taegu) are found in its basin (Bartz 1972:22). The gradient of the rivers becomes low toward their mouths, creating long estuaries. Navigation is thus possible seasonally for some distance up the major rivers. The major cities tend to be located at the ends of the estuaries, rather than on the coasts, and they are frequently not even directly on a river, but a few kilometers back from it protected by hills. These topographic features made prehistoric travel in Korea difficult, but they have failed to isolate any part of the peninsula more than others, so that striking regional differences have not developed, and similar adaptations are found throughout.

Dividing lines between Korean provinces follow the major rivers and mountain ranges to a large extent. Traditionally, Korea was divided into eight provinces, of which all but three are subdivided into northern (Puk) and southern (Nam) halves (Fig. 2.3). They will be described briefly in their historical configuration without regard to the present division of Korea into north and south, which is marked by the 1953 truce line following natural features near the 38th parallel.

Hamgyong Puk Do and Hamgyong Nam Do lie in the northeast, the most forested and most rugged part of Korea. Most of the archaeological sites known in this region have been discovered along the Tumen river and near the coast. The Kaema plateau in north central Korea, characterized as "cold, forested, and forbidding" (McCune 1956:124), is the most sparsely populated region. North and South Pyongan provinces cover the northwestern region, divided by the

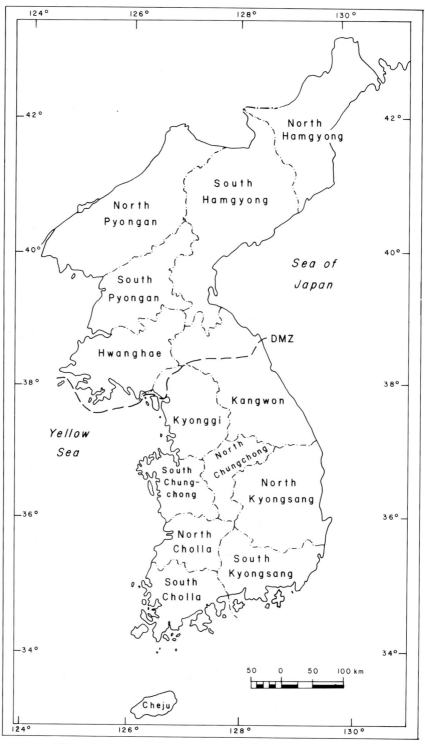

2.3 The traditional Korean provinces.

Chongchon river. Mountain ridges trend southwest to northeast, with arable land in the valleys between. Rice can be raised in these basins, but other crops, such as maize and millet, cover more acreage (Vreeland and Shinn 1976). South of Pyongan lies Hwanghae Do, with the Taedong river forming the northern border. Pyongyang, the capital of North Korea and a historic capital city as well, is situated on the Taedong river at the end of its estuary. A part of Kangwon Do in the east is also in North Korea. This region contains coastal fishing villages and medium-sized towns.

The Imjin and Han river drainages are largely in South Korea, in Kyonggi Do. Seoul, the capital city of South Korea, lies on the Han river, 30 km inland at the edge of its estuary. Chungchong Nam Do includes the Kum river, with the cities of Puyo and Kongju, both former capitals of the Paekche kingdom. North and South Cholla are divided from North and South Kyongsang provinces by the Sobaek range. The Cholla provinces include much rugged terrain, but because of the warmer southern climate they can be double-cropped. The Naktong river runs through the Kyongsang provinces, also a region of double-cropping. Kyongju, the former capital of Silla, is in a side valley of a tributary to the Naktong, and is protected from the east coast by a mountain ridge. The present major port of Pusan contains many archaeological sites, including both shell mounds and burial grounds. At the mouth of the Naktong stood Taekaya, the capital of one of the small Kaya polities, in the vicinity of present day Kimhae. Archaeological sites abound in this region as well. Cheju Do is a large volcanic island, some 100 km off the south coast of Korea, with Mt Halla rising more than 2,000 m at its center.

Climate

Korea's climate is basically continental, although extremes are usually tempered by the presence of water on three sides. McCune (1956:17) characterizes the climate as a "humid, mid-latitude monsoonal climate." The winters are cold and dry, while the summers are hot and subject to monsoon rains. The cold winds blowing from the continent alternate with warmer Pacific air in the winter, creating a cyclic pattern in the winter temperatures – a regularity which is expressed in the Korean proverb, "three days cold, four days warm."

The pattern of dry winters with little snow alternating with markedly rainy summers has an important effect upon river flow, accounting for the lack of wide alluvial plains. Rivers that are shallow enough to wade across in spring and fall, and frozen over in winter, become raging torrents during the rainy season, sweeping many tons of soil, gravel and boulders along their beds and out to sea. In the rainy season a single day's rainfall may exceed 200 mm (Kim S.J. 1978:24). It is estimated that 400,000 tons of silt are annually deposited in the Yellow Sea by Korean rivers (Bartz 1972:6).

Large deviations from the mean precipitation are also a characteristic of

Korean weather. For instance, in Seoul the recorded maximum is 2135 mm (in 1940), while the recorded minimum was 634 mm in 1949 (Kim S.J. 1978:4). Approximately one year in eight the annual precipitation falls below the minimum required for rice cultivation (Kim S.J. 1978:26), making unirrigated farming chancy.

Flora

Before it was cleared for cultivation, most of the land in Korea was forested. The major habitat for grasses and herbs was on narrow alluvial banks, where annual floods prevented larger plants from taking hold. The natural vegetation of most of Korea is classified as deciduous summer forest, East Asian Formation (Eyre 1968). Five main types of natural vegetation are found in Korea, of which the major three are varieties of mixed deciduous pine forest: maple, basswood and birch in the north, deciduous oak in the center, and mixed mesophytic forest in the south (Fig. 2.4). In the far south, a narrow belt of evergreen broadleaved forest can be found, and in the highest mountains, mostly located in the northeast, the montane coniferous forest is dominated by spruce and fir (Wang 1961, Yim 1977).

Perhaps because of the lack of glaciers, which eliminated flora in other settings, plant variety is great, with about 4,500 species known in Korea. This is an impressive number – for comparison, it is more than twice the number listed for England (Kim S.J. 1978:31), which is about the same size. Forest trees important for the prehistoric inhabitants include oak, birch, fir, pine, beech and many kinds of fruit and nut-bearing trees. Many other native species are useful plants, including hemp, ramie, willow, bamboo, mulberry, ginseng and several trees containing sap suitable for making lacquer.

Fauna

The wild animals of Korea are almost entirely creatures of the forest. Deer and wild boar were available for meat, and bear and tiger for pelts. These animals can still be hunted, especially in the north (Zaichikov 1952). The tiger figures conspicuously in ancient spirit worship – the Mountain God and his tiger appear in side shrines of many Buddhist temples. Folklore too honored the tiger, as protector, jester and fearsome creature (Zozayong 1972). The tiger only ceased to be a real and ever-present menace to villagers in this century. One traveler reported that leopards were shot even inside the walls of Seoul (Bishop 1905:73).

Although archery with stationary targets is a traditional gentlemanly sport, hunting has not traditionally been a prestigious occupation (Bergman 1938:73). The famous hunting scene from the tomb of the dancers, a Koguryo tomb in Jian showing nobles hunting deer and tigers with bows and arrows from horseback, suggests that this attitude was not always present. Wild fowl of various kinds are

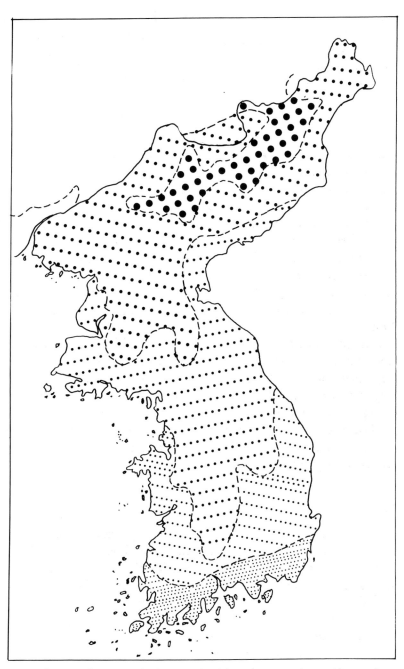

2.4 Natural vegetation types in Korea. From north to south: coniferous forest, mixed hardwood forest, deciduous broadleaved forest, mixed mesophytic forest, evergreen broadleaved forest.

numerous and the Silla Kingdom was especially noted for its domesticated fowl. Both freshwater and marine fish are important foods, as well as the many and plentiful varieties of shellfish. Fish and squid are commonly sold in the market dried and salted.

Domesticated animals in traditional Korea included dog, pig, horse and ox. Dog skeletons are found in various Early Villages locations, as well as pig bones. The wild horse of this region, *Equus przewalski*, was called the Mongolian pony because of its small size. Domesticated versions are depicted in sculpture and painting in the early centuries AD. Mandibles of this creature were discovered in a late paleolithic site in Inner Mongolia, as well as the neolithic site of Banpo, suggesting that domestication of the horse may have taken place in northern China (Olsen 1984).

Paleoclimate

Most of what is written about Korea's climate in the Pleistocene is inferred from studies in nearby regions, or even world-wide trends, because so few local studies have been made. This situation is slowly changing, but much more work needs to be accomplished before local environments at various times in the past can be described with precision. In general, cold and warm stages have been demonstrated in China and Siberia, corresponding roughly to the four major glaciations in Europe and North America. The customary terminology used by Korean archaeologists is that of the Alpine glaciations – Gunz, Mindel, Riss, Würm, from early to late. I shall follow that convention, although a direct correspondence is not implied. In Korea itself there was no significant glaciation at any time; therefore, the Alpine terminology merely indicates world-wide alternating cold and warm periods and a general time frame.

Direct evidence in Korea for temperature changes in the Pleistocene has been found in pollen profiles and fauna from cave sediments. However, since the sediments and pollen have been dated largely by means of relative depth and reference to sites in China and Siberia, there is not yet any firm Korean Pleistocene chronology. A start, however, has been made with the study of the pollen and fauna in Chommal Cave. The results show a warm period earlier than 20,000 BC, followed by a warmer period of perhaps a thousand years, and a short return to cold from 9500 to 8000 BC (Sohn and Park 1980). A pollen study in the Liaodong peninsula of China shows climate fluctuation in the Holocene (Chen, Lu and Shen 1978).

Ho (1975:31) states that the forests of north China have been essentially the same throughout the Late Pleistocene, and the same may have been the case for Korea. Pearson (1974:228) suggested that pine and artemisia could result from "human disturbance of the forests," but evidence from caves in the Korean Pleistocene shows a preponderance of pine through tens of thousands of years.

Frenzel, who studied the Pleistocene vegetation of all of northern Eurasia, describes the Korean flora during that era as chiefly composed of mixed forest dominated by conifers (Frenzel 1968: Fig. 5). Pearson (1977) has gathered together evidence that Korea and Japan fit into the pattern of alternate warmer and cooler eras that have been documented for Europe. The chief effect of these climate changes on flora seems to have been a slight shifting of the borders of the deciduous forest, southward in cooler times and northward in warm swings.

Post-Pleistocene climate changes in Korea have been little discussed or tested. According to a study by Yasuda and Kim (1980), from 15,000 to 11,000 BC the climate was still cold, lingering from the final glacial period. The warmer Neothermal period, 11,000 to 8000 BC, is characterized by deciduous broad-leaved trees, especially oak. At the beginning of this warming trend, sea level was more than 16 m lower than at present, but as the continental ice melted the sea gradually rose to its present level. These findings are similar to those of Sohn, cited above, except that they do not include a cooling trend around 9000 BC.

Another pollen study which focused on somewhat later times (Oh 1971) indicates that arboreal pollens have been dominant in central Korea since at least 3000 BC, but that the relative abundance of various trees has changed over time. A cool, moist climate is suggested for 3000 BC, the lowest level of the peat bog studied by Oh. On the other hand, Park Y.C. (1976) believes that the temperature of south coastal Korea was actually 2 degrees centigrade warmer, based on the presence of subtropical shells at the site of Tongsamdong (cited in Choe 1986:16). Studying the clues to be found in the oracle bone inscriptions in China, Li (1983:24) concludes that the mean annual temperature in China from 3000 to 1000 BC was higher than at present by approximately 2 degrees centigrade.

The major Pleistocene change affecting the Korean peninsula was marked fluctuations in sea level, making the Yellow Sea into dry land or at most an inland lake during glacial maxima, and joining Japan to Korea in the region of the Tsushima Straits. During interglacials, some of the present Korean coastline may have been drowned. But there is little agreement on sea level changes in the few studies that have been conducted. One study of the ria coasts of south and west Korea indicates ancient beaches which have reemerged, perhaps corresponding to the Eemian beaches of northern Europe (Guilcher 1976). In the Last Glacial maximum, about 18,000 BP, sea level was 110 to 140 m lower than today. By 12,000 BP, sea level in the Bering Strait had risen to 40 m below its present stand, and the temperature was lower than the present by only 5 or 6 degrees centigrade (Aigner 1972:53). According to Minato and Kumano, at about 6000 BC, sea level was 1.7 m lower than at present, rising 1.4 m more by 2000 BC (cited in Choi M.L. 1984b:37), but some excavators have found evidence for sea levels higher than the present in neolithic sites (e.g. Sohn 1982).

A pollen study on the Yellow Sea coast suggests that the coastal area is still submerging at a slow but steady rate, and that this subsidence began at least 7,000 years ago (Pak 1977). The change in beach line is more than can be accounted for by gradually rising world-wide sea level, and therefore, Pak concludes, the west coast of Korea is still subsiding.

If the phenomenon of the Yellow Sea coast submergence is independent of sea level changes, it may be caused by the shifting of the underlying block of the peninsula. Bartz (1972:12) suggests that such tilting is due to the weight of the sediments which accumulate in the Yellow Sea annually from major rivers flowing from China, Manchuria and Korea. Guilcher (1976:664), however, believes that tilting is a process which ended in the Eemian period. This problem is in need of further study.

Coastal changes on the China side of the Yellow Sea have been charted (Huang 1984). Aigner (1972:53) suggests that during the Eemian interglacial there was a major increase in the size of the Yellow Sea, flooding parts of Shandong and Manchuria. At the time of the Würm maximum, around 18,000 BP, sea level was 116 to 140 m below its present level, which would have dried up the Yellow Sea completely, except for a major river running down its length. By 12,000 BP, sea level was only 40 m lower than the present but the Yellow Sea is so shallow that the distance between China and Korea is still very short. Huang (1984) has calculated coastlines between 15,000 and 6,000 BP, based on C14 dates. Extrapolation from these dates suggests that at roughly 10,000 years ago none of the Korean west and south coast islands was submerged.

Geographical referents are not always clear in ancient Chinese documents, and interpretations of them are varied. For instance, Legge (in Waltham 1971:43, fn) remarks that some commentators believe the area called Qing Zhou not only included the Shandong peninsula of China but also "crossed the sea and extended into the Liaodong peninsula as far as modern Korea." An (1974:51) cites the *Shi Ji*, Vol. 2, as asserting that the Gulf of Bohai was smaller before the time of Confucius, and says that parts of Qing Zhou sank into the sea, as well as parts of the territory of Yan, a northern kingdom in China.

Kao-li-chai, an archaeological site on the edge of the Liaodong peninsula, is known to have been abandoned owing to a rise in sea level, and later re-occupied when the island emerged again (Okladnikov 1965:160), while a study of sediments in southern Liaoning suggests that the highest sea level occurred about 6000–3000 BC (Chen, Lu and Shen 1978). Chang (1986) suggests that the area of central Shandong only gradually built up from river silts, and that it was still marshy in the Yangshao period. All of this indicates a complex coastal history, of which we do not yet have a detailed record on the Korean side.

Summary

Korea is a mountainous, forested peninsula which has not changed drastically in these features since the first arrival of human beings. Thus, the archaeology of

Korea is a study in adaptation to a rugged environment, with habitable pockets more common than broad areas of desirable land. Transportation and communication had few obvious routes, which meant that the creation of polities larger than villages encountered special problems. The environment of Korea was surely a factor in its development.

CHAPTER 3

FOREST FORAGERS 500,000 to 10,000 BC

Archaeological sites with chipped stone flakes and tools are scattered both geographically and temporally in the Korean peninsula, including open-air as well as cave sites. The population which created these sites is designated "forest foragers" for two reasons. First, the rugged terrain of the Korean landscape seems to have been largely wooded throughout the Pleistocene, as has been discussed in the preceding chapter. Although fruits, nuts and herbs, deer, wild boar and other game were probably plentiful, they are dispersed resources which could not continuously support large local populations. Second, the archaeological evidence is consistent with this view. Other than some extensive (but not intensive) areas of lithic tools and debitage along interior rivers (which probably reflect repeated campsites rather than a large population), there is no evidence for either large groups of people or extended residence at any time in the Korean Pleistocene.

Paleolithic archaeology in Korea is barely a quarter of a century old, but the study of paleolithic sites in Korea burgeoned in the 1980s, with the secure establishment of the fact of Pleistocene habitation in the peninsula. In a summary paper published as recently as 1982, Lee Yung-jo listed only eleven excavated paleolithic sites. The number was expanded to twenty-five in a 1986 publication by the same author (Lee Y.J. 1986a), and perhaps another twenty-five sites have doubled the paleolithic inventory again since then (Fig. 3.1).

History of paleolithic discoveries

Although Tonggwanjin in North Korea was described as paleolithic in the 1930s (Kim J.H. 1978b), this interpretation was treated with skepticism by most archaeologists. In any case it was not a particularly productive or informative site. Not until the 1960s, when the stratified site at Sokchangni revealed many layers of preceramic occupation demonstrating the increasing complexity of tool

3.1 Approximate locations of sites in Chapter 3.
 1 Changnae, 2 Chommal, 3 Chon'gongni, 4 Daehyundong (Yokpo), 5 Hukwuri (Komunmoru), 6 Imbulli, 7 Kulpori, 8 Kumgul, 9 Mandalli, 10 Myongori, 11 Saemgul, 12 Sangmuryongni, 13 Sangsi, 14 Simgongni, 15 Sokchangni, 16 Suyanggae, 17 Tohuari, 18 Tonggwanjin, 19 Tok-chong, 20 Turubong, 21 Yokchi Do, 22 Yonggul Cave, 23 Yonggongni.

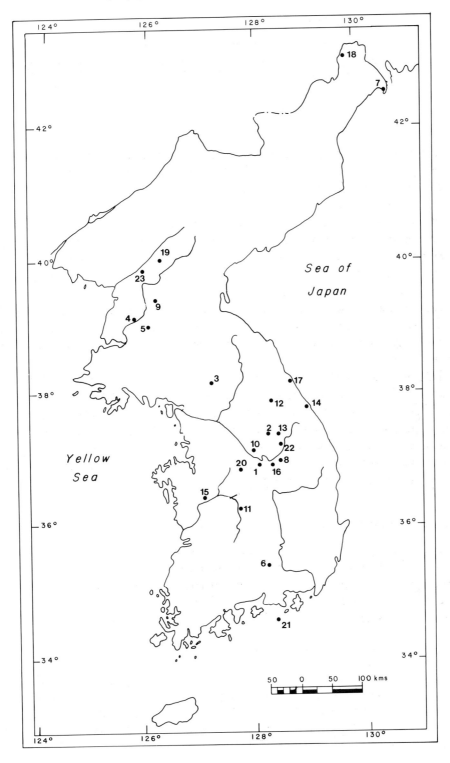

technology through time, did the occurrence of paleolithic sites begin to be acknowledged in the Republic of Korea. Meanwhile, in the north, the discovery of two distinct lithic occupations beneath a shell mound at Kulpori near the mouth of the Tumen river gave impetus to further discoveries in the northern half of the peninsula (To 1964). Since that time, many more lithic sites have been discovered, and their attribution to the Pleistocene confirmed.

With the general agreement that these sites are genuine, debates have shifted to the interpretation of the data. For example, certain stones and bones regarded as artifacts by their excavators are viewed with skepticism by other Korean archaeologists, and the chronological placement of a few important sites is in dispute. Possible paleolithic art is the least accepted factor of all. These discussions should not obscure the fact that great strides have been made in paleolithic archaeology since 1970. Although the earlier periods are not free from controversy, the late paleolithic can be described with some certainty.

The numerous new finds in the paleolithic of Korea have solved a few problems but raised more. Although it is by now beyond question that makers of stone and bone tools inhabited Korea during the Pleistocene period, the correlation of sites with fluctuations in sea level, especially in the Yellow Sea, along with climatic changes related to continental glaciations, is not fully established.

Terminology used in South Korea to describe paleolithic tools comes mainly from Europe, especially France, and assumptions about the age of stone tool assemblages are often made on the basis of resemblances between tool morphology in Korea and Europe. This practice has its obvious dangers. Terms most often used are "Acheulian" (Chung 1984b) which applies to hand-axe forms assigned to the lower paleolithic, "Mousterian" for middle paleolithic (Choi M.C. 1984), and "Aurignacian" for upper paleolithic (e.g. Chung 1984a, Choi M.C. 1987). It is usually not made explicit whether the terms are meant to designate evolutionary stages at roughly equivalent time periods in addition to morphological similarities, but it seems that no direct connection with Europe is implied by the use of these terms. These designations are used to describe morphological tool types either to the exclusion of other chronological or functional considerations or assuming their concurrence. For example, Yi believes that the East African system is the "most feasible system to accommodate Korean Paleolithic materials" (Yi 1986:279). However, it is my observation that, although some specific tools bear similarities to European stone tools, Korean *assemblages* have no striking relationship to Afro-European assemblages (see Chung 1986b for extended illustrations of individual tools). North Korean usage has created such terms as "Kulporian," but little light is shed in this way on either chronology or areal extent, since the characteristics of the style are not well specified.

Archaeologists in each of the regions contiguous to Korea use their own sets of terms for both geological and archaeological stages, which are usually transliterated rather than translated into western languages. The geological eras in the nearby regions may be comparable to the European glacial sequence, but the only attempt which has been made to align them is not annotated (Sohn 1988), so it is of less value than it might be. The Korean peninsula was not glaciated in the Pleistocene, in spite of significant temperature fluctuations. Therefore, associating archaeological sites with world-wide Pleistocene divisions, except on a gross scale, is very difficult. Since it is Korean practice to use the terminology of the European glaciers – Gunz, Mindel, Riss and Würm, in order from early to late – to stand for world-wide glacial phenomena, with the underlying assumption of equivalency in Korea, this practice will be continued here, simply for convenience, although it is to be hoped that more study of the Korean Quaternary period will refine this usage or replace it with another tailored to the local situation. Yi Seon-bok (1988) has made a solid beginning in this direction. Other summaries of the paleolithic environment include those of Choi Mou-chang (1986) and Lee Yung-jo (1986b).

As a result of a conference in 1973 on the paleolithic in East Asia, terminology distinct from that of Europe was created, dispensing with the term middle paleolithic altogether and substituting the terms early paleolithic and late paleolithic for lower and upper paleolithic. The latter terms are associated with specific hominid forms, geological periods and artifactual assemblages, while the terms early paleolithic and late paleolithic are intended to apply to tool morphology and lithic technology rather than to time period, although "early" does begin earlier than "late." Omitting the concept of middle paleolithic in Asia allows for the overlapping and coexistence of early and late paleolithic and the possibility of functional as well as chronological differences (Ikawa-Smith 1978:6).

Although I follow the early/late convention here, it has *not* been universally accepted in Korea. Yi Seon-bok (1986) has argued vehemently against using these alternative time divisions for Asia. He equates Asian tool types with specific hominid forms, and argues for the association of *Homo erectus* with lower paleolithic, *Homo sapiens neanderthalensis* with middle paleolithic, and *Homo sapiens sapiens* with upper paleolithic. Yi dates the boundary between lower and middle paleolithic in Asia at 75,000 BP, and the onset of late paleolithic at 40,000 BP, with a margin of error of 10 percent, based largely on data from China.

Hominid forms, geomorphology and lithic technology need to be studied separately in order to discover how they coincide in Asia, rather than preempting this discussion with the assumption of identity between tool types and hominids. Although the data in Korea are not sufficient to decide this debate, it is possible to examine with which models the data are consistent (and which inconsistent). Therefore the Ikawa-Smith convention of using the terms early paleolithic and late paleolithic with reference to tool assemblages will be followed here. However, I will consider the question of whether or not there is a recognizable Mousterian period, and whether "Neanderthals" existed in Korea.

Early paleolithic

Evidence for early paleolithic in Korea is sketchy, although several sites have been assigned on typological grounds. These include two open sites, the lowest levels at Sokchangni and the entire site of Chon'gongni, and two cave deposits, Kumgul Cave in central South Korea, and Hukwuri Cave near Pyongyang in North Korea (but see the discussion below). New layers unearthed at Dae-hyundong Cave and Yonggongni have produced several complete skulls reputed to be *Homo erectus*, but there is as yet no scholarly report. Even cave sites which have been published are disappointingly sketchy, and all the sites have been challenged on one ground or another (Yi and Clark 1983). Hominid remains are limited to a broken skull cap, 5.4 × 3.5 cm, said to represent *Homo erectus* (Sohn 1984a), from Kumgul Cave on the Namhan river, and the unreported sites mentioned above (Sohn 1990). The Kumgul Cave attribution to *H. erectus* has been questioned, but whether or not this particular cranium stands up to scrutiny, it is not unreasonable to suppose that Korea was populated by hominids in the Lower and Middle Pleistocene (Kwon 1990), since several sites with hominid fossils have been found nearby in northern China (Wu and Dong 1985).

A limestone cave containing the unusual combination (for Korea) of both fauna and stone tools is Hukwuri Cave (also called Komunmoru) in Sangwon County, 40 km southeast of Pyongyang in Pyongan Nam Do. (See Fig. 3.1 for locations of sites.) The Hukwuri finds are indisputably Middle Pleistocene in geological age. This limestone cave contains deposits 2.5 m in depth in an area 30 m long but less than 3 m deep. The lowest deposits are believed by North Korean archaeologists to be at least 400,000 years old. Evidence adduced for the time depth is the presence of *Mimomys* sp., which became extinct shortly after that time (FLPH 1977:3). Sohn (1988) places the find at 600,000–550,000 BP. Five layers were excavated, of which Layer 1, just above bedrock, and Layer 4 had possible tools made of the local limestone. They included one hand-axe-like core tool and five other large, heavy tools, crudely made and without retouch (Fig. 3.2). Many have questioned whether these are tools of human manufacture (e.g. Bae 1989b, Yi S.B. 1986, Yi and Clark 1983). Fossilized animal bones are abundant, including rhinoceros and megaloceros. Monkey, bison, boar, horse, elephant, tiger and cave bear were also identified.

A limestone cave with deep deposits in south central Korea, Kumgul Cave has bronze age, neolithic and possibly mesolithic materials in its upper levels. Below are three paleolithic layers of uncertain time depth, of which the lowest (Unit VIII) is estimated to belong to the early paleolithic (Choi M.C. 1987, Sohn 1984a, 1988). A few core tools, including choppers, crude chopping tools and "Abbevillian type" hand-axes (Sohn 1984a), were found in this layer. Fragments of deer bones were also collected. Unit VII contained the same kind of core tools (Fig. 3.3), but in addition contained large flakes created by the block-on-block

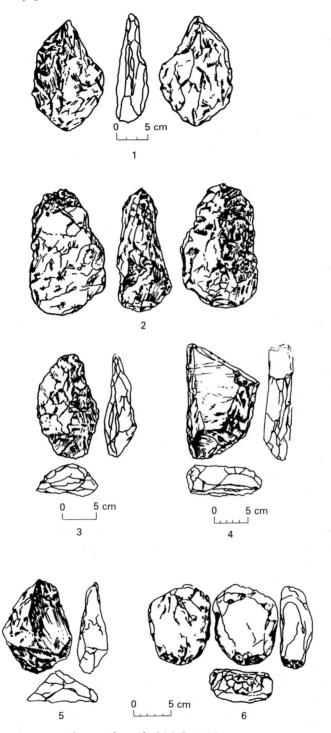

3.2 Hukwuri artifacts. After Choi M.C. 1987.

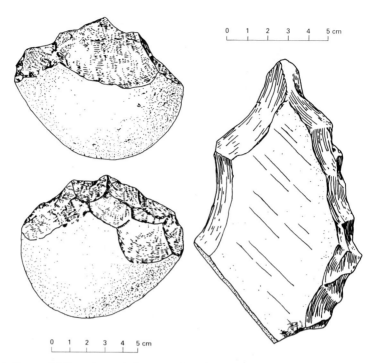

3.3 Kumgul biface (r) and chopper (l). After Choi M.C. 1987.

technique. Bolas stones were present, as well as anvil stones. Faunal remains include *Bos primigenius, Pseudaxis grayi, Dicerorhinus, Panthera* and *Hyaena*.

The next two units were devoid of cultural material. Unit IV was divided into A and B horizons. The lower one contained core tools and heavy scrapers, similar to those from the layers below but tending to be smaller in size. The A horizon included tools made of flakes struck from a prepared core. A wide variety of fauna was represented, including *Ovis, Cervus, Elephas, Hydropotes, Sus scrofa, Meles, Mustela, Vulpes, Dicerorhinus* and other animals such as panther, bear, hyena, horse, macaque and moose. This layer is believed to have been laid down in a mild climate, probably an interglacial (Sohn 1984a). This is an important site because of the presence of both tools and fossil fauna, but its attribution to the early or even middle paleolithic has been questioned (Choi M.C. 1987).

The discovery of hand-axes at Chon'gongni in central Korea, on the side of the "Movius line" which was believed to exclude hand-axes (Movius 1948), has required a reassessment of the early paleolithic in East Asia (Yi and Clark 1983). In an area more than 16 km in length along a terrace above the Hantan river (Yi 1983, 1984), bifacially flaked core tools (Figs. 3.4 and 3.5), as well as tools made on flakes (Fig. 3.6), were found in abundance (Kim W.Y. and Chung Y.H. 1979, Bowen 1979, Hwang 1979, Yi S.B. 1986, Bae 1989b).

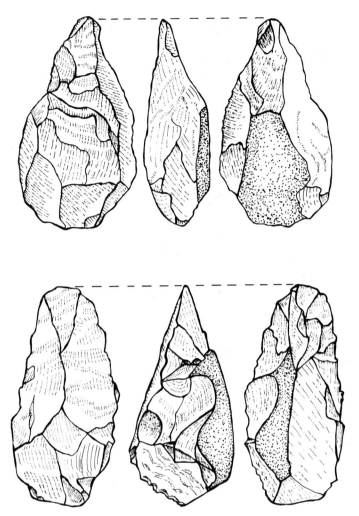

3.4 Hand-axes, Chon'gongni. (Prehistoric Stone Tools, Seoul National University.)

The bedrock at Chon'gongni is paleozoic gneiss, covered by 20 to 25 m of volcanic basalt. On top of the basalt is a layer of reddish clay, up to 3 m thick, in which the artifacts were found. The Hantan river eroded through the clay and the basalt, leaving a terrace about 30 m above the river. The basalt has been dated by the Potassium/Argon method, with results varying from 270,000 and 300,000 to 600,000 BP (Chung 1984a). The basalt is probably the result of several flows, accounting for the variation in the dates. Deep downcutting of the stream began after the formation of the clays, followed by another period of alluvial deposits. A final downcutting of the river through the basalt to the present level left a former tributary with hanging sediments (Clark 1983). Clark concludes that the

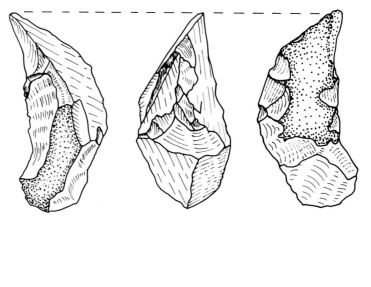

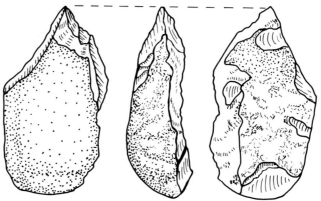

3.5 Pointed tools, Chon'gongni. (Prehistoric Stone Tools, Seoul National University.)

last stage probably occurred when the sea level was lowered during the last glaciation. This interpretation would date the clays (and the artifacts) to the Riss/Würm Interglacial, from 125,000 to 80,000 years ago, an intermediate date between those of Bae and Yi, discussed above.

The lowest stratum in the excavated grids shows basalt gravel in a matrix of red clay, and even in this level some stone tools were found. Above the gravel/clay layer the "reddish compact loamy clay" (Kim W.Y. 1983a:6) contained many artifacts, as did a lighter clay layer above that. Before the site was discovered, bulldozers largely removed the humus layer, preparing to utilize the clay in the local brickworks. Possibly as a result of the bulldozing, the whole surface area is littered with stone tools, lying helter-skelter and out of context.

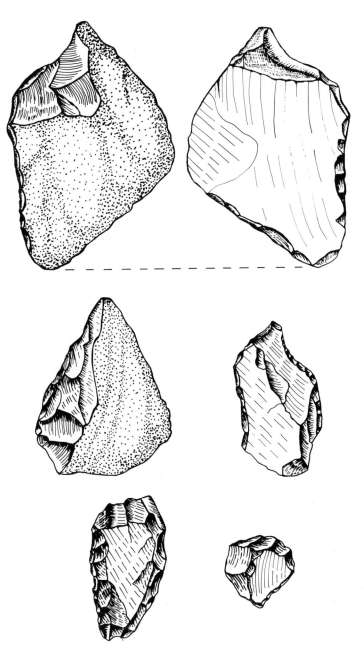

3.6 Tools on flakes, Chon'gongni. (Prehistoric Stone Tools, Seoul National University.)

The red clay of the site has been variously explained as analogous to similar beds in China known to be of Pleistocene age, and as a process that is still continuing in Korea. Bae (1987a:795, 1989a) sifts all the evidence, and comes to the conclusion that the site should be dated around 200,000 BP. Yi S.B. (1986:236), however, citing thermoluminescence dates of 46,500 ± 543, and 48,200 ± 6,690 from the fluvial channel bed and equating them with the actual deposits, believes that 50–40,000 BP is more accurate. Korean geologists (cited in Yi 1984) have suggested that the clays were deposited in depressions in the surface of the basalt, where many small lakes had formed. Slopewash and alluvial deposits are also considered possible origins for the clay. The site was formed in a time of rapid temperature decline, such as the beginning of a glacial episode (Yi 1986:236). Prehistoric foragers would surely have been attracted to an area of small lakes where animals would come to drink.

Four universities took part in the excavation of Chon'gongni, examining different parts of the site (Fig. 3.7; Kim W.Y. and Bae K.D. 1983, Hwang 1983, Chung Y.H. 1983, 1984b, Choi M.C. 1983a). At Locality 1, six test pits, each 5 m square, produced 292 quartzite cores and flakes (Kim W.Y. and Bae K.D. 1983). Thirty-two pits in Locality 2 yielded 1,126 stone implements, "including four bifacially worked hand-axes of Acheulian type" (Kim W.Y. 1980a:3). This is not an impressive percentage of hand-axes, but it was the presence of hand-axes that was important, not their dominance in the sites. Choi M.C. (1983a) reports mostly tools in the chopper/chopping tool tradition, all found in the darker clay layer. Locality 3 produced large numbers of choppers, and has been interpreted as a workshop, while 85 percent of the tools from Locality 4 were choppers (Hwang 1979). Hwang (n.d.) and Clark (1982) have both identified these groupings of artifacts as workshops rather than as camps. Their proximity to appropriate sources of raw material supports this view. The stone for the tools probably came from the nearby Baeguiri formation, transported by the stream (Yi 1984).

There is no question that the tools at Chon'gongni are genuine human artifacts. The complexity of the flaking, with sinuous edges on some bifacial tools produced by alternate flaking of the faces, and use of quartzite, which is not naturally found above the basalt layer, both make convincing evidence. The question of whether the tools could properly be called Acheulian, however, is still open. François Bordes, judging from photographs, concurred that some of the hand-axes are entirely consistent with the Acheulian type (Kim W.Y. and Chung Y.H. 1979). However, the tool morphology in the entire assemblage suggests a number of different paleolithic traditions. The bifaces include a variety of shapes: lanceolate, almond and rhomboid, and all are characterized by thick butts which are unlike the classic Acheulian (Hwang 1979:37). Four of the cores found by Choi M.C. (1982) exhibit what he believes to be a Levallois technique, and he designates the industry Mousterian of Acheulian tradition. The quartz and quartzite from which the tools are made do not flake as regularly as flint used

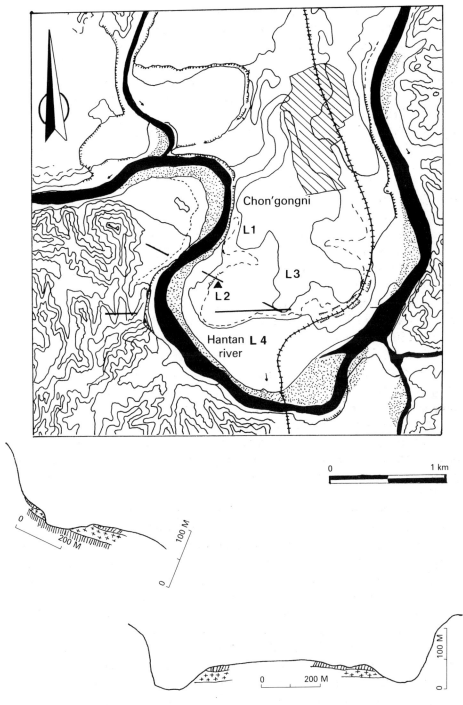

3.7 Location of excavations at Chon'gongni. After Kim W.Y. and Bae K.D. 1983.

for Acheulian tools, and this fact may have contributed to some of the differences. Ayres and Rhee (1984) relate the hand-axes to the North Asian heavy tool tradition, but this does not seem to get us any farther, begging the questions of both tool functions and assemblage similarities.

In addition to core tools (which include picks, scrapers, polyhedrons and spheroids as well as hand-axes), tools made on flakes are common (Bae 1987b). These are minimally flaked, usually unifacially, to become side or end-scrapers, borers or notches. Few of the cores show signs of multi-stage preparation, and the retouch appears to have been accomplished by means of a hard hammer. Hammerstones show use-battering, as do anvils. There is little patterning; in Clark's words, "informality is the keynote of the industry" (Clark 1983:595).

Animal bones are lacking at this site. The only pollen identified was a single grain of pine (Kim W.Y. 1983a:591). This tenuous clue suggests a wooded environment for the time of occupation (Yi 1984). Studies of the geology (Lee S.M. 1983), soils (Pak 1983) and biological environment (Chang 1983) of Chon'gongni are useful but have not yet allowed a cultural interpretation of the site.

The site of Sokchangni, the first paleolithic site to be excavated in South Korea, was a pioneering study of the paleolithic in South Korea (Sohn 1972, 1974, 1978a). Situated beside the Kum river in Chungchong Nam Do, this deeply stratified open site has twenty-seven strata identified above bedrock, of which eleven strata contained artifacts. Two areas were excavated, designated Locality 1 and Locality 2. The levels were correlated and numbered accordingly, so that there is only a small overlap of levels in the two localities. Locality 2 had the deeper excavation, continuing even below the present river level. Layers 10 to 27 in Locality 2 are the earliest deposits. The excavator refers to these layers as middle and lower paleolithic with the implication that Layer 15a and below should be assigned to the lower (early) paleolithic (Sohn 1978a). The artifact-bearing strata in Locality 2 are Layers 10, 12, 13, 15, 15a, 17, 19, 21 and 27. This group of strata were 4 to 11 m below ground surface, contained in a gravel matrix in all cases except Layers 10 and 13. This circumstance suggests to Sohn that the site was used only in cold periods in the early paleolithic. The stone artifacts found in these layers are designated as choppers, pointed tools, scrapers, hammerstones and flakes. Tools from the uppermost of these layers are said to be more "sophisticated" than those below, implying prepared cores, patterned tools and in some cases retouch. The predominant stone used for tool making was quartz, but granite-gneiss and pegmatite, which form the local bedrock, were also used. The lowest level, below the water table, had to be continually pumped to allow excavation to proceed. The excavation unit became quite constricted at the bottom as well, owing to the depth of 8 to 9 m below the river bed. The basal layer rested on Pre-Cambrian bedrock.

These lower strata have been designated early paleolithic on the basis of the morphology of the stone tools and their position at the base of the excavations.

Clark (1983:138) suggests that the deposits are likely to be contemporary with the Last Glacial (Würm) lowering of sea level, since they are below the present channel, but Sohn believes them to be much earlier. Until the early geomorphology of Korea is better studied, this must continue to be moot. Yi Seon-bok (1986) has doubted the human manufacture of these alleged artifacts from the lower levels. However, published drawings of the lithics in question appear to be credibly artifacts and not "geofacts."

The stone tool designations have also been challenged by Hwang (n.d.), who doubts that the technology is necessarily early paleolithic, although he characterizes the tools as very crude. These points, cleavers, scrapers and picks belong to the "chopper/chopping tool" tradition described by Movius (1948); the problem pointed out by Hwang is that such tools are known to have been made right down to the neolithic in some parts of Asia, and cannot be assigned to a time period by morphology alone.

The tools at Sokchangni were produced either by percussion flaking or by a technique called anvil hurling, which involves throwing a stone nodule onto a stationary rock, in order to split off usable flakes. Pairs of hard and soft anvils were found in one layer, apparently used together. It may be that the parent material of the tools, especially quartz, along with these inelegant techniques, contributes to the simplicity of the tools.

Although Hwang believes that the tools from the lower layers at Sokchangni are late paleolithic, Kim Won-Yong (1983a) has characterized the quartzite tools in the lower levels as belonging to the chopper/chopping tool tradition of Zhoukoudian in northern China, concurring with the early paleolithic designation on these grounds. Kim notes that the bipolar tool manufacturing technique is similar to that of Zhoukoudian. Obviously, tool morphology alone cannot solve the question of placement in time – only the geomorphological context and/or radiometric dating could provide indisputable proof of age. However, in the case of Sokchangni, the depth and relative position of the finds lend weight to the argument that they belong to the early paleolithic.

Tohuari is a very rich site near the east coast in central Korea. The lithics found on the surface include bifaces as well as tools manufactured on flakes. More than 4,000 lithics were collected in an area about 100 × 200 m. This was either a site near a quarry or primary manufacturing, since preforms abound (Yi 1986). The age of the site is not determined (Yi S.B. 1986:254–6, Ro 1986).

Early paleolithic comparisons in East Asia

The early paleolithic is well established in China, with many sites containing the bones of *Homo erectus*. Among these is the site of Yiyuan, on the Shandong peninsula across the Yellow Sea from Korea. In times of lowered sea level, when the Yellow Sea was a large plain with a meandering river, the Korean peninsula would have been easily accessible and probably attractive, rising in tiers to the east above the plain. Other sites near Korea are Jinniushan and Benxi, limestone caves with early paleolithic strata, beyond Korea's northwest border (Zhang 1985).

According to a recent review of Chinese early paleolithic, the Chinese sites should be dated from one million years ago to 200,000 BP. The associated tools are made by simple techniques, and most are multi-functional implements. "Typologically classifiable tools are relatively scarce" (Zhang 1985:147). There are more tools made from flakes than from cores, and three of the four flake production techniques involve anvil stones. The four methods identified by Zhang are: (1) simple direct percussion, (2) anvil-supported direct percussion or "crushing" (known in Korea as the bipolar technique), (3) anvil percussion or block-on-block, and (4) throwing, often called "anvil hurling" in the Korean literature. None of these techniques tend to produce regular and patterned flakes. Some flakes obtained by such methods were utilized without further attention. Where there is retouch, the same techniques listed above were used except for throwing, which would have been ineffective.

The best known early paleolithic site in China, Locality 1 of Zhoukoudian, included six morphological tool categories: scrapers, points, choppers, gravers, awls and spheroids (also referred to as bolas or stone balls). Of the total number of tools, 71.3 percent were made on retouched flakes. Small tools characterize the assemblage – 75.2 percent of the tools are scrapers of various types, mostly less than 40 mm long (Zhang 1985). Although small tools on flakes occur in Korean sites, none has such a high percentage.

Jinniushan Cave, in the Liaodong peninsula, contained much Middle Pleistocene fauna in its lowest three levels, along with evidence of fire including burned bones, fire-cracked rock, reddened clay and ash. Flake tools, made with bipolar percussion, were characteristic. Tools included six scrapers, one point and one graver (Zhang 1985). This collection is not unlike the finds in Korean caves, especially Hukwuri.

The regions directly north of Korea, including parts of Jilin Province and the Soviet Maritime region, contain a few sites with chopper/chopping tools made on pebbles. They are mostly found in gravel beds, and are believed by some archaeologists to be early palaeolithic, although supporting evidence of human fossils or animal bone is lacking (Aigner 1978). Derevianko (1978) believes that *Homo erectus* penetrated into the Amur basin as well as into Japan during the Second Interglacial, bringing the pebble tool technology. This conclusion is based on the rare (and questionable) tools found in gravel beds, and the evidence that severe climatic changes did not occur in northeastern Asia to the extent that they did in Europe. The ameliorating effect of the Pacific ocean even during the most severe cold period is seen as accounting for survivals of Tertiary subtropical flora such as cork and gingko, in the Maritime region, China and Korea. Yi and Clark (1983) hold the opinion that none of these sites stands up to scrutiny as early paleolithic occupations, however.

The case for early paleolithic in Japan is as unsettled as in Korea. The main proponent of early dates is Serizawa (1978), who believes some Japanese sites go back to 130,000 years ago. The dates are based on the finds of artifacts in the Tama loam, which underlies strata that have been geologically dated by fission-track determinations as 66,000 to 132,000 BP. Few of the chipped stone pieces from the three sites which Serizawa believes to be lower paleolithic are convincing artifacts, because they lack patterning and have only a few flakes removed. Nevertheless, the Sozudai site has hand-axes and ovate tools much like Chon'gongni. Even these are questioned, for example Ohyi (1978) does not accept them as artifacts at all. Thus, no Japanese site is universally accepted as lower paleolithic.

In the interglacials, Japan was separated from Korea, but joined to the mainland by a lowering of sea level in the glacial periods. During the times of maximum glaciation, sea level was lowered to the extent of exposing the floor of the Yellow Sea, connecting the Korean peninsula directly to China and making Korea easily accessible. It seems not unlikely that *Homo erectus*, known to have been so near by, found the way to Korea, as the skull cap from Kumgul Cave seems to indicate.

Stratigraphically, the Sokchangni materials imply an early date, and they are typologically the equivalent of early paleolithic tools. Yet these "crude" tools persisted in Asia right up to the neolithic, so caution must be applied in dating by typology alone. The Chon'gongni site has a reddish clay layer that may correspond to a geological layer said to be on the Holocene boundary throughout East Asia (Larichev and Grigorenko 1969:129), rather than earlier red clays. Until it is known whether the red clay layers were formed at several different times when there was a warm and humid climate, the red clay does not make a secure time determinant. Detailed study of the Pleistocene geology of Korea is likely to aid greatly in placing components in their proper places. At present, it can only be said that the existence of early paleolithic in Korea seems increasingly probable.

The hand-axe question is important mainly to remove once and for all the "Movius line," along with the implication that South and East Asia were culturally retarded compared with Europe and Africa. The first report of Chon'gongni (*Han'guk Ilbo* 16 October 1979) made much of the discovery of hand-axes in East Asia beyond the "Movius line" (Movius 1948) which separated the chopper/chopping tool tradition from the hand-axe tradition. This find, however, was not unique for East Asia even at that time. Other hand-axes have been discovered in north China, for instance at Dingcun (Tingts'un), even though these tools are often called points or pointed tools and contrasted to hand-axes. "Breuil interpreted many of the Tingts'un chopping tools as bifaces similar to the late Acheulian" (Aigner 1978:203). Aigner cites both Pei and Bordes as believing that these tools are independent of European traditions. Furthermore, there is no distinct *assemblage* of hand-axes and other tools.

Where hand-axes are found they are added to the other characteristic tools (Bae 1989b). The much-admired patterning of Afro-European tools is probably related in part to raw materials which could be more elegantly flaked than most of the stone found in Asia. Bae (1989b) argues that cruder stone tools in Asia might also reflect the use of more perishable materials for refined and specific tools, an idea that has had wide currency in Southeast Asia (Hutterer 1977, Pope 1990).

The functions of "hand-axes" of various shapes is another question which needs to be addressed. For example, Binford (1972:142) has stated that hand-axes tend to occur in sites with "little or no fauna," and that they are unlikely to be related to meat processing. It is likely that the forested environment of Korea did not promote big game hunting, lacking extensive grasslands for groups of large grazers such as mammoth and horse, which were utilized more extensively in the north and west. On the other hand, Watanabe (1985) makes an ecological argument for the use of large, crude stone tools, relating them to the rain forests and the exploitation of smaller fauna. Directly contrary to Binford's observation about the inverse relation between hand-axes and faunal remains, Watanabe assumes that hand-axes are cutting tools indicating specialization in big game hunting. Use-wear analysis would be important to solve this problem. Watanabe explains what he believes is the lack of hand-axes in East Asia by the missed opportunity for diffusion of the technology into an ecologically appropriate niche. In any case, it is clear that there is complexity in the East Asian early paleolithic, but it has its own character and is not identical to that of Europe.

Recent research in China has suggested two separate traditions of stone working techniques, beginning in the early paleolithic and continuing into the neolithic. These traditions are represented by the Kehe/Dingcun series emphasizing large tools on the one hand, and Zhoukoudian with its flake industry on the other (Jia and Huang 1986). However, the large pointed tools illustrated at Dingcun are not hand-axes in the classical sense – they are more elongated with sharper points. And the term that is frequently translated from the Chinese as "microliths" just means small tools; it does not imply specially prepared cores. The two-tradition division in China is related to the hand-axe question in that it is another attempt to declare that Chinese paleolithic is not backward and boring, à la Movius, and should be evaluated in that light.

Another example of East Asian "hand-axes" was reported by Okladnikov (1978). A workshop in eastern Mongolia near Mount Yarkh has "excellent specimens of Acheulian-like tools," specifically disassociated from Dingcun. Okladnikov finds the likeness to Acheulian so striking that "there are reasons to believe that not only the Acheulian technique but its carriers had penetrated from the areas of the classic Abbevillian and Acheulian cultures of Afro-European origin to the central regions of Asia" (Okladnikov 1978:321). This remains an unsolved riddle.

The Neanderthal question

Quite aside from the problem of middle paleolithic tool industries, discussed above, there is the question of the existence of Neanderthals. A few human fossils of *Homo sapiens neanderthalensis* are claimed in Korea. More frequently now they are being designated early *Homo sapiens*. To date they are too few and too sketchily published to lead to any firm conclusions (Kwon 1990). Some scholars (e.g. Yi 1986) have doubted that these bones are properly to be attributed to the Neanderthal line. However, the finds, which are dated to the Riss/Würm Interglacial period and the Early Würm, have been discovered in cave sites in both North and South Korea.

Tokchon Cave in Sungnisan, 75 km northeast of Pyongyang in North Korea, is a site with abundant faunal material (Kim K.K. 1979) including two human molars and a clavicle assigned to *Homo sapiens neanderthalensis* (Kim W.Y. 1973) and associated with typical Riss/Würm Interglacial fauna, although Choi M.C. (1987) includes it with late paleolithic. Yokpo, a cave near Pyongyang, yielded the skull of a child (Kwon 1986, 1990).

The series of caves at Turubong, in Chungchong Puk Do, have a great deal of published information. In the cave named Hungsugul, one nearly complete skeleton of a six or seven-year-old child was unearthed (Park 1990). It is an extended burial, supine, with the legs slightly bent. A square plaquette had been placed on its midsection. Another skull and lower mandible were found a few meters away. At the entrance to the cave, anvil and hammerstones were found. Other tools included bolas, cleavers, choppers and end-scrapers made of quartz, quartzite, felsite, granite and porphyry. Associated fauna were *Sus scrofa* and various cervids (Lee Y.J. 1990).

Daehyundong is a limestone fissure rather than a cave with a living floor. This North Korean site has abundant bones, including human remains. Two pieces of human cranium are believed to be from the same individual, a juvenile. Some traits of archaic *Homo sapiens* include low forehead and supraorbital ridge, and it is reported as Neanderthal (Kim Y.G. and Suk K.J. 1984). Many extinct species were identified among the fauna.

Cave 2 at Turubong is assigned to the Riss/Würm Interglacial, also on the basis of warm-climate fauna, 20 percent of which represent extinct species (Lee Y.J. 1983). The animals represented include *Dicerorhinus kirchbergensis*, *Hyaena ultima*, *Pseudaxis grayii* and *Macaca robustus*. Cervids are represented in most of the 10 cm levels. Pollen analysis indicates a warm stage at 20,000 years ago and older. Pine is present throughout, suggesting that the mixed forest environment, although it may have varied somewhat in its composition, basically persisted throughout the Pleistocene climatic changes (Sohn 1978b). Some tools were made from fractured long bones, including scrapers, awls, gravers and denticulates (Lee Y.J. 1986a). Layer 7 contains a living floor with a hearth. Charcoal in the hearth was identified as pine, alder and maple. Annual rings of the wood indicated irregular rainfall. Pollen in this level all turned out to be from a flowering plant, *Ericaceae*, a kind of heath. Since the pollen from this plant is not wind-borne, its presence indicates that an armful of blooms was brought into the cave. Lee Y.J. (1986a) believes that this is earlier than the famous Shanidar Cave, and therefore *these* are the first "flower children." According to Lee's analysis of the amount of animal bones, a family of five could have lived here for nearly ten years.

Turubong Cave No. 9 has Middle Pleistocene fauna, unassociated with artifacts in its fissures, and two habitation layers with Upper Pleistocene fauna in higher cave sediments. The lower of these two habitation layers is contained in a yellowish matrix, with a few stone tools. It includes bones of four animal species, of which two are extinct. The upper level has thirty-three species, of which nine are extinct. A spectrometry date of 32,500 ± 2,500 BP was calculated (Lee Y.J. 1983:68). The layer is reddish clay, and includes both bones and stone tools (Fig. 3.8). The majority of the fossils are of *Pseudaxis grayii*, *Macaca* and *Panthera*. Estimates were made of the total amount of meat available on the animals (presumably) hunted, and it was concluded that this was an occupation of less than two months, if continuous. The upper layer could have been inhabited for four months and occupation was presumably a winter one, for the young deer are four to six months of age (Sohn 1983).

Saemgul Cave included bones of *Elephus antiqitatus*, *Dicerorhinus kirchbergensis*, *Macaca robustus*, *Hyaena ultima*, *Ursus arctos* L. and *Pseudaxis grayii*. This is the first time the ancient elephant has been identified in Korean cave faunas (Lee Y.J. 1986a:98). Within 1 sq m in a corner thirteen skulls of *Pseudaxis grayii* were grouped, along with two sawed antler pieces interpreted as pendants. Chongyo Cave nearby has one area of scattered cervid bones, and another with an articulated skeleton of a cave bear adorned by a deer antler placed on top of it, possibly indicating ritual behavior. Only Cave No. 15 produced a habitation area, with a line of limestone fragments demarcating a living area of 9.6 sq m. In the center was a 30 × 30 cm hearth, and scattered around it were "kitchen tools," scrapers and points made of quartz.

Chommal is yet another limestone cave. No stone tools have been found, but some of the bone is reported as worked (Sohn 1975, Sohn and Park 1980). The artifactual status of these bones is not entirely accepted (Bae 1989b). Inconsistent dates were obtained from bone, with a 40,000 date on a feline tooth from Layer IV and a date of 66,000 ± 3,000 BP on the jaw of a bear from the layer above. Charcoal from Layer VI gives a C14 date of 13,700 ± 700 BP.

Myongori, an open-air site on the Namhan river, includes a layer (Layer 3) which contains chopping tools, cleavers, six side-scrapers and a burin. This layer is assigned to the end of the middle paleolithic. Layer 2 contains many more artifacts, totaling 163, including large hand-axes up to 14 cm long, a pick made of slate, cleavers and many small tools made on flakes. These are called side-scrapers, end-scrapers, points, notches, denticulates, borers, burins and knives

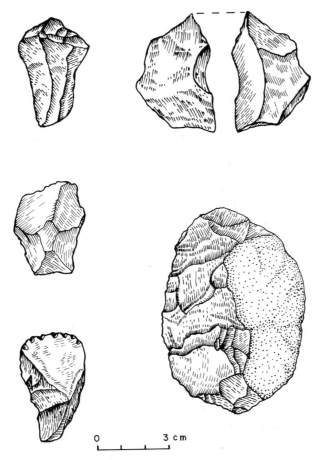

3.8 Artifacts from Turubong Cave No. 9. After Sohn 1983.

(Fig. 3.9). On the basis of a "Levallois" core, the whole layer is assigned to the "late Mousterian" (Choi M.C. 1984), and dated around 40,000 to 50,000 BP (Choi M.C. 1987).

Lying underneath the neolithic shell mound referred to as Sopohang, the two tool-bearing layers of Kulpori are variously described as "Acheulian" (Kulpo I) and "Mousterian" (Kulpo II) (Hwang n.d.), and ascribed to Neanderthal at 100,000 BP and *Homo sapiens* at 40,000 BP (FLPH 1977:4). Located on the northeast coast near the mouth of the Tumen river, the site when it was active was close to a bay which has now receded some 300 m. Two terraces on the hill slope rise up from the bay; the lower one is connected with the paleolithic layer (Larichev and Grigorenko 1969:128).

The stratigraphy of the site includes a basal layer of loose gravel, above which is a layer of pebbles, stone blocks and fire-cracked stones. This is Kulpo I. Kulpo II is in a layer of dark reddish clay, with tiny pebble inclusions. This kind of

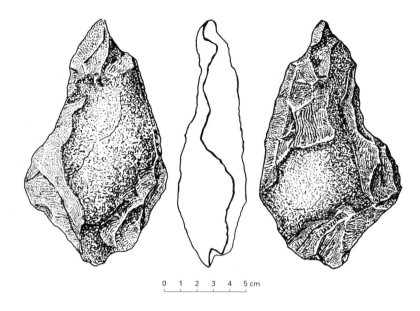

0 1 2 3 4 5 cm

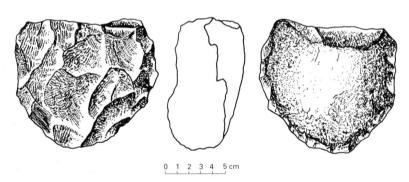

0 1 2 3 4 5 cm

3.9 Artifacts from Myongori. After Choi M.C. 1987.

clay, with much iron oxide, indicates a humid and warm climate. Kulpo II has tools of hornfels (Kim W.Y. [1981] calls it slate), including choppers, chopping tools, scrapers and burins. They tend to be made on flakes with unifacial retouch. Kulpo I features quartzite tools which are larger and heavier. A workshop area includes a large (92 × 96 × 40 cm) porphyrite anvil stone and porphyrite hammerstones, along with numerous flakes. To Yu-ho (1964) regards the flaking method as anvil hurling. A stone enclosure about 15 cm high has been interpreted as the base of a windbreak. It outlines an area of 11.5 × 8 m, which is larger than other such enclosed areas in paleolithic Korea.

East Asian comparisons

"Middle paleolithic" in China is marked more by the presence of *Homo sapiens neanderthalensis* remains than by a shift in tool technology. Associated with Neanderthals are "new species including *Equus przewalskiy, Ethemionus, Bos primigenius, Cervus elephas* and *Megaloceros ordosianus* which appear for the first time" (Qiu 1985:190). Techniques of tool making are still the same: simple direct percussion, bipolar percussion and anvil hurling. Like the earlier finds, the majority of tools are made on flakes. In addition, there are large, heavy points, including trihedral forms and picks.

The Japanese site of Hoshino contains both hand-axes and tools made on flakes in "Cultural Strata" 2 and 3. Aikens and Higuchi (1982:39ff.) suggest a date of 50,000 to 35,000 BP for stratum 3, which according to them contained most of the artifacts. Serizawa (1986:192), however, describes thirteen layers, and dates the lowest at 80,000 BP. The presence of a middle paleolithic in Asia is yet to be demonstrated.

Late paleolithic

Radiocarbon dates of 30,690 ± 3,000 (AERIK 5) and 20,830 ± 1,880 BP (AERIK 8) at Sokchangni, 32,500 ± 2,500 BP at Turubong, 30,000 ± 7,000 BP at Sangsi Rockshelter, and two dates of 13,000 and 66,000 BP at Yonggul Cave help to place the late paleolithic sites more firmly in a time scale. Many more dates are needed, however, before even the relative chronology is secure. A few bones of *Homo sapiens sapiens* have been unearthed, although not yet thoroughly described. Some interesting features of the recent finds include obsidian tools, tanged points and microcores which had not previously been discovered in Korea.

The open-air site of Suyanggae was discovered during the survey for the Chungju Dam project, and subsequently excavated (Lee Y.J. 1984a, 1988b, 1986a, 1989). It covers at least 1,250 sq m and is being investigated with a large continuous excavation instead of in smaller discontinuous units. Three layers contain cultural materials. The lowest level, IVb, is designated middle paleolithic. There are well-made hand-axes with sinuous edges as well as less definite multi-purpose tools made on "Levalloisian" flakes, and some flakes resulting from anvil hurling. Much charcoal was found as well, and radiocarbon dating is awaited. The wood is identified as camellia, pine and larch. Level IVa is assigned to the late paleolithic and is distinct from the layer below. The raw material used is quite variable – quartzite, shale, rhyolite, quartz felsite and obsidian. The tools include rectangular knives (Fig. 3.10), side-scrapers, end-scrapers, burins and tanged points (Fig. 3.11), as well as "ski-shaped" spalls. Microblades and prepared microblade cores (Fig. 3.12) are also found. The cores

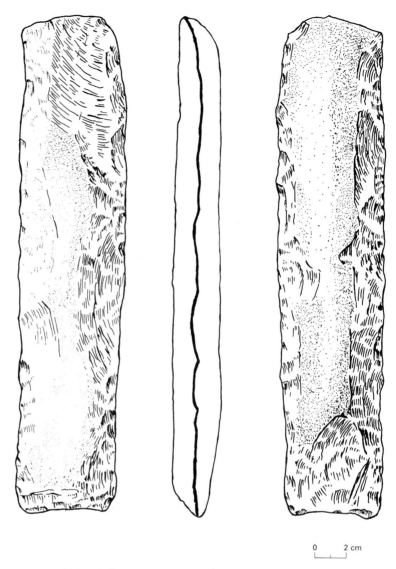

0   2 cm

3.10 Rectangular knife from Suyanggae. After Lee Y.J. 1989.

appear to have been used as tools after they were exhausted (Lee Y.J. 1989:4). Some of the microblades are retouched. The whole assemblage is similar to the very late paleolithic assemblages with the Yubetsu technique of microblade production first recognized in Japan.

Nearly fifty workshop areas were noted with sandstone anvils, hammerstones and large numbers of flakes. A whole core was reconstructed from the flakes in one of these features. Seeds of *Chenopodia*, *Compositae*, *Rutaceae* and *Cruci-*

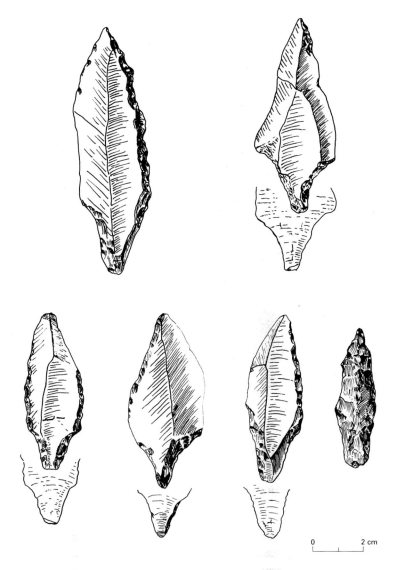

3.11 Tanged points from Suyanggae. After Lee Y.J. 1989.

ferae were collected, as well as animal fur which may be from wild boar (Lee Y.U. 1986a). A tibia of *Bos primigenius* was carved with a fish-like outline.

A habitation floor at Sokchangni has been radiocarbon dated to 20,830 ± 1880 BP (AERIK 8). Pollen from this level included *Pinus, Lingustrum, Osmunda, Liliacea, Magnolia* and *Alnus*, indicating a climate at least as warm as the present, or possibly warmer. Sohn (1973) suggests it may represent the last interstadial of the Würm glaciation. However, fossils in Chinese sites indicate a mild period

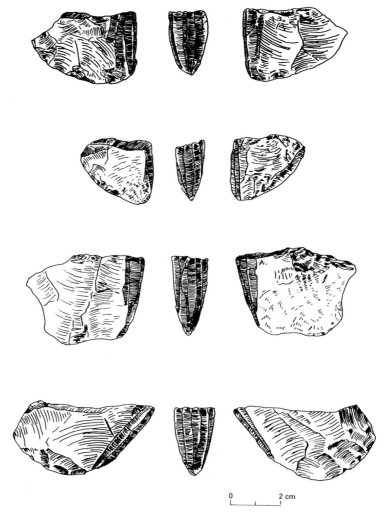

0 _____ 2 cm

3.12 Microblade cores from Suyanggae. After Lee Y.J. 1989.

around 40,000 BP with mixed deciduous forest in the Ordos region. By 30,000 BP the mean annual temperature had dropped considerably, leading to the last glacial maximum at 22,000 to 13,000 BP (Sohn 1984b).

The dwelling found at Locality I was outlined by two lines of stones, which indicate a hut or a windbreak. Behind this formation lies a hearth, and behind the hearth five post holes were found. The space is adequate for the living area of about 10 people. Stone tools were mostly made of local quartzite, and consisted of 63 percent core tools (Fig. 3.13). Few of the tools had regular edge retouch (Fig. 3.14). Several oddly shaped stones were found inside the habitation, some with minimal chipping. Sohn has interpreted these as animal forms. Limonite

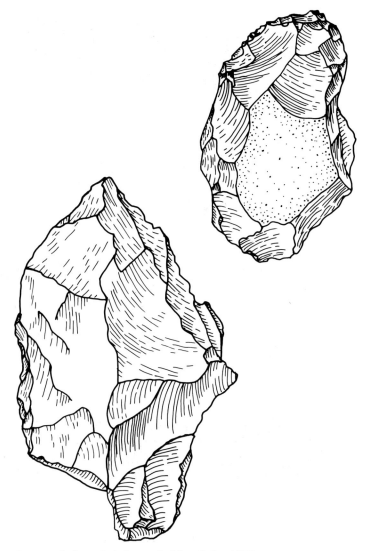

3.13 Core tools from Sokchangni. After Sohn 1973.

and hematite pigments were found in several shades – bright red, dark red, pale brown and black – and some pebbles had traces of paint on them. Painting on perishable materials must have taken place here.

Changnae is another open site which lies on a small tributary to the Namhan river. The site has eight layers and covers 240 sq m. The basal layer consists of river gravels, with an upper paleolithic dwelling in the layer just above. Flake tools dominate the assemblage. Scrapers are the most common tool, made with edge retouch. A hearth, surrounded by post holes enclosing an area of 10 sq m, is an interesting feature of this site. From the angles of the post holes, a tent-shaped

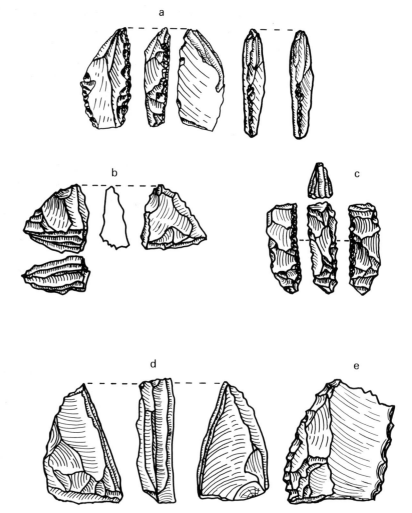

3.14 Small tools from the upper layer of Sokchangni. *a* burin, *b, c, d* wedge-shaped microblade cores, *e* scraper. After Sohn 1973.

structure has been reconstructed. Tools are found near the hearth, made from several kinds of raw materials: chert, rhyolite, felsite, porphyry, quartz and obsidian (Pak 1984, 1990).

Mandalli, a limestone cave near Pyongyang, contained human and animal bones. A human skull is identified as that of a male twenty-five to thirty years old. The bulk of the artifacts were made of obsidian, including microblade cores. Worked antler was made into a knife handle, and bone points from deer were also found.

Yonggul Cave is a small shelter only 13 × 3 m. Five meters of deposits have been excavated, divided into seven layers, of which the top is neolithic. The next layer has a date of 13,000 BP associated with two human metatarsals. A long erosional period appears to follow, for the next layer is dated 66,000 BP. Although the excavator finds evidence for working on the bones (direct fracture and retouch), stone tools are extremely scarce (Sohn, Park and Han 1990).

Simgongni is near the central east coast of the Korean peninsula. The site has predominantly choppers, largely made of quartz, but also contains flake scrapers and other small tools. It lacks any of the late paleolithic features such as tanged points, but is found in red-clay sea-terrace deposits that are considered to be Quaternary (Ro 1986).

Sangmuryongni is a site in an area deep in the mountains near the spine of the Korean peninsula which has a number of paleolithic localities strung along small streams. This region, near Chunchon in Kangwon Do, was surveyed before the construction of the Paraho Dam. In all there are more than 7,000 artifacts, especially pointed tools and burins. The presence of obsidian is notable here, with about 250 implements (Jin 1989c).

Near Taejonni in the southwest, in the region surveyed for the Juam Dam, a number of late paleolithic sites were found. Boat-shaped cores reminiscent of those found in Japan are dated about 25,000 BP (Lee Y.J. 1988a).

Late paleolithic in East Asia

Late paleolithic sites in Korea are beginning to appear in sufficient number for generalization about some of their characteristics. The use of obsidian was widespread, possibly from newly discovered sources in central Korea, and blade tools appear at many sites, including tanged points and burins.

Some similarities with other sites in East Asia can be noted. Parallels can be found with a few sites in Japan, including the Iwajuku site in Honshu and the Yubetsu technique found in Hokkaido. The chronology and distribution of the Korean sites need to be studied further.

The paleolithic/Holocene boundary

The radiocarbon gap which formerly divided the latest late paleolithic date from the earliest dated ceramic level in Korea is closing rapidly. An isolated date of 12,000 BP from Osanni may be suspect, but at Sangnodae Do, a preceramic level seems to indicate Holocene coastal foraging, and some of the Juam Dam sites with microcores in southwestern Korea have been described as resembling the Japanese early Holocene microcores (Kim D.H. 1984). The important site of Yokchi Do, off the southern coast, has a preceramic component with small tools (Choe 1986:20, Chinju National Museum 1989), and some 500 microliths made of obsidian and quartz were found at a site on the Hongchon river in Kangwon Do.

Chommal Cave has a reported "mesolithic" layer consisting of scrapers and knives, dated at 11,700 ± 700 BP (Choi M.C. 1987, Sohn 1974). Microcores and microliths have been reported at sites in the Juam Dam survey region, at the southeastern site of Imbulli (Kim K.U. 1974), and in three sites on the south coast.

In sites described as microlithic in East Asia, microcores are common, especially in north China, Mongolia and Manchuria (Tong 1979). The terminology, however, becomes problematical, because tools described as "microlithic" may simply be small stone tools, not necessarily made on microblades. Many Chinese sites feature microcores like those at Sokchangni and elsewhere, including locations near Korea in the Shandong and Liaodong peninsulas. Microblades were also discovered in Fukui Cave in Kyushu. Between 50,000 and 12,000 BP, a vast plain extended where the Yellow Sea now lies, and a land bridge connected Japan to the continent with a small gap through the Tsushima strait to Kyushu. Forest animals and broadleaved deciduous trees are attested in the Korean sites, also similar to Japan. Pottery sometimes accompanies the microliths in both Japan and China, suggesting a widespread late paleolithic horizon to which pottery was added. Two basic industries producing microblades, represented by wedge-shaped cores and conical cores, are found in China, although both of these, and some other variants as well, may be found together in many sites. Microblades were also discovered in Fukui Cave in Kyushu.

The Dyuktai assemblage in eastern Siberia has been widely viewed as a possible link with paleo-Indian sites, but its relationship to sites farther south in Korea is less often noted. The accepted dates are 18,000–10,500 BP (Yi and Clark 1985). The pressure blade technique (Flenniken 1987) which produces ski-spall flakes and microblades is also found in Korea. It would be interesting to understand the functions of this technocomplex (Aigner 1984), since its distribution appears to be so wide. The time period seems to be on the Pleistocene/Holocene boundary (Michael 1984).

Microblades are found in Japan rather late, appearing with the earliest pottery (Serizawa 1986), but in China they are dated as early as 30,000 BP (Tong 1979), and as late as 9000 BP (Chen 1984). Similarities over the vast region of East Asia suggest cultural continuities, but regional and temporal differences abound (Chen 1984) and have not yet been sorted out.

It seems unlikely that, as temperatures warmed and sea levels rose, the Korean peninsula would have been uninhabited, as previous models have suggested. Rather we might expect that sites have been invisible or unrecognized, perhaps buried under silt on the continental shelf or under the Yellow Sea. Other sites are gradually coming to light as more subtle signs of human occupation are becoming recognized in Korea, and as shell mound sites are excavated more deeply.

Conclusion

Although the evidence is fragmentary, it is important to attempt to view the paleolithic materials in Korea as evidence of living human systems. A few generalizations can be made regarding the subsistence base, the settlement system and the size of the social groups represented in these sites.

Subsistence

All the evidence points to opportunistic exploitation of deciduous forest resources, regardless of the time depth in the Pleistocene. Little is known of the subsistence base except for the faunal component, and it is not wise to assume that all bones found on the sites represent animals eaten by the human inhabitants. However, animal bones are the best primary evidence for hunting, especially when they bear traces of butchering. The most likely food sources include various cervids (deer) and *Sus scrofa* (wild boar) from the late paleolithic, and macaques and cervids from earlier periods.

Processing tools are of too general a nature for a distinction to be made between faunal-processing and vegetal-processing tools. There are no definite projectile points, and relatively few of the large stone utensils that would be expected in a "butchering" tool kit. Perhaps animals were taken in traps and butchered on the spot. Overall, the impression is that of forest animals in the sites, regardless of the time period, with a preponderance of deer throughout the paleolithic.

Vegetal resources are even more difficult to pin down from the archaeological record. Containers for gathering were made of perishable materials, and the plant remains themselves decay as well. Pollen in sites helps to describe the environment, but pollen profiles are not likely to reflect the daily diet. It can be safely inferred, however, that the rich vegetal resources of the deciduous forest were not overlooked. Lee Y.J. (1986a) suggests that jujubes and persimmons were collected near Suyanggae. Sohn (1974) believes the people at Sokchangni were exploiting the river fish, to judge from the location of the site above the Kum river and some possible representations of fish. Other sites on large river banks are also situated to take advantage of fish, including a number of sites only surface-collected so far. Sites such as Kulpori were located to exploit marine resources.

Although climatic conditions were variable in the Pleistocene, the changes in vegetation that took place in Korea seem to have been relatively minor: a shifting north and south of the boundaries of the various types of forest. This shift would not have any profound far-reaching effect on the fauna, leaving the foraging adaptation unchanged. During the height of each glacial period, Korea's wooded, mountainous terrain rose above the vast plain covered at present by the Yellow Sea. Populations might have preferred to live in these lowlands, making only seasonal excursions into the mountains for forest fauna such as deer and boar and for the gatherables of the deciduous forest: nuts, fruits and herbs. As sea level gradually rose in the interglacial periods, populations would have become restricted to the forested mountains. Their food base might well have been augmented by increased access to resources from the sea, with a greatly expanded coastline, but there is no direct evidence of such marine adaptations until the end of the Pleistocene.

Dwellings

Four paleolithic shelters have so far been discovered. At Sokchangni, a wind-break in front of a hearth appears to be indicated, while the shelter at Kulpori seems to represent an enclosed dwelling. Both are small, and could have sheltered an extended family at best. Cave sites in general allow for a larger local group, but the Korean caves excavated so far provided only restricted areas, and appear to have been the homes of small families at best. Thus, the scanty evidence points to small foraging groups. Places for macrobands to gather have so far not been located, unless extensive lithic scatters can be shown to be contemporaneous.

Population size

A band-level organization is frequently hypothesized for paleolithic groups in general (Service 1962), although the European paleolithic shows considerable complexity. However, few Korean sites imply that they were created by large aggregates of people. Although the extensive open-air sites of Chon'gongni, Suyanggae and Sangmuryongni are possible exceptions, it remains to be seen whether they represent multiple occupations or synchronous gatherings. The evidence, admittedly scanty, points to minimal bands, even family groups, as the social units that occupied most of the sites.

The forest habitat supplies a likely explanation for the small size of human groups: forest animals do not travel in large groups like the grazing herbivores, and are best hunted by a single person or only a few hunters at most. They are effectively trapped or snared. Vegetal resources in deciduous forests vary by season, and also would not support large numbers of people without some form of food storage. How thickly the bands were to be found upon the landscape cannot be estimated with the data at hand, but the finds to date suggest that they were few and widely separated.

The study of paleolithic sites in East Asia has concentrated so far on description of stone artifacts, but reconstructing the local environment from the local fauna, geomorphology and pollen or macroflora is being increasingly attempted. Research focusing on the function of artifacts, the size of the social group, or the behavior and cognition of these early hominids is minimal, and based on scanty evidence, but it is leading in more productive directions. The presence of *Homo erectus* in China is established, but the extension of the range to Korea is not universally accepted. However, the evidence for an early paleolithic stage in Korea is increasingly convincing. The existence of middle paleolithic is predicated on a few human bones said to have Neanderthaloid features, and a flake tool industry described as Mousterian. Only the late paleolithic is securely dated, and acknowledged to have been widespread throughout East Asia. Early Holocene discoveries with microcores are beginning to close the gap between the early foragers and the settled villages.

CHAPTER 4

EARLY VILLAGES

The era when pottery and villages with semi-subterranean dwellings make their appearance in Korea is often called neolithic. An agricultural subsistence base is not necessarily implied by writers who use this term, as there is no conclusive evidence of domesticated plants and/or animals at the beginning of this stage. I would prefer to leave the discussion of the subsistence base to later in the chapter, and defer the neolithic issue. The Early Villages period has also been referred to as the Chulmun ("combware") period, in reference to the incised pottery, decorated on the exterior with geometric patterns. With the discovery of earlier raised-design (Yungkimun) pottery, the use of the term Chulmun to designate the entire period has also become problematical. Semi-subterranean dwellings, however, do seem to be a peninsula-wide characteristic, and these houses are grouped into villages. Therefore, I prefer to call this stage simply Early Villages, focusing on the settlement pattern rather than on any specific artifact type.

Based on radiocarbon dates, the time frame of the Early Villages period is approximately 6000–2000 BC (Nelson 1992a). The beginning of the Early Villages period coincides with the first appearance of pottery, and the end is marked by the addition of megaliths and the appearance of plain, or Mumun, pottery types.

The entire peninsula is thought to have been sparsely inhabited by paleo-Asiatics (Kim W.Y. 1983a) at this time. These inhabitants are usually regarded not as the former paleolithic foragers metamorphosed into villagers, but as a new group of pottery producers who came from the north bringing with them an advanced foraging technology (Kwon 1990). Originally, a simple migration from Siberia was proposed (Fujita 1930), but with new discoveries of a variety of pottery styles and ever earlier radiocarbon dates, an intricate series of events must be postulated in order to preserve the theory of migrations from the north (e.g. Kim W.Y. 1986a:83). Regional variations in styles of containers and kinds of stone and bone implements further complicate the picture. Discussions of the origin and development of these early inhabitants of Korea is necessarily complex. I will present the site data first, and then consider interpretations, in order to facilitate an orderly discussion.

Sites

Early Villages sites contain hand-made pottery and chipped stone tools found in and near semi-subterranean dwellings which were heated by central hearths. The sites are mainly located on river terraces or sea coasts, each site as a rule having contained only a few houses at any one time.

Although the term Chulmun means "comb-marked," implying decoration applied with a toothed implement, this designation should not be taken as a literal description of all the pottery from 6000–2000 BC. Only a few of the decorative patterns on the incised ware were made with a comb-like tool, although repetitive designs were often drawn sequentially with finger nails, bird bones, shells or sticks. In addition, pottery adorned with raised lines (Yung-kimun) rather than incising is the dominant type in some layers of east and south coast sites. Radiocarbon dates confirm that the raised designs belong to the same time frame as the incised styles, or somewhat earlier. The designation "Chulmun," as frequently used, should be understood not merely as a description of a decorative technique used on pottery, but as a general term covering the first 4,000 years or so of settled villages in Korea, analogous to the use of the term "Jomon" in Japan.

Distribution

Early Villages site locations are closely related to particular features of the landscape, and it is reasonable to infer that sites were positioned to exploit specific habitats. In general, villages were situated on river banks, along the coasts, and on west and south coast islands (Fig. 4.1). Coastal and island sites are located above the present high-tide mark (which can be nearly 10 m on the west coast), but they tend to be directly on the coast rather than on a hill slope away from the sea or even farther inland. Riverine sites, especially those in the lower reaches, occupy terraces situated about 10 m above the present river-bed. Similar elevations on rivers and coasts are an interesting coincidence, for which no geomorphological explanation has been offered. The recently discovered sites farthest inland do not share this characteristic, although they are also found on river terraces.

The elevation of coastal sites just above the present high-tide line suggests relatively stable sea levels since the Early Villages period. However, some scholars believe that a significant number of Early Village sites may have disappeared beneath the rising level of the Yellow Sea (e.g. Hewes 1947), since the coastline at 8000 BC appears to have been up to 50 km west of the present shoreline (Huang 1984: Fig. 4.2).

An important characteristic of the site distribution is the tendency to cluster. Sites are not found continuously at roughly equidistant locations along the coasts, but in small groups of sites, separated by long stretches with no known

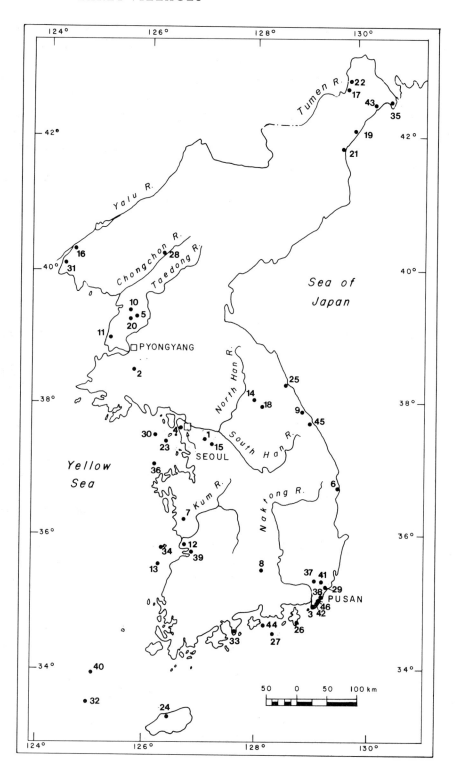

sites at all. The same pattern can be perceived along the rivers, although less clearly than on the coasts (Im and Pak 1988). While it is likely that other sites will be discovered, the clustering does not appear to be either a result of random finds or an artifact of skewed discovery. Recent archaeological activity in South Korea has included survey and excavation for a dozen or more dam projects. These were carried out in inland areas hitherto little known archaeologically. In spite of a large number of new discoveries, the clustering pattern found in the early surveys (Kim W.Y. and Im H.J. 1968, Chase 1960, Pearson and Im 1968, Sample and Mohr 1964) has not been altered, although new clusters have been found. (See Fig. 4.1, and the neolithic map in Seoul National University Museum 1984:13.) The relative dating of these inland and upland sites has yet to be clarified.

Regional pottery styles

Chulmun pottery has been packaged into geographical groupings by several scholars, although neither the regions chosen nor the dividing lines between them are consistent. Arimitsu (1962) was among the first to suggest regional types for Korean Chulmun. His four divisions are Central Korea, including the Han river and adjacent coasts and islands; the Taedong river and nearby coastal sites comprising Western Korea; Northern Korea, in which he includes the far northeast on the Tumen river as well as the east coast, and Southern Korea. Kim Jong-hak (1978b) grouped all the northwest together from the Yalu river as far south as Hwanghae province, with the northeast forming a separate region. A central group includes a section from coast to coast across the peninsula, above and below the 38th parallel. Finally he names a southern group, encompassing North and South Cholla and North and South Kyongsang provinces. Kim Won-yong (1981) perceives three "natural" groups rather than four – the west coast, the southeast and the northeast, with the Yalu river sites as perhaps a special case (Kim W.Y. 1967a). This variety could lead one to suspect that there are no "real" regional groups at all. At the very best the groupings are polythetic sets.

Although these classifications were partly made for the sake of convenience in presentation, they imply relationships that may not be supported by other data.

4.1 Approximate locations of sites in Chapter 4.
1 Amsadong, 2 Chitamni, 3 Cho Do, 4 Chojiri, 5 Chonghori, 6 Hupori, 7 Hyuamni, 8 Imbulli, 9 Katunji, 10 Kumtalli, 11 Kungsanni, 12 Kunsan, 13 Kyehwa Do, 14 Kyodong, 15 Misari, 16 Misongni, 17 Musan, 18 Naepyongni, 19 Najin, 20 Namgyongni, 21 Nongpodong, 22 Odong, 23 Oi Do, 24 Orali, 25 Osanni, 26 Sandal Do, 27 Sangnodae Do, 28 Sejungni, 29 Shinamni, 30 Si Do, 31 Sinamni, 32 Sohuksan Do, 33 Song Do, 34 Sonyu Do, 35 Sopohang, 36 Soya Do, 37 Sugari, 38 Tadaepo, 39 Taehangni, 40 Taehuksan Do, 41 Tongnae, 42 Tongsamdong, 43 Unggi, 44 Yondae Do, 45 Yongjilli, 46 Yongsandong.

Temporal differences become obscured in these schemes, and the temptation to propose sweeping diffusionist or migrationist explanations for the origin and spread of early pottery is intensified. A more detailed examination of the potsherds, as well as other artifacts and features of the sites, reveals more complexity. The following site descriptions, therefore, are presented in geographic order only as an organizational convenience, beginning on the central east coast (because the earliest dates come from there) and proceeding in a clockwise direction around the peninsula.

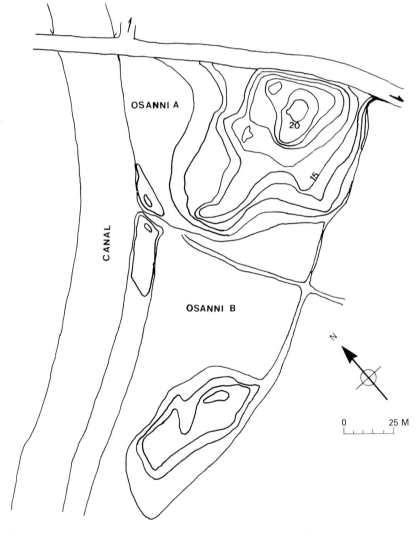

4.2 Site map of Osanni. After Im and Kwon 1988.

Central east coast sites

Several Chulmun sites have been discovered in the region around Yangyang on the central east coast. The sites are in the narrow coastal plain, often associated with sand dunes. Osanni is the only site in this group which has been both excavated and published.

Osanni is in an area of active dune formation beside an ancient lake which formed as a lagoon behind a sand bar. The Namdaechon river empties into the East Sea about 3 km north of the site. Two areas were excavated, designated A and B (Fig. 4.2) (Im 1982b, 1982c, Im and Kwon 1984, Kim, Im and Kwon 1985, Im and Lee 1988). Locality A covers the highest part of the site, while Locality B is approximately 50 m distant in the direction of the lake. Six soil layers were encountered. The uppermost layer (I) was 40 cm thick, existing only at the summit of the site. The soil is composed of humus mixed with clay. Layer II, varying in thickness from 20 to 65 cm, was made up of fine sand, which extended over almost the entire excavated area. A thin (5 cm) layer of black sand lies beneath Layer II separating it from Layer III which is a dark-brown fine-sandy layer. Layer IV is of fine yellow-brown sand, varying in thickness from 20 to 80 cm. This layer is devoid of artifacts. Layer V contains all the dwelling floors in a matrix of brown sand mixed with humus. It is differentiated into thin lenses, containing the seven floors that were discovered. Layer VI is sterile soil.

Layer V in Locality A was the most productive. Dwelling floors, unusual pottery and artifacts, and a series of radiocarbon dates that place it in the time range of 6000 to 4500 BC (Table 4.1) make this site important. New C14 determinations have confirmed the earlier dates, but also include a puzzling outlier at 12,000 BP. This date is not surprising in the larger context of East Asia, including sites associated with pottery in Japan, but it is the first such early date in Korea.

The shapes of the living floors vary from round to oval (Fig. 4.3). All but one have central hearths. The smallest floor, only 2.3 m across, is probably not a dwelling, as it contains no hearth and few artifacts. Perhaps it was some kind of storage building, birthing hut or other special-purpose building. Three stone pavements identified as house floors in the most recent excavations (Im and Lee 1988) may have had a special function also, for cooking, or for baking pottery, for example. The two largest oval houses (about 32 sq m) each contain two hearths, perhaps indicating extended families. Each hearth, outlined with flattened river cobbles, is square in plan, slightly depressed in a basin shape. The stones are fire-cracked and blackened from smoke. Around the hearth a clay layer 5 cm thick had been pounded into a hard surface. One hearth is lined on the surface with small pebbles, in addition to having the usual outer upright ring.

Pottery and stone tools are found associated with the floors, as well as in the fill. The most common type of stone implement is a composite fishhook made of a slender stone cylinder which was probably lashed to a bone or wood point in a

Table 4.1. *Early Villages period radiocarbon dates*

	Site	Location	Sample no.	Half-life 5568 BP	5730 BP	CRD 1 σ BC	Material	References
1.	Osanni	Locality B	KSU-515	7050±120	7255	6150–5573	Carbonized wood	Im 1982b
2.		Layer V1	KSU-492	7120±700	7325	6075–4675	Carbonized wood	
3.		Layer V1	KSU-494	6780±1000	6975	6025–4025	Carbonized wood	Im 1984b
4.		Layer V2	KSU-619	6080±211	6255	5260–4735	Carbonized wood	
5.		Layer V7	KSU-616	6130±50	6305	5235–4955	Carbonized wood	
6.		Layer V1	KSU-615	6070±30	6245	5210–4920	Carbonized wood	
7.		Layer V3	KSU-620	5740±210	5905	4920–4415	Carbonized wood	
8.		House 1988		4360±50				
9.		Cobble		5690±120				
10.		Structure B3 House and flat-based pots		12000±50				
11.	Tongsamdong	Level E	GX-0378	5890±140	6060	5050–4560	Carbonized wood	Sample 1974
12.		Layer V	Gak-6666	5820±140	5895	4950–4540	Shell	Choi S.N. 1982a
13.		Layer V	Gak-6667	5500±100	5660	4445–4320	Shell	
14.		Layer V	Gak-6669	5190±130	5340	4145–3795	Shell	
15.			N-1132	5180±125	5330	4140–3790	Shell	Kim W.Y. 1977a
16.		Layer V	Gak-6668	5160±120	5310	4115–3800	Shell	Choi S.N. 1982a
17.		Layer V	KAERI-?	4950±100	5090	3885–3650	Shell	Lee Y.J. 1977
18.		Level C	GX-0379	4950±125	5080	3880–3650	Carbonized wood	Sample 1974
19.			N-1213	4880±160	5020	3875–3510	Carbonized wood	Kim W.Y. 1977a
20.		Level III	Gak-6664	4690±120	4825	3655–3360	Shell	Choi S.N. 1982a
21.		Level III	Gak-6662	4510±120	4640	3380–3035	Shell	
22.		Level IV	Gak-6665	4490±110	4620	3375–3020	Shell	
23.		Layer 3	AERIK-27	4400±90	4525	3360–2910	Carbonized wood	Yang 1972
24.		Layer 2	AERIK-22	4170±100	4290	2930–2640	Carbonized wood	
25.		Layer III	Gak-6663	4140±120	4260	2910–2630	Shell	Choi S.N. 1982a
26.		Layer 3	AERIK-23	4020±100	4135	2680–2515	Carbonized wood	Yang 1972
27.		Layer 3	AERIK-24	3980±100	4095	2660–2385	Carbonized wood	

No.	Site	Context	Lab no.	Age	bp	Range	Material	Reference
28.		Layer 3	AERIK-25	3930±100	4040	2645–2310	Carbonized wood	Choi S.N. 1982a
29.		Layer 3	AERIK-26	3880±100	3990	2550–2185	Carbonized wood	
30.		Layer III	Gak-6661	3800±100	3910	2415–2130	Shell	Sample 1974
31.		Level C	GX-0493	3400±120	3495	1885–1645	Carbonized wood	Sohn 1982
32.	Sangnodae Do	Layer V	KAERI-?	6430±180	6615	5540–5195	Carbonized wood	Kim D.H. 1984
33.		AU		6622±180				Chung, Shin and Im 1981
34.	Sugari	Level V	N-3448a	4380±105	4510	3555–2905	Shell	
35.		Level V	N-3448b	4360±70	4490	3170–2910	Carbonized wood	Im 1985a
36.		Level III	N-3457	4250±70	4380	3015–2865	Carbonized wood	
37.		Level V	N-3452	4200±90	4330	2980–2665	Carbonized wood	
38.		Level III	N-3456	4170±90	4290	2930–2640	Carbonized wood	
39.	Amsadong	1975 excavation	N-2337	6230±110	6410	5300–5020	Carbonized wood	Im 1985a
40.		1975 excavation	N-2336	6050±105	6225	5210–4895	Carbonized wood	Im 1985a
41.		House 10	KAERI-188	5510±110	5670	4445–4325	Carbonized wood	Kim W.Y. 1975a
42.		1974 excavation	AERIK-?	4950±200	5090	3910–3525	Carbonized wood	Im 1985a
43.		House 2	KAERI-189	5000±70	5145	3890–3760	Carbonized wood	
44.		House 4	KAERI-?	4730±200	4865	3690–3350	Carbonized wood	
45.		House 5	KAERI-?	4610±200	4740	3655–3045	Carbonized wood	
46.		1967 excavation	Washington U.	3430±250	3525	2010–1550	Carbonized wood	Lee Y.J. 1977
47.	Misari	Layer VI	KSU-497	5100±140	5245	3990–3770	Carbonized wood	
48.	Sonyu Do		AERIK-?	4812±45	4945	3675–3510	Carbonized wood	Lee Y.J. 1977
49.	Sandal Do		KSU-618	4440±40	4565	3360–2995	Shell	Im 1983
50.	Oi Do		KSU-617	4080±45	4195	2870–2545	Shell	
51.	Cho Do			4190±120	4310	2950–2560	Shell	Pearson 1980
52.	Soya Do			3860±40	3970	2420–2290	Shell	Im 1983
53.				3750±40	3860	2325–2110	Shell	
54.	Taehuksan Do			3240±120	3515	1900–1660	Shell	Pearson 1980
55.	Si Do	Cairn	AERIK-13	3100±60	3190	1450–1330	Carbonized wood	Yang 1972
56.		Area III	AERIK-11	3040±60	3125	1405–1240	Carbonized wood	Han 1970
57.		Cairn	AERIK-14	3040±60	3125	1405–1240	Carbonized wood	Yang 1972
58.		Cairn	AERIK	2870±60	2950	1125–1015	Carbonized wood	
59.	Chojiri	Shell mound		2290±90			Carbonized wood	Kim W.Y. 1979b

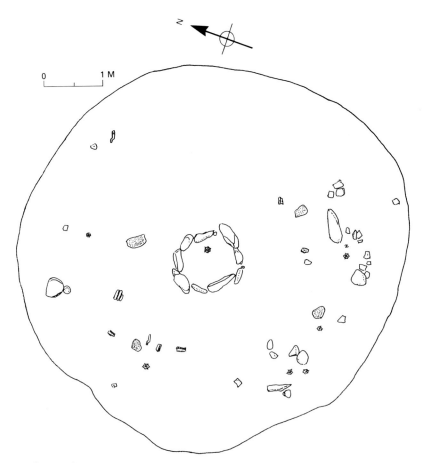

4.3 A house floor at Osanni. After Im and Lee Kwon 1988.

V-shape. The unit that attaches to the fishline is grooved around the top. These fishhook shanks are found in profusion around the site (Fig. 4.4). Fragments of similar fishhooks have been found at Tongsamdong near Pusan (see below), and in Siberia. Late Jomon equivalents in Japan were made of bone (Im 1982b:13). The stone fishhooks found at Osanni are quite large – up to 9 cm long – implying deep-sea fishing. One small polished projectile point was found, as well as several stone knives, hoes, milling slabs and milling stones, net sinkers, scrapers, and grooved stone weights that resemble plumb bobs (Fig. 4.5). One denticulate saw-like tool was found, with analogs in other sites along the east coast such as Tongsamdong and Nongpori. Obsidian flakes were said to match the obsidian flows at Paektusan on the northern border, some 700 km away (Im and Kwon 1984). Recently cores of unworked obsidian have been found at the site. Obsidian has been discovered in the Taebaek mountains closer to the site, providing another possible source.

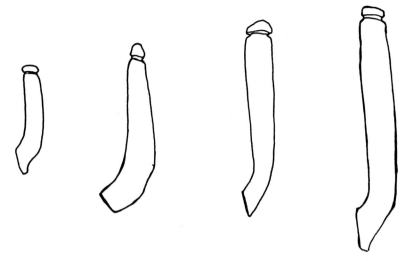

4.4 Fishhook shanks from Osanni.

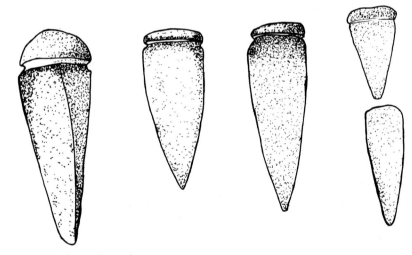

4.5 Weights from Osanni.

The pottery styles of the lowest level had elaborate stamped and raised designs, some of which were unknown in Korea before they were found at Osanni. Locality B contained raised-design (Yungkimun) pottery with flat bases (Fig. 4.6), while Locality A, Layer V featured bowls with small flat bases and elaborate stamped decorative patterns (Fig. 4.7). Small vertical loop handles were attached in pairs to many of the vessels, and the stamping continued across the

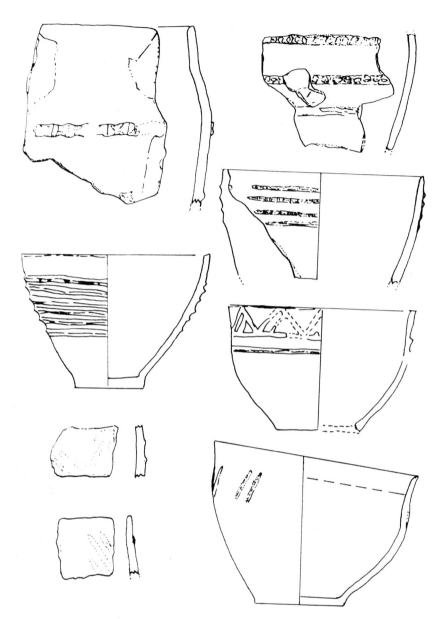

4.6 Yungkimun vessels and sherds. After Chung J.W. 1985.

handles. Two necked jars were found, one of which has vertical loop handles at the curve between the neck and the shoulder. Another jar with vertical loop handles on the shoulder has no neck. Miniature vessels were found on the floor of House 4. One of these was a bowl and the other a broken jar.

The middle cultural layer (Layer III) contained an unusual structure outlined with cobbles, each about 30 cm long, resembling the hearth-ring cobbles. Some

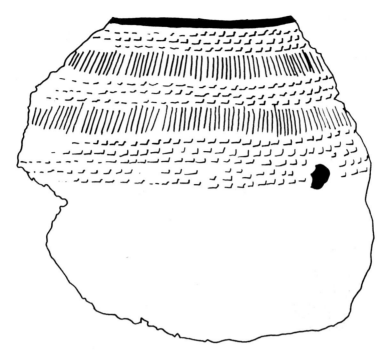

4.7 Impressed sherd from Osanni.

decorated pottery was found inside this ring of stones, but no trace of a fireplace was found. The vessel bases from this layer are all flat.

Four restorable plain pots were found, of which the largest is 23 cm in diameter at the mouth, 7 cm at the base and 18 cm high. The clear impression of a large leaf was left in several of the bases. Decorated sherds were impressed with patterns of punctates and short slanting lines around the mouth in bands, like some sites on the northeast coast of Korea (Im 1982b:14). Also in this layer was a small face or mask of clay, very simply executed with a pinched-up nose and punched-in mouth and eyes. Other crude human faces have been found along the east coast – a bone face from Sopohang in the northeast, and a shell face from Tongsamdong in the southeast. Pinched clay figurines of humans and animals were found at Nongpodong in the southeast and various northeastern sites.

Composite fishhooks continued in Level III, as well as objects made of smoky topaz, which outcrops at a number of locations in Korea. These pieces, 3 to 4 cm long, may be amulets, since only the ends are chipped, and the sharp edges of the crystal facets had been rounded by polishing. Cutting and scraping tools made of granite-gneiss complete the stone assemblage in this layer.

The uppermost culture-bearing layer at Osanni still contains Yungkimun sherds with raised decorations and sherds from flat-based decorated pottery, but predominantly classic Chulmun sherds indicating vessels with pointed bases and incised band patterns around the mouth.

Excavations in 1986 and 1987 uncovered a floor in Locality A strewn with stones and a central stone-filled pit, in addition to a small house that had been burned. Locality B produced three round areas densely packed with fire-cracked stones or cobbles, with blackened potsherds and stone tools. Chulmun pottery was found in the layer, with dates of 4360 ± 50 and 5690 ± 120 BP. A piece of charcoal from a house floor in Locality A yielded a date of 12,000 ± 50 BP (Im and Lee 1988). This date fits well with dates from Jomon Japan, but so far it stands alone in Korean sites. The conclusions which the excavator draws regarding the site are as follows. From 6000 to 4500 BC (and perhaps earlier), the site was a fishing hamlet, closely connected to northeastern Korea, where similar pottery is found in the lower levels of several sites. This culture continues in the middle level. Bases of vessels are larger, giving them more stability, but this is seen as representing local evolution and not as a radical change (Im 1983). In this layer, Im (1983) perceives connections with both the Soviet Maritime region and Japan. Leaf impressions on the bases of pots are found in both of these areas, as are composite fishhooks, and flat-based Yungkimun pottery.

The uppermost level represents a different cultural tradition, with the introduction of classic Chulmun sherds (Fig. 4.8) and pebble net sinkers. This complex closely resembles the central western sites. Other pinched and impressed pottery continues, but this may be an admixture from below. The upper level is therefore interpreted as representing an intrusive new group, although a composite culture could also be postulated.

Other east coast sites. Chulmun sherds have been found in other sand dunes in this area of the coast. Several of these sites are not far from Osanni, including a surface scatter along the Namdaechon river. Coastal sites appear to be small – both Yongjilli and Katunju cover only 30 sq m or so in surface scatter. Both contain Chulmun potsherds of central Korean style, having the pointed bases and rows of short parallel lines combined with a horizontal herringbone pattern on the body, but sherds from flat-based containers have also been found on these sites. Some body sherds are decorated with rows of oblique dots like some found in Tumen river sites, and an incised lattice pattern that turns up all along the west coast, as well as elsewhere in Korea (Sample and Mohr 1964).

The south coast

Shell mounds are characteristic of sites in the south and southeast, including the well-known site of Tongsamdong (Sample 1967, 1974) and many other excavated sites (Chung 1980). Although no dwellings have been identified, midden material has been analyzed. The shell mounds are particularly important for the preservation of bones due to the shell matrix, allowing calculations regarding the subsistence base to be more soundly based at these sites.

The site of Tongsamdong lies on Yong Do island near Pusan, in Pusan Bay. This large island is close to the mainland and joined to it by a bridge. The site

4.8 Chulmun sherds from Osanni.

consists of an extensive (80 × 28 m) shell mound which abuts the water on the bay side of the island. A few pits were excavated by Japanese archaeologists, Yokoyama in 1930 and Oikawa in 1932. Yokoyama (1933) identified four layers in his trench, approximately in the center of the mound. The upper two layers, described as a light gray and a dark gray humus, had relatively few artifacts. A shell layer about 1 m thick contained most of the finds, including a denticulate saw, a projectile point and some obsidian debitage. Under the shell, about 30 cm of clay lay directly on the bedrock. Oikawa excavated the edge of the mound near the sea, where the shell layer was only 30 cm thick. A large, well-made stone spearhead was unearthed, along with grinding stones and another obsidian saw. Three shapes of pottery are described, all with either rounded or pointed bases – a shallow bowl, a cone-shaped pot and a necked bottle. Hatched areas in the band designs are noted, and raised strips, as well as a "sawtooth" design, which is probably that which is described elsewhere as herringbone.

Sample's excavations were designed to examine the stratigraphy with more rigor than the previous attempts. Trench A and Trench B were sunk parallel to each other in different parts of the site. Combining the natural stratigraphy with the results of the ceramic study, Sample described five layers, which she named Cho Do, Mokto, Pusan, Tudo and Yong Do, in order from the bottom. Trench B contained no Pusan layer, while in Trench A Pusan rested on bedrock, followed by Tudo and Yong Do. The various occupation levels were located in different places over the site's duration, according to this scheme. Sample found plain and pinched sherds on the lowest levels, followed by Chulmun pottery which she called Tudo Bold (Sample 1967, 1974). The Yongdo pottery belongs to the megalithic age, to be discussed in the next chapter.

The most recent probe into the site was conducted by the National Museum of Korea in 1969–71. Although never entirely published, the radiocarbon dates and associated assemblages have been reported (Kim W.Y. 1975b:66–70). A reddish-brown clay lies at the bottom of the site and is the "original occupation floor." TSD I consists of a 50-cm layer of mixed soil and shell containing undecorated and Yungkimun sherds, which Kim calls Pre-Comb Pottery. The well-fired plain pottery was constructed with both flat and pointed bases. Chulmun is represented in this layer, but the designs are restricted to the rims. Some sherds were coated with a red ocher wash. Yungkimun pottery is decorated with plain and zigzag lines, similar to patterns found at the Osanni site and nearby Shinamni, as well as Japanese sites on Tsushima Island in the Korea Strait, at Fukui Cave in Kyushu, the Iwakage site, Kamikuroiwa in Shikoku, and at several sites in Honshu. Linear relief pottery is assigned exclusively to Initial Jomon (Aikens and Higuchi 1982:96). Associated dates include 12,700 ± 500 BP at Fukui Cave and 12,165 ± 700 BP at Iwakage (Esaka 1986).

The bases of some Tongsamdong pottery are flat and very small, about 5 cm in diameter, similar to those of the lowest level at Osanni.

From TSD II, several trade sherds have been identified as Todoroki type, an Early Jomon style dated to approximately 4500–4000 BC. The C14 dates are consistent with this postulated relationship.

Obsidian flakes were found in this lowest layer. The nearest source for obsidian was across the Korea Strait in Kyushu, but the flakes have not been tested for trace elements. Stone tools included several chipped stone axes made on pebbles, with the working edge polished bifacially. Bone and shell implements are not plentiful in this layer.

Numerous bones of large fish were found, such as shark, sea bream, tuna and cod. Sea lions and whales were represented, as well as river deer (a small native species) and wild boar. An ox-horn-shaped pottery vessel indicates familiarity with cattle, and a clay figurine of a boar is reminiscent of pig figures found throughout northeastern China by this time (Kim W.Y. 1986a).

The uppermost level, TSD III, contains Chulmun and plain pottery in approximately equal proportions. The top layer of Tongsamdong features fishhooks, small projectile points, harpoons, borers, spatulas and awls. It is in this layer that a shell mask was found, with three holes arranged like eyes and a mouth. A similar shell mask is reported for Japan (Kim W.Y. 1983a). The Chulmun is identical in design motifs to pottery from central Korea, but the incising is deeper. Sample called this type Tudo Bold. Trade sherds from Japan include Early Jomon of the Sobata type, dated between 3500 and 3000 BC, agreeing with the C14 dates. Im (1982b) has suggested that Sobata pottery found on the northern coast of Kyushu is derivative from Chulmun, and not vice versa.

The second layer of the site is dominated by Chulmun pottery, including large vessels up to 40 cm in diameter. Radiocarbon dates fall in the range of 2500 to 2000 BC, dates that are corroborated by finds of Middle Jomon Adaka sherds, C14 dated in Japan between 2290 and 1860 BC. The date of 1850 BC is early for Mumun but late for Chulmun pottery, suggesting a transitional stage at this site. Sherds of a Late Jomon type called Nishibira, which is dated around 1300 BC, are also present, indicating the continual deposition of midden at least to the middle of the second millennium BC. Semi-lunar stone knives and Mumun pottery sherds with doubled over rims are reported in other southeastern sites as early as 2000 BC, and will be discussed in the next chapter. Bones of large fish indicate that deep-sea fishing continued, along with an increase in the bones of land fauna, especially Manchurian deer.

Yongsandong is another shell mound on the same island as Tongsamdong. The shell layer was only 20–50 cm thick, but it contained several whole vessels including two shallow bowls with spouts decorated in Yungkimun style and a narrow-necked jar. Many of the styles found at Tongsamdong are also present here. Some sherds are decorated with cord impressions, uncommon in Korea, and perhaps related to Jomon. The site of Tongnae, also a shell mound, produced Yungkimun pottery with very small bases and raised lines parallel to the rim, as well as diagonal and vertical pinching (Im 1968). At Tadaepo, located on the left bank of the Naktong river, Chulmun sherds were found, some of which appear to have come from a very large pot. Yungkimun sherds were also present (Kim Y.K. 1971). Most of the shell mound sites in this area combine roughly chipped stone implements with well-made pottery (Chung 1982b).

The Shinamni site just north of Pusan is not a shell mound, although the site is near the coast. Three areas were excavated, of which two have been reported (Chi and Lee 1988a, Chung 1989). At Locality 1 a line of rocks which may relate to a house floor was uncovered. It is a single component site, with stone artifacts and Yungkimun sherds found largely inside the structure. Pottery bases are flat or slightly rounded. Stone tools include retouched flakes, ground stone axes and grinding stones. Locality 2 also contains a single cultural layer; but in this case the predominant style is Chulmun, with only a few examples of Yungkimun. A small broken figurine of a nude female was a notable item from the assemblage (Fig. 4.9).

The Sugari shell mound produced a sequence similar to that of Tongsamdong. Five layers were described: Incipient, Early, Middle, Late and Final. Incipient pottery is flat-bottomed, either plain or Yungkimun. Early pottery has pointed bases, and is either plain or decorated with incised lines. Deep grooves, as in Sample's Tudo Bold from Tongsamdong, are characteristic of Middle ceramics, while the Late layer has various incised motifs, and Final has pots with everted or double lip, decorated on the upper half or not at all. Spindle whorls were an unusual find at this site, as well as a pot with a crude drawing which might represent a spouting whale (Chung, Shin and Im 1981).

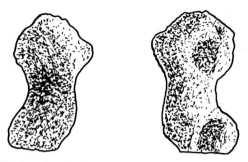

4.9 Broken female figurine, Shinamni. After Chung 1989.

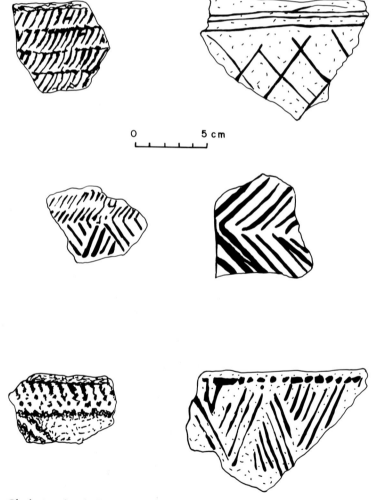

0   5 cm

4.10 Chulmun sherds from Sandal Do. After Chung J.W. 1986.

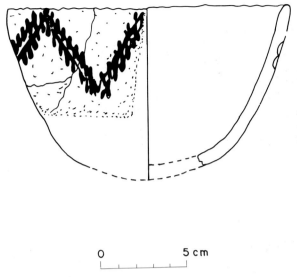

0   5 cm

4.11 Round-based vessel from Sandal Do. After Chung J.W. 1986.

About half of the faunal remains found at the site are bones of *Sus scrofa* (probably wild boar, although this is the same species that was domesticated in Asia). Deer are also common, especially in the upper layers. Also present are elk, dog, badger, cat, ox, whale and dolphin.

Sandal Island is another shell mound off the southern coast. The pottery is largely incised, with conical bases, which the excavator refers to as Amsadong style, and believes to be the latest (Fig. 4.10). Round-based vessels also occur (Fig. 4.11). Plain jars with constricted necks and sherds of burnished red pots reported from the site may belong to a later time. No stratigraphic sections are presented in the report (Chung J.W. 1986).

Another important site, still in the process of excavation, is Sangnodae Do (Dong-A 1984, Sohn 1982). The lowest level in the Yonsei excavations, discussed in Chapter 3, appears to be transitional from a mesolithic way of life to settled villages. Of the ten layers, V through VIII were deposited when sea level was lower than at present, and Layers II through IV represent a time when sea level was approximately 5 m higher than the present. A radiocarbon date from Layer V (6430 ± 180 BP) recalibrates to approximately 5000 BC. The layers beneath this dated level, deposited at lower sea level, must then date back into the early Holocene period, perhaps as early as 10,000 years ago.

Pottery is found all the way to the lowest level in one sounding (Sohn 1982). If datable material is ultimately found in the lowest level, Korean pottery may be found to be as old as the Japanese discoveries at Fukui Cave, as the earlier date at Osanni suggests. The Dong-A University team uncovered a preceramic layer which is not yet dated although a date of 6622 ± 180 BP from a pottery-bearing

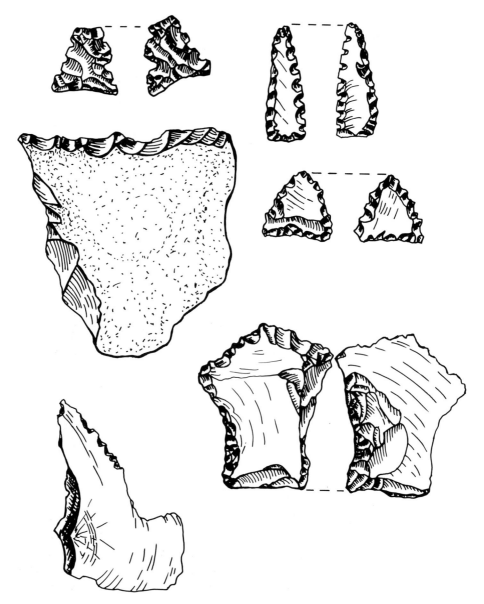

4.12 Chipped stone tools from Sangnodae Do. After Sohn 1982.

layer has been published. In the lower layers some chipped stone tools, such as large nosed scrapers and gravers, indicate woodworking. Throughout the lower layers tools were made of chipped stone (Fig. 4.12), contrasting with the upper four layers which contained polished celts, grinding stones and grinding slabs, and mortars and pestles. Raw materials for the tools included obsidian and porphyry. A human molar was found in the bottom layer – a rarity in Korean sites. The tooth was identified as belonging to a middle-aged male (Sohn

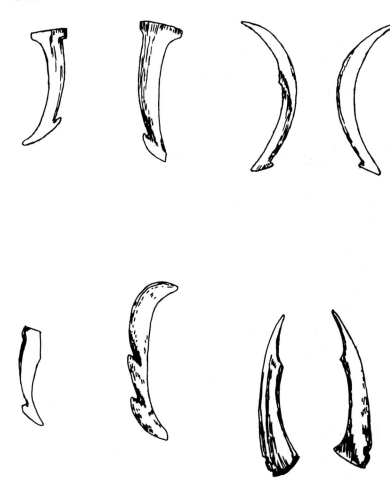

4.13 Bone tools from Sangnodae Do. After Sohn 1982.

1982:142, Sohn and Shin 1990). Both flat-based and round-based sherds occur from the lowest layer. All the pottery types that we have already seen in southeastern sites were represented, as well as an unusual pot decorated with stingray spine impressions. Bone tools include fishhooks, drills, needles, awls, scrapers, paddles and spatulas which increased in numbers in the upper layers (Fig. 4.13).

The midden analysis identified forty-three species of shellfish, of which eight were collected continuously from Layer VII through Layer II. Fauna represented include boar, otter, fox, dog, baleen whale, sea lion, seal and turtle. Several species of fish and birds were also present.

Imbulli is an inland site which has yielded an interesting sequence including mesolithic, Chulmun and plain pottery in stratified sequence (An 1989). There are several other inland sites with Chulmun pottery, for example Kangnuri on the Nam river (a tributary to the Naktong from the west), which contains incised geometric patterns as well as flat-based plain pottery and polished stone implements belonging to a later stage (Cho 1987).

Chung Jing-won (1985) seriated the Yungkimun pottery, assigning the raised line with indentations as earliest, followed by plain raised lines and ending with raised and impressed lines. He suggests that the styles traveled from north to south. However, since this scheme is not grounded in C14 dates and only weakly supported by stratigraphy it is not entirely convincing.

Southwestern sites

Early Villages sites are scarce in the Cholla provinces, and tend to be on islands. In one recent survey, several Chulmun sherds were collected from surface sites on the mainland, but none of these sites has been excavated (Kim B.M. 1983). The Juam Dam survey turned up a few Chulmun sherds in inland areas as well, but they were scarce compared to both paleolithic and megalithic sites. Offshore islands, including Sohuksan Do, 160 km from the mainland, contain several sites with the classic Chulmun pottery. Rim sherds are decorated in bands around the rim only, and body sherds are plain. The oblique lattice design, herringbone and rows of dots are other motifs described. Kim W.Y. (1975b) calls these styles late neolithic but, as we have seen from the east coast sites and their associated C14 dates, that is not necessarily the case. Since they are found on distant islands, they may well be earlier.

The first shell mound of the southern coast of Cholla Nam Do to be excavated was Song Do. Four layers contained Yungkimun pottery dominant throughout, although some Chulmun and plain sherds were also present. Spindle whorls, shell bracelets, composite fishhook shanks, grinding stones and scrapers were found. In Layer 3 a hardened clay floor, oval in shape, was encountered. The excavators believe the site should be dated around 4500 BC, based on comparisons with other sites (Chi and Cho 1989).

A shell mound on Taehuksan Do was partially excavated. The mound is small, only about 30 sq m, and like the south coast shell mounds no dwellings were found. For such a small site, presumably a midden, the pottery is quite variable. Round bases, and rims with rows of oblique dots, are characteristic. Designs in the shape of the letter "W," incised in double outline and hatched in the middle, are found on some sherds. Other vessels have shell impressions. There are also sherds from the megalithic age – folded-over rims, with oblique elongated dots at the border between the body and the rim. Both polished axes and simple choppers were found. A C14 date of 1900–1660 BC has been reported. Surprisingly, on this large island of 30 sq km no other shell mound has been located.

Sohuksan Do, Taehuksan Do and Hatae Do are along the coastline of about 10,000 BC. If they were settled at that time, rather than later as islands, the interpretation of population movement would become rather different. It is unfortunate that C14 dates are rare for these island sites.

Cheju Do, the large volcanic island 96 km off the south coast, has few excavated Chulmun sites. Only two were found during a survey of the island. One is the site of Kosan, which has brown pottery and "pecked basalt celts with rectangular cross-section," the other is Orali, with the unusual combination of Chulmun pottery and a polished slate knife (Pearson and Im 1968).

Cholla Puk Do contains a few shell mounds on the coast and off-shore islands. Kunsan and Taehangni near Puan are coastal shell mounds, and Sonyu Do and Kyehwa Do are island sites. The latter appears to have been a cache rather than a waste dump, as it was found on top of a hill almost 250 m high. In addition to some Chulmun sherds and small flake scrapers, seven miniature polished adzes were found, two of them of chalcedony. Rhee (1984:140) interprets this as a cult center.

Central western sites

Sites on the Han and Taedong rivers appear to be the original home of the "classic" Chulmun pottery: wide-mouthed vessels having conical bottoms, with incised decorative patterns in the form of a rim band and body designs. The pottery from these river-bank sites, especially Amsari (now renamed Amsadong because it has become part of Seoul city), was perceived by Fujita as strikingly different from the Mumun (plain) pottery found on hill slopes in the same region. Fujita (1933) explained the different pottery styles at first as two contemporaneous cultural adaptations; later he believed they belonged to successive eras. The latter interpretation still stands, in spite of the variability now perceived in both Chulmun and Mumun.

First exposed by a flood in 1925, Amsadong is more than a kilometer away from the present river channel, nestled against the hills in an area that may have once been if not on the river bank at least much closer to the river than it is now. Yokoyama made a surface collection, and Fujita reported that there had been shells of both freshwater and marine mollusks (Kim W.Y. 1983a). Whatever may have remained immediately after the 1925 flood, there is not a trace of a shell mound today, nor have shells been reported from the excavations. The site was occupied through many eras. Mumun and Samguk potsherds are found there as well as Chulmun. Yokoyama's surface collection included both simple and complex Chulmun patterns. In some cases the decoration consists of a band of one motif and a different motif on the body (Fig. 4.14), while others feature a third decorated area between the band and the body. This extra motif consists of concentric rows of dots making semicircular swags toward the lower decoration, and is known as the wave pattern. All the pottery is reddish-brown in color, with mica inclusions in the paste, reflecting the composition of the local soil.

The site has been tested several times by various institutions, but no comprehensive site report has ever been published (Kim W.Y. 1962, Kim K.S. 1970, Im 1982a, 1985a). At least twenty dwelling floors have been uncovered, some of

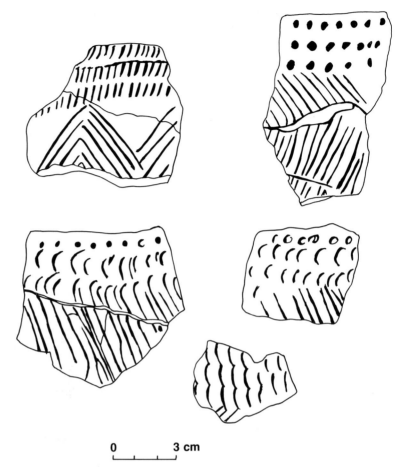

0 _____ 3 cm

4.14 Chulmun sherds from Misari.

them overlapping. Radiocarbon dates have become progressively earlier over the years, which suggests that deeper levels of the site are being reached in the later excavations. The houses are subrectangular and semi-subterranean, with squared central hearths similar to those from Osanni. Associated stone tools include slender slate hoes (Fig. 4.15), small weights usually referred to as net sinkers (Fig. 4.16), grinding stones, a stone plow, and various unpatterned chipped tools (exhibit in the National Museum, Seoul).

In at least one area, the vessels were rather large, averaging more than 50 cm in diameter. Lim Byung-tae (personal communication) made a wide cutting, and located on a site map every artifact on the dwelling floors; it is one of the glimpses of distributional patterns in the Chulmun period. One group of large pots suggests a storage area, similar to groups of *kimchi* pots on the *matang* in traditional Korean houses.

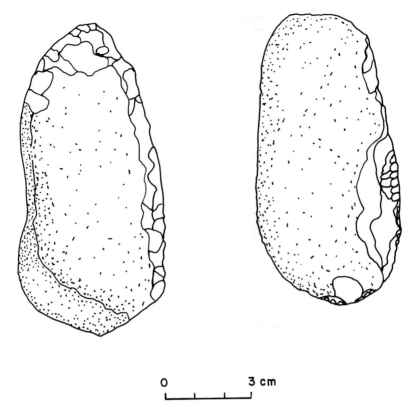

O ⊢———⊣———⊣ 3 cm

4.15 Slate hoes from Han river sites.

Misari is a site on an island in the Han river, about five kilometers from Amsadong. The river has eroded away a large part of the site, leaving an edge exposed in a sandy bluff about 100 m above the river. The site is stratified, with at least two Chulmun layers on the bottom, and Mumun, Wonsamguk and Samguk layers above (Im H.J. 1981). Thus, everything collected from the base of the bluff does not necessarily belong to the Chulmun occupation, as is sometimes implied. The decorative motifs echo those of Amsadong. Many small pebble weights were found and a long pointed porphyry tool with a pierced hole and notches along the side is identified as a netting tool. Stone axes and grinding stones are also common (Kim W.Y. 1961). Some quite elaborate designs on Chulmun pottery may reflect a later stage, but since they were excavated before the stratigraphy was perceived, no definitive statement can be made about superposition (Kim C.C. 1966).

Naepyongni, near Chongchon on the North Han river, was found to have house floors with pottery somewhat different from the central Han sites. The vessels have beveled lips and are decorated with several rows of slanting lines below the mouth, leaving the body undecorated (Fig. 4.17).

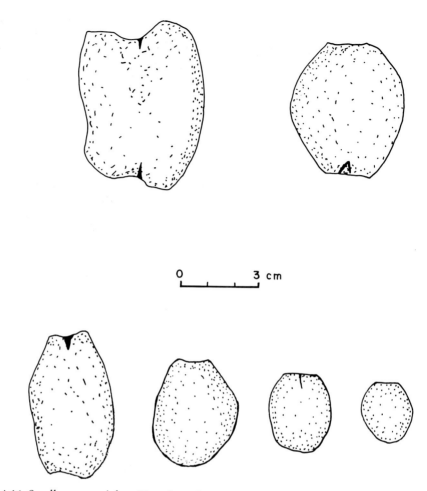

4.16 Small stone weights, Han river sites.

Chojiri shell mound, on the coast, contained typical conical Chulmun pots, as well as some sherds of Kimhae pottery from the proto-Three Kingdoms period (Kim W.Y. 1979b). Many shell mound sites have been located on the smaller islands off shore. Oi Do, dated 4080 ± 45 BP (2860–2620 BC) (Im and Pak 1988), produced several areas of stone scatter in addition to distinct shell heaps. In the excavations and surface collection, some 400 sherds were obtained, but few implements. The tools included two stone axes, one stone and one bone projectile point, and a flat pointed stone tool that may be an oyster pick. Overall pottery designs were favored in the upper layer, with separate band and body decorative patterns in the layer below. Other islands have one or two shell mounds but at Soya Do, seven have been discovered (Han and An 1983).

The site of Si Do appears to represent a late survival of Chulmun, judging from the recalibrated C14 dates, which range from 1540 to 1020 BC. The lowest level

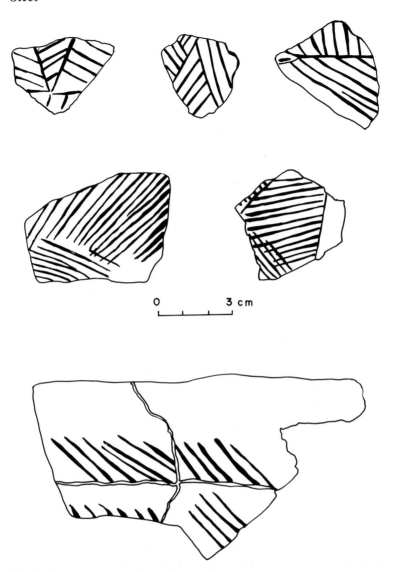

4.17 Sherds from Naepyongni, on the North Han river.

of this shell mound contains Chulmun pottery, with some of the more elaborate designs, such as the lattice pattern and the wave pattern. The stone tools include a triangular slate arrowhead with indented base, slate knives and a polished axe. An unusual feature consisting of an oval pit, 1.5 × 1.2 m, filled with stones, was reported as a burial (Han B.S. 1970) but might have been a cooking device. The pit was 20 cm deep, excavated into the weathered granite bedrock. It contained a few Chulmun sherds in addition to stones, charcoal and ash.

0   5   10 cm

4.18 A typical all-over herringbone pattern Chulmun vessel. From Yongdori. After Arimitsu 1962.

Taedong river sites

Sites adjoining the coast or beside the mouth of the Taedong are shell mounds, but further inland, along the river bank, sites are found in the sandy alluvium like those on the Han river. Kungsanni, located on a hill 200 m from the coast, is a good example of a shell mound site. A 10-cm layer of humus overlies a 50-cm layer of shells, which are reported to be mostly oysters. Beneath this is a clay layer less than 50 cm in depth, resting on another 60-cm shell layer where clam shells predominate. The excavation was divided into six levels, of which only four had cultural remains. House floors had been excavated into each level. The lower shell layer, estimated to date around 4280 BC (Choe 1986:41), contained classic Chulmun pottery, with pointed or rounded bases, incised band decorations, and herringbone on the body (Fig. 4.18). Associated stone tools included polished stone axes, polished triangular arrowheads with indented base, and grinding stones. Antler hoes and perforated boar tusk sickles were abundant (Fig. 4.19). Faunal remains in the lower level include red deer, roe deer and water buffalo.

Pottery from the upper layer, which Choe (1986) cross-dates to 3100 BC, had flat bases, but was decorated with the wave pattern, as well as W-shaped hatched bands. Antler hoes are not found in this layer, being replaced by stone hoes. Other stone artifacts include weights, adzes, stone saws and spearheads, while bone artifacts include drills, spatulas, hoes, needles and awls. The fauna from the

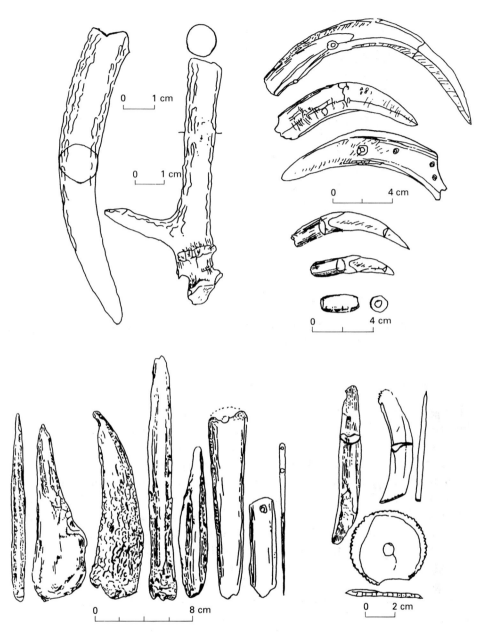

4.19 Bone and antler tools from Kungsanni.

upper layer have been identified as deer (which was well represented), as well as antelope, boar, water buffalo, dog, cat, and several kinds of fish and mollusks (Han Y.H. 1978). Nephrite microcelts may represent trade items (Choe 1986:103).

The site of Chitamni, on the banks of the Chaeryong river, a tributary to the Taedong river in Hwanghae Do, is well-known for the discovery of grains inside a Chulmun jar. The site covers a large area with several occupation layers. Two excavated localities have produced Chulmun remains. An undisturbed Chulmun layer about 1 m thick was encountered beneath 1 m of alluvium inside a medieval town wall, and designated Locality 1. An unusually large dwelling floor was excavated, measuring 7 m on each side. The semi-subterranean floor, dug 50–70 cm into the sandy soil, was coated with clay. Traces of burned wood, the remnants of the house frame, lay on the floor. A central hearth was demarcated by the usual encircling large stones. Six large pots rested near the hearth. These were typical Chulmun pots with rounded bases and herringbone designs. Fragments of pottery with handles were also found, as well as grinding stones, arrowheads, spear points, knives, axes, sinkers and chisels. Locality 1 is considered to be the earlier part of the site.

Some 700 m distant, a second excavation unit produced two smaller dwellings, also with central hearths. Each house was about 4 m long. Pottery vessels were set into the floor for storage in this house as well. The pottery design motifs included herringbone and rows of short slanted lines, as well as dotted wavy lines. Stone artifacts included polished leaf-shaped projectile points of varying lengths, grinding stones and grinding slabs, polished axes, sickles, stone plowshares and sinkers (To and Hwang 1957, Chard 1960). One dwelling, designated House 3, contained twenty-two partially finished projectile points. Choe (1986) has suggested that this may be evidence of craft specialization.

Kumtalli has a layer containing mostly incised pottery beneath a layer of "top-shaped" vessels (see Chapter 5). The lower level has one dwelling. Associated with it are pots with rim and body decorations having rounded bases. Punctates and triangles also appear. The upper layer has four semi-subterranean houses. The decorated pottery still has conical bases, but horizontal herringbone pattern covers the entire pot. Some vessels are globular, with everted rims and a few handles. Plainer pots are also found. Net sinkers, hoes, slate arrowheads of willow-leaf shape, axes, adzes and ornaments are also reported (Kim Y.G. 1964, Townsend 1975).

The presence of Yungkimun pottery makes the site of Chonghori especially interesting. The site is 9 km east of Pyongyang in sandy alluvium on the banks of the Taedong river. Four cultural layers of dark brown clay were separated by narrow banks of sand. All the layers have some Chulmun, some Yungkimun, and some plain vessels with rounded bases and straight sides, but the Chulmun is more common in the lowest two levels. Chipped stone bifacial axes and flake scrapers were characteristic finds in the lower levels, while polished axes, two shapes of arrowheads and rectangular knives replaced them in the upper layers. Pebble net sinkers, notched on each end, were common in all the layers (Kim J.H. 1978b).

Northwestern sites

Near the Chongchon river, in the next major river drainage north of Pyongyang, an extensive site has been excavated at Sejungni. A dwelling floor (House 7) on the lowest level contains Chulmun pottery marked with herringbone designs, rows of dots and rows of short slanting lines. Many bases are round or pointed, in classic Chulmun style, but there are some flat bases as well. The only complete vessel was decorated over the entire surface with incised patterns. Zones of hatching are seen on some sherds. The temper is sand and mica, similar to Han river pottery. The house floor is 4.5 m in one direction; the other dimension is unknown. A square central hearth defined by cobbles was roughly in the middle of a floor of hardened clay. An unusual perforated stone was found which presumably was an ornament or amulet (Kim J.H. 1978b).

The Yalu river region contains another series of sites rather different from other Early Villages (Kim W.Y. 1967c). None of these appears to be a classic Chulmun site, although some of the familiar incised patterns were used on the pottery. At Sinamni, on the coast near the mouth of the Yalu, two areas were excavated. Locality 1, on a hill west of the village, contained pottery featuring incised herringbone designs along with the squared spirals that are called the "lightning pattern," which probably belong to the megalithic age (see Chapter 5).

Locality 2, on a hill to the north, has three occupation layers. The uppermost is a Koguryo layer, while the middle one contains incised ceramics with complicated shapes, such as mounted cups. The lowest level, containing House 6, has potsherds resembling those of Locality 1. More complex pottery shapes include tall, necked jars as well as vessels with handles on the shoulders, and plain globular jars. The accompanying stone tool inventory is also more sophisticated, including polished projectile points with a flattened hexagonal cross-section and semi-lunar reaping knives. These implements are usually associated with megalithic age sites. Also unusual in the stone utensil inventory were axes and adzes, circular "axes" (these are thick disks with a central perforation – they are found more commonly in Mumun sites in North Korea and are often described as "stone money"), spindle whorls, net sinkers and ornaments. It is not clear which level these were associated with, but it is likely that they belong largely in the middle layer (Kim J.H. 1978b).

The location of the Misongni site in a small limestone cave is unusual, although a few other cave sites with Chulmun pottery have been discovered in recent years. This site is 16 m above a small tributary of the Yalu river. Of the two cultural layers, the upper one appears to be of megalithic age (although some of the pots have incised designs), while the lower one is definitely Chulmun. No vessels could be reconstructed. Potsherds were decorated with rows of dots or short incised lines, as well as herringbone. Two net sinkers were found, along with three bone drills and one tiny ornament made of white jade. This site is so fragmentary it may represent a disturbed burial (Henthorn 1966).

Northeastern sites

Along a stretch of the Tumen river near Hoeryong a number of sites have been located, but few have been excavated. The pottery is decorated with the squared spirals called the lightning pattern, and other areas which are filled with hatching or dots (Arimitsu 1962). The Odong site has remains of deer, pig, rabbit and bear (Choe 1986).

The site of Musan Pomuigusok is primarily noted for its bronze and iron components, but the lowest level is from the Early Villages period. Square dwellings with central hearths contain a variety of stone tools, including polished axes and shouldered hoes and finely flaked obsidian tools. Bone awls and spindle whorls are also in the assemblage. The pottery has flat bases or sometimes a short pedestal – perhaps the earliest *dou* form in Korea. Globular jars are also in the assemblage (Hwang K.D. 1975). This site is included in Lin's (1985) Tuanjie culture, to be discussed further in the next chapter in connection with the megalithic age.

The coastal sites tend to be clustered in the far northeast. Not surprisingly, they bear a close relationship to sites further up the coast in the Soviet Maritime region.

Sopohang is a large mound of oyster shells right at the mouth of the Tumen river very near the border with Russian Siberia. The paleolithic site beneath it is called Kulpori, causing some confusion. Four neolithic cultural layers were delineated (Kim Y.G. and So G.T. 1972). The lowest level contains a house floor which is subrectangular, 12 × 6 m, with a clay floor. Some traces of possible rock dividing walls exist and five hearths line up more or less in a row along the length of the dwelling. Three of the hearths are paved with small stones in a circular form, while the other two on each end are outlined with stones only (Fig. 4.20). Artifacts were located near the hearths. The pottery is simple, with flat bases and direct rims. A reconstructed pot has four rows of impressed geometric design around the mouth, and is plain on the body. Stone tools include polished axes and chipped hoes which are seen as evidence of incipient agriculture. Bone tools consist of various sizes of awls, a barbed end of a toggle harpoon and an object with a hooked end (Fig. 4.21). Knives made from boar's tusks are also present. Faunal remains include dog, deer, wild boar, various kinds of fish, and sea mammals such as sea lion and dolphin.

Four dwellings were found in Layer II, ranging in diameter from 3 to 4 m. Each was circular, about 4.2 m in diameter, shallowly excavating into contemporaneous ground level. The floor consisted of a baked mixture of clam and oyster shell. Post holes were found around the outer edge, and a fireplace containing ash and burned bone was in the center, demarcated by a layer of

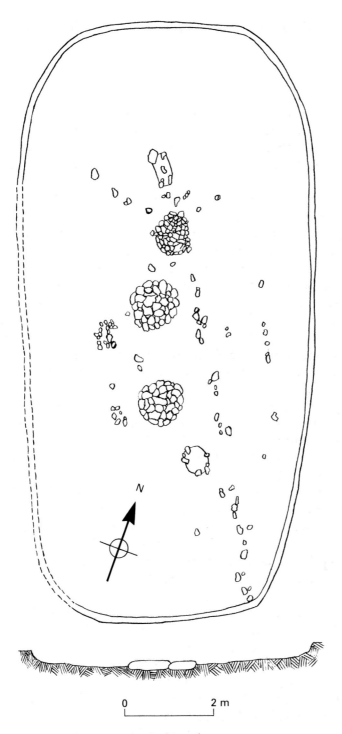

4.20 House in the lowest level of Sopohang.

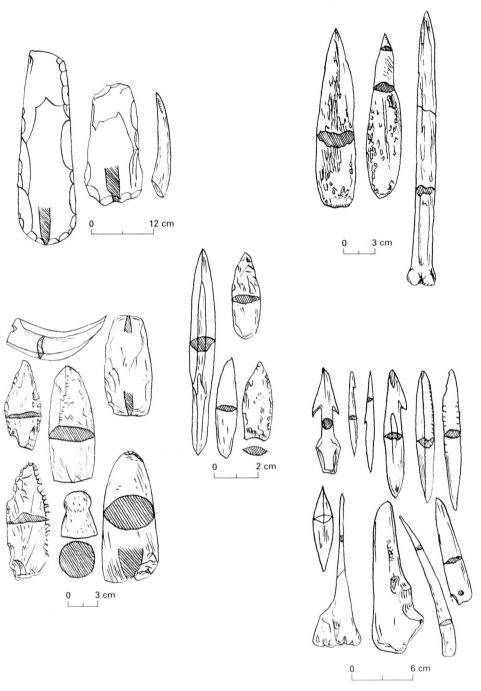

4.21 Stone and bone tools, northeast coast of Korea.

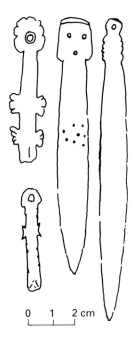

0 1 2 cm

4.22 Bone "idols" at Sopohang.

stones (Henthorn 1968). Stone and bone tools were of the same types as the layer below, but there was one house which contained forty awls, suggesting a basketry specialist or an awl-maker (Choe 1986:82). Reconstructed pots all have flat bases. Some vessels have wide mouths but narrow-necked jars also appear. Decoration tends more toward overall geometric designs, although one completely undecorated jar was found. The possibility of domesticated pigs at this site has been raised (Choe 1986:82).

Dwellings in Layer III are squarish with rounded corners. House 26 has a clay-plastered floor and the hearth uncharacteristically in the southeast corner. Both chipped and polished small obsidian projectile points make their appearance, along with geometric-patterned biconical spindle whorls (see Fig. 5.30), grinding stones and some oddly carved bones that are interpreted as idols (Fig. 4.22). A representation of a snake head and perhaps a dog or bear head were also found, carved from antler. Two complete dog skeletons had been placed under house floors. Decorative objects, such as rings, bracelets and pendants, became popular. Pottery shapes include bowls, tall pots and jars. Geometric decoration covers the top half to two-thirds of the exterior of the vessels. Curvilinear designs are rarely found.

In Layer IV, increasing numbers of carved bone items, arrowheads with indented bases and notched stone sinkers were found. Oblong obsidian blades with dentate edges appear, like the stone saws of Osanni and Tongsamdong. The previous pottery shapes continue, but additionally include jars with long necks, ring bases and handles, and a low bowl with outflaring sides and handles (Kim Y.G. and So G.T. 1972). Many of the vessels are plain, but squared spirals in zoned designs (the lightning pattern) are also common.

The Najin site, 20 km to the south along the coast, is a shell mound 90 m long which was discovered underneath 2 m of sand dune. The cultural layer is thin, only 15 cm, suggesting that it may represent a single occupation. Some of the sherds collected have short lines and punctates around the rim. Other sherds suggest beaker shapes, with recurved bodies and elaborate rims. The surface of these vessels is covered with fine impressed designs resembling cord-marking. Chipped and polished axes, obsidian arrowheads, harpoons, drills and sinkers were also found (Arimitsu 1962). Flat-based, wide-mouthed jars, typical of this region, were found at Songpyongdong (Fig. 4.23).

Yokoyama made some cuttings in the shell mound at Nongpodong, near Chongjin, but the major excavation of the site took place in 1956, organized by the Chongjin Historical Museum. Four areas were probed, three of which were thought to be redeposited from higher up the hill. Only on the south slope did they find undisturbed shell midden and what was designated as an occupation layer although no dwellings or hearths were found. The ceramic vessels have a number of different shapes including jars, tall wide-mouthed pots, cylindrical vessels, bowls and plates. Bases were mostly flat, but some have a ring foot. Few vessels are entirely undecorated. The designs do not begin at the mouth, but farther down the pot, leaving an undecorated band around the rim. Designs include the ubiquitous herringbone, rows of short slanting lines and punctates, as well as squared spirals filled with hatching or dots. There are a few painted pots.

The number of stone tools and flakes is astonishing, including 2,546 pieces of flaked obsidian (Fig. 4.24). The site has been interpreted as a workshop because of the large quantity of flakes. Triangular projectile points with notched bases were made by pressure flaking, as were end-scrapers, knives, large projectile points and daggers. Ground stone tools included rectangular axes, small projectile points, grinding stones and grinding slabs. Abundant pebble net sinkers, ceramic spindle whorls, and harpoons, fishhooks, needles and awls made of bone were also reported. Thirteen crudely sculpted zoomorphic and anthropomorphic clay figurines were an unusual discovery as well as an implement made of boar's tusk for stamping pottery (Kim J.H. 1978b).

Burials

Few burials have been found in neolithic Korea, and those that have been discovered are too disparate to suggest any pattern. A cemetery of inhumation burials in the northeast, a mound with secondary burials in the southeast, a cave in the central region with three bodies each oriented in a different direction, and an unpublished burial under a shell mound constitute the sample. Choe (1986)

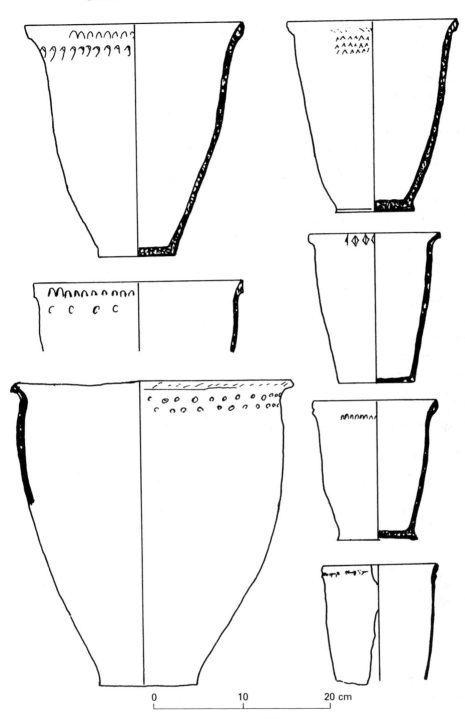

4.23 Flat-based vessels from Songpyongdong, Unggi.

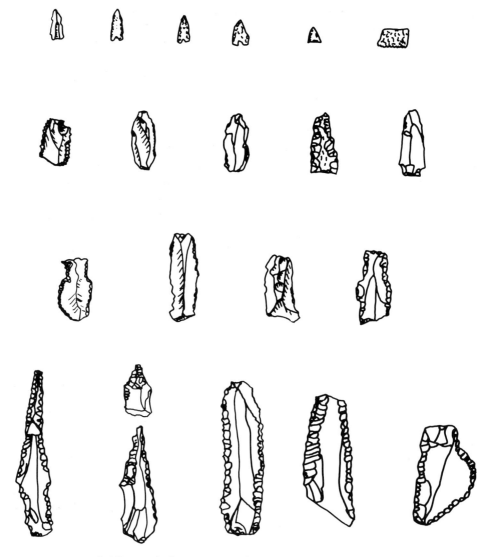

4.24 Obsidian tools from Nongpodong. After Arimitsu 1962.

mentions two others, neither of them applicable to this chapter. I believe the feature at Si Do discussed above is more likely to be an oven than a grave, as it is too low to be a tumulus and in any case cairn burials began much later.

At Unggi, a group of fourteen burials was found, each skeleton extended on its back with head to the east. Four of the burials were male, one female, and the rest are unknown (Kim W.Y. 1986a:21). Burial goods were decorative only – bone hair ornaments, shell necklaces and jade rings. Some of the pottery from this site is incised.

In contrast, the burial at Hupori near Kyongju included about 130 beautifully polished stone implements – axes and celts – all neatly placed in parallel rows. The largest axes were more than 80 cm long. The human remains included skulls, teeth and long bones. Heads were oriented to the southeast, and red ocher was found on the leg bones. The reconstruction displayed in the National Museum in Seoul appears to depict bundle burials. A circle of stones was placed around the burial (National Museum of Korea 1986).

At Kyodong three extended skeletons were found in a cave, each with feet pointing toward a central hearth. Five very small pots with flat bases accompanied the burial, along with large and small ground slate projectile points, five polished celts, three long flat axes, an unworked piece of quartz and a long polished tubular bead (Kim W.Y. 1968a). A newly discovered site on Yondae Do appears to contain bones of three individuals, accompanied by potsherds and stone tools (*Korea Newsreview* 22 Dec. 1990:30).

This long recitation of the particulars of the sites was needed to demonstrate the variations within the Chulmun period. Now it is necessary to attempt to sort out the sources of variation – space, time, function and perhaps ethnicity.

Chronology

Radiocarbon dates

The sites of Osanni, Tongsamdong and Amsari each have a series of dates, and other isolated dates from scattered sites in South Korea help to fill in the picture (Table 4.1). Osanni's date of 10,000 BC, if confirmed by further work, brings the Korean sites more in line with those of Japan. The other recalibrated dates for this site place it firmly in the range of 6000 to 4500 BC. Sangnodae Do also may have very early deposits, implied by its date of about 5000 BC in approximately the middle layer of the excavation (see Nelson 1992a for an extended discussion of the radiocarbon dates). In the north, Kungsanni and Sopohang have been divided into four stages each, unfortunately not anchored with C14 dates.

The Tongsamdong sequence is particularly interesting. Although there have been several excavations at this large shell mound near Pusan, the dates are mostly from Sample's (1967, 1974) expedition and that of the National Museum, which has never published a site report. In addition, one date was "obtained on shell collected by ... Esaka" (Kim J.B. 1978b:52). Since the published Japanese excavations were by Yokoyama and Oikawa (see Sample 1967:320), the context of this date is not clear. It is the oldest published date for Tongsamdong (5180 ± 125 BP, or more than 4000 BC), and is attributed by Lee Y.J. (1977:12) to the lowest level of the site.

The dates from the Tongsamdong shell mound published by Sample (1974) relate to four of the five levels she distinguished by means of pottery frequencies and natural stratigraphy. No datable materials were found in the lowest level (Cho Do) resting on bedrock. Sample's Mokto period, which includes mostly pinched and plain pottery types, is dated to 5890 ± 140 BP (GX-0378), or 4745 BC. The stratum which contains the Mokto period is Level E from Trench B, a thick shell stratum containing large quantities of bone refuse and many artifacts (Sample 1967:68). The date from the Pusan period, 4950 ± 125 BP (GX-0379), is recalibrated to 3780 BC. This sample came from Stratum C, a dark soil layer with a shell lens intruding into it, in Trench A which was about 2 m higher up the hill than Trench B. Presumably the dated charcoal came from Lower C, the part below the shell lens, since only the lowest area was designated Pusan. The excavation unit labeled Pusan contained mostly plain pottery, but did include a number of decorated types as well. Finally, incised pottery recognized as classic Chulmun was called Tudo Bold, and the associated date is 3400 ± 120 BP (GX-0493), or 1770 BC. This was in a soil layer at a depth of 130 cm. The date seems to be too late in comparison to the others at this site. It is also exactly the same as the date from the level that contains Mumun pottery, 3400 ± 215 BP (GX-0592), or 1770 BC, from Trench A at a depth of 40–5 cm.

Excavations by the National Museum were divided into only three levels. The lowest of these, designated TSD I, had Yungkimun pottery, TSD II contained Chulmun pottery, and TSD III was marked by Mumun ware. Five dates from Level II in various pits ranged from 4400 ± 90 BP (3175 BC, AERIK-27) to 3880 ± 100 BP (2430 BC, AERIK-26). The range of Chulmun dates at Tongsamdong is quite reasonable, if Sample's date for the Tudo level is discounted.

The two earliest dates at Amsadong are at present among the earliest published dates for the Chulmun period, and they are associated with incised pottery rather than with Yungkimun as at Tongsamdong and Osanni. The youngest date of 3430 ± 250 BP (1810 BC; Lee Y.J. 1977) is from the 1967 excavations with several universities cooperating. The coverage was wide but not deep. From 1970 to 1975, the National Museum's excavations produced dates of 4950 ± 200 BP (3785 BC; Kim W.Y. 1975a), 6050 ± 105 BP (4975 BC, N-2336), and 6230 ± 110 BP (5155 BC; Kim W.Y. 1976a).

Single dates from two island sites in the southwest fit into the late end of the Yungkimun pottery (Sonyu Do) and the middle of the Chulmun pottery (Cho Do). One island site in the southwest (Taehuksan Do) is in the later part of the Chulmun series. The dates from Si Do are the latest of those associated with Chulmun. This either represents a late remnant of Chulmun pottery or is simply an error.

These radiocarbon dates indicate a much earlier establishment of Chulmun than previously thought. While these dates do not yet bring Chulmun completely into line with Incipient Jomon and the earliest Chinese dates, it appears more and more likely that Chulmun represents a local style within the early pan-Asian ceramic horizon (Nelson 1990).

Relative dating

Several attempts have been made to sequence Chulmun sites (Kim J.H. 1968, Kim W.Y. 1975b, Han B.S. 1974, Han Y.H. 1978, Im H.J. 1983, 1984a, Kang 1975, Kim Y.G. 1979). An Sung-mo (1988) compares several of these. Archaeologists in the north tend to place the beginning of the Early Villages around 5000 BC, which is congruent with the C14 dates from the south. With the exception of Im's study, the subdivisions have been heavily dependent on pottery styles, and only presence or absence of decorative traits, not their relative abundance, has been used as the criterion for ordering.

There are several problems with the use of ceramic attributes as a basis for an Early Villages chronology. One is the amount of regional variation, which seems to outweigh temporal differences in many instances. The apparent variation in design motifs and placement, decorative techniques and pottery shapes within the same level of the same site presents another problem. Present evidence suggests that the strong regional differences and weak stylistic change through time is real, and needs to be understood in cultural terms. At least three regional traditions are indicated. Yungkimun appears earliest on the east coast, at approximately the same time as Chulmun occurs in the west central sites. Flat-based pottery is a third tradition, most prevalent in the north.

Chronological divisions of Chulmun which are based on ceramic types have one strike against them at the outset, as seen above. Other problems compound the difficulties. Chulmun, when first discovered and named, was assumed to be an offshoot of Baltic *Kammkeramik*, by way of Siberian Pit and Comb Ware. Although this theory is not supported by C14 dates, it continues to influence interpretations of archaeology in Korea. For example, types in the north are assumed to be earlier than those in the south, and the sequence is presumed to follow a pattern similar to that of the Baikal region. This mind-set has hampered the understanding of the Chulmun period.

Im's (1984a) examination of Early Villages pottery in Korea led him to suggest that the neolithic can be divided into three stages, Period I (Early) 6000–3500 BC, Period II (Middle) 3500–2000 BC, and Period III (Late) 2000–1000 BC. Choe (1986) also follows this division. However, I consider late neolithic as used by these authors to be best discussed with the megalithic period sites because the pottery is Mumun. In Im's formulation, sites along the east coast share the earliest part of Period I, from 6000–5000 BC. West coast comb ware appears by 5000 BC, and changes in east coast sites, including long-necked jars, are found from 4500–3500 BC. Then the classic Chulmun from the west coast spreads out and covers all of Korea, along with millet cultivation (Im 1988, 1989).

Subsistence

Actual food refuse is very rarely found in Korean sites. This is largely a result of the acidic soils and the alternating seasons of hot/wet and cold/dry, which accelerate the decomposition process. With rare exceptions, bones are preserved only in shell mounds, which potentially skews the faunal data strongly in favor of marine resources. Additionally, few sites published before the last decade have reported the faunal materials in terms of quantities rather than merely presence, with the result that knowledge of the relative use of various faunal resources is limited. Nevertheless, in all sites with preserved bone, the major land animals represented are deer and boar. Two species of deer are found, Corean river deer, which is small and similar to roe deer, and the larger Manchurian deer, analogous to red deer or elk. At Tongsamdong, Manchurian deer outnumber Corean river deer by about 2.5 to 1 in the site as a whole, but the Corean deer seem to have been more important in the earlier layers (Sample 1974). Boar bones are rare at Tongsamdong, but they are found in larger numbers in northern sites. It is not clear at what stage domesticated pigs appear in the south, but a North Korean scholar, having studied the bones from shell mounds on both coasts, believes that pig domestication occurred during the Chulmun period (Kim S.K. 1966). It has been suggested that pigs were domesticated in Japan by 1000 BC (Nagamine 1986:261). Boar tusks and deer antlers were frequently used as raw material from which to fashion tools. Antelope, dog and cat have also been identified from the Kungsanni site near the mouth of the Taedong river (Han 1978). Dogs are reported from Kulpori on the northeast coast in addition to deer and pigs (Choe 1986), and both dog and cat were found at Tongsamdong (Sample 1974). The subsistence picture gleaned from these sites indicates that land animals were important even in coastal shell mound sites, but the state of animal domestication is unknown.

Sea mammals appear in larger quantities than land mammals among the identified bone at Tongsamdong. Especially prominent are whale and sea lion (Sample 1974). The same is true of Sopohang. Among the fish bones, large species are clearly the most important. Shark and seabream are the most common fish, but tuna, yellowtail and cod are also found in large quantities (Choe 1986). Skilled fishing is indicated, with boats venturing some distance from shore on a regular basis.

The shell mounds themselves are composed of many varieties of shell. One receives an impression in general of mussels being important in the lowest levels, with oysters taking precedence next, and finally clams. There may be significant regional variation, but it has not been studied.

Floral remains are even rarer than bones. "Manchurian nuts" were noted by Yokoyama at Wonsudae in northeast Korea (Sample 1967), acorns were found at Misari, Amsadong and Osanni, and horse chestnuts (*Aesculus turbinata*) were found at Amsadong (Kim W.Y. 1962). Nuts are known to have been important in Jomon Japan (Nishida 1983, Akazawa 1986) and it is likely they were widely used in Korea as well. Grains, presumably domesticated, have been found in several sites. The best-known site yielding grains in association with Chulmun is Chitamni, where half a liter of carbonized grain was found inside a Chulmun vessel. The grain is referred to as millet (*cho* and *susu*), and assumed to be *Panicum crus galli* and/or *Setaria italica*, although no scientific description was published (Kim W.Y. 1975b). Namgyongni near Pyongyang also yielded millets, although it is not clear whether they were associated with the Chulmun pottery layer (SSI 1986). Kungsanni also yielded a small amount of grain (Henthorn 1968).

It seems not unreasonable that horticulture was being practiced in Korea. In nearby Japan, the evidence is increasing rapidly. Grains of several sorts have been found in Jomon sites, dating as early as 3500 BC (Ikawa-Smith 1986). Other important remains from Early Jomon sites include gourds, peas, and the paper mulberry at Torihama shell mound in Fukui Prefecture (Esaka 1986:226). Crawford and Takamiya (1990) have pointed out that discussions of the origins of agriculture in Japan are focused on rice; and I believe the same is true for Korea.

Other food resources were probably exploited, but direct evidence is not yet forthcoming. Identified charcoal from the Naepyong site included plum, elm, oak, pine and spruce (Nelson 1973), indicating a variety of woods utilized from the deciduous forest environment. This must have included many kinds of edible fruits, nuts, herbs and berries. Nishida (1983) points to the importance of nuts in the Jomon diet, and it is reasonable to suppose, given the occasional discovery of nuts in Early Villages sites, that they were important in Korea also.

Stone and bone artifacts

Some inferences about the food sources for the Chulmun period can be made from the inventory of tools found at various sites. The number of stone tools reported per site differs widely and the inventory of tool types is variable throughout the Korean peninsula in the Chulmun period. Some sites contain unique tool types, for example the pointed weights at Osanni and the antler hoes at Kungsanni. Tools made of bone are less common than stone tools, for only in the shell mounds have they been preserved. No Chulmun site has preservation of wooden tools, but one might surmise that bone and wooden tools were used throughout Korea.

Stone projectile points have been found in small numbers in virtually every site. The most common shape is triangular with a markedly concave base. In the northeast, particularly at the Nongpodong site, arrowheads are carefully flaked from obsidian. Elsewhere they tend to be made from the local slate, and polished. Polished types have six faces, with beveled edges on both sides and flute-like bifacial concavities. There are two sizes, presumably the smaller ones are arrowheads and the larger are spear points.

Ground stone axes are frequent, especially in the north, central west, and east. They may be either rectangular or lenticular in cross-section; in either case the cutting edge is biconvex. At Kyehwa Do off the southwest coast and Kungsanni in central Korea, small polished axes of nephrite or agate point to distant sources of raw material. Larger polished nephrite axes were also found in Hupori, an east coast burial (National Museum of Korea 1986:17).

Grinding stones are found everywhere, frequently on house floors, with both an upper and a nether stone. The upper stone is round to oval, and the lower has a semi-circular to ovate cross-section. No study has been made of grinding patterns, but the shape of the stones suggests a back and forth motion, as in grain grinding, rather than a circular motion, such as might be used to crush pigments. There is slight evidence for pounding, in the form of hammerstones and stone mortars and pestles. In Korean peasant homes in the recent past mortars and pestles were made of wood, so perhaps their rarity in Korean sites is only a reflection of the perishability of the raw material.

Cutting tools consist of sharp-edged stone flakes with no standard pattern. Scrapers are also unpatterned, identifiable only by an area of steep retouch on an otherwise amorphous tool. Choppers and denticulates are occasionally mentioned in reports. At Kungsanni, twenty-six sickles of boar's tusk were discovered.

Net sinkers are commonly reported, but their actual frequency is problematical. They seem to be more numerous in the central sites than elsewhere. It is possible that these artifacts represent loom weights rather than net sinkers (Kent and Nelson 1976). Spindle whorls are not universally found, and are more frequently reported from northern sites. They may be made of broken sherds, as at Kungsanni, or manufactured of clay, as at Nongpodong.

Artifacts identified as agricultural tools differ from region to region. In sites along the Yalu and Tumen rivers, and at Amsadong, large, flat, chipped stone implements with large tangs for hafting have been called plowshares. They resemble similar implements found in China. In the Kungsanni shell mounds, hoes or picks are made of antler in the lower level, but stone hoes are found in upper strata. Central Korean sites feature bifacial shale pebbles chipped on both sides, but with much of the cortex remaining. The hoes are most often made of selected river pebbles of approximately the desired shape. These have been called axes, or "hoe-axes," but their thinness suggests their use as hoes, probably for weeding (Nelson 1975a, 1975b). Choe (1986) points out the similarity to a metal tool called *homi*, used by modern Korean women to gather wild plants.

Reaping tools are very rare. Six perforated boar's tusk sickles were reported from Kungsanni; four stone sickles were reported from Chitamni, and one from

Osanni. Sopohang, Osanni and Tongsamdong have rectangular obsidian tools with serrated edges, exactly like tools found in Manchuria. Harvesting of grains may have been accomplished with tools of perishable materials. Bone awls, needles and possible netting tools are preserved in shell mounds. Several sites also are reported to contain bone harpoons and fishhooks.

Pottery sizes and shapes

Pottery styles have already been discussed in connection with space-time systematics, but, in the context of the subsistence base, other characteristics of the pottery become salient. Size and shape are particularly important in this context. Although occasional site reports indicate that some Chulmun vessels are large, only two studies have actually measured vessels (Nelson 1975a, Im and Nelson 1976). These studies made use of measurements of whole pots which established a constant relationship between height and rim diameter. Volume was calculated within a reasonable margin of error. Histograms revealed a trimodal distribution of small pots (10–30 cm in diameter), medium pots (35–45 cm), and large pots (50–70 cm).

The different sizes may represent three different functions of the pots, or perhaps three different foodstuffs being stored. The vessels containing grain from Chitamni belong to the medium category. No extension of this study to other regions has been possible. Few site reports contain vessel measurements, making extrapolation from drawings, photographs and narrative necessary. Very large vessels do appear at a number of sites.

In terms of shape, most Chulmun vessels are roughly conical, with pointed bases, no necks, and uncurved rims ending directly in a mouth that is the maximum diameter of the vessel. They are best described as pots, being neither narrow-necked like jars nor wider than their height like bowls. Yungkimun pottery runs heavily to jar shapes with flat bases, although bowls also occur. Whether the variability in shape is related to different functions is untested, but it is interesting to note that the larger and medium-sized pots appear to be storage jars, since a few have been found with grains or other items inside, and the grouping found together at Amsadong strongly suggests storage for a lean season (Nelson 1975b).

Houses, settlements and distributions

No complete village has been excavated in Korea; consequently, the arrangement of contemporaneous houses must be hypothesized on the basis of partial evidence. Several sites in North Korea have been well reported including house plans and artifact content. In the south, at least twenty house floors have been unearthed at Amsadong, one Chulmun house was excavated at Naepyongni, and several dwellings were reported at Osanni. Throughout the peninsula the dwellings are more consistently alike than either the pottery or the stone tools (Kim C.K. 1968, 1976). A few specific examples will be instructive.

Sopohang, in the northeastern part of Korea, contained a longhouse in its lowest level, and smaller, roughly circular dwellings above. In the northwest, on the bank of the Chongchon river at Sejungni, one rectangular semi-subterranean dwelling was identified, 4.5 m wide on the intact side. It is thought to have been longer on the side eroded by the river. The floor of hardened clay was 2.7 m below ground surface, with a central hearth outlined with river cobbles which contained burned clay to a depth of 30 cm (Kim J.H. 1978b).

On the west coast north of the Taedong river, in the shell mound site of Kungsanni, six houses were unearthed of which four were round and two subrectangular (Arimitsu 1962). Each house is about 6 m in diameter (Kim W.Y. 1975a), with central hearths and post holes along the sides. Floors were made of burned clay plastered on the weathered granite surface under the shell mound or in the shell layer. Storage pits inside the dwellings contained inverted Chulmun pots with bases removed.

In the site of Chitamni, near the Taedong river, three houses were identified. The largest is subrectangular, about 7 m on each side, and approximately 0.5 m deep. Floor and walls were coated with clay, and an entrance ramp can be traced in the southeast corner. A central hearth, slightly depressed, was surrounded by cobbles. Six storage pits were found, and near the hearth a pit was lined with an inverted pot with the bottom knocked out (Kim C.K. 1968, 1976). Two other houses were smaller, about 4 m on each side and 0.4 to 0.6 m deep. They also contained central hearths and storage pits, with large pots for storage. Both have southeast entrances, and one has steps leading down into it. Contents of the storage pits included one with unidentified green organic material, one with grain, one with red sand and ocher, one with grinding stones, and one with net sinkers, attesting to a surprising degree of prehistoric tidiness.

At least twenty dwellings have been excavated at Amsadong on the left bank of the Han river in west central Korea. In general, the houses are subrectangular, about 6 m in diameter, and about 1 m deep. Central squarish fireplaces are outlined with cobbles. At least one has a burned clay floor (Kim K.S. 1970), and another had corner steps, with charred posts along the edges.

Osanni's house floors have already been described in detail. They are circular to subrectangular, and excavated shallowly into the sand or shell. The main features are central hearths outlined with river cobbles.

Other features

Features in addition to dwellings have been identified in a number of Early Villages sites. Outdoor hearths and ovens have been found at several sites. At Osanni there are five large areas, one circular, 3.3 m in diameter, another rectangular, 1.8 × 2.7 m. The excavator believes they are fireplaces used to broil meat. Since they belong to a fishing village, the features might equally be interpreted as fish smoking or fish cooking areas. A smaller feature which might be an earth oven was mentioned earlier, found at Si Do (Han B.S. 1970) on the west coast, and four shallow oval areas filled with burned rocks at Amsadong are believed to be outdoor ovens. So far unique in the Early Villages period is a stone floor covering 320 sq m at Hyuamni in Chungchong Nam Do (Yun, Han and Jung 1990). Chulmun sherds are found scattered in the stones, but otherwise that site is from the megalithic period. It is possible that the floor was created by the later inhabitants, using the earlier sherds for extra fill.

Storage pits are occasionally found outside the dwellings, for example a large circular storage pit at Amsadong, 3.4 m in diameter and 1.7 m deep, with earth steps leading down into it (Im 1985a).

Summary of subsistence and settlement

Combining the data on flora and fauna, artifacts, pottery and dwellings, Early Villages sites can be characterized as having residential stability, similar to sites in Japan (Watanabe 1986). The adaptation to the environment was relatively consistent, and included the ability to store food, and perhaps to grow it. The sites located on sandy river banks, spaced with a few kilometers between villages, are better interpreted as agricultural villages than simple hunting and fishing camps (Nelson 1975b). Hoes and grinding stones tend to support this interpretation as well.

Hunting, fishing and shellfish gathering were clearly important in the overall subsistence strategy, whether or not any plants were domesticated. Forest animals, especially deer, were a prominent source of food, for projectile points are found even where no bones have been preserved. Large fish and sea mammals were favored on the coasts, and shellfish also played an important part in the diet.

Nuts, berries, fruits and herbs were surely collected from the abundant forest. In a brief and unsystematic study of wild plants still utilized in Korea, thirty-seven plant species were identified by a native informant in two habitats (river bank and swamp edge) in the course of a short afternoon (Nelson 1975a). It is reasonable to assume that at least as many plants were collected and utilized in the Chulmun period. A piece of hemp thread strung through a needle has been found in the north (Kim Y.G. 1979).

Mixed strategies were thus used in the Early Villages period. At some point there was a transition from purely foraging behavior to incipient agriculture but the timing is not clear. Priority for planting cannot be firmly established for any region either, although the stone tool inventories point to the central west coast as the initial area for food production.

Social organization

Ethnologists, ordering living societies in evolutionary stages, have placed groups occupying permanent settlements in the category of "tribe" (Service 1966, Sahlins 1968). Tribes are described as basically egalitarian, with households and villages loosely integrated into a larger society by means of sodalities, age-grade societies or other mechanisms that cross-cut kinship, while kinship and marriage remain the basic social ties, and political and economic structures are embedded within the social structure. It would be pleasant and simple to use these descriptions to interpret the archaeological record, but evidence that these generalizations are applicable to the distant past must be adduced for each case, rather than assumed. Furthermore, the current controversy among ethnographers regarding the reality of the category "tribe" as an evolutionary stage should give us pause. Morton Fried (1975) has argued that tribes are a creation of state-level societies which exert pressure on groups that are not yet organized in any formal way. Extrapolating this argument to the past, one would not expect to find any self-conscious groups with clear boundaries marking them off from other such groups at the same cultural level, unless a more highly organized society was within their sphere of interaction.

The limited artifactual inventory of Chulmun sites makes it impossible to consider entire assemblages for the purpose of establishing bounded groups. Bone tools must be eliminated, since they are only preserved in shell mounds, and most stone tools are too crude to indicate much stylistic variation. Furthermore, functional differences will not reveal levels of interaction. Only the pottery seems to lend itself to this exercise.

The first effort along these lines was intended to test a different hypothesis: whether the central Han sites and the sites on islands in the Yellow Sea were part of an annual transhumant pattern (Nelson 1975a). Resembling ethnographic patterns of "affluent foragers" such as the Ainu or the Northwest Coast American Indians, each village on the Han river might have moved seasonally to the coast or an island. If this were the case, similarities in styles between pairs of sites should emerge. Variables used in that study were selected stylistic elements, such as band and body design and number of band rows. Expected similarities between the riverine and island sites were not found. Additionally, river sites and island sites were clearly separable statistically on the basis of the attributes included in the study. Bounded groups of villages self-consciously using the same style within a small region is a reasonable explanation, although temporal differences might cause the same pattern and the late radiocarbon dates from Si Do show that this possibility cannot be discounted.

Im (1977) followed up on the Han river study by quantifying another set of attributes, many relating to manufacture but some reflecting function and style, using many of the same sherds. He found that both paste and temper could be used to discriminate between central Han river, island and east coast sites.

Another study (Nelson 1987) applied Chi-square tests to Im's data. Techniques of decoration, separately recorded for rim and body sherds, are less discriminatory than paste and temper but all attributes are significantly different by region. The data were also used as a negative test for an underlying clinal structure as implied by Renfrew's (1978) model. Discriminant analysis, using the geographic groups which emerged from Im's tables, showed the west coast island and river sites distantly separated, with the east coast sites forming a distinct third group (Nelson 1987). Stylistic and technological variables do cluster in the manner predicted by Spaulding (1982). More impressionistically, the geographic clusters of sites appear to be stylistic clusters as well.

The second problem concerns whether these apparently bounded units are "tribes." Renfrew (1978) has offered three general propositions against which this example can be tested. The first is that "the basic social group is defined by the habitual association of persons within a territory." Early Villages, being stable, fit this definition. Secondly, "human spatial organization is...cellular and modular." The villages follow this form, being to some extent linearly related to each other in units of roughly equal size along coasts and rivers. "Basic social groups do not exist in isolation, but affiliate into larger groups, meeting together at periodic intervals." Since even hunter-gatherer bands may have such periodic gatherings, this fact alone is not sufficient to differentiate tribes from bands. Perhaps the nature of the event changes when groups become sedentary. The location of the periodic gathering may become fixed, and accrue to itself economic and political functions as well. Such places are often marked archaeologically by shrines. Unhappily, in the Korean case early shrines had no architecture, but consisted of clearings in the forest marked by bells and drums (Joe 1972). In any case, villages with central functions are not evident in Korea at this stage.

It can be suggested, however, that although groups of villages may have been bound together loosely by ties of intermarriage, and although the gathering places may have been ephemeral, a social group beyond one's own village can be a hedge against crop failures for sedentary groups. To be dependent upon a crop is to be dependent on the weather, and Korea's climate is notoriously variable (Bartz 1972). At first glance this may not seem like an ecologically sound suggestion. Since Korea is characterized by rugged terrain, with villages isolated even from each other by sharp ridges, one might look for ecological diversity, rather than sameness, to explain bounded groups. Farming disasters, however, can strike differentially even nearby villages, whether the problem is too much water or too little. The presence of other villages nearby, considered part of the larger group and therefore obligated to help in the case of flood or late spring rains, might be the edge that would allow an incipient farming group to survive.

Not only does culture change involve "fundamental and irreversible changes in structure" (Renfrew 1978:109), so does the domestication of plants and animals (Hole, Flannery and Neely 1969). The irreversible effect on the local ecology requires new social forms, both to hedge against the increasing dependence on domesticated plants and to integrate peacefully the larger number of people living closer to each other. Thus it seems likely that we can reasonably postulate tribes in the Early Villages, each occupying a major river valley or coastal region (Nelson 1987).

Symbols and styles

Very few sites have produced ornamental objects. Several shell mound sites have the remains of shell bracelets, mostly fashioned from whole glycemeris shells. Nongpodong produced shell beads and perforated fish vertebrae. Beads of pottery, animal teeth, shell and jade were found at Sopohang, as well as three bracelets and eight small rings of nephrite and marble. Occasionally a piece of unusually shaped bone is reported as a pottery stamp.

Figurines have been discovered at two sites in the northeast and on the south coast, and masks or faces have been discovered in the east and south. Nongpodong contained a total of thirteen clay figurines, of which some are birds and dogs, and one is a headless female figure, 6 cm long, with its hands crossed over the chest. Sopohang has stylized bone objects which are said to represent females, but they could be decorative pins. There are also clay figurines of other creatures, identified as snake or bear. A broken female torso was found at Shinamni and a crude pinched pottery face at Osanni (Im 1982b), and a shell with three holes in it from Tongsamdong is said to represent a mask. Kim W.Y. (1986a:38) considers that these representations "probably represent shamanistic deities, the protectors of households and the communities who assured peace and a good harvest."

East Asian relationships

Jomon Japan

As I have suggested elsewhere (Nelson 1975a), the simplest explanation of the origin of Chulmun that fits the known data is that the first pottery making in this region (and perhaps the pottery makers) was influenced by Yungkimun pottery from southern Japan. The new pottery makers created new settlements as appropriate locations were found, spreading along the Korean coast. The earliest dated ceramics in Japan, at Fukui Cave and Kamikuroiwa (both older than 10,000 BC), are of the Yungkimun type (Ikawa-Smith 1976). Kim W.Y. (1986a:83) draws attention to parallels between undecorated conical pots from Kawarada Cave in northeastern Kyushu (as well as other sites farther east in Japan) and some southeastern Korean pottery. He considers that there may have been a "common stage" of Initial Jomon pottery in the regions of Japan and Korea which are nearest to each other. Im (1986) draws attention to the similarity of Sobata ware to Chulmun, while Choe (1986:49) notes the similarity with Natsushima as well as Hime, Todoroki and Sobata types. The Yungkimun from Tongsamdong and Osanni can be reasonably related to the pinched ceramics from Initial Jomon (Chard 1974, Sample 1974). At the Tongsamdong site, the few sherds that are positively identified as intrusive from Japan include Early and Middle Jomon types, indicating continued relationships with western Japan. Triangular projectile points are sometimes associated with this pottery in Japan (Aikens and Higuchi 1982) as well as in Korea. On the other hand, Sample (1978) argues against diffusion or migration between Korea and Japan in the early neolithic.

The rare find of dugout canoes in Jomon Japan (Aikens and Higuchi 1982:124) shows that the means for communication was present. Ikawa-Smith (1986:201), after examining the evidence for early marine transport in Japan, concludes that "this technology was most certainly present by about 9000 BP, and may have been present in the Late Pleistocene as well." Non-local obsidian may be yet another connecting link between the southeast Korean sites and southwestern Japan. Sakata (according to Kim W.Y. 1981:29) believes that the Koshidaka site on Tsushima Island was "produced by immigrants from Tongsamdong." Interestingly, Aikens and Higuchi (1982:114) express the opinion that "ceramics were introduced [to Japan] from the continent via Korea and spread northward," although the known dates do not support such a conclusion at present.

Grains of cultivable plants, especially buckwheat and millets, have been found in Middle to Late Jomon sites, although few would describe Jomon as an agricultural society (Anderson 1987). Native plants of many sorts may have been cultivated (Crawford and Takamiya 1990, Ikawa-Smith 1986). It is unnecessary and probably incorrect to connect the early Japanese experiments in plant cultivation with those in Korea, but it is interesting to note likely parallels.

The evidence suggests intermittent rather than continuous contacts. Although boats were efficiently used, each region seems to have been basically self-sufficient, with little need to interact.

Liaoning

When the northern hypothesis for the peopling of Korea from Siberia was proposed, the archaeology of northeastern China (Manchuria) was little known. With new discoveries in this region, the similarities with Korean sites have been noted and discussed. Functionally, the pottery vessels are similar, with the differences mainly stylistic – flat bases in Manchuria rather than pointed or rounded ones and a high incidence of rocker-stamping, for example. The use of jade is another characteristic usually found in Manchuria but seldom in Korea. Square hearths outlined by upright cobbles are an interesting similarity (Nelson 1990).

Im (1987) finds relationships with the flat-based, incised pottery of Xiao-zhushan, and sees it as the antecedent of all Korean neolithic sites. Certainly there were boats, as reported from a later site in Shandong (Wang 1987). Harking back to the likelihood of a narrower Yellow Sea in 7000 BC, it seems not only possible but likely that Korean west coast Chulmun is related to the Liaodong sites. At the moment, the earliest date in Liaoning comes from the Cahai site near Fuxin. Although there is no incontrovertible evidence of domesticated plants, no other subsistence base is suggested by the finds (LICRA 1986). Definite evidence of millet is found at Xinle, dated around 5000 BC (OAPSPM 1985). While I perceive close relationships between central western Chulmun sites and the Liaodong peninsula, I would not suggest that Liaodong is the forerunner of all Korean Early Villages sites. A distinction between the origins of east coast and west coast sites must be made. The earlier east coast sites cannot be derived from Liaoning on the grounds of either site similarities or absolute dates; rather, their affinities appear to be with Japan. Southern Chinese relationships seem less likely. Not only is the pottery different, but the rice agriculture attested at Hemudu and earlier sites (Yan 1990) has no counterpart in Korea during the Early Villages period.

The Soviet Maritime region

Similarities between northeast Korean sites and the Soviet Maritime region are frequently noted (Chard 1974). However, radiocarbon dates from this region do not suggest that the sites are earlier than similar Korean sites such as Sopohang (Ackerman 1982). It is to be hoped that more studies of this important region will be made available to the western world.

Summary

The maritime adaptation of the earliest Korean sites implies boats. Coastal settlements could have been founded by sea from anywhere in East or Southwest Asia. A model that derives each decorative pattern from a similar site elsewhere (Kim W.Y. 1986a) would soon have to be mapped as a mass of lines diverging from the same parent site to several locations on the Korean coast, with each Korean site likewise a recipient of many convergent lines. What could such a model reveal about population movement? If the rocker stampers from Manchuria joined raised-line potters from Kyushu and many others at Sangnodae Do, for example, did each group maintain ties with the parent settlement? Shall we imagine deep-sea fishermen bringing pottery-making wives (or vice versa!) to their settlement? None of these seems to be a very satisfying model of population movement. Only faint echoes of long-distance trade, in the form of obsidian, jade, jasper and smoky topaz, are found at one or at most a few sites. More evidence would be expected if these groups of fishers were voyaging widely.

What of plant cultivation? If millet was being grown in Manchuria as the archaeological discoveries demonstrate, why not Korea? Increasing early complexity is suggested by sites in Manchuria; is it consistent to expect extreme simplicity on the Korean peninsula? Rindos' (1984) model of incidental domestication would be consistent with the known data from Korean sites at an early date. By 3500 BC, at the start of Im's middle neolithic, the west coast Chulmun pottery appears to spread rapidly everywhere. Sohn Pow-key (1982) explains this occurrence at Sangnodae Do as a shift from the iconography of fisher folk to that of planters, from water representations to images of plants (Sohn and Shin 1990). Whether or not this interpretation can be sustained, some explanation of this circumstance is required. An increase in net sinkers (or possibly loom weights) as well as grinding stones accompanies the spread of Chulmun. Were the west coast "Chulmun" groups growing hemp and weaving it in addition to growing millets? Should a whole complex of plant domestication and its consequent industries be seen as spreading across the peninsula? If so, was there a population explosion in the west that sent out daughter colonies, or did a good idea catch on? The climate was still warm, but we cannot even guess at what minor perturbations might have pushed people from the west or pulled them to the south and east.

It seems reasonable to posit mobility in boats at the very beginning of the Early Villages period with daughter colonies from many places springing up along the coasts. Although we cannot know exactly which sites spawned which newer ones, the ability to send out colonies and to stay in contact with the original group seems likely for all sites. No hostilities between groups are evident in the archaeological record. However, as agriculture became more and more intensified, it may have been necessary to form groups for mutual insurance against capricious weather. At this stage the present national boundaries were wholly irrelevant, and networks of trade and other interaction probably characterized the entire region.

CHAPTER 5

MEGALITHS, RICE AND BRONZE 2000 TO 500 BC

The appearance of dolmens and other megalithic monuments, along with a significant change in pottery styles and in location strategies, began about 2000 BC. Differences in the rate of change and variations in the styles of the plain pottery are found throughout the peninsula, but by 1000 BC the new way of life had taken hold everywhere. Other new traits made their appearance also, especially stone cist graves, polished stone tools, rice cultivation and bronze. (For site locations see Fig. 5.1.)

Discussions of the period from 2000 to 1000 BC are couched in Korea in two mutually exclusive ways. On the one hand, some archaeologists include the beginnings of Mumun pottery as late neolithic (e.g. Im H.J. 1984b, Choe 1986), regarding the change as merely a shift from incised to plain surface pottery, from Chulmun to Mumun, rather than a revolution in subsistence base or socio-political organization. On the other hand, Mumun may be equated with a bronze age (Kim W.Y. 1981, Lee C.K. 1988a, Riotto 1989), and any appearance of Mumun is so designated. It seems to me that neither approach is helpful in understanding the process of change. The megaliths, which appear to co-exist with Mumun, suggest that profound alterations in the social, political and economic structures were taking place, although it is hard to know whether changes in these structures are consequences or causes of an intensified subsistence base. Since the megalithic monuments are firmly associated with the Mumun pottery, and the presence of bronze at the beginning is questionable, I prefer to take dolmens as the time marker, and call this the megalithic period rather than the bronze age, or even the Mumun period, since pottery designated Mumun by some archaeologists lasts into protohistory.

Although local developments were surely important, it seems unlikely that the changes in Korea in this era were unrelated to those in China, especially northern China. During the millennium from 2000 to 1000 BC, a pristine state was forming in the central plain of northern China. The rise of the Xia and the Shang dynasties occurred in this millennium, and by the time of the Shang (traditionally 1766–1122 BC), a writing system, intensive agriculture, highly developed bronze technology and long-distance trade were well established (Chang 1986). The archaeologically visible changes in Korea at this time may represent a distant echo of China's expanding civilization, even though there is little that is reminiscent of Xia or Shang in the Korean peninsula. An intermediate group of sites, loosely classified as Xiajiadian Lower Culture, provides the transition from Xia and Shang to Korea (Shao 1990).

A common Korean interpretation of the time period after about 1000 BC is that a nomadic group, sometimes specified as the Ye-Maek, an ethnic group mentioned in Chinese histories (Wang M.H. 1990), entered the peninsula from the north, bringing new pottery styles and rice agriculture with the stone tool technology to carry it out. In this interpretation the Ye-Maek also buried their dead in stone cists and erected enormous dolmens to mark their chiefs (e.g. Choe 1986, Kim W.Y. 1986a, Choi M.L. 1984a, Kwon 1988, Kim J.B. 1987). This is a simplistic argument based loosely on historical sources, which will be discussed further below. The archaeological data cannot so easily be fitted into a Ye-Maek pigeonhole, and as Manchurian archaeology becomes better known, the mosaic becomes more complex, not simpler. Many of the sites of Liaoning, Jilin and Heilongjiang provinces appear to be those of settled farmers (Nelson 1990), not the nomads we are accustomed to picturing on the Zhou dynasty's northeastern frontier. After examining the archaeology in Korea and China, it will become evident that a variety of factors are at play in the new cultural configuration in the Korean peninsula. Various elements probably entered Korea separately, with different groups, and mingled together at a later time.

The archaeological materials, with the exception of pottery types, do not lend themselves easily to regional treatment, as in the preceding chapter. The addition of burial forms and the uncertainty of the association of the elements of Mumun pottery, dolmens, rice and bronze throughout the entire period, make the megalithic era difficult to explicate. Examination of the dates, the settlements, the subsistence base, burial styles and bronze metallurgy will highlight the diversity within the often asserted cultural uniformity, and allow an exploration of what this broad period may mean in terms of socio-political development.

A relatively consistent assemblage of artifacts in the megalithic period of Korea suggests a similar way of life for ordinary villagers throughout the peninsula. The pottery has regional and temporal variants, but two basic shapes – a wide-mouthed pot and a narrow-necked jar – are frequently found together. It seems likely that this consistency in shape indicates dietary similarities of the people throughout the peninsula. Ground stone technology was used to create implements for subsistence tasks: reaping knives, axes, adzes, chisels and projectile points of several sizes and shapes. Increasing use of wood is implied by the adzes and chisels. In unusually favorable circumstances bone tools have been preserved, notably awls and needles. Along with spindle whorls, these suggest woven and tailored clothing.

In this society, bronze artifacts and gemstone beads appear to function as status markers for the elite. Necklaces of tubular beads were often deposited with the dead. Occasionally one or more of the comma-shaped beads known as *gokok*, which became an important symbol in the Silla kingdom as well as in Yamato Japan, appear in burials, usually in conjunction with tubular beads,

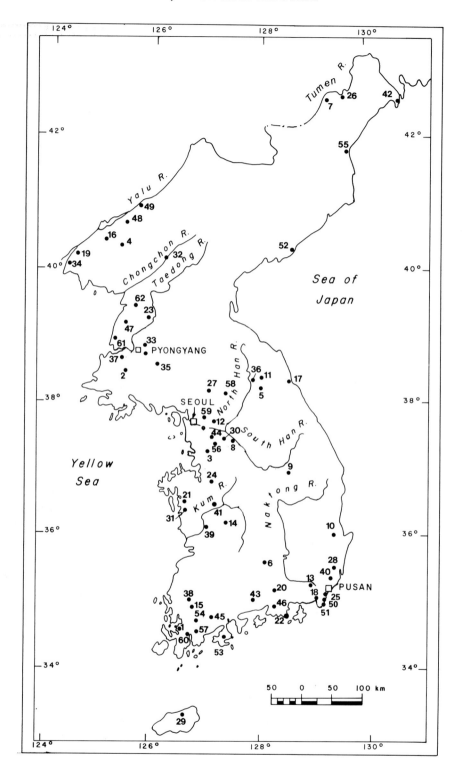

perhaps signifying some specific role or status. Bronze was used both for weapons and for non-utilitarian items, such as mirrors, bells, buttons and horse-trappings. Overall, the artifact assemblage bespeaks more diversity than that of the preceding Early Villages period. As time went on, craft specialists were needed for metal production and stone working, pottery may have been mass produced and traded, and probably other items made of perishable materials were created by specialized industries. Traditions and documents imply a state-level society (Kim J.B. 1979), although some have argued for chiefdoms (Choi M.L. 1984b), and yet other archaeologists see little to suggest central organization of any kind (Kang 1990, Pai 1989b).

Chronology

Radiocarbon dates associated with Mumun pottery, dolmens or bronze demonstrate interesting patterns, but fail to provide secure footing for subdivisions of the megalithic age. A group of dates in the southeast ranges from about 2800 to 800 BC (Table 5.1), with a tight central cluster of sites between 2100 and 1750 BC. These sites all contain Mumun pottery of the Ichungko (doubled rim) type, mostly with rounded rather than flat bases. In central Korea there is one date (from beneath a dolmen) at about 1900 BC, then a long hiatus of a millennium, except for one possibly spurious date of 1550 BC from Hunamni. From the fourteenth century BC a continuous string of dates is associated with Mumun pottery. Published dates from the north are limited to two from different houses at Musan (see Fig. 6.1 for location), both in the sixth century BC, which North Korean archaeologists believe to be an iron age layer.

It is often said that the earliest Mumun is found in the north (e.g. Rhee 1984:80), but the range of south coast radiocarbon dates suggests otherwise, establishing the presence of Mumun pottery and associated ground stone tools as early as 2000 BC along the south coast. Since there is no evidence of bronze at

5.1 Approximate locations of sites in Chapter 5.
1 Changchonni, 2 Chitamni, 3 Choburi, 4 Chonjindong, 5 Chonjonni, 6 Chopori, 7 Hogokdong, 8 Hunamni, 9 Hwangsongni, 10 Innidong, 11 Jung Do, 12 Karakdong, 13 Kimhae, 14 Koejongdong, 15 Kubongni, 16 Kuksongdong, 17 Kumgangni, 18 Kumgokdong, 19 Misongni, 20 Mugyeri, 21 Naedongni, 22 Namdongmyongni, 23 Namgyongni, 24 Namsongni, 25 Nongsori, 26 Odong, 27 Oksongni, 28 Pan'gudae, 29 Pobchonni, 30 Sangjapori, 31 Sangnimni, 32 Sejungni, 33 Simcholli, 34 Sinamni, 35 Sinhungdong, 36 Sinmaeri, 37 Soktalli, 38 Songamdong, 39 Songgungni, 40 Songsan, 41 Songwonni, 42 Sopohang, 43 Sunchon, 44 Susongni, 45 Taegongni, 46 Taepyongni, 47 Taesongni, 48 Tangsan, 49 Tobongni, 50 Tongnae, 51 Tongsamdong, 52 Tosongni, 53 Undaeri, 54 Usanni, 55 Wonsudae, 56 Yanggulli, 57 Yangpyongni, 58 Yangsuri, 59 Yoksamdong, 60 Yongam, 61 Yongdori, 62 Yonghungni.

Table 5.1. *Megalithic period radiocarbon dates*

Site	Location	Sample no.	Half-life 5568 BP	5730 BP	CRD 1 σ BC	Material	References
Osanni	Layer 1	KSU-?	3360±180	3455	1945–1420	Carbonized wood	Im 1982b
Tongsamdong	Level B	GX–0492	3400±215	3495	1980–1530	Carbonized wood	Sample 1974
	Layer 2	Gak–6660	3470±100	3570	1905–1680	Shell	Choi S.N. 1982a
Sugari	Layer 1	N–3453	3290±70	3390	1700–1545	Carbonized wood	Chung, Shin and Im 1981
Kumgokdong		N–3451	3040±80	3130	1430–1225	Carbonized wood	Kim J.H. and Chung J.W. 1980
		N–2135	3580±75	3680	2120–1865	?	
Tongnae	40–54 cm deep	AERIK–3	3570±80	3570	1965–1680	Carbonized wood	Yang 1970
Namdong-myongni	1 m deep	AERIK–7	3573±50	3670	2110–1860	Carbonized wood	
Yangsuri	Dolmen	KAERI–95	3900±200	4010	2665–2140	Carbonized wood	Pak and Yang 1974
Songsanni		AERIK–16	2880±120	2960	1260–885	Carbonized wood	Yang 1972
Yangpyongni		GX–9079	2875±165	2860	1125–795	Carbonized wood	Lee Y.J. 1977
Taegongni	Dolmen	KAERI–80	2560±120	2630	820–795	Wood	Pak and Yang 1974
Hwangsongni		GX–0554	2360±370	2425	835–0	Bone	Lee Y.J. 1977
Yanggulli		KAERI–81	2760±70	2840	920–815	Carbonized wood	Pak and Yang 1974
Naepyongni		AERIK–29	2930±60	3015	1265–1045	Carbonized wood	Yang 1972
		AERIK–39	2590±60	2665	815–765	Carbonized wood	
		AERIK–28	2290±60	2355	415–380	Carbonized wood	

Site	Feature	Lab no.	bp ± SD	bp	Calibrated date	Material	Reference
Hunamni	House 12	KAERI-70	3210±70	3300	1660–1410	?	Kim W.Y. et al. 1978
		RIKEN	2980±70	3065	1365–1210	Carbonized wood	Kim W.Y. et al. 1978
		RIKEN	2920±70	3000	1260–1040	?	Kim W.Y. et al. 1976
	House 8	KAERI-154[1]	2696±160	2775	930–775	Carbonized wood	Kim W.Y. et al. 1976
		KAERI-154[4]	2660±160	2735	910–760	Carbonized wood	Im H.J. 1978
		KAERI-169	2620±100	2695	865–760	Carbonized wood	Kim W.Y. et al. 1976
		KAERI-153	2540±150	2610	830–410	Carbonized wood	
	House 7	KAERI	2520±220	2590	800–405	Carbonized wood	Kim W.Y. et al. 1978
		KSU	2290±60	2355	415–380	Carbonized wood	
		KAERI	2145±60	2200	255–145	Carbonized wood	
		KAERI	2110±60	2170	195–20	Carbonized wood	
	House 14	KSU	2089±60	2150	190–10	Carbonized wood	
	House 7	KAERI	1810±190	1860	15 BC–AD 430	Carbonized wood	Kim W.Y. et al. 1976
Songgungni	Pit 54–1	KAERI-186	2665±60	2735	870–785	Carbonized wood	Kim W.Y. 1982a
		KAERI-187	2565±90	2630	820–585	Carbonized wood	
Oksongni	House under dolmen	GX-0554	2590±105	2665	830–745	Carbonized wood	Lee Y.J. 1977
Susongni	House 3	M-?	2340±120	2405	595–385	Carbonized wood	Kim W.Y. 1969
		M-?	2230±280	2290	625 BC–AD 30	Carbonized wood	
Sangjapori	Dolmen 4	KAERI-91	2170±60	2230	390–160	Carbonized wood	Pak and Yang 1974
Si Do	Top level	AERIK-10	2470±60	2540	650–425	Carbonized wood	Yang 1972
Musan Hogokdong	House 15	?	2430±110	2500	645–405	Carbonized wood	Kim W.Y. 1969
Pokchonni	Layer 5	KSU-1512	2920±25			?	Lee C.K. 1988

this date in the south, the first thousand years of Mumun is often designated late neolithic (e.g. Choi M.L. 1984b:55). North Koreans also date the first Mumun to about 2000 BC. This is based on similarities to pottery types in Manchurian sites, some of which contain bronzes.

Whether the early Mumun sites in the south represent rice agriculture is impossible to know at present, for no rice grains have been found in this group of coastal sites. If rice should be found, it would strengthen the assumption that it came across from southern China, rather than down from the north. Although millet had been cultivated in northern China for millennia, it is unlikely that rice was a major crop there between 2000 and 1000 BC (Chang 1986), even though the average annual temperature was warmer than the present. But rice had been grown in south China for thousands of years (Yan 1990), and could have been brought directly across the Yellow Sea to a similar ecological niche in southern Korea (Chon 1989a). Rice pollen is dated to 1500 BC in the southwest, and actual rice grains were found in a site at 1050 BC (Kim W.Y. 1982a, Choi M.L. 1984b:122). The problem of the introduction of rice to Korea will be discussed in greater detail below.

Bronze smelting may have occurred in Korea as early as 900 BC, the date (recalibrated) associated with a clay mold found at Yanggulli (2760 ± 70 BP, AERIK-81). North Korean archaeologists date the origins of bronze manufacture in Korea much earlier than South Koreans do, placing the beginnings of bronze metallurgy around 2000 BC (Hwang K.D. 1975:226), co-eval with the development of bronze in Liaoning and central China. There is no inherent reason to reject this as a hypothesis, although so far the evidence is thin. The earliest bronze artifact in Korea is said to come from Shinamni, where bronze buttons and a knife were cross-dated with Manchurian sites at 1300 BC (Kim J.H. 1978b:124).

In the south, at Taegongni, bronze ritual bells, horse bells, mirrors and swords, along with an axe and a chisel, have an associated date of 2560 ± 120 BP, or 610 BC. Bronze ornaments and weapons continued to be manufactured and used after iron appeared in the last few centuries BC, but bronze tools became uncommon. A new complex appears at that time, including different pottery types; therefore, this chapter ends at 500 BC. (For a more extended discussion of the radiocarbon dates, see Nelson 1992a.)

Artifacts

Ceramics

The ceramics from this period are designated Mumun, meaning undecorated, in contrast to the preceding Chulmun or "comb decorated" pottery. Korean writers often use the term Plain Coarse Pottery to refer to Mumun in English, to distinguish it from other plain pottery both later and earlier (Kim W.Y. 1968b),

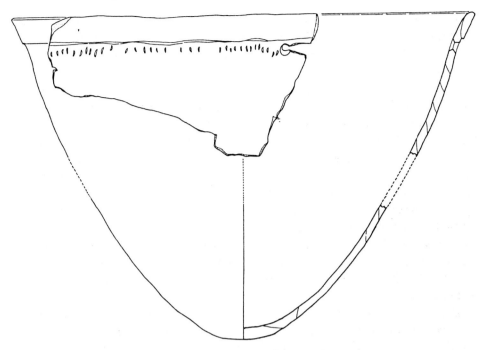

5.2 Ichungko vessel from Sugari. After Chung, Shin and Im 1981.

but the term is nevertheless too broad (Nelson 1991a). Mumun is not always entirely undecorated, as some variants have incising on the rim, on the neck or around the base, and painted designs also occur. Furthermore, the types with the squared spirals (lightning pattern), seem to belong with Mumun rather than Chulmun. Mumun is easily distinguishable from Chulmun by means of several attributes other than its lack of decoration. Differences in wall thickness, temper and paste make it unlikely that even an incised Mumun sherd would be confused with Chulmun. The paste contains coarser temper, resulting in thicker walls, so that sherds give the impression of crudeness when compared to the Chulmun pottery. Mumun ranges in color from buff to medium brown to ashy gray, probably depending on local clays and firing techniques.

Mumun pottery was fabricated in a wider variety of shapes than Chulmun, including jars with handles, bowls on pedestals (called *dou* in Chinese), and steamers, a characteristic which makes whole vessels seem more evolved. The several regional variants of Mumun can be grouped together on the basis of overall shape and differences in treatment of the rim.

Many varieties of Mumun have a collar, or double rim. The Ichungko (double rim) type with a rounded base occurs predominantly in the south (Fig. 5.2). The upper layers at Tongsamdong and Sangnodae Do (see Fig. 4.1 for location) contain some examples, as do at least seven other sites along the coast (Chung J.W. 1982a). This is the earliest dated Mumun pottery, from the second millen-

5.3 *Karak* style vessel from Hunamni.

nium BC. For example, Kumgokdong, a small rock shelter near the south coast, is dated to 2120–1865 BC and the Mumun layer at Tongsamdong to 1885–1645 BC (Choi 1978). Other shell mounds with similar plain pottery include Songsan (Kim Y.K. and Chung J.W. 1965) and Nongsori (Kim Y.K. 1965).

Even Cheju Do has a rock shelter with Ichungko, dated 2920 ± 25 BP (KSU-1512). Wide-mouthed vessels and necked jars are the usual shapes. The jars are globular with S-curved sides, and tend to be completely undecorated. Some specimens have handles (Lee C.K. 1988). Farther north, other variations of Mumun are found. Named after a site in metropolitan Seoul, *Karak* pottery also was made in two basic forms: a wide-mouthed, flower-pot shape (Fig. 5.3) and a globular jar with a short constricted neck. The bases are flat and small but not unstable. Rims are often collared and incised at the lower edge of the doubled rim, but *Gongyul* is a variant of the *Karak* style which lacks the double rim, and is characterized by a row of punctates just under the rim, accompanied by a scalloped lip (Fig. 5.4). *Karak* type pottery is found predominantly in the Han river basin (Lim 1968), but it has also been recognized as far south as the Kimhae site (see Fig. 5.1 for location) on the southeastern shore (An 1977, Kim W.Y. 1987:15).

Paengi (top-shaped) pottery is so designated because the base of the wide-mouthed pot or necked jar is almost as narrow as a child's spinning toy, making

5.4 *Gongyul* style vessel from Hunamni.

the overall shape similar to that of a top (Fig. 5.5). The narrow flat base was created by attaching a small clay disk to the round bottom of the vessel. The usual pot has a collar. Short slanting parallel lines are frequently incised into the collar where it meets the body, suggesting an affinity with *Karak* vessels. *Paengi* pots range from about 16 to 25 cm in height. A hole was bored in the narrow base of some of the pots before firing. Occasionally an auxiliary hole nearby, placed asymmetrically, is also found. The jar form, with a constricted neck and

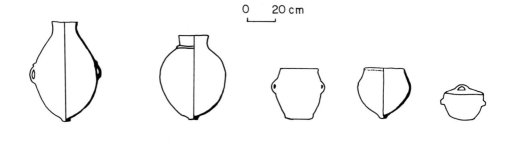

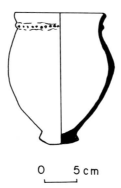

5.5 *Paengi* pottery, Pyongan Puk Do.

everted rim, is usually entirely undecorated. Some examples have a low ring base rather than a disk, and others have narrow flat bases with no additions at all. Han Y.H. (1983) dates *Paengi* pottery from about 1100 to 300 BC, suggesting that it has both regional and temporal variants.

Paengi pottery is found in greatest abundance in Hwanghae Do and the neighboring South Pyongan Do. Sites in this region are relatively dense. Kim J.H. (1978a) believes *Paengi* is the earliest style of Mumun ceramics, partly because of the sparseness of associated bronze artifacts and partly because of characteristics which seem to him to be closer to Chulmun than the other Mumun styles, for example rounded bases and residual incising. Radiocarbon dates at present do not bear out this interpretation, but few dates from the north have been published, so the relative dating remains unclear.

The wide-mouthed pot with basal perforation is sometimes cited as evidence of rice steaming. The pot would fit into the jar to make a functional pair, and the two forms are frequently found together. However, other explanations are possible. For example, the pot with a hole in the base could have been used as a funnel. Alternatively, Okladnikov (1965) has suggested that similar vessels in the Soviet Maritime region were used for making cheese, although this use seems unlikely in Korea since milk and its products are not part of the traditional cuisine. Rice usage is confirmed by finds of actual grains as far north as Pyongyang, so rice steaming seems to be the most reasonable explanation, unless there was some process in making *makkolli* (rice wine) which required such an arrangement.

Pon'gae pottery is called "neolithic," or even Chulmun, by some North and South Korean archaeologists (Kim J.H. 1968, Kang 1975) but I have included it in this chapter because the shapes echo those of Mumun and not Chulmun, and similar designs are found in Manchuria associated with Mumun-like vessels. Furthermore, associated artifacts include polished stone types more often found with megaliths than Early Villages. Pon'gae means lightning, referring to designs of squared spirals. Although this design is usually incised rather than painted, it does bring to mind some Upper Xiajiadian culture motifs, and might well belong to the same period.

For instance, the upper level in the cave at Misongni, on the Yalu river, has pottery with long funnel-shaped necks, gourd-shaped bodies and small lug handles (Henthorn 1966). Other northwestern sites with ceramics of the same shape but with *Pon'gae* decoration are Tangsan, Sejungni, Tobongni, Shinamni (Fig. 5.6) and elsewhere. This type is also found in the northeast, along the Tumen river at Musan, and on the coast including the sites of Sopohang, Nongpodong and Wonsudae. It also appears in the Soviet Maritime region, for example at Gladkaya I (Okladnikov 1965, Kang 1975).

In a comparative study of pottery types in Manchuria, Miyamoto (1985) places the Pon'gae pottery level of Shinamni at 2000 BC, comparing it with the lowest level of Shuangtouce in Liaodong. The upper level of Misongni is considered to be about 1,000 years later, along with the upper layer of Shinamni. These sites are grouped with the upper layer of Shangmash on the Liaodong peninsula and sites in Shenyang (Miyamoto 1990).

In the region where Koguryo arose, on the central Yalu river and its tributaries, there is evidence of plain pottery and agriculture by 2000–1500 BC (Rhee 1989). Several shapes occur, including jars, bowls and wide-mouthed pots. Clay spindle whorls and net sinkers are also found, along with chipped hoes, polished axes, arrowheads and knives (Chen 1965).

On the Tumen river in the northeast, bowls on high pedestals (*dou*) are a distinctive element of the assemblage (Fig. 5.7). This area is included in the Tuanjie culture of eastern China (Lin 1985), which also is found in the Soviet Maritime region, associated in all cases with stone cist graves. Northeastern wide-mouthed pots were made with unusually broad flat bases, and the jars are more globular than elsewhere. Miyamoto (1985) considers these sites to be only slightly earlier than Western Han. In addition to those in northern sites, a few other *dou* are found in association with late Mumun types in the south, for

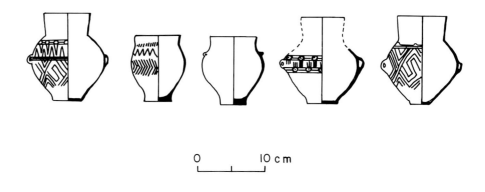

0   10 cm

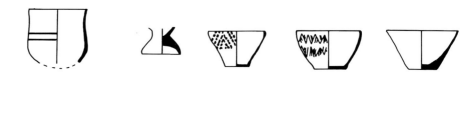

5.6 *Pon'gae* pottery from Sinamni.

5.7 Pedestal vessels at Musan Pomuigusok. After Hwang K.D. 1975.

example a broken pedestal at Jung Do in central Korea (National Museum of Korea 1981), a site on the campus of Yongnam University (Chung 1985, 1986), and a late-looking low pedestal vessel at Kumgokdong (Kim J.H. and Chung J.W. 1980). It is clear that the vessels on pedestals were a late addition in Korea.

Jungdo pottery is yet another variety of Mumun, which was first found on the North Han river in central Korea, and has since been located in Cholla Nam Do in the southwest as well. The *Jungdo* style features a row of impressed ovals or circles above the base (Fig. 5.8). Choi M.C. (1983b) considers this style to be the final form of Mumun, sequencing the site of Hunamni with *Gongyul* pottery as Early Mumun, Karakdong as Middle, and Jung Do (the site) as Late Mumun. Generally *Jungdo* pottery is seen as iron age, and it will be discussed more fully in the following chapter.

Burnished red pottery seems to have been used as a status marker, as it is discovered far more often in burials than in dwellings. The most common shape is a small globular jar with a short neck (Fig. 5.9). The bright red-orange color is said to derive from iron oxide (SSI 1986), and much labor was expended to accomplish the high sheen. The distribution seems to be largely in the south and the far northeast (An 1977). Black or gray burnished pottery is also found, but it is rarer than red pottery (Kim W.Y. 1966a, 1967b). Its form is often a narrow, long-necked jar. In dated contexts black pottery ranges from very late in the megalithic period to early Wonsamguk age and it too will be discussed in the next chapter. Painted jars are occasionally found in the northeast, and painted vessels have recently been excavated in the far southwest as well. The painted designs are simple and monochrome.

Lithics

Specific stone tool shapes have little continuity from Chulmun to Mumun, although functionally similar tools occur. Not only were previously utilized implement types such as projectile points and net sinkers manufactured in new shapes, but also several altogether new implements appeared. The most obvious difference is that whereas most Chulmun assemblages were characterized by chipped stone tools, polished stone artifacts are the rule in Mumun sites.

Among the new tools, the semi-lunar knife, associated with intensive agriculture, is particularly notable (Fig. 5.10). This two-holed crescent-shaped reaping knife is by far the most prevalent stone artifact in Mumun sites. These knives were most often made of polished slate. In shape they are similar to knives found in Longshan and Longshanoid sites in China (An 1955, 1980), while the typical Yangshao rectangular knife with side notches used to harvest millets is not found. Some variations occur, with the two holes on either the straight or the convex side of the tool. Okladnikov (1965:121) and Leroi-Gourhan (1946:306) associate the semi-lunar knife with harvesting of kaoliang (grain sorghum) or millet, but scholars more often have connected the semi-lunar knives with rice

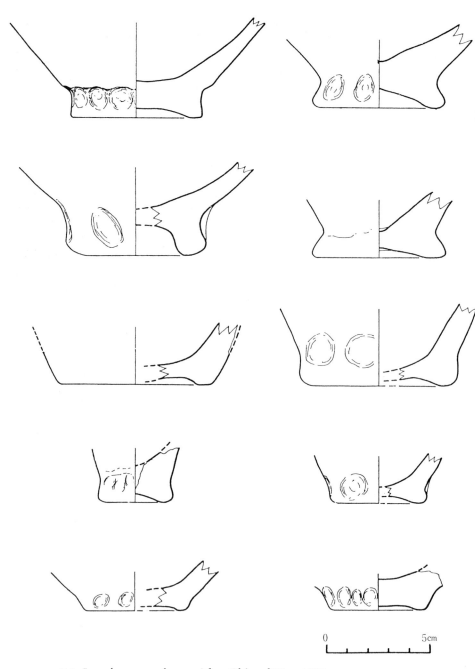

5.8 *Jungdo* pottery bases. After Chi and Han 1982.

5.9 Burnished red vessels from Hunamni.

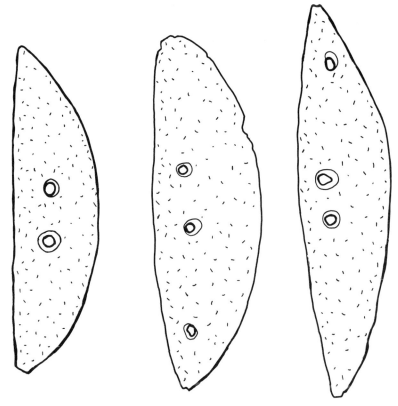

5.10 Semi-lunar reaping knives.

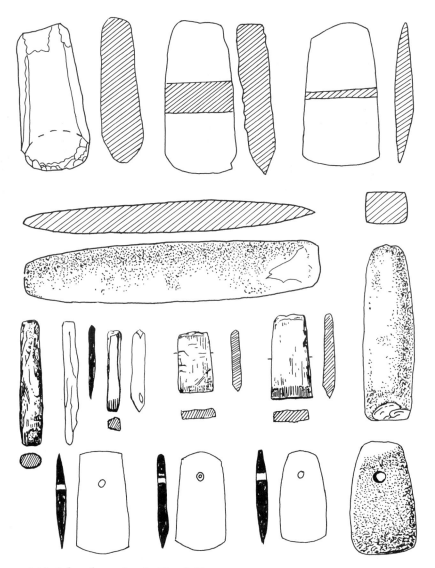

5.11 Adzes from sites in North Korea.

cultivation (e.g., Choe 1982, An 1955). Thus the distribution pattern of semi-lunar knives is often used as surrogate evidence for the diffusion of rice. Triangular knives are usually seen as a separate type, and their locations are often mapped to indicate the direction of diffusion (Chon 1983). However, it seems to me that they may be resharpened semi-lunar knives which were finally discarded when they reached the triangular stage.

Stepped adzes are frequently present (Fig. 5.11). The step is for the purpose of hafting, as is shown by the one wooden handle which has partially survived at

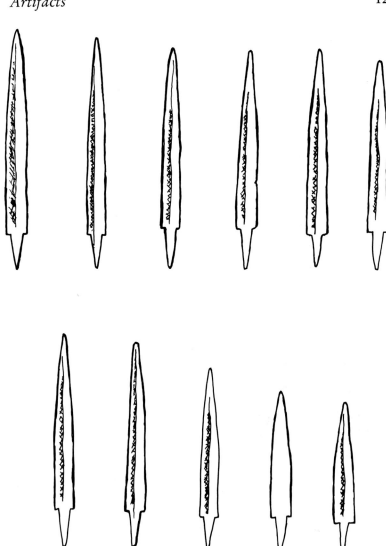

5.12 Stone spear points from Taepyongni dolmen in Puyo.

Sinhungdong (Kim J.H. 1978b). Some adzes have two steps, for reverse hafting. Ground stone axes and chisels appear at most sites, as do grinding stones, whetstones and net sinkers. Decorated pottery spindle whorls also occur in many sites.

Stone projectile points and daggers are more numerous than their bronze counterparts. Stone spear points were long and narrow, stemmed, and had diamond-shaped cross-sections (Fig. 5.12). Arrowheads occur in two contrasting shapes (Choi S.N. 1982b). Those with diamond-shaped cross-sections are stemmed like the spear points, while the flattened hexagonal variety has no stem

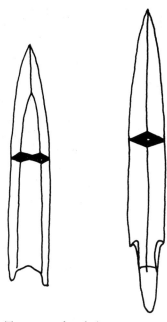

5.13 Two arrowhead shapes.

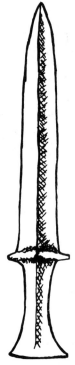

5.14 Simple stone dagger.

5.15 Stone daggers from Hunamni.

but pronounced tangs (Fig. 5.13). The latter probably was hafted into a split stick. These two arrowhead shapes are frequently found in the same site, even in the same burial, suggesting functional rather than spatial or temporal differences. However, possible uses of the two types have not been investigated.

Polished stone daggers are constructed with the handle and blade fashioned from a single piece of stone (Figs. 5.14, 5.15). Frequently they are made of a

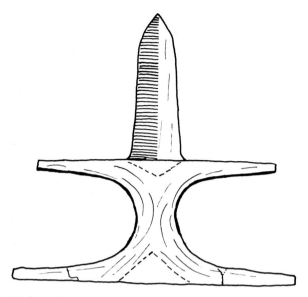

5.16 X-shaped stone dagger from Pusan Koejongdong.

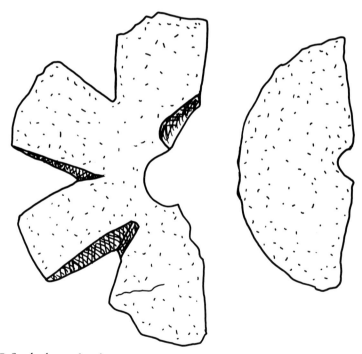

5.17 Spoked macehead.

5.18 Perforated stone disks from Hunamni.

striated limestone producing elegant effects. The stone daggers vary from rather simple shapes (e.g. from a dolmen in Sunchon [Im 1967]) to elaborate, highly polished pieces with such wide flanges that they must have been intended for ceremonial use only (Fig. 5.16), appearing too fragile for use in battle or any other practical function. A dwelling pit at Paju containing a stone dagger was radiocarbon dated to 640 BC (Kim W.Y. 1980a).

Spoked maceheads are most common in the north, although a few have been found in east coast sites as well (Fig. 5.17). Some of these implements appear to be very businesslike battle-axes, but others were made with such slender spokes that they too must be ceremonial. There is little evidence of warfare in sites other than the possible battle-axes. Settlements are not walled, nor are there other signs of fortifications, although it must be admitted that the beginning date of many hill forts is unknown.

Stone disks with central perforations are referred to as "stone money" by some North Korean archaeologists, but they appear to be very similar to Yang-shao digging stick weights from north China (Chang 1977:160). These objects occur commonly enough to have had some utilitarian value, and were not found in hoards or in burials as one would expect if they were used as media of exchange or stores of value (Fig. 5.18).

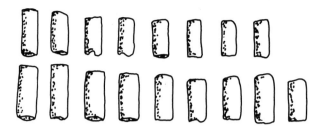

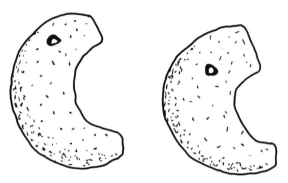

5.19 Tubular beads and *gokok* from Taesongni.

Polished stone beads of fine-grained stone such as amazonite or nephrite occur in both dwellings and burials. Amazonite tends to be replaced by nephrite through time. Early beads were drilled by hand, while later ones were made with mechanical drills (Francis 1985). The usual shape is tubular, but *gokok*, curved comma-shaped beads, are not uncommon, often as the central gem in a necklace (Fig. 5.19). A few beads were found which are semi-circular with two perforations, for example at Yonghungni in South Pyongan Do and at Koejongdong in South Chungchong Do. This shape may be transitional to the *gokok*. The curved shape is sometimes said to represent animal claws or teeth, although Han (1976) associates it with the crescent moon. Whatever its symbolic meaning may be, the *gokok* seems to function as an indicator of high status. The earliest date for one of these ornaments is eighth to seventh century BC (Table in Lee I.S. 1987:368–9).

Bronze artifacts

The dates of the appearance of bronze artifacts and the beginning of bronze manufacture are still under discussion. Even the terminology regarding bronze and iron ages in Korea is unsettled. Any occurrence of bronze or iron may cause the site to be designated bronze age or iron age, thus the two "ages" may co-exist, if one burial has only bronze and its neighbor contains iron. When iron appears, bronze continues to be used. Since we are not concerned here with a bronze age as such, only early bronzes will be discussed in this chapter, up to about 400 BC.

Artifacts made of bronze are more frequently found in burial sites and hoards than in dwellings. Many burial sites are covered by dolmens, making them relatively easy to discover and plunder, which may explain the fact that few bronzes have been found *in situ*. Large numbers of the bronze artifacts in museums as well as private collections are of unknown provenance. Even with this uncertainty in provenance, it seems that the quantity and variety of bronze artifacts increased throughout the last millennium BC. Bronze of course continued in use along with iron into the Three Kingdoms period, but was used for sword blades and tools. Ro (1989) believes that the bronze indicates newcomers to Korea. This topic will be considered below.

Bronze daggers, spear points and arrowheads are all found in the megalithic period. (The daggers are sometimes called swords, but they range from 25 to 40 cm in length, shorter than the term sword implies.) Although it is sometimes asserted that the polished stone daggers and arrowheads are copies of bronze prototypes, the shapes of these implements in bronze and stone are far from identical. The stone daggers in particular have been the subject of controversy, seen alternatively as a lower-class copy of bronze daggers or as a marker of high status.

While stone daggers have been discovered in settlements as well as burials, the bronze daggers have been found exclusively in hoards or in burial contexts (stone cists or pits). This suggests either that bronze daggers were worn on the person and not kept in dwellings or that the houses of the dagger-wearers have not been found. The dagger blade was cast separately from the hilt, and frequently only the blade is found. Presumably their hilts were made of perishable materials. When the hilts were metal, they could be cast in several pieces, including handle, hand guard and end ornament. Blade shapes have been classified into two basic types: the Liaoning dagger which has wide bracket-shaped projections on the sides near the hilt (Fig. 5.20), and the slender dagger in which these projections became progressively attenuated (Fig. 5.21) (An 1983, Lee C.K. 1982). The Liaoning type, which is earlier, has been further subdivided into three types, with the protuberance progressively closer to the handle through time. The Liaoning dagger is found abundantly in the Liaodong peninsula and around Bohai Bay, as well as in Korea, but it is not found in China south of the Great Wall. Several cist graves with Liaoning daggers have been found in the Cholla provinces, for example several were recently discovered in the Juam Dam excavations (Yoon D.H. 1988). The narrow dagger is also divided into types and subtypes, continuing into the time of the introducton of iron. Three molds for

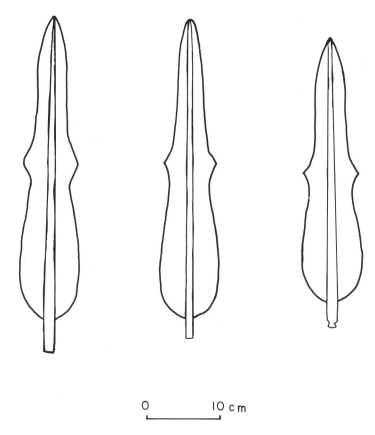

0   10 cm

5.20 Liaoning-type bronze daggers.

casting slender bronze daggers were found at Choburi in Kyonggi Do, near several dolmens (National Museum 1986).

Ge-halberds (weapons hafted at right angles to the staff) have broader blades than daggers with conventional hafting (Fig. 5.22). The ge was a common form of weapon in China beginning in the Shang dynasty, but was discontinued in the Western Han (Wang 1982:123). The Korean ge tends to be a late form. The halberd was not socketed but was attached to a pole with rivets or lashing through cast holes. On the other hand, spearheads were always socketed. A reputed Chinese spearhead, datable to the fifth century BC, was found in southwestern Korea (Kim W.Y. 1978:9). Kim Jong-hak (1978b) notes that neither bronze spearheads nor ge-halberds are found associated with Liaoning daggers, suggesting that the Liaoning daggers have a different derivation. Twenty-six Chinese daggers with the handle and blade cast together, dating to the sixth century BC, were discovered in a cache near Sangnimni in southwestern Korea (Chon 1976). The Chinese daggers are clearly imports, not locally manufactured.

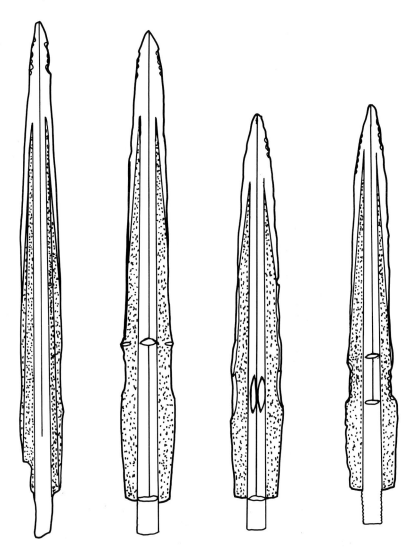

5.21 Slender bronze daggers.

Bronze axes were made in two forms, one with flaring sides and a rounded cutting edge and the other narrower with a straight cutting edge. In the upper level of Misongni these two shapes were found together. Neither form resembles the broad axe of central China, but both could be derived from types found in Manchuria. At least some of the Korean axes were locally made, for sandstone axe molds have been found in the peninsula.

Bronze projectile points are stemmed, and have multiple facets and grooves. Bronze knives are rare, resembling those of the Karasuk culture, with ring handles and angled blades. Similar bronze knives also occur in Shang dynasty sites in China.

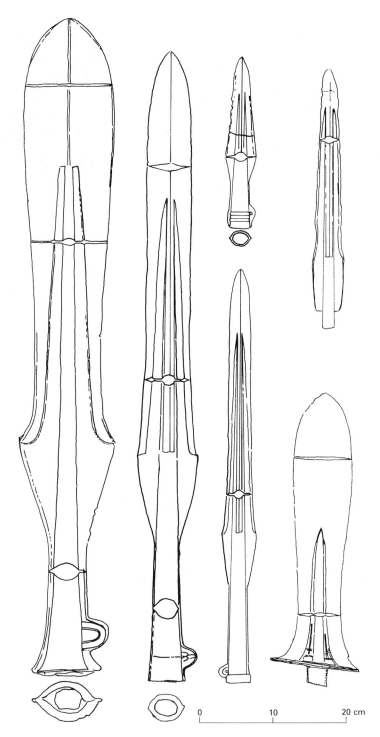

5.22 Bronze *ge*-halberd and spearheads.

5.23 Bronze geometric mirrors from Korea: *a* coarse lines, *b* fine lines.

Mirrors are the most common form of non-utilitarian bronze artifacts. Korean mirrors are decorated with geometric patterns composed of zigzags or triangular hatched zones. They are distinctively different from Chinese mirrors (Fig. 5.23) (Lee N.Y. 1983), but it is interesting to note that mirrors from the Fu Hao grave in Anyang have geometric line designs, including hatched triangles (Lin 1986:252). The Fu Hao mirrors have a single knob, unlike the two perforated knobs, placed together off-center, which characterize the northeastern and Korean mirrors. Korean mirrors have been seriated on the basis of fineness of the linear patterns, with broad zigzags leading to large triangles, and finely executed triangular patterns in the latest examples. Chon (cited in Kim W.Y. 1978:8) dates the earliest mirrors to the sixth to fourth centuries BC. Kim Jong-hak (1978b) suggests that the mirrors developed from bronze buttons which are common in Siberia and Manchuria, because the button attachments are similar to the mirror loops. He believes that bronze buttons are among the earliest bronze artifacts found in Korea.

Bells, belt hooks, horse trappings and chariot ornaments are bronze items not found in cist graves but often occurring in pit burials so that they seem to be later developments. They will be discussed in the next chapter.

Many of the bronze artifacts found in Korea were locally manufactured. Molds for daggers, arrowheads, mirrors, fishhooks, axes and other bronze items have appeared in sites throughout the peninsula, indicating the widespread manufacture of bronze weapons and implements. The Soongsil Museum (1986) exhibits several such molds. An interesting pair of flat steatite molds, found in Yongam, South Cholla province, includes one that is constructed to form a dagger on one side and a spear on the other. The second mold has an axe form on one side and fishhooks on the other. Also indicative of local production is recent evidence that Korean bronze is significantly different from Chinese bronze in chemical composition, containing a greater admixture of zinc. According to Jeon, "the oldest surviving relic of zinc-bronze alloy in the world is what may be called Korean zinc-bronzewear [sic] which was discovered in North Korea and which dates from the tenth century BC" (Jeon 1976:35). The zinc content of Korean bronzes varies from 7 to 13 percent (Jeon 1974). However, a significant amount of lead (5 to 9 percent) is also found in the Liaoning-type dagger alloys (Kim W.Y. 1986a:99) and a bronze disk from a Yangshao site has been found to be 25 percent zinc (Chang 1980a), so perhaps future analysis will require a further reassessment of the uniqueness of Korean bronze.

Specific sources of metal ores for Korean bronze have not been located. Copper is found in several regions in mountainous Korea, although no ancient copper mines have been identified (Kim W.Y. 1986a:102). Copper is not uncommon in East Asia, but tin is more restricted in its distribution. One of the world's "tin belts" goes across northern Asia, with a branch running through Korea and Japan (deJesus 1977). Zinc is also found in northern Korea and in the Taebaek range in the south (Vreeland and Shinn 1976). Thus the raw material was locally available once the technology to smelt it had been developed.

Settlements

Locations

A shift in location strategy accounts for the fact that relatively few sites contain both Mumun and Chulmun ceramics. For the most part the river banks were abandoned, and hillsides were chosen as village sites, as indeed they still are. The valleys and areas adjacent to small streams were left free for fields. The clustering of sites, so obvious on distribution maps of Chulmun sites, disappeared and the pattern of site locations became similar to the present placement of villages. Sites are sparser in the northern and eastern mountains, with increasing site density to the west and south where the best cultivable land and the longest growing season occur. However, Mumun sites are found even in the more rugged areas.

Villages and dolmens are usually found together. After an intensive survey in the southwest, Rhee (1984:321) predicted that a village site could be found about 500–1500 m away from any group of dolmens. The habitations would also be within 100 m of a good-sized stream, "on a ridge facing south next to a broad valley floor, commanding a good view of the dolmens."

Dwellings

Although many single dwellings containing Mumun pottery have been excavated, only a few entire villages have been explored, ranging in size from tens to hundreds of houses. The dwellings continue to be semi-subterranean, but they are larger on the whole than Early Villages houses, and many have two or more hearths. Both round floor plans, as at Songamdong (Choi 1978), and rectangular floors are found in these sites (Fig. 5.24). Some evidence of household clusters with shared storage facilities suggests complex intra-village arrangements (Lim 1985). Examples of small villages with several excavated dwellings include the site of Hunamni on the South Han river and Sinmaeri on the North Han river in central Korea. Songgungni farther south, and Soktalli in the northwest are examples of larger villages.

The *Hunamni* site was excavated by a team from Seoul National University over several field seasons (Kim W.Y. *et al.* 1973, 1974, 1976, 1978). The site is on a hill slope above a small stream near its confluence with the Han river. Fourteen houses were excavated on the slope of a hill (Fig. 5.25). Three were on the north slope, while the other eleven dwelling pits were some distance away on the southern side. Several houses overlap, indicating that these dwellings were not all contemporaneous. Although other houses might yet be uncovered, this site seems to represent a small village occupied over some length of time, at least several centuries according to the radiocarbon dates.

Three dwellings stood toward the summit of the north slope of a hill. The foundation of each house had been shallowly excavated into the hillside in a rectangular shape. House 2 was about 1 m distant from House 1, and House 3 had been partly destroyed by the erection of House 2. House 1 measured 8.2 × 4.2 m. An entrance in the center of a long wall and a layer of fire-hardened clay forming the floor were the only features. The fact that neither hearth nor postholes were present might suggest some use other than a dwelling. It has been interpreted as a communal storehouse (Choi M.L. 1984b). However, the artifacts on the floor were items of daily use, including a chipped stone axe, stone daggers, a semi-lunar knife, potsherds and pottery, net sinkers and spindle whorls. Similar items, additionally including whetstones and small triangular stone projectile points, were found in the lower house fill. House 2 was featureless like House 1, but House 3 contained a stone-lined hearth on the eastern side. Two hollows had been scooped out of the floor on the west side, and a rectangular depression, 1.1 × 0.3 m and 0.4 m deep, abutted the west wall.

On the southern slope of the hill, House 5 overlapped House 4, and the building of House 10 partially destroyed House 9. The other houses are dispersed down the hill slope, with distances of 2 to 7 m between them. The houses are rectangular, usually about twice as long as they are wide. The larger houses range from 5.9 m to 9.6 m in length, and 2.8 to 4.5 m in width. Three small houses each have a length of about 4.5 to 5 m and vary from 2.5 to 3.9 m in width. The larger

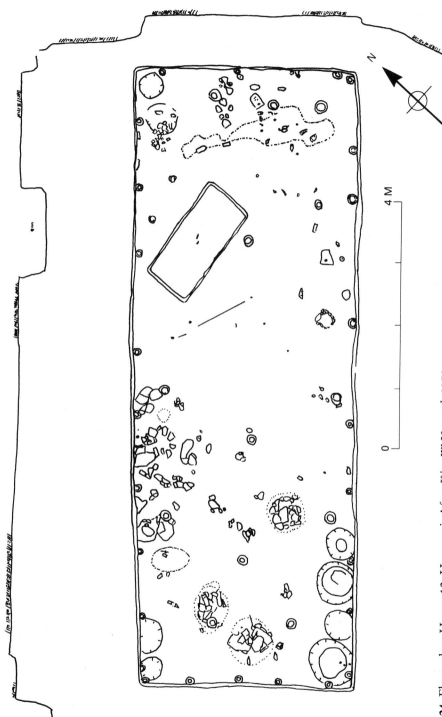

5.24 Floor plan, House 12, Hunamni. After Kim W.Y. *et al.* 1978.

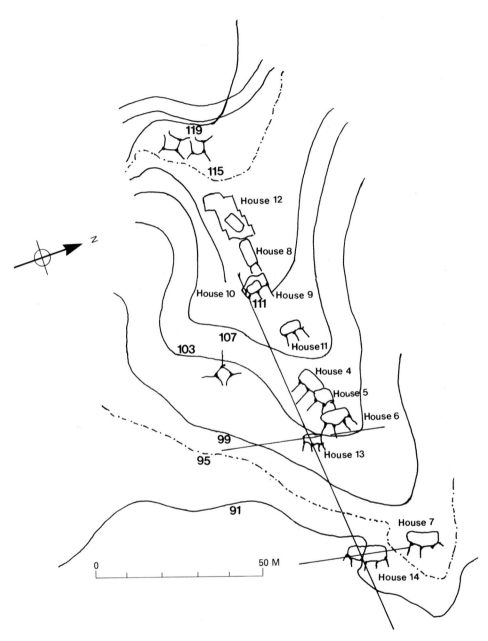

5.25 Houses on hill slope, Hunamni. After Kim W.Y. *et al.* 1978.

dwellings could have housed extended families while the smaller ones would only have accommodated nuclear families. Some of the houses had hardened clay floors, while others were plastered with a hard limy substance similar to that reported from Longhan sites in China (Chang 1977). An oval depression, 1.73 × 1.39 m and 30 cm deep, was found in the center of House 4, and a group of depressions clustered together in the southwest corner. House 5 had two hearths and a small square projection in the east corner of the north wall. Houses 6, 7 and 8 each contained a row of post holes. House 7 had a burnt area but no hearth, and House 8 featured a clay-lined hearth near the southwest corner. The houses thus had considerable variation in their construction and internal appointments. However, there is no single building which is clearly larger, more complex or otherwise distinct from the others. Hunamni was a small village without internal stratification whose inhabitants farmed the lower slopes near the river. The site appears to have been continuously occupied for at least several generations.

The site of Sinmaeri on the North Han river in central Korea allows a glimpse of a late village pattern. An outdoor fireplace 1.4 m in diameter and 60 cm in depth was unlike any hearth feature of Early Villages. Two stone cobbles were in the center, surrounded by large potsherds. Charcoal and ash filled the area between. Whether this feature represents cooking or other uses is uncertain, but food preparation is most likely since it was close to a pithouse. The pithouse remains were rectangular, with slightly rounded corners. The largest house, 5.5 × 4.5 m, contained two hearths not outlined by stones, but merely oval depressions about 50 cm long and 10 cm deep, filled with ash and charcoal. Associated pottery is of the *Gongyul* and *Jungdo* types. Nearby three dolmens were excavated. The burials beneath included one in a stone cist and two surrounded with irregular stones. Mumun pottery, hexagonal arrowheads, polished stone axes, a chisel and a pottery bead were found with the burials. This site is estimated to date to the fourth century BC (National Museum of Korea 1981, Chi and Lee 1984).

Changchonni in southwestern Korea similarly has round house floors. Spindle whorls and a simple Mumun jar were associated with one floor while others contained oval firepits with a post hole at each end (Mokpo University Museum 1986).

The large village of Songgungni near Puyo in southwestern Korea neatly ties together many elements in the same site. The village covers more than 8 ha of land, and includes house floors, dolmens, a jar burial, a cist burial containing a Puyo dagger, and a kiln site (Kang *et al.* 1979, Chi, An and Song 1986, An, Cho and Yoon 1987).

The pit houses have several shapes: circular, rectangular and irregular. The rectangular example has an oval pit in the center flanked by two post holes, and rows of post holes down the long sides. The circular examples average about 5 m in diameter, but have no features. House 1 contained rice grains, which are of the *japonica* variety. Artifacts recovered include a stone dagger, stone arrowheads and spearheads, semi-lunar knives, a saddle quern, a plane, whetstones, spindle whorls and a ground axe. A wooden spade and a wooden shaft for a stone dagger were found here for the first time (An, Cho and Yoon 1987). The projectile points are diamond-shaped in cross-section.

Potsherds are plain, red polished and black. The Mumun shapes include both deep and shallow bowls. Some vessels are *dou*-shaped on pedestals. A globular jar with a small flat base is unlike any other pottery found so far in Korea. Red burnished pottery includes an unusual long-necked jar. Two sherds of unpolished black pottery were also found (Chi and Lee 1988b).

The nearby stone cist was made of four or five vertical stone slabs per side with flat slabs for a floor. A single flat oval stone served as the cover (Han 1977). The head was oriented to the north. Contents included a Liaoning style dagger, about 30 cm long, a bronze chisel, seventeen large tubular beads of amazonite, two *gokok*, one stone dagger and eleven stone arrowheads (Rhi 1976). Urns appear to be associated with this site as well, standing upright in a pit with slab covers. One jar contained dozens of tubular jades; the others were found empty. Since vertical pots are not the usual mode of jar burial, these jars may represent caches rather than burials.

A stone mold for a fan-shaped bronze axe was found in the village, indicating production as well as consumption of bronze. A kiln site where pottery was produced was higher up the hill on the north edge of the village. It appears to have had an open fire in a circular area. Sherds of Mumun and red polished pottery along with clods of burnt earth identified the site as a pottery firing area. A small polished stone dagger was also found near this feature (National Museum of Korea 1979). Dates from Songgungni are 2665 ± 60 and 2565 ± 90 BP, or 715 and 615 BC.

The site of Soktalli in Hwanghae Do is an example of a much larger village. Settlement debris covers an area of 100,000 sq m, and it is estimated that there were at least a hundred dwellings at the site. Of these, twelve have been excavated. No village plan was published. The excavated houses are similar in detail and contents to those of Hunamni. For example, House 2 is 6.6 × 4 m and 40 cm deep, with post holes along the walls and a hearth delineated by a depression. Fired clay created a smooth floor. In several houses floor depressions of various sizes and shapes were discovered (Pak and Li 1965). Artifacts associated with each house were quite variable. Two stone cist graves were also excavated, 35 m from the nearest house, but quite close to each other. Unfortunately, no artifacts remained in these burials to strengthen the inference of relationship to the village. Other sites, however, have established conclusively that the stone cists contain the burials associated with the Mumun culture.

At Simcholli in Hwanghae Do the dwellings are somewhat disturbed. Although the extent of the village cannot be ascertained, the houses that have been excavated are similar to those already discussed. The village must have been of considerable size, judging from the fact that dolmens and associated cist graves have been found in large numbers, on nearby hill slopes as well as on the valley floor (Pak and Li 1965).

Taepyongni is a village site near the south coast. Clay spindle whorls, net sinkers and beads were found along with the usual set of polished stone implements. The pottery ranges from *Karak* style with perforated rim and burnished jars to later types such as triangular rim bowls and jars with painted egg plant design (Chinju National Museum 1988). Another Mumun village was found at Hapchon Chopori, with dolmens nearby in which rather plain polished stone knives were found (Pusan University Museum 1988).

Longhouses

Some sites seem to consist of a single dwelling, of longhouse form. Yoksamdong, on the Han river in central Korea (Fig. 5.26) (Kim Y.S. and Lim B.T. 1968), and Oksongni farther north in Kyonggi Do, are examples of this house type. The dwelling at Oksongni is 15.7 × 3.7 m, while that at Yoksamdong measures 16 × 3 m. These houses have post holes closely spaced along the edges, but are otherwise similar to the more typical house. The Oksongni house has two oval fire basins on the long axis of the house, both in the eastern half. The house was found under a dolmen, but the two are thought not to be associated (Kim C.W. and Yun M.B. 1967). At Yangpyongni, the remains of a low wall 1.5 m long were found on the east side of a large oval house, about 6 × 4 m. A radiocarbon date of 920 BC (2870 BP) was obtained from this dwelling (Choi and Im 1984).

Subsistence

Many of the artifacts found in Mumun dwelling sites, and the locations of the villages, point to farming as the basic subsistence strategy. The small semi-lunar knives are probably grain-reaping implements. Grinding stones are a frequent find, and weights for digging sticks are very common. Stone axes for clearing fields complete the agricultural tool kit, except for the rare find of large flat stone implements which have been identified as plows.

Actual remains of grains and legumes are known from several Mumun sites. At the small settlement of Hunamni in Kwangju, Kyonggi Do, four different kinds of grains were identified: rice, foxtail millet, barley and sorghum. Rice pollen was identified near Naju in Cholla Nam Do and near Kimpo in Kyonggi Do, while rice grains were discovered in the village of Songgungni, and at Namgyong near Pyongyang, along with millets and soybean (Kim Y.G. and Suk K.J. 1984). The rice grains are all of the *Japonica* type (Kim W.Y. *et al.* 1974). Flour identified as made from millet was found in a broken jar on the floor of a dwelling at Hogokdong, in Hamgyong Puk Do near the Tumen river, and similar flour was found in four other dwellings nearby (Hwang 1960). Another site in

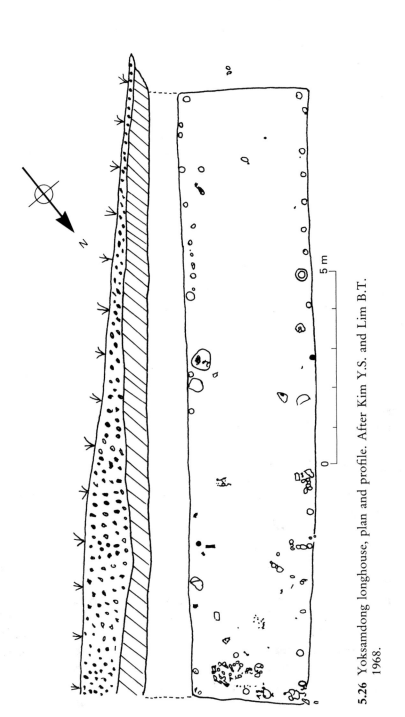

5.26 Yoksamdong longhouse, plan and profile. After Kim Y.S. and Lim B.T. 1968.

Odong, Hoeryong, produced red beans and soybeans. These sites are dated in North Korea as early as 1200 BC. Since rice has been identified in phytoliths in the Late Jomon of Japan (Fujihara 1976), these early dates seem quite acceptable. (See Nelson 1982, Choe 1982, Kim W.Y. 1982a, Im H.J. 1988 and Choe 1986.) Although most discussions of agriculture from this period have focused on rice, it is clear from the above finds that monocropping of rice is not an appropriate model for the agriculture of the megalithic period.

Only rare sites in Korea produce animal bones, due to the combination of alternating wet/warm and dry/cold seasons, and the acidic soil. Rarely, burial offerings of cattle, deer and pig have survived, for example in the Hwangsongni dolmens (Lee Y.J. 1984b). According to a North Korean analysis, pigs, dogs and cattle were domesticated in the Early Villages period (Kim S.K. 1966), as described in the previous chapter. Hogokdong contained the bones of at least twenty domesticated pigs. Some water buffalo bones were found as far north as the Yalu river, a fact which has been thought to indicate a milder climate at the time. It is possible, however, that the bones represent an attempt to import water buffalo as draft animals, along with other rice technology from the south.

Pigs are used as scavengers of human waste, and are ecologically appropriate in the forest environment of Korea. According to Watson (1971), in northeast Asia pigs were kept near the homestead and fed scraps, rather than being allowed to root in the forest. Pigs are common in present-day rural Korea, and wild boar still roam the northern forests. No enclosures for animals have been identified in archaeological sites. Dogs were sometimes raised for food in Korea as they were in China, but there is no archaeological evidence that dogs constituted a basic food resource.

Ovicaprids are entirely missing. The humid forest of Korea is not an ecologically appropriate environment for sheep, and by United Silla times, when sheep became important for sacrifices in the Chinese manner, they had to be imported from China for specific ceremonies.

Projectile points suggest hunting, and large net sinkers imply fishing. Spindle whorls attest to a textile industry, probably based on hemp, ramie or similar native plants. It is possible that silk worms were raised as well, although no hard evidence has come to light.

The creation of polished stone implements is extremely labor intensive. Some daily tools may have been made within each household, but one house at Chitamni with far more its share of arrowheads suggests specialization (Choe 1986). Ceramic specialists may have made the pottery for clusters of villages. Choi Mong-lyong (1984b) believes that craft specialization and itinerant pedlars were part of the Mumun system. Lee Y.J. (1984b:17) suggests that the different colors of slate used to make the polished stone knives which are found in a single site are evidence of trade in raw materials or finished products.

Ceramic vessels differ in shape somewhat, but everywhere there are two general forms – one with a wide mouth and the other with a constricted neck.

Some of the wide-mouthed jars have small holes in the bottom, which has led to the speculation that they might be rice steamers. The appearance of pedestal vessels in the northeast implies a ritual association, since *dou* are used to this day in shamanistic ceremonies in Korea, set on the altar with offerings of rice, fruit or cakes.

Burials

Stone cists and dolmens are the commonest forms of burial associated with Mumun pottery. Jar burials do occur in Mumun pots, but they are few, mostly confined to the southwest, and seem to be quite late. Either jars or cists may be found under dolmens.

Dolmens

Above-ground constructions of large unworked stones are called dolmens in Europe, and this word is often used to translate the Korean terms *koindol* and *chisokmyo*. Although the constructions look similar, there is no reason to postulate connections between the dolmens of Europe and those of Korea, since the gaps between them are temporal as well as spatial. In Asia, megaliths are found ranging from India to Manchuria, but the northeast Asian dolmen is found in greatest numbers in Korea (Kim B.M. 1981a), and seems to be a local invention. Earlier, estimates of several thousand dolmens in the Korean peninsula were made, but the recent identification of over 5,500 dolmens in the southwest corner alone (Choi M.L. 1984b:113, Yi Y.M. 1987) suggests that 100,000 may be a more appropriate number.

Three styles of dolmens are recognized in Korea (Fig. 5.27) (Hwang 1981). The "northern style" is made of four upright stone slabs placed to create sides of a cube, and topped with a much larger horizontal capstone which protrudes on all sides. Many of these upper stones are of vast proportions, weighing up to 300 tons (Rhee 1984). Only a few northern dolmens have been found to contain evidence of burial within the upright stones, but it is probable that grave goods were placed there and have been looted, since traces of human bone cannot be routinely expected in burial sites, and at least one northern-style dolmen in Manchuria contained a burial (Mikami 1961). However, the table dolmens may simply represent markers, territorial or commemorative.

The "southern style" consists of a large boulder covering a pile of small stones, while the "capstone" type lies directly on the ground as the cover of a stone cist burial. Southern dolmens are always burial markers most commonly covering an extended burial in a stone cist, but jar coffins also occur.

Although there are more "southern" dolmens in the south and "northern" dolmens in the north, the distribution of the two types of dolmens overlaps considerably. For example, there are large numbers of southern style dolmens in

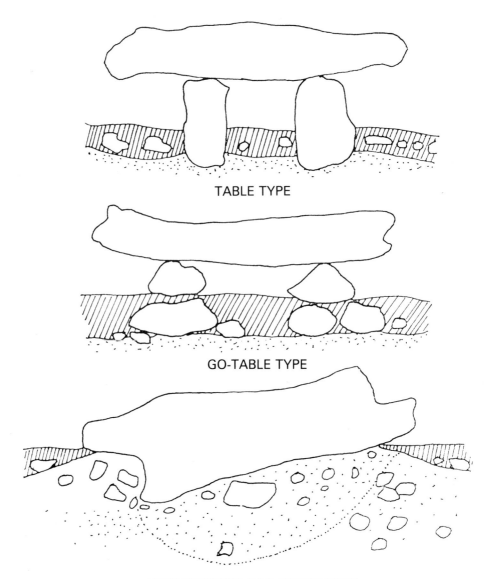

5.27 Three types of dolmens. After Hwang Y.H. 1981.

the vicinity of the Taedong river. The northern style is found scattered in the south, where the two types may be found together, apparently associated, for instance, at Naedongni where three dolmens of the southern type and one of northern type were excavated (Chi 1977a), and at Kumgangni near Yangyang on the east coast.

Southern dolmens are almost always found in groups, often in neat rows, curved or straight (Lee Y.J., Ha M.S. and Choi S.K. 1988, Lee Y.J. *et al.* 1988). Three lines of dolmens were found at Usanni, for example (Lee Y.J. 1988a). Northern dolmens may occur in isolation, but more often than not a dozen or so are found together (Torii 1926, Kim B.M. 1981a:180). Often they too are lined up along a river or stream, as are several groups of dolmens near Hwangsongni. These are particularly interesting, since animal bones were preserved in the burials – ox, deer and pig, in the manner of many stone cist graves in Liaoning. Burial No. 7 was a burial of a woman aged about 40–50, with her head to the east, wearing a bead necklace (Lee Y.J. 1984a).

In both north and south there are regions where dolmens are connected to each other by stone pavements, for example at Chonjindong and Kuksongdong in the northwest, believed to date to 2000 BC, where tubular jade beads and polished stone projectile points are the most common artifacts (Sok 1979). Those in the south are assumed to be later since they contain more bronze, although some examples at Changchonni in the southwest are remarkably similar to those in the north (Mokpo University Museum 1984). Songgungni has also produced a circular area of stones covering cists beneath (Chung *et al.* 1988).

The capstone type of dolmen has been identified in the Unggok valley of North Cholla as well as elsewhere along the southwest coast and in Cheju Island. A large capstone is placed directly on the underground cist, completely lacking propping stones. It seems to be a late form (Chon 1984).

Southern dolmens may cover jar burials as well as stone cists. The jar burials, which are quite late, may be related to similar configurations in Kyushu, Japan, assigned to the Yayoi period (Shim 1981).

Burials were usually single, although occasionally one dolmen covers two or more graves. Rarely, double burials occur, often consisting of a large and a small cist side by side. Perhaps mothers and infants were buried concurrently, or perhaps they represent a married couple, with the bones of the earlier deceased compacted into a bundle burial. The stone cists were made of local stone: granite, slate or sandstone depending on the area. Occasionally one or more dolmens lie atop a pebble layer which covers several stone cists. Mikami (1961) calls these family tombs. They tend to be late – 400 BC or so, and therefore around the end of the time period of this chapter.

Dolmens have been found on many of the small but inhabited islands off the south and west coasts (Im 1966, Kim W.Y. and Im H.J. 1968). The largest Korean island, Cheju Do, contains dolmens as well (Pearson and Im 1968, Lee C.K. 1985). Occupation of large and small islands may indicate that all available space was needed by a continuously increasing population. Perhaps the dolmens functioned as territorial markers, as suggested for the opposite side of the Eurasian continent by Renfrew (1973). Once expansion is no longer possible, it may become necessary to stake out inalienable ancestral lands for the descent group.

Dolmens are interpreted as graves of the upper class only, based on their special burial goods, and the fact that there are too few of them to account for the entire population (Nelson 1982, Choi 1984a). The largest estimate of the total number of dolmens in Korea is 100,000, which only allows for fifty or so to be erected each year in the entire peninsula over a 2,000 year period. If there were fewer dolmens, even fewer people were given such burials.

One or more egg-shaped depressions, known as "cup marks," are sometimes found on Korean dolmens. Although more than 1,000 such cup marks have been found, there is no consensus about their meaning. Hwang (1974) points out that sometimes they occur with rock carvings of daggers, geometric designs or human activities (Yi K.M. *et al.* 1985) and suggests that they may be associated with a fertility rite similar to one performed by women in Korea up to recent times. Kim B.M. (1981a) connects the cup marks with the oviparous myths of the founders of the Three Kingdoms, several of whom were said to be miraculously born from eggs.

Single standing megaliths, called menhirs, are also found in Korea, presumably dating to this same period. Some menhirs were converted to Buddhist monuments in the subsequent Samguk period, especially in the southern part of Korea. These standing stones are called *miruk*, the Matreiya of the future. The simplest conversion of a menhir to a *miruk* was the creation of rough features to make a standing human figure, and the placement of a flat stone across the top of the head representing a hat. This flat hat is common on standing outdoor Buddhas in Korea, whatever the time period of their creation, and is a unique feature of Korean Buddhist iconography, possibly dating back to pre-Buddhist times.

Occasionally groups of menhirs are arranged in a pattern, such as a circle or the constellation Ursa Major (Holt 1948). The Great Bear or Big Dipper constellation is still important in shamanistic rites, and the *Chilsong*, the seven stars, are powerful deities in the *mudang*'s pantheon. Rituals may take place beside sacred stones in Korea, indicating an animism with deep roots in the ancient past. An interesting find at Hwangsongni is a pair of standing stones, interpreted as a male and a female (Lee Y.J. 1984b) in the manner of the wooden *changsung*, or village guardians, which were found in all villages before the present century, and exist in a few locations even today (Kim T.G. 1983). These menhirs are associated with forty-six dolmens aligned along the river over a distance of more than 1 km. Another pair of menhirs is found not far away near the Pukhan river.

Stone cists

Stone cist burials were the most frequent form of interment in megalithic Korea. Actual skeletons are very rare, since the podzolic soil tends to destroy bone rapidly. For this reason little is known regarding sex ratio, age of death or other demographic variables. However, it is notable that most stone cists were long enough for extended adult burials, and the few skeletons that exist (for instance at Hwangsongni in Chungchong [Lee Y.J. 1984a, 1984b]) are extended and supine. Cists tend to be about 2 m long and 30 cm wide, but graves as small as 60 × 26 cm have been reported. They may have contained children, or secondary bundle burials (Rhee 1984). Occasionally small jar-coffins are associated with stone cists, possibly representing infant burials.

Although many stone cists have been looted, a sufficient number have been found intact to allow some generalizations. Tubular beads and *gokok* are frequently present in stone cist burials, as are polished stone daggers and burnished red pots.

The earliest stone cists are often said to be those of the northeast, in the region of the Tumen river. Stone artifacts, especially polished stone daggers, characterize the grave goods, although a bronze button was found in one stone cist in this area. These burials seem to be in continuous distribution with the stone cists of central and eastern Manchuria. Mikami (1961) noted their similarities with what is now Jilin province in China, and Lin (1985) includes stone cists as a characteristic of the Tuanjie culture of eastern Manchuria. Rhi (1976) notes different directional orientations with different styles of stone cists in Manchuria. A type he believes is early consists of a stone-lined grave made of several stone slabs, on a northeast–southwest axis. A slightly trapezoidal shape, also made of stone slabs, directs heads to the east, while in another style with thinner stone slabs heads are aligned toward the south. Decorated spoons and heads carved on sticks are found in these sites (Fig. 5.28). Further study of such differences will help to identify the boundaries of various ethnic groups.

In the southern part of Korea, many stone cists are covered with southern style dolmens. Their orientation is to the direction of the river, varying as the river curves. In the southeast, heads tend to point to the east in stone cists burials. At the site of Hapchon Chopori, the usual assortment of polished stone tools and burnished red pots is accompanied by wide bowls (Fig. 5.29). At Sincholli, burials from many time periods were encountered – stone cist tombs included burnished red vessels and stone projectile points, while pit graves contained tubular jades (Choi and An 1983). Choi M.L. (1984a) believes that stone cist burials and dolmens have different distributions and different histories. However, stone cists often have dolmens for markers, especially in the south. This is a point that requires clarification.

Cist burials were sometimes quite rich. At Songgungni in southwestern Korea, as noted above, a Liaoning dagger was found in a stone cist accompanied by bronze, stone and a necklace made of two amazonite *gokok* and seventeen tubular beads. The Undaeri site also contained a Liaoning dagger along with a stone dagger and several polished stone projectile points. The Mugyeri burial included three tubular jade beads, both bronze and stone arrowheads, a stone dagger with wide flanges, and burnished red pottery. At Namsongni an unusually long (2.8 m) stone cist included more than one hundred bronze artifacts, some so far unique (Yoon 1978). A suggestion that the unusual bronzes are shamans' paraphernalia seems likely (Kim W.Y. 1986a). Two early mirrors, ten

5.28 Spoon-shaped objects and carved faces from stone cist burials in northern Korea. After Mikami 1961.

daggers, a socketed axe, a chisel, a *gokok* and 106 tubular jade beads, and fragments of lacquer on birchbark, probably pieces of a scabbard, also accompanied the dead (National Museum of Korea 1977). In southwestern Korea, at Kubongni, a rich burial was unearthed with many bronzes including eleven daggers, two *ge*-halberds, one chisel, two socketed axes, two fine-line mirrors and one spear. A stone axe and Mumun pottery also accompanied the deceased (Kim W.Y. 1986b). Kongpyonni produced *ge*-halberds, narrow swords, fine-line mirrors and an axe (Yi K.M. 1989). Yet another example is the pit grave at Tosongni which yielded eight bronze daggers, one of the Liaoning type, three hilt-shaped ornaments, two trumpet-shaped objects which may be harness parts, two mirrors, a disk, and 103 greenstone beads (Kim W.Y. 1979a:4). Some of these burials may belong to a later stage.

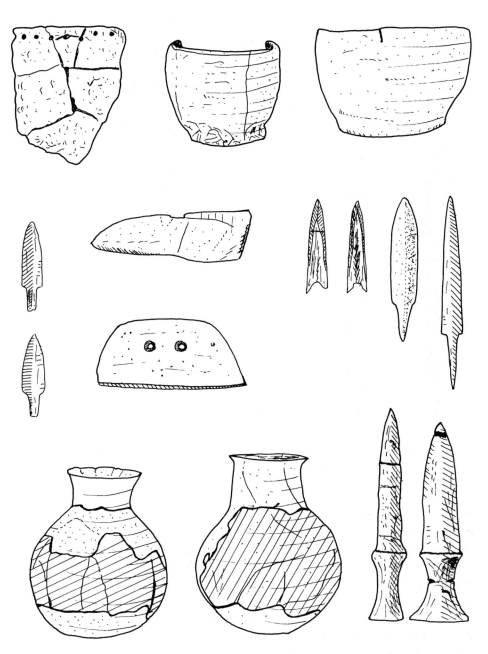

5.29 Artifacts from dolmens in Hapchon Chopori.

Rock art

Several large panels of pecked rock drawings in southeastern Korea are believed to date from the megalithic period. The panels at Pan'gudae are thought to be earlier because of the pecking technique (Hwang Y.H. 1975, 1987; Kim W.Y. 1980b). At Chonjonni, geometric patterns such as spirals, circles and lozenges decorate a large smooth rock, along with deer, reindeer and other mammals. Near Taegongni a large area about 2 × 8 m is covered with animal drawings, mostly whales and dolphins on the left, and land animals on the right, including tigers, goats, deer, dogs, cats and wild boar. Several men in a boat can be seen, and other drawings appear to be men with weapons (Mun 1973, Kim W.Y. 1977b). On the basis of the type of bow depicted, the petroglyphs are assigned to the megalithic period. A few petroglyphs have been found on dolmens, strengthening the association, for example two stone daggers and an arrowhead engraved on a dolmen at Innidong in southeastern Korea (Kim W.Y. 1985:2).

Social organization

Some richly furnished burials are the main evidence for a degree of social ranking. No special dwellings that can be ascribed to high-ranking persons have been identified, although differences in house sizes and contents are noted. Monumental civic-ceremonial architecture is lacking. The burials, however, give ample evidence for high-status individuals. Hwang (1965) proposed a relationship between the size of the dolmen capstone and the power of the chief. Burials of children with presumed indicators of rank, such as *gokok*, also imply hereditary status. The occasional richly furnished graves contrast with other burials accompanied by pottery only, although Choi Mong-lyong (1984b) suggests there were only two classes, of which the nobility received burial and the others were disposed of by excarnation. Polished stone knives are often found in stone cist burials, suggesting ritual meaning.

Jade and other precious stone ornaments are relatively rare, but when they are found they usually comprise beads for necklaces, frequently accompanied by bronze artifacts. For example at Taesongni, 110 bluestone beads were found in a stone cist along with a geometric twin-knobbed mirror and four bronze disks (Kim W.Y. 1977a) and at Yonghungni a bronze sword and knife were found with a semi-circular jade bead (Han B.S. 1968). The sources of these stones may be outside Korea, although a recent study (Choi Un-ju, cited in Kim W.Y. 1987a:20) suggests that Korean nephrite mines existed in the Chunchon area. Another relatively rare item often found in a burial context which might be a status marker is the red burnished pottery. Occasionally sherds from these small well-made jars are found in houses, but they occur most often in burial contexts.

Little is known of gender relationships. In the rare cases where human bones remain, the sexes are approximately equally represented and equally treated. In sites along the North Han river, males are said to be accompanied by weapons and females by jewelry (Lee Y.J. 1984a), but as noted above, weapons and jewelry co-occur more often than not. Apparently the people of highest rank owned bronze weapons – daggers, spears and arrows – and wore jade necklaces, regardless of sex. Horse trappings and chariot fittings in burials might imply an aristocracy, but they are not found in megalithic period burials.

Craft specialization is implied by the local bronze metallurgy. Both the presence of casting molds and the singularity of the Korean bronze alloy indicate a bronze weapon and tool industry in Korea. Some polished stone tools and the ground beads suggest craft specialists as well. Most of the pottery is simple enough to be locally made, but analysis suggests regional manufacture (Choe 1982). The burnished red ware in particular required time and skill to construct and polish.

Rhee (1984) states that some megalithic period villages are much larger than others, and might even be considered towns, although the larger villages bear no obvious indications of being central places. Specialized economic, administrative or religious activities, if they existed, have left few traces. Whether this reflects a lack of hierarchy in settlements or merely accidents of archaeological investigation remains to be seen. One hint of possible greater importance of the larger villages, however, is that they seem to be associated with larger groups of dolmens. If dolmens imply a ruling class, the elite were more numerous in the larger villages (or, of course, the villages lasted longer). This suggests that there were extra functions for the emerging elite to perform in these large villages. The considerable variation in dolmen capstone size also suggests ranking among those buried. The capstone size may be dependent upon the amount of manpower which could be assembled to move the required boulders (Choi M.L. 1984b). Rhee (1984) suggests the importance of one valley as a *sodo*, or sacred place.

Myth, legend and history

The Tangun legend is sometimes regarded as history in Korea. The origin of the Korean calendric date (2333 BC) is said to be the same of Tangun, perhaps not coincidentally the same time as the legendary Chinese Emperor Yao (Hwang 1967). The story belongs to the tradition of culture heroes, including a miraculous birth. A common version of the story begins with a female bear and a tigress who lived together in a cave, both aspiring to become human. Hwan-in, the chief god, gave them mugwort and garlic to eat, and instructed them to stay in the dark and not see the sun for a hundred days. The tigress became restless and failed at the task, but the she-bear persevered and became human, married the son of Hwan-in, and bore a son named Tangun Wanggom. Perhaps the she-bear was the tale's original hero. Tangun, the originator of millet cultivation (a gift from his deity father), set up a kingdom in Pyongyang and named the country

Choson. He lived for 1,000 years and became a spirit in Chonji, Heavenly Lake, in the crater of Paektusan. Although this legend does not appear in written form until the eleventh century AD, it probably reaches back into antiquity. There are several interesting facets of the Tangun story. First, it is clearly a legend of forest-dwelling peoples, not steppe nomads; thus, it seems to be indigenous to Korea (although it has been used to tie Korea's ancient religion with that of the steppes [Allen 1990]). The tiger and the bear are still hunted in the forests of Korea, and tigers have been a menace even into this century (Bishop 1905, Kim S.J. 1978). Second, it seems to reflect distantly the circumpolar bear cult.

Another legend, this one on the verge of history, is that of Kija (Chitzu), a nephew of the last king of the Chinese Shang dynasty. The traditional date for the end of the Shang is 1122 BC, and although the precise date is disputed by scholars, a round figure of 1100 BC will suffice for the less precise comparisons with archaeological sites. According to the tradition, Kija departed with a retinue of 5,000 people and went in exile to Korea, where he founded a state called Choson. Nothing further is recorded about Kija, except to note that the Koguryo kingdom revered him as an ancestor. No bronze ritual vessels, which a Shang prince could be expected to take with him in order to attend properly to his ancestors, have ever been found in Korea.

Chinese references to the Dong-I, Eastern Barbarians, have been taken as applying to Korea. According to Chinese sources, in prehistoric times Shandong was the homeland of some Dong-I. Battles between the Shang and the Dong-I of Shandong are mentioned in oracle bone inscriptions. Shandong sites which could be associated with the Dong-I include cemeteries which have megalithic constructions in the center; these megaliths do not closely resemble Korean dolmens, as they are smaller and without capstones, but Mikami (1961) reported some northern-style dolmens in Shandong. The term Dong-I has been interpreted as applying to a wide area, including the inhabitants of Korea, the area around Bohai, and southern Manchuria (Sohn, Kim and Hong 1970, An 1974, Kim J.B. 1975b). With the Korean population included as Dong-I, the use of the direction east to describe the location of this group of non-Chinese peoples becomes more understandable. This interpretation meets with some archaeological problems, however. The fact that tripods are found profusely in Shandong and Liaodong, but never in Korea, suggests a profound and important difference between these two areas – differences in ritual or cuisine, or both. Of course the Chinese writers may have lumped several groups together as Eastern Barbarians, but the point is that there is a noticeable break in probably symbolic artifacts between the Korean peninsula and Liaodong. Other traits, however, tie the two regions together.

Migration, diffusion or local development?

Any discussion of the ethnicity of the megalithic people must take into account a number of variables. If Ye-Maek peoples came galloping in with Liaoning daggers, planted rice, and buried their dead in stone cists under dolmens, as is often stated, then it should be easy to trace their beginnings. The data suggest a less straightforward sequence of events.

The Kija legend can be disposed of without too much difficulty. Obviously, it requires a site or area in Korea that is distinctively Shang Chinese. If a Chinese nobleman went to Korea with a retinue of thousands, one would expect to find clear evidence of the Shang ruling class, including such distinctive traits as bronze ceremonial vessels, writing and oracle bones. No trace of bronze vessels or writing exists at any Korean site in this period, although a few oracle bones without writing have turned up in the north. To accept the Kija story as applying to Korea, it must be assumed that bronze vessels were created by specialists who did not accompany the group into exile, or that the vessels represented royal perquisites to which Kija was not entitled. Either, of course, is possible. Chang (1977:351) makes this point with regard to bronze as restricted to the aristocracy in China from 1750 to 500 BC.

Another possibility is that Kija may indeed have joined the "Korean" ancestors, but the region they lived in is not part of present-day Korea. In western Liaoning, evidence of Shang lineages has been found with inscriptions on bronze vessels (Chang 1980b:310).

The source of Korean rice

Since rice itself is not native to Korea, it is reasonable to suppose that seeds were brought to Korea from China. Actual finds of rice grains (*Oryza sativa*) have been dated to about 1200 BC at Hunamni (Kim W.Y. 1982a:515). Rice grains have also been found at Songgungni on the Kum river (National Museum of Korea 1979) and at Namgyong near Pyongyang in the north. The grains are the *Japonica* variety, which is adapted to northern climates, with shorter growing seasons. Rice was cultivated in southern China at a much earlier date, at least by 5500 BC (Li 1983). New finds along the Changjiang river have a series of dates of 8500–7000 BP (Yan 1990). In northern China, where millet was the major crop, rice was not grown much before the Shang dynasty (Chang 1986).

Rice is seen as arriving in Korea by way of Manchuria on the evidence of semi-lunar reaping knives. Reaping knives of rectangular shape with end notches are the common type found in Yangshao sites in northern China, while semi-lunar reaping knives are characteristic of the Longshan culture in the Shandong peninsula. This has been interpreted to suggest that millet knives are rectangular, while semi-lunar knives were used for gathering rice. This argument is complicated by the fact that in Manchuria the shape of the semi-lunar knives becomes inverted, with the cutting edge on the straight side rather than the convex side (An 1955). Some Korean semi-lunar knives share this trait with Manchuria, although the distributions are complex (Choe 1982). On the Liaodong peninsula, sites with semi-lunar knives, polished arrowheads and other artifacts identical to those of Korean megalithic sites have been excavated (Chon 1989a); for example, Shuang-touce which is dated to about 2000 BC (Xu 1989a). Sites with similar reaping knives are found in north Asia from the Soviet Maritime region to the middle Sungari valley.

Spoked maceheads, digging stick weights and stepped adzes are other stone tools which are found both in Korea and in Longshan sites in northern China. Perhaps the weights and adzes are related to cultivation, and not to any one ethnic group.

Identifiable Longshan pottery does not appear in Korea. Polished black vessels do occur, although rarely, associated with late Mumun or early Wonsamguk sites. They are similar to Longshan in color, but do not attain the eggshell thinness typical of the fine black Longshan ware, and if the present dating (not earlier than 500 BC) is correct, they are far too late to be considered Longshanoid.

Pottery from many sites in Manchuria, particularly Liaoning and Heilong-jiang, is similar to Mumun pottery. Plain brown or buff pots with flat bases and simple shapes are found nearly everywhere. If the vessels with basal perforations are indeed rice steamers, they constitute further distant echoes of China, and not connections with steppe nomads. Also common in Manchuria, however, are tripods of the *ding* and *li* types, which, as already noted, do not occur in Korea until much later. The total lack of tripods in Korea, although they are found nearby in Liaoning and the Shandong peninsula, implies different cuisines in these areas, or perhaps different rituals. The variations in Mumun pottery suggest several distinct cultural groups, perhaps each forged from diverse elements.

Polished stone artifacts from Manchurian sites are also much like those of Mumun sites: multifaceted arrowheads, crescent reaping knives, pottery net sinkers, and even polished stone knives. The Tuanjie culture, described by Lin (1985), includes sites in northeastern Korea around the Tumen river, as well as in the Soviet Maritime region. *Dou* vessels are prevalent, sometimes raised on extravagantly high pedestals, but tripod vessels are lacking.

Stone cist graves in the north

Korea's stone cist burials are probably a variant of the widespread stone slab burials of northeast Asia (Tong 1982, Lee H.K. 1988). Construction of the burial chambers appears to be similar throughout, with long narrow chambers made of thin slabs of local stone, or piles of stone to create the walls. There are regional differences, however, such as the occasional projection of the slabs above the ground surface in Siberia, and the practice of covering of the stone cists with dolmens in Korea.

Watson (1971) divided the slab grave cultures into three regions, of which the western region corresponds to the distribution of the Upper Xiajiadian culture. The middle group with many sites on the Songhua river near Jilin is now known as Xituanshan, and the eastern group is called the Tuanjie culture, as noted above.

Nineteen cist tombs were excavated at the type site of Xituanshan (Dong 1964). Both flexed and extended inhumations occurred. Grave goods often included pig mandibles, as well as pendants of pigs' teeth. White tubular beads appear to be ceramic, not stone, although stone beads also occur. The semi-lunar stone knife is common, along with leaf-shaped projectile points. The brown sand-tempered pottery includes a *guan* jar with lug handles and handled jars with recurved sides. Other sites also have tripods with both baggy and solid legs, and *dou* vessels on stands (Liu 1982). The Xituanshan culture is dated from the beginning of Western Zhou to the beginning of the Han dynasty (Dong 1983). A simple farming economy seems to be indicated.

In northeastern Korea, and on the north side of the Tumen river as well, the Tuanjie culture has many features in common with Xituanshan, not the least of which is the cist graves. *Dou* vessels are common, and sometimes have very high pedestals. No tripods appear but *guan* jars are common. Small projectile points are found, both chipped from obsidian, or made from slate and polished. Spindle whorls (Fig. 5.30) and semi-lunar knives were also present (Lin 1985).

Megaliths in Asia

Although Korea is the site of the highest density of dolmens, several attempts have been made to relate them to similar constructions in Manchuria, as well as less obviously related megaliths in South and Southeast Asia (Kim B.M. 1981a, 1981c, Chi 1982). The most parsimonious explanation of the dolmen distribution is that the dolmens arose in Korea. The number of dolmens in Korea suggests both indigenous origin and local development. Their appearance could have been in response to the need of a ruling elite to mark their territory by means of their burial places, as occurred in the British Isles (Renfrew 1973).

Bronze types in Siberia and China

Similarities between Korean bronze weapons, tools and ornaments and those of northeast China are far more numerous than similarities between Korea and the Yellow river region. On the other hand, a few bronze weapon shapes seem to derive directly from China. These include *ge*-halberds, socketed spearheads and socketed axes, all forms that do not appear in China before the Zhou dynasty,

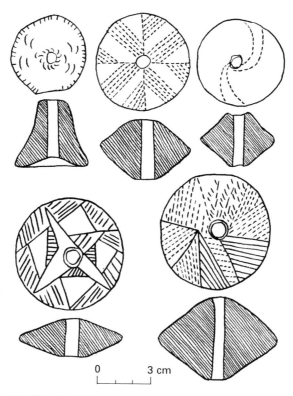

5.30 Spindle whorls from Sopohang.

and appear to be even later in Korea. Bells, mirrors and knives are found in one Shang burial, that of Fu Hao (Lin 1986), but that anomaly may be explained by linking Fu Hao herself to the north. Bronze vessels, most characteristic of the Shang, are not found in Korea at all before the Three Kingdoms period, as has been noted above.

Early cultural complexity in Liaoning province suggests the need for a re-appraisal of the development of complex society in northern China. The Hong-shan culture of 3500–2000 BC included a walled town, a temple and high-status burials. This was followed by the Lower Xiajiadian culture, which has many apparently intrusive traits (Chang 1986:374), echoing in this distant region the questions of migration or diffusion that have been posed for the Korean peninsula.

The ill-defined Lower Xiajiadian culture is found as far east as the Bay of Bohai, with C14 dates ranging from the mid-third to the mid-second millennium BC. Copper artifacts from this region are "among the earliest metal objects in Chinese archaeology" (Chang 1980b:294). Associated stone artifacts resemble those of Mumun, and the pottery is similar except that in Liaoning tripods are included, linking the area more to mainland China than to Korea.

Lee K.S. (1979) has compared the Korean bronze age to two groups of sites in Manchuria, the Upper Xiajiadian culture and sites belonging to the "Liaoning" culture. Several kinds of artifacts in the two areas have different styles, as he points out. Sword handles, sword blades and knives were made in different shapes, and sites with types of one set rarely have any examples of the other. The most interesting finding, however, is that the Liaoning assemblages include trappings for riding horses, while the Upper Xiajiadian culture features decorations for carriages and traction horses. The distribution of these different styles is seen to be distinct, overlapping only at the site of Nanshangen. Lee believes that considerable influences from China can be seen in Upper Xiajiadian, but little Chinese impact occurred in the Liaoning sites.

Questions of the relationship of Dongbei bronzes to Shang China and the Karasuk are still being debated in China (Wu 1985) and by Sinologists outside China. Barnard (1983) suggests that metallurgy began in China around 2500–2000 BC, and Meacham (1983:166) argues for the existence of bronze technology in the peripheral areas, including "parts of Korea," as early as 2000–1500 BC.

The Northern Complex is the name Lin (1986) gives to the bronzes of the Upper Xiajiadian culture. At the site of Nanshangen, the Liaoning dagger first appears, at about 700 BC (Jin 1983). Sites farther east containing Liaoning daggers have distinct cultural differences, however (Lee K.S. 1979). Jin (1983, 1987) argues that these are Donghu people, and that the Xituanshan culture represents the Ye-Maek. Kim W.Y. (1986a) suggests that the Donghu and Ye-Maek are one and the same, while Lin (personal communication) suggests that the Liaoning dagger makers are Dong-I, not Donghu. Physical anthropological evidence links the Tungusic population ("Northern Mongoloids") to the Xituanshan culture. However, "in the province of Jilin and Liaoning, as well as in neighboring Korea, skulls dating to the late second and first millennium B.C. have been found in graves ... [which] could belong to ancestors of the Altaians and Paleosiberians" (Jettmar 1983:221).

Even with the plethora of new discoveries in China, Kim Y.O. (1981) suggests that the designs on Korean bronze artifacts, with fine-line geometric designs and deer and bird images, are a link to the Amur region. Relationships between Korea and its northern neighbors are far from solved.

Summary

The realization that Mumun pottery, the "index fossil" of the megalithic period, had a long span of manufacture and use, has led to various schemes for separating the Mumun period into sequential stages. Choi M.C. (1982) considers that the bronze age in Korea lasted from 1300 to 200 BC, but this does not include the earlier Mumun before bronze. North Koreans tend toward earlier dates than South Koreans, suggesting 2000 BC as a starting point not only for Mumun but also for bronze (Kim Y.G. and So G.T. 1972). North Korean bronze is thus seen as contemporary with early bronze in China. While there is no *a priori* reason to grant precedence to China, there is insufficient evidence for such an early date in Korea. However, bronze manufacture did occur in Manchuria in the Lower Xiajiadian culture, making the transition to Korea shorter than was previously thought.

Radiocarbon dates indicate that some sites with Mumun pottery are indeed as early as 2000 BC. These sites do not contain bronze, or any indication that bronze was known or used. A lack of dates from the north hampers any assessment of the North Korean assertions. However, the earliest sites with Mumun ceramics also contain semi-lunar reaping knives, making it not unreasonable to believe they represent the beginnings of rice cultivation in Korea, even though C14 dates do not confirm rice before 1500 BC or so. Rice is not an indigenous plant in Korea; it follows that the rice itself came from elsewhere, presumably China. Millet cultivation, and probably other plant domestication, already had a long history in Korea, making it unnecessary to postulate a migration of people on the basis of rice agriculture and its associated tools. On the other hand, the intrusive pottery tradition itself may indicate the arrival of a new group (or groups) of people. There is no conclusive evidence of craft specialization, ranking or central places at the beginning of this stage. The major variations are in pottery styles, stone tool types, and the cultivation of rice, requiring some water control in the form of small-scale terracing but no large-scale cooperation in the building of dams.

Choi M.L. (1981) believes that stone cists and megaliths should be conceptually separated. Burial in stone cists may be earlier in the northeast, in the Tumen river region, and may indicate a movement of peoples from the Xituanshan or Xinkailiu cultures in Manchuria, where stone cists are widespread. Given the varieties of stone cists and the different orientations of burials, it seems likely that small groups from the north and northwest gradually moved into the Korean peninsula to settle. The apparent addition of the new elements of megalithic monuments, elaboration of burial traditions, and the use of bronze may or may not be simultaneous. The present evidence, however, suggests that they are.

Dolmens of the northern style are found in Shandong and Manchuria as well as Korea (Torii 1926, 1930). This suggests to some scholars a migration (or diffusion) pattern from the northwest. As noted above, the center of dolmens appears to be in Korea, however, possibly representing the origin of the form. Small amounts of bronze have been found associated with both stone cists and dolmens in these early contexts.

The formation of ranked society in Korea has been attributed to horse-riding warriors with better weapons and more mobility becoming the overlords of an indigenous agricultural population (Choi M.L. 1984a). Bronze-using groups in Manchuria (Upper and Lower Xiajiadian for example) appear to be associated with horses, although no direct evidence for horses at this date has appeared in Korea.

Choe C.P. (1982) has argued for continuity from Chulmun to Mumun styles, suggesting evolution in place. While continuity of population is likely, local evolution cannot account for either rice agriculture or bronze technology, and migration or diffusion must be invoked to explain their appearance. Both stone cists and dolmens probably reflect ranked societies (Choi M.L. 1981), and both are found outside the Korean peninsula. Some evidence of long-distance trade appears at this stage, in the form of beads made of nephrite and other stone, and craft specialization is suggested by molds to make bronze items, as well as possible pottery-making villages (Choi M.L. 1980).

The southern style dolmens are associated with an advanced bronze culture, and the amount and quality of grave goods became markedly unequal. In the south, this bronze culture may be contemporaneous with the beginning of iron manufacture in the north, as North Korean archaeologists claim. However, examples of southern style dolmens and large cemeteries occur as far north as Hwanghae and South Pyonghae provinces, perhaps earlier than the first appearance of iron. These large groups of dolmens suggest expanded populations.

Multiple influences impinged on megalithic Korea. A major new population influx may have come from the north, but precisely from where and with what stop-overs and for how long are the wrong questions. There is no evidence that a single ethnic group swept into Korea with bronze/rice technology. It seems much more consonant with the evidence at hand to postulate that over the course of 2,000 years various groups entered the peninsula and found a niche in the mosaic of a developing complex society.

Postscript: Dates for rice recently reported from western Korea are 2400 and 2100 BC (Choe C.P. 1991: 37).

CHAPTER 6

IRON, TRADE AND EXPLOITATION
400 BC TO AD 300

Iron technology, advanced ceramic technology and an above-ground house style appeared in the Korean peninsula by 400 BC, or perhaps earlier, heralding a new stage of social and political complexity. These characteristics are not independent, for stoneware and iron production depend on methods for making hotter fires, and the ground-level house with *ondol* floor (subfloor heating) required iron tools to make planks for floors. These new technologies reflect increasing interaction with the mainland, if not actual migration of both Han Chinese and groups of "barbarians" from the northern frontier of China into Korea.

Some Koreanists may find the beginning date of this chapter too early, arguing that an "iron age" must include iron production, not just iron use (e.g. Taylor 1989). Others may judge it too late, pointing to possible earlier iron in the north. But this is not a chapter on an iron age as such; rather, it considers iron as only one factor in the increasing inclusion of polities on the Korean peninsula within China's orbit. I have avoided the concept of an iron age because as it is used in Korea it is slippery at best. For example, the last three centuries BC, when iron was not only present throughout the peninsula but was mined and worked as well, is known as Bronze Age II in an influential periodization of prehistoric Korea (Kim W.Y. 1986a). The first three centuries AD are considered iron age according to this scheme, but most often are called *Wonsamguk* (Proto-Three Kingdoms). Although this period may not be usefully conceptualized as an iron age (implying the dominance of iron technology), iron is an important element in the changes in the peninsula's political economy of this time, and a causative factor in some of the changes.

During this time the Korean peninsula came more and more to the attention of an increasingly unified China, as the Warring States period gave way to the Qin and Han dynasties. The concentration and centralization of power in China had important repercussions in Korea. In particular, the extension of Chinese trade and warfare impinged upon the Korean peninsula both directly and indirectly. In the Warring States period (the final division of the Zhou dynasty), Chinese influence spread in ever wider circles. Under the Chin unification of China and the ensuing Han expansion, locating and utilizing important raw materials, as well as pacification of the frontier, were major motivations for the interest of the Chinese states in their northeastern neighbors. Chinese armies besieged forts and cities on Korean soil, ostensibly because they were blocking trade between China and the southern part of the peninsula. Eventually China conquered the state of Wiman Choson and established commanderies, giving the Han dynasty a foothold in the peninsula which would last more than 400 years. The Korean peninsula cannot be considered as a single "culture" in spite of increasing incorporation into the Chinese Interaction Sphere. Regional differences were exacerbated by the Chinese effect, and the distance of various regions, coupled with difficulty of access, allowed regions to develop quite distinctive patterns. Sites mentioned in the text are located on Fig. 6.1.

Documentary sources

Beginning in the first century BC, Chinese documents provide important information about Korea. However, these documents are neither chronicles nor meticulous ethnographies. They offer tantalizing snippets, allowing latitude for interpretation, as can be seen in the varying discussions of this period by Chinese and Korean historians in the present.

Chinese historians were interested in the curious peoples who lived beyond their borders, and maintained a long tradition of describing the appearance and behavior of the barbarians in distant lands. Lively accounts of groups in the Korean peninsula, no doubt much abridged over the centuries, are full of ethnographic detail. However, the Chinese documents should be treated with caution for many reasons. Errors in transcription or translation have probably crept in; embroidering on facts by the Chinese for their own purposes (to point a moral, for example) may have occurred; and the original observers of the "barbarians" might have misunderstood what they saw.

The state of Choson in northern Korea was mentioned in the early Chinese documents *Shan Hai Ching* and *Changuo Tso* (Henderson 1959:148), but the sketchiness of these reports demonstrates the slight importance accorded to Choson by Chinese historians. It is not even universally agreed that the Choson of the Chinese histories was in the Korean peninsula (Yoon N.H. 1986). The sections from the *Wei Ji* and the *Hou Han Shu* pertaining to Korea, recounted below, are nevertheless sources of great interest. Not until they clashed directly in battle with Korean forces did the Chinese preserve records of specific events in Korea in their histories (Gardiner 1969a). The amount of credibility given these histories and geographies varies from one author to another. Many Korean historians (for example, Li Ki-baek [1984], Sohn, Kim and Hong [1970], Choi H.C. [1971]) tend to rely on the documents literally, while Gardiner (1969a) is skeptical on many points. Without taking a position on the accuracy of every word, the Chinese histories can be used as a framework in which to consider the archaeological evidence. Gardiner (1969a) discusses these sources in some detail, as do Kayamoto (1962), Wheatley and See (1978) and Hong (1988). Here we will synthesize the histories and then discuss the relevant archaeological finds by

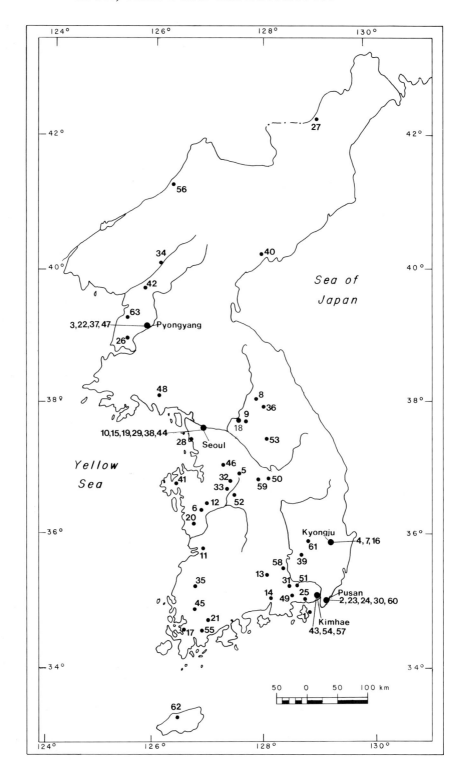

region. A word of caution about names of the Chinese sources: the first thirty chapters of the *San Guo Ji* are called the *Wei Ji* or the *Wei Shuy* (e.g. Gardiner 1969a). A much later document is also called *Wei Shu*. I have used the term *Wei Ji* throughout to refer to the earlier document.

The state of Wiman Choson

According to the *Wei Ji*, groups of ethnic Chinese were already living in Korea when Wiman, a general from a nearby Chinese state, "adopt[ed] the mallet-shaped hairdo and dress of the eastern barbarians" (Watson 1961:258), and fled into the peninsula with about a thousand followers. In Korea, Wiman created his own state in 198 BC, establishing his capital at present-day Pyongyang. In doing so he drove out the local leader, Kichun, purportedly a descendant of Kija, mentioned in the preceding chapter. Kichun fled in boats with his family and set up a new kingdom in the south, taking the family name of Han.

The polity of Wiman Choson lasted for three generations, until in 109 BC the Han Chinese sent forces by both land and sea intending to annihilate it. This attack must be seen in the context of Han expansionism, in addition to the search for sources of iron and salt which became government monopolies (Gale 1931). After a year of struggle described in some detail (Watson 1961), the capital fortress capitulated, conquered more by trickery than by force. Chinese commanderies were established to rule the northern half of the peninsula.

The area now claimed by China was vast, covering the northern half of the Korean peninsula and parts of Manchuria. It was so large that four Chinese commanderies (called in Korean Nangnang [Lelang], Imdun, Hyondo and Chinbon), each with its own central administration, were required to govern it. The time of the Chinese colonies is generally referred to as the Lelang period after the largest and longest-lasting of the Chinese commanderies. The location of the exact boundaries of the commanderies is a matter of scholarly debate. The

---

6.1 Approximate locations of sites in Chapter 6.
1 Achisom, 2 Cho Do, 3 Chongbaengni, 4 Choyangdong, 5 Hachon, 6 Hapsongni, 7 Hwangnamdong, 8 Jung Do, 9 Kapyongni, 10 Karak-dong, 11 Kimje, 12 Kobu, 13 Kongpungni, 14 Kosong, 15 Kuidong, 16 Kujongdong, 17 Kungongni, 18 Majangni, 19 Mongchon, 20 Myong-jiri, 21 Naksuri, 22 Namsuri, 23 Nangmingdong, 24 Nopodong, 25 Nuk Do, 26 Oksongni, 27 Pomuigusok, 28 Pungchongni, 29 Pungnamni, 30 Puwondong, 31 Samdongdong, 32 Samnyongni, 33 Sansuri, 34 Sejungni, 35 Sinchangni, 36 Sinmaeri, 37 Sogamni, 38 Sokchondong, 39 Songsan, 40 Sorari, 41 Sosan, 42 Suksangni, 43 Sugari, 44 Susongni, 45 Taegongni, 46 Taesimni, 47 Taesongni, 48 Tang Tosong, 49 Tahori, 50 Tohwari, 51 Toiraeri, 52 Tokchong, 53 Tunnaeri, 54 Ungchon, 55 Wauri, 56 Wutuoling, 57 Yangsan, 58 Yangdongni, 59 Yangpyongni, 60 Yeanni, 61 Yongchon, 62 Yongdamdong, 63 Yonggangni.

commanderies of Chinbon and Imdun collapsed in 82 BC, leaving the main Chinese presence at Lelang.

The Chinese commanderies did not extend to the southern half of the peninsula, stretching perhaps as far south as the Han river at the greatest extent, but they did reach the northeast coast. It is important to note here that the state of Wiman Choson must have covered (or at least extracted tribute from) this same extensive territory for the Chinese to consider that they had conquered it by taking the citadel at Pyongyang. The *Wei Ji* relates that when Ugo, Wiman's grandson, was put to death, "his territory was divided into four prefectures" (Ikeuchi 1929:88). Wiman and his descendants would have needed a bureaucracy to govern this region.

The *Han Shu* records a population of 406,748 in the Lelang colony, while the *Hou Han Shu* lists 257,050 (Kayamoto 1962:104). It is impossible to know whether there was real depopulation due to dissatisfaction with Chinese rule, or whether the smaller population figure only reflects reduced territory under Chinese control (Sun and de Francis 1966), but this apparent population decline may illustrate the disarray of the later Lelang colony and allow an inference of better government by Wiman. In either case, one may infer that Wiman's government was at least as effective as that of the Han commanderies.

The Lelang commandery

The inhabitants of northern Korea proved difficult for the Han dynasty to govern. By 75 BC, a generation after the conquest, only the Lelang commandery, centered at Wiman's old capital near present-day Pyongyang, remained in Chinese control. This area presumably had the largest number of expatriate Chinese, and perhaps was more amenable to the Chinese administration. It was accessible from China by boat as well. Although there are some scholars who doubt the reality of Lelang at all (Pearson 1978, Yoon N.H. 1986, 1987), it seems wiser to adhere to the Chinese historic documents as long as the archaeological evidence is interpretable both ways. In spite of periods of rebellion and turmoil, the Chinese maintained their presence in northwestern Korea for about 400 years – approximately the length of the Roman occupation of Britain, but with fewer identifiable archaeological remains, largely because no counterpart to the Roman villa exists among the Han remains. Wood, brick and stone tombs under earthen mounds are the most lasting remnant of this Chinese outpost.

Incidents illustrating the relationships between Lelang and the southern Korean groups, known collectively as the Three Han (Mahan, Pyonhan and Chinhan), are recorded in various documents. For example, in the early part of the first century AD, a southern Korean polity raided Lelang (presumably by boat) and carried off 1,500 Chinese as captives (Gardiner 1969a:21). Large ships were then dispatched from Lelang to Chinhan. A thousand Chinese were rescued, a third of the captives having died in the meantime. Reparations consisted of sending 15,000 people to Lelang from Chinhan, and 15,000 lengths of cloth from Pyonhan, apparently considered to be somewhat less guilty. Even allowing for considerable hyperbole, it seems inappropriate to refer to people capable of this level of organization as "wild tribes" (Ikeuchi 1930), and the lengths of cloth demanded as payment suggest an organized textile industry. Corroborating evidence comes from the *Samguk Yusa*, in which a tale of weaving competitions between villages is told, relating to the first century AD (Ilyon 1972).

After a number of decades of waning power and shrinking territory, resurgence on the continent created a new commandery called Taifang, with its headquarters north of Seoul (Gardiner 1969a:24). The rulers of this commandery were the Kungsun family from Liaodong, who had acquired control through warfare and political maneuvers. During this time, leaders from the Han tribes were given nominal titles, and leaders of the first and second degree were issued hats establishing their status. An "uprising" of Chinhan occurred when the Taifang prefecture attempted to appropriate about half of their territory, which they were unwilling to cede. The Taifang commandery lasted only until AD 313, when Koguryo attacked from the north and the Chinese formally withdrew all pretense to colonies in Korea.

Koguryo and Puyo: barbarians in the north

The founding myths of Koguryo and Puyo are so similar that the Chinese assumed they represented essentially the same cultural group. The Puyo homeland was probably along the Songhua river in the north Manchurian plain, where, the documents tell us, the five cereals were grown, pigs and oxen were kept, and famous horses were raised. Red jade, sables, marmots and large pearls were among the trade or tribute items. Cities were surrounded by wooden palisades instead of earthen walls, and buildings included palaces, granaries and prisons (Parker 1890).

The chiefs (the Chinese characters mean "big man") were named after the five domestic animals, and each village also bore such a name. A supreme king received special burial treatment, being buried in a jade coffin which was prepared well before his death. (This is reminiscent of the jade burial suits found in China, but no jade *coffin* burials have so far been unearthed.) Other dead were buried in simple pits without an inner coffin. Those guilty of crimes for which capital punishment was prescribed were not buried at all, but their bodies were exposed on a hill, suggesting beliefs about afterlife associated with a proper burial.

The king of Puyo paid his respects to the Chinese emperor at times, but occasionally led several thousand warriors to plunder Lelang instead. Paying tribute to the emperor usually meant receiving a great many gifts, a deliberate policy which the Chinese pursued in an effort to eliminate barbarian raiding. In the year AD 120, for instance, we read of Puyo receiving a seal, sash, gold and brightly colored cloth (*Wei Ji*).

The five tribes of Koguryo, before they coalesced into a state, inhabited the high mountainous region near the upper Yalu river, and according to the *Wei Ji* did not practice agriculture. However, archaeological discoveries show that farming was known in the valleys of the Hun river and its tributaries (Rhee 1989).

Transgressors were punished by their own clan, suggesting a lack of state-level power. They practiced matrilocal marriage, but after the first child was grown the father could return to his own village and build a house. Koguryo, like Puyo, alternated tribute and raiding in their relationship to China.

Ye-Maek and Ok-cho, barbarians in the east

The documents describe a group called Ye-Maek living north of Chinhan, in a narrow strip along the east coast. They were said to have laws and customs similar to those of Koguryo, and to speak the same language. Tribal areas were marked off according to natural boundaries such as mountains and streams, which were considered sacred. The people were agricultural, raising hemp and silkworms. Horses and oxen were also part of their economy. They were known as good foot soldiers, and had special spears 30 feet long which took several men to hold. (How this could be efficient for warfare is hard to imagine!) They were also famous for the production of superior bows. They worshipped the tiger, and feasted enthusiastically. The region was noted for spotted leopards, small horses and particularly tasty fish (Parker 1890).

The Ok-cho were located east of the Kaema plateau, and north of the Ye-Maek, bordering the ocean. They cultivated the "five cereals," including rice. In customs and language they too resembled Koguryo. Each clan owned a long wooden hall, in which the dead were buried with carved memorial tablets for each deceased family member. When subject to Lelang or Koguryo, taxes were paid in sables, cloth, fish, salt and seafood. Seven cities and military posts were to be found in this region east of Lelang (Parker 1890).

The un-Sinicized south

The name Chin'guk appears in the *Wei Ji* as a designation for the southern part of the peninsula not included in Wiman Choson. Some scholars (e.g. Kim J.B. 1976) have suggested that Chin'guk was the state formed by Kichun, but the governing apparatus to hold it together was lacking, so the state could not maintain its cohesion. Thus Chin'guk degenerated into the three Han: Pyonhan, Mahan and Chinhan. These southern groups are mentioned in other documents, especially the *Hou Han Shu*. If Chin'guk did exist as a state, we have no details of its structure, nor is there indisputable archaeological evidence for its existence.

Some bronze sites near Iksan are believed to be related to the reign of King Chun, however (Kim J.B. 1976).

The most extensive accounts of the Sam Han groups in southern Korea are in the *Wei Ji* and the *Hou Han Shu*. It is perhaps useful to point out here that the Han of the Sam Han is written with a different character from that of the Chinese Han dynasty, and there is no connection between these names.

The Mahan group was the largest of the three Han, consisting of fifty-four "states." It is the most extensively described in the Chinese histories, and perhaps was the best observed, being the closest of the Sam Han to China. According to the documents, the Mahan people wove cloth, practiced agriculture and raised silkworms. Some of them decorated themselves with tattoos. Unlike the other Hans, they were said to have walled cities. Their clay houses were dome-shaped, entered through a hole in the roof. Their way of life included gender equality, but ranking existed in the political arena. A custom is described which distantly echoes a feature of the American Indian Sundance: "the young men ... would take a rope and run it through the skin of their back, and trail a huge log by it" (Parker 1890:208). Two annual agricultural festivals were held, with much drinking, dancing and singing. (One assumes that the demon rice-wine must have been known by this time.) A shaman was appointed to arrange the ceremonies, which took place in sacred clearings called *sodo* marked by bells and drums but no ceremonial buildings. Rhee (1984) suggests that the Ungok valley, with its natural beauty and continued use by Buddhists and Confucianists, might have been a *sodo*.

An island in the sea "west" of Mahan is described as a separate state. This island is usually identified as Cheju Do, the large volcanic island to the southwest of the main peninsula. The people of this island were short, wore skin clothing and kept their hair short. They raised cattle and pigs, taking the animals by boat to trade with the peninsular Han groups.

The Chinhan were located east of the Naktong river, and included twelve tribes, of about 50,000 households. They had "stockaded city-like enclosures," and five ranks of chiefs (Parker 1890:209). The people were fully settled and agricultural: they raised silkworms, and they used both oxen and horses to pull carts. Iron was produced, smelted and used as a medium of exchange. Head-flattening was practiced (an archaeological example has been found at Yeanni), and the people were tall. Many of the old people of Chinhan were said to be refugees from China. Examples of their pronunciation of words are given, suggesting derivation from a dialect of northwest China (Parker 1890:213).

Pyonhan, along the Naktong river and the coast and westward to the Sobaek range, also consisted of twelve states. Similar to Chinhan in clothing and customs, it differed in language. People who lived in the south, nearest the Wa, followed the custom of tattooing themselves. The Wa (or Wae in Korean) are usually thought to be exclusively in the Japanese islands. However, it has been argued that some of the confusion over the interpretation of various acts of the

Wa is related to location: some Wa lived on the Korean peninsula (Yi C.H. 1977). This is a thorny problem, which can only ultimately be resolved with more evidence than the written documents provide, as well as attention to place without reference to current national boundaries.

Archaeological evidence

Chronology

C14 determinations are rarely made for this time period on the grounds that it is historical, but chronological issues could be greatly clarified with more dates. Black pottery jars, equated by Korean archaeologists with the presence of iron (e.g. Kim J.B. 1975a), establish dates of about 400 BC in central Korea, as at Susongni on the Han river (Kim W.Y. 1966a, 1967b). Along the Han river, Mumun pottery and semi-subterranean houses were still in use when iron technology appeared, and in the Naktong river basin shell mounds were still accumulating when iron became important.

C14 dates associated either with iron artifacts or with sites containing iron are few. Those that do exist range from about 480 BC (at Musan on the Tumen river) to the early centuries AD (Table 6.1). Although there are some claims for earlier iron production in northern Korea (Hwang 1965) and the Siberian coast (Oklad-nikov 1965), it is generally believed that iron entered Korea during the Warring States period (476–221 BC) shortly after iron began to impact the technology of China. Coins cast in the shape of knives, minted in the "semi-barbarian" state of Yan in the vicinity of modern Beijing, found their way to northwestern Korea along with iron tools during this era.

Some Korean scholars offer very early dates for iron in Korea. Kim Jong-bae (1975b), for instance, believes that iron came into Korea directly from Manchuria by the sixth century BC. On the other hand, Kim Won-yong (1986a:39) suggests that iron casting using the local iron ore began only in the third century BC, and Yi Nam-kyu (1982) would place it two centuries later than that. Recent studies on the iron implements themselves have explained much about iron technology in Korea, but have failed to solve the dating debate (Yoon D.S. 1984, 1986, 1989; Yoon and Lee 1985a, 1985b; Yoon and Shin 1982).

Relative chronologies based on typologies are as common as those based on C14 dates are scarce, but they are not all compatible. Several archaeologists have worked on seriating late "Mumun" styles. Kim Chong-won (1989:139), Choi Sung-nak (1988a) and Chung and Shin (1987) argue that the undecorated pottery from this time period (still called Mumun) can be ordered chronologically according to the rim style. They find round rims to be earlier, dating as early as 200 BC. Examples include Layer II of the Cho Do site and Susongni on the Han river. The triangular rim type lasts from 175 BC to 100 AD, including such sites as Cho Do Layer I. This dating is based on comparisons with Yayoi, in Japan.

Table 6.1. *Radiocarbon dates in the Womsanguk period*

Site	Sample no. or ref.	C14 date	Recalibrated calendar date
Achisom	Lee Y.J. 1977	2200±70	210–370 BC
Yangsan	AERIK 4	2169±122	225, 320, 335 BC
	N–239	1840±120	AD 175
	N–236	1750±120	AD 245
	N–238	1750±120	AD 245
	N–237	1520±120	AD 450
Si Do	AERIK 9	1980±60	AD 20
Ungchon	M–1181	1910±75	AD 110
Kumgokdong	N–2110	1870±85	AD 160
Kosong	AERIK 15	1730±70	AD 260
Pungnamni	N–240	1720±110	AD 265
Majangni	M–303	1700±250	AD 280
Kimje (irrigation)	KAERI 149–3	1620±110	AD 330
	KAERI 149–1	1600±100	AD 350
	KAERI 149–2	1576±100	AD 374
Jung Do	Chi and Lee 1983	1835±90	AD 115
	Chi and Lee 1983	1535±95	AD 415

Chung, Shin and Im (1988) also seriate the southern sites into early, middle and late according to pottery types, again on the basis of lip shape. Pak (1989a) examines the Han river pottery and seriates the sites on the basis of the percentage of *Kyongjil* plain ware (see below), paddled vessels and black pottery.

A few artifacts, mostly from the Lelang region, are inscribed with dates. For example, a halberd found near Pyongyang bore an inscription dating it to 222 BC (Gardiner 1969a:8), and a painted lacquer bowl is dated AD 69 (Hamada 1936). A Chinese mirror with a 28-character inscription, made in the imperial factory around the BC/AD turning point, was found at Yangdongni, near Kimhae in the southeast, accompanied by both iron and bronze weapons (Munhwajae 1987).

Coins are also found in some sites. As far south as the upper reaches of the Taedong river, knife-shaped coins were found (Choi M.L. 1989), manufactured in the north Chinese state of Yan, between the late sixth century BC and 222 BC when Yan was conquered by the Chin emperor (Yang 1952:15). Wang Mang coins (AD 9 to 23) are found in a number of sites in the south.

Iron use and manufacture

With so few chronological anchors, it is difficult to be definitive about the beginnings of iron use or iron manufacture in Korea. South Korean archaeologists look to China for the antecedents of Korean iron. Meteoritic iron sword blades "recorded as having been presented as tribute from abroad" (Hirth 1908:237) are known from the Shang period. Smelting and cast iron began as early as the seventh century BC in China (Rostoker 1982–3). Iron manufacture of weapons was followed by the production of household and agricultural implements at least by the fourth century BC (Ho 1975:83). Iron was common and widespread in China by the Han dynasty (Needham 1958), revolutionizing agriculture, boat building, house building and warfare (Wang 1982:122).

Abundant evidence that iron ore was locally smelted and cast has been found in various sites. Iron slag was unearthed at several sites in South Korea, including Kapyongni and Kosong. The site of Musan in the north is located near one of the largest iron mines in Korea, and iron-rich sands are found near the southern Korean sites (Yoon D.S. 1986).

Recent studies of Korean iron demonstrate that iron objects were manufactured locally. Iron-making sites in North Korea include half-a-dozen villages in Hwanghae Do, two sites near Wonsan, and Musan on the Tumen river in the far northeast (Yoon 1984). Iron artifacts were produced in small furnaces which have been found along the North Han river, dating to the third century BC or earlier. These sites are all near sources of iron (Yoon 1984:47). In the southeast as well, sites containing iron slag are not far from iron-rich sands or iron ore deposits. Recently a site with iron furnaces has been discovered at Hwangsong-dong near Kyongju, in southeastern Korea. Clay bowls for casting are an important discovery at this site.

Chemical analysis shows that some iron artifacts were forged while others were cast (Yoon and Lee 1985b). Implements made of cast iron were mostly tools such as axes (Fig. 6.2) and plows (Fig. 6.3), which received heavy use. Although some of the iron tools made in these villages may have been traded to villages elsewhere and even outside the peninsula, they were also used locally, as their presence in dwellings and graves attests.

Metal artifacts

Iron weapons such as iron daggers, arrowheads and spears were manufactured in shapes similar to those previously made of bronze. An important difference in iron production, however, was the extension of the use of metal to implements of daily use, especially for farming and woodworking. At Musan, for example, iron axes, sickles, crescent-shaped adzes and fishhooks were found associated with dwellings (Hwang K.D. 1975). Iron agricultural implements were precious enough to be used as grave goods. Some iron ingots may date to this period (Taylor 1989:430), suggesting trade in iron.

Bronze, in the meantime, appears to have acquired more symbolic meanings, while continuing in use for weaponry. The broad-bladed Liaoning dagger was replaced by a slimmer weapon, with attenuated points along the edges. This change in dagger form is attributed by Chung (1982a) to the fourth century BC. The blade was still cast separately from the hilt, relating the slender daggers unmistakably to the Liaoning form rather than to Chinese weapons, which were

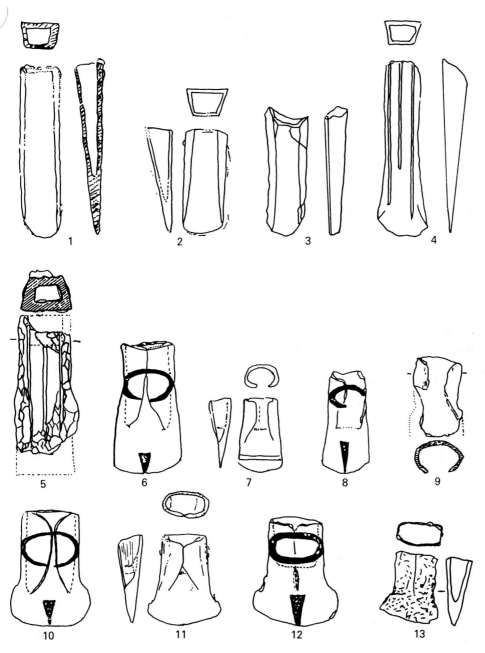

6.2 Iron axes. 1, 9 Hachon F House I; 2, 7, 11 Nopodong Grave 16; 3, 4 Taesimni; 5 Mongchon fortress; 6, 10 Yangpyongni Dolmen 2; 8, 12 Tohwari dolmen; 13 Pungchongni Grave 33. After Pak 1989.

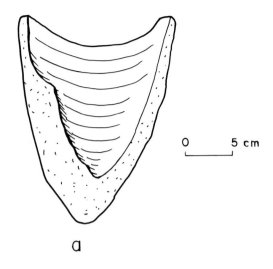

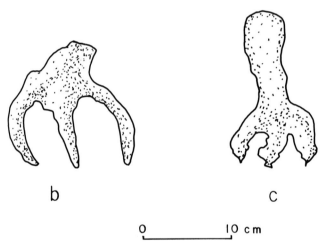

6.3 Iron artifacts from Kuidong. *a* iron plow, *b, c* iron forks.

cast with the handle and blade together. Seventeen southeastern sites are seriated by means of these increasingly slender daggers. Lee C.K. (1982) also classified these daggers using 140 examples, but offers later dates, beginning around 300 BC. It is interesting to note that 63% of all the known slender daggers have been found in South Korea (Lee C.K. 1982:17, Table 6.2), suggesting that the evolution of this dagger may have occurred there, not in the north.

Along with the changing dagger shapes, increasingly well-crafted fine-lined

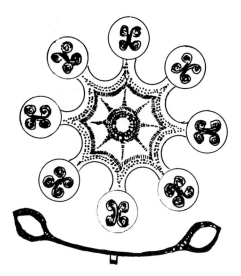

6.4 Bronze bell, possibly shaman's equipment.

mirrors are found. These mirrors have a high tin content, as well as significant amounts of zinc and iron (Jeon 1974). Chinese-style mirrors appear in the Former Han period (206 BC–AD 7), while native Korean geometric mirrors decline. Apparently the imported mirrors were valued more highly than the locally manufactured ones, for inferior copies of Han mirrors were made in Korea instead of the highly developed fine-line mirrors which had been found earlier (Yun 1981).

A number of bronze artifacts with unusual, apparently non-utilitarian shapes have been cited as examples of shaman's equipment (Kim W.Y. 1986a) (Fig. 6.4). Bells and rattles are particularly convincing, as such implements are still in use by Korean *mudangs*. The mirrors themselves probably played some role in the spiritual beliefs.

Many horse-shaped bronze belt buckles were found in graves and caches along with a few tiger-shaped buckles (Fig. 6.5). The horse buckles range from a very fine example from a remote village near Yongchon, in the southeast, to some rather simplified castings. Nearly every museum in Korea, large or small, has one or more horse buckles on display (Fig. 6.6). The buckles may be symbols of rank, but they are so common that the rank of the horse buckle wearer cannot have been a very high one. Based on scarcity alone, one might suppose that the wearer of a horse buckle is inferior to the wearer of a tiger buckle.

Korean style iron artifacts were found at Yongdamdong in Cheju, confirming the relationship of Cheju to the rest of the Korean peninsula as described in the *Sanguo Ji*. Most of the weapons are like those found in northwestern Korea, but the arrowhead types resemble those of the south. Wushu coins of AD 8–23 were also found there (Lee C.K. 1985), as they have been in other Korean sites. Large

6.5 Horse and tiger buckles from Yongchon.

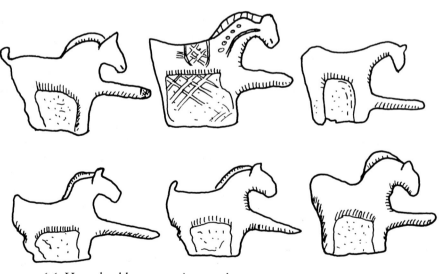

6.6 Horse buckles, provenience unknown.

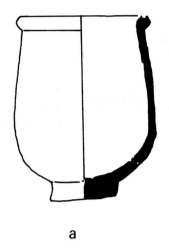
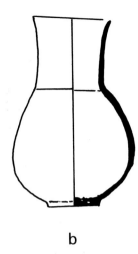

a
b

6.7 *a* Rolled rim and *b* long-necked vessels.

quantities of knife-shaped coins and some spade-shaped coins were found in the northwest.

Ceramics

Pottery of this age is easily distinguished from that of the preceding period, although several varieties of wares were produced (Choi M.L. 1983b). In the southeast an early type is brownish or reddish ware similar to Mumun, but fired at a higher temperature. It is referred to as *yonjil*. One typical shape has a rounded base and horn-like projections for handles (Kim W.Y. 1982c); another has a rolled or triangular rim (Fig. 6.7a). Black jars with long necks are also found (Fig. 6.7b). The surface is undecorated but polished (Kim W.Y. 1967a).

Kimhae decorated pottery, now often called *kyongjil*, is finer and harder than the horn-handled pottery. It ranges in color from blue-gray to light brown. The surface has cord or lattice patterns, sometimes appearing to be paddled (Fig. 6.8). Pedestal vessels (*dou*) made of unpaddled gray ware thrown on a wheel are common (Fig. 6.9). The gray ceramics fired in a reducing atmosphere may be a result of the application of kiln technology associated with iron smelting to pottery kilns as the vessels were fired in a closed kiln with a reducing atmosphere (Kim W.Y. 1986a:42). Several kilns have been excavated, including Samnyongni, Sansuri and Taegongni (Barnes 1989, Choi, Kwon and Kim 1989). Globular gray jars with paddled surfaces are known from Han dynasty China, and are thought to be the inspiration for Kimhae pottery.

A newly discovered pottery type called *wajil* (brick-clay pottery) emerged from pit graves in the southeast (Shin 1982). A softer pottery, it might have been

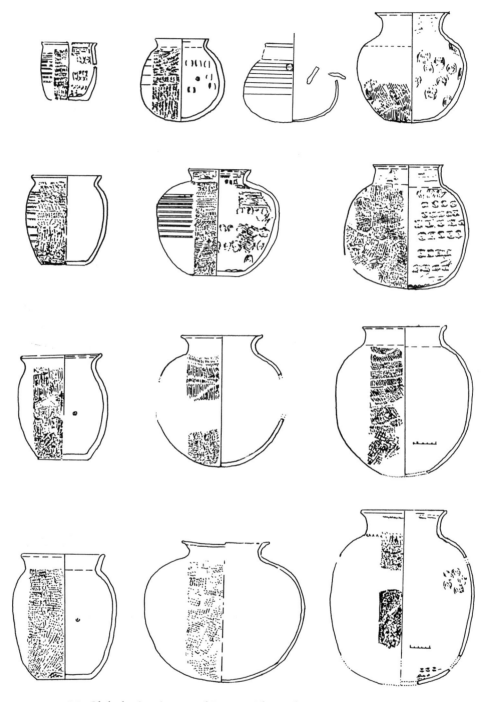

6.8 Globular jars in central Korea. After Pak 1989.

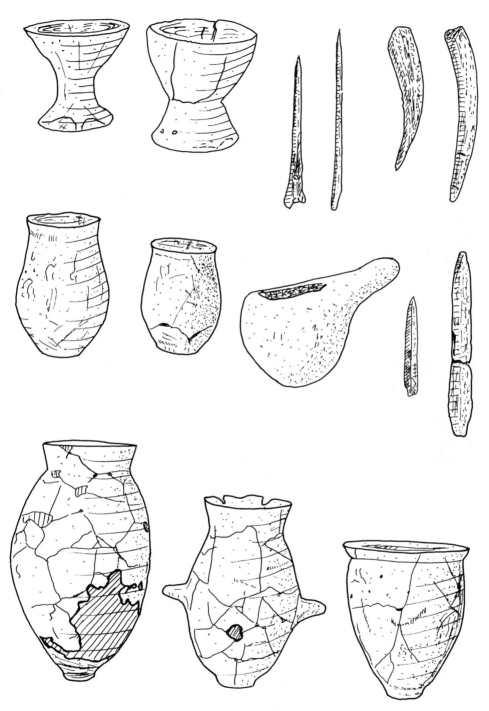

6.9 Artifacts from Samchonpo, Nuk Do.

produced only for mortuary purposes, especially since it has not been found in non-tomb contexts (Kim W.Y. 1982b). It has no surface decoration, but is characterized by complex globular shapes, horn handles and short pedestals. Regional divisions of this pottery have been noted; for example, the Songju area is characterized by vessels having three or four handles (Han B.S. 1984).

The temporal ordering of these pottery types is in dispute. One sequence moves from the black long-necked jars to jars with handles and everted rims to more globular jars, some of them with attached pedestals (Choi J.G. 1982b). Other schemes focus on the rim style, as noted above. Additional C14 dates could move the discussion beyond competing typologies.

Tripods are not characteristic of Korean pottery. A tiny, poorly made pottery tripod was found associated with Mumun sherds, a tubular bead, a spindle whorl and iron axes at the Hachon F site in central Korea (Yun 1984), and is the only ceramic tripod found in Korea from this period. It must have been made in imitation of Chinese styles, where tripods had been prevalent for many millennia. Some ceremonial importation is implied by this circumstance, for the tripod is likely to reflect either kitchen or altar usage, and Chinese-style cuisine never supplanted local Korean food habits.

Glass

Early glass in Korea dates to the first century BC (Lee I.S. 1989). Two types are discriminated by the constituent elements, rather than by visible characteristics (Lee I.S. 1989). Glass beads were found in a number of places, including Kungongni shell mound and Yongdamdong on Cheju island. The earliest glass found so far in Korea was in a stone cist tomb at Hapsongni, dated to the second century BC (Puyo National Museum 1989). Many of the early beads are tiny, including those found at Kimhae Yangdongni and the original Kimhae shell mound. Jeon (1976) believes the glass was locally made in Korea. The technology possibly came from China, although early glass in China is lead glass (Francis 1986:7), while the first Korean glass is a potash silicate type (Lee I.S. 1989). Glass vessels were produced in China as early as the Western Han in the first century BC (An J.Y. 1984), while glass ornaments and beads are still earlier (Sarton 1936, Francis 1986). Engle (1976) suggests that glass came into China along with the use of iron and gold, imported from the nomadic cultures on the northwestern frontier. It is possible that glass bead making came to Korea from the northern steppe rather than by way of China.

Stone and bone artifacts

Implements of stone and bone continued to be manufactured and used after the introduction of iron, although with decreasing frequency. For a few examples, stone knives and adzes were found at Kosong; bone needles, awls and arrowheads as well as the antler handle of an iron knife were preserved in the shell mound at Kimhae; and the Cho Do site produced a polished stone dagger and a triangular stone projectile point. Scapulae with burn holes, apparently for divination purposes, were found at Kungongni (Choi S.N. 1988b), and at Musan (Hwang K.D. 1975).

Burials

Iron artifacts have been found associated with several burial modes, including stone cists, pit burials without any stone lining, jar-coffins, and cairns covering stone-lined pits. Iron in stone cists is rare, and when it occurs it may represent the earliest iron in Korea. Pit burials differ from stone cist burials chiefly in lacking stone slabs or piled stones outlining the narrow grave. Perhaps a wooden coffin was substituted, but if so there are few surviving examples. More pit burials are found in the north than in the south. The grave furniture frequently included both bronze and iron weapons. Specific examples of burials will be discussed regionally, after examining the documents pertaining to this period.

Regional differences

Northwest

When megalithics disappear in the north, hoards of *mingdao* coins (Fig. 6.10), "knife money," minted in the state of Yan in Hebei province, China, begin to be found. Several interpretations of these hoards have been proposed. Yoon N.H. (1987, 1986) and Choi M.L. (1984a) argue that the coins are firm evidence of a state-level society tied into a network of long-distance trade. Choi M.L. (1989) suggests that horses are particularly important items of trade for Ko Choson, along with iron, dried fish, silk and long arrows. Pai (1989b), however, dismisses this evidence as unconvincing.

Mingdao coins have been found in fifteen sites in North Korea (Choi M.L. 1989), and occasional pieces of spade money and other coins have also turned up. Although many of the sites are either stray finds or hoards, Sejungni on the Chongchon river contained more than 2,500 coins in Layer III, a layer with iron implements which also features above-ground houses with *ondol* floors.

The *ondol* is a heating system which sends heat from the cooking stove through channels under the floor to warm the house in winter. A photograph of an excavated *ondol* floor from North Hamgyong Province appears in Han Woo-keun (1970:12–13), and a house floor beneath a Paekche burial at Sokchondong near Seoul likewise had provisions for subfloor heating. Okladnikov mentions two Siberian sites with *ondol* floors, one of which is dated to 99 BC (Okladnikov 1964:69, 81).

Pit burials are found throughout Korea, but the largest concentration is in the

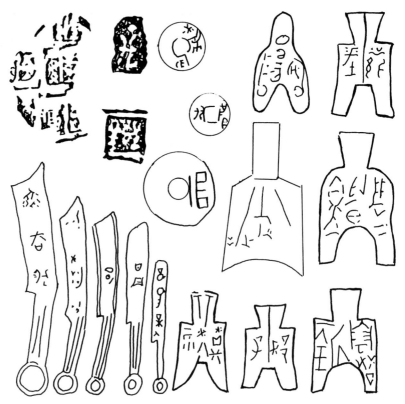

6.10 Early Chinese coins.

northwest. North Koreans place the pit graves, for example at Suksangni, in the third to fourth century BC, while Japanese scholars find a date near the end of the second century BC more acceptable (Yi N.K. 1987). This question remains under discussion. Yi examines the pit graves in the northwest, and finds them congruent with the Liaodong culture area, except that he believes double burials are a result of Han influence. These graves show traces of wooden coffins and frequently contain evidence of two burials, a male and a female, presumably a married pair (Fig. 6.11). Horse fittings and chariot parts are often present. For instance, of the twelve excavated tombs at Taesongni, eight have evidence of wooden coffins, five are double burials, and one (Tomb 11) is probably a woman alone (Kim J.B. 1978a:40–1). Lee Soon-jin (1983) notes the large number of native Korean bronze weapons found in the wooden coffin burials. These burials were made over a period of perhaps two centuries. Probably the earliest are two graves with more bronze than iron. Other graves contain either a short iron sword, which is intermediate in age, or a long iron sword, the latest of all. When first excavated, these were interpreted as Lelang tombs, but mounting evidence suggests that they are earlier than Lelang, from the time of Wiman Choson or

6.11 Double grave in the northwest. After Lee S.J. 1983.

even his reputed predecessor King Chun. An inscription on one weapon dates it to the "25th year of the First Emperor of China," or 221 BC (Kim J.B. 1978a:43), before Wiman's arrival. Of course it could have been an heirloom placed in the grave many years after its manufacture, but it is at least suggestive of a previously existing polity.

An example of a pit tomb without a mound is that of Pujo Yegun, whose name is inscribed on a silver seal in his tomb. The inscription is interpreted to mean Prince Ye of Pujo. Pujo was a province of the east coast, named in the *Han Shu*. Metal artifacts found in the grave have a marked leaning toward the military – a bronze dagger, two iron swords, one bronze and one iron spear, an iron knife, an iron axe and fifteen bronze arrowheads. In addition, bronze chariot hubcaps, twelve bronze bells and other chariot fixtures were found. Ceramic vessels were of the utilitarian sort, covered with mat impressions. A wooden floor could be traced, but no coffin was found. Kim Jong-hak (1978b:142–4) interprets the silver seal as that of the ruler of the Ok-cho, before the establishment of the Chinese commanderies. If that is the case the grave belongs with the pit grave group, rather than Lelang. A Prince of Ye (as in Ye-Maek) is described as surrendering to the Chinese in 128 BC.

The tombs in the vicinity of Lelang, at Namsuri, Sogamni and Chongbaengni, are of several kinds (Fig. 6.12). The earliest are typical of iron age pit tombs, without a mound. As noted above, they are interpreted as native Korean burials. Later tombs, covered by mounds, have burial chambers constructed of wood or brick, in the style of the Han dynasty of China. Some Koreans argue that these are not Chinese burials, but Korean officials (e.g. Son 1985). In the 1930s a survey noted 446 wooden tombs and 926 brick tombs, mostly looted (Kayamoto 1962:106). Of these, the wooden chamber type is earlier, according to dated inscriptions found in many tombs, but the two overlap in time. Kayamoto (1962) believes that the earliest form of wooden chamber tomb belongs to the "middle period" of Lelang. The typical tomb has partitions containing two or three separate lacquered coffins and chambers for burial goods. In one case a coffin made from a single split and hollowed log was noted (Kayamoto 1962:113), a circumstance also found in Kaya territory and in Japan. The all-bricks tombs date from Later Han times, and stone chambered tombs are the latest of all, probably representing Koguryo's reconquest of the region.

Since most tombs under a mound contain coffins of a man and a woman, and several have additional (often child-size) coffins, the tombs can be seen as burial places for the nuclear family unit. An entrance passage allowed the tomb to be reopened to receive family members later deceased, or for ancestor worship. Only the more spectacular tombs have been reported in detail, but these demonstrate the richness of life on one fringe of the Chinese empire. Much lacquer work survived, as well as wood, fragments of cloth, leather and other usually perishable items.

An example of a wooden tomb under a mound is that of Wang Kuang, whose two wooden seals established his identity. As is frequently the case, both Wang and his wife were interred in black lacquer coffins, heads to the north. Wang occupied the western coffin. In the coffins, Wang Kuang still wore a hat, leather shoes, a ring and a belt buckle. Buried beside him were a sword in a lacquered sheath, a knife and two wooden seals. His wife was accompanied by hairpins, jewels and rings. Outside the coffins, burial goods were ranged in neat rows along the north and west sides. Seven lacquered tables, ten pottery vessels, more than sixty lacquered plates, lacquered cups and other dishes probably held the remains of the final funeral feast. Additional grave goods included five bronze

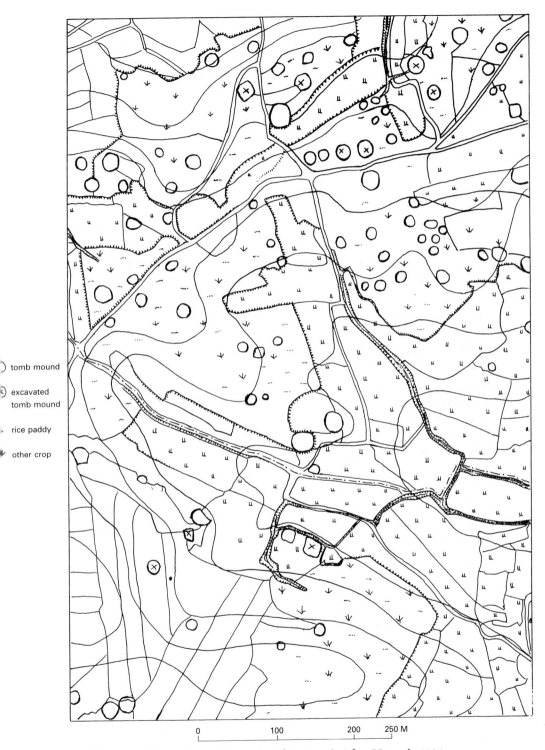

tomb mound

excavated
tomb mound

rice paddy

other crop

0   100   200   250 M

6.12 Lelang cemeteries at Namsuri and Sogamni. After Hamada 1934.

mirrors, a lacquered cosmetic box, a chest and a tray painted with the motif of dancing bears (McCune 1962).

Another tomb with two seals, these of silver, is that of Ko Sang-Hyon. It is dated by an inscription on a lacquered chariot canopy pole to AD 14. Two wooden coffins were unearthed, the woman lying in the western coffin. The metal objects were typically Korean in form: a slender bronze dagger, a fine-lined mirror, horsemask, bell, crossbow and chariot fixtures. Pujo Chang, the inscription on the seals, is interpreted by Kim J.H. (1978b:144–6) as referring to an Ok-cho official after the establishment of Lelang.

The tomb of Wang Kun is an example of a partitioned tomb. It was covered by a mound over 20 m in diameter and about 5 m high. The wooden interior was divided into rooms, each with its own coffin. The western one contained an elegantly arrayed male, with a silk gauze hat decorated with jade beads, a wide silk sash with silver ornaments, silver rings, a necklace, combs, an iron sword, a wooden pillow and a seal with a tortoise-shaped knob. The eastern, woman's coffin, had gilded copper ornaments on the outside of the coffin, and within lay jade beads in a hairnet arrangement, pendant earrings, a broad sash, jade bracelets, silver rings and a lacquer box containing glass beads. Outside the coffins were the usual weapons, horse trappings and chariot parts, as well as much tableware (McCune 1962).

The Painted Basket Tomb, a late wooden tomb built around AD 100, contained two chambers. The main room housed three lacquered coffins, while an anteroom contained the burial offerings. The famous painted basket after which the tomb was named is made of wicker with painted lacquer panels depicting lively figures in bright colors. In one coffin, the male had a dagger by his side and wore leather shoes, while the woman and child were accompanied by various ornaments of tortoise shell, silver and gold. Remnants of yellow silk, hemp and a rush mat were also found (Hamada and Koisumi 1934). A wall painting could be dimly discerned, showing men on horseback. Wood and clay burial miniatures of horses, dolls and chariots were also included, reflecting a widespread custom of the Han dynasty not found in earlier graves. In the outer chamber, a wooden tablet bears an inscription announcing that Tien Kung sent an underling to sacrifice with three rolls of yellow silk, implying that the occupant of the tomb was a high official of Lelang (Kayamoto 1962:111).

Many graves contained unusual or unique items. A gold buckle with turquoise inlays, made in a granulated technique rarely found in China but similar in technique to some Silla earrings, is one such object. An almost identical buckle has recently been found in Tomb No. 7, Shizhaishan in Yunnan, China (Pirazzoli-t'serstevens 1982). Another unusual item is a pair of table legs in the form of bears, made of gilt copper and decorated with turquoise (Umehara 1926). A drinking cup of lacquered birch bark, a coral bead and an amber bead were additional grave goods of this particular burial (McCune 1962:42).

Although some North Korean archaeologists have attempted to deny the presence of the Chinese commanderies and assert that the Lelang finds represent an indigenous Korean development (Pearson 1978), in my opinion the written documents are too substantial to be dismissed when considered in conjunction with the archaeological finds. While an argument of *in situ* progression of grave types cannot be entirely ruled out, the archaeological discoveries are not incompatible with the presence of Chinese families, gradually becoming Koreanized (Pai 1989b). Wang and Han are two family names which the documents relate were chosen by Chinese-descended Korean families (Sun and de Francis 1966:55).

The artifacts deposited in the graves were manufactured in many different places, some as far away as Szechuan, and others locally made, as would be expected in a trading center, regardless of the overlordship. The shift, rather late, to Han Chinese burial customs including brick tombs and mortuary figurines, could be explained simply as diffusion from China, but on balance seems more likely to indicate actual Chinese officials following their own customs. While the archaeological discoveries fail to tell us whether or not the Chinese were really in charge, the documents do not leave much room for doubt, since they include detailed chronicles, tax rolls, population statistics and the like, unlikely to have been invented later for the purpose of verisimilitude.

Although tombs account for the bulk of the archaeological finds from Lelang, some forts and buildings have been excavated. The capital city of Lelang, lying on a hill on the south bank of the Taedong river, across the river from the present city of Pyongyang, has been partially excavated. An area of about 700 × 600 m was surrounded by mud walls, the footing of which is still visible. Rather than rectangular city walls, according to Chinese custom, the walls followed the contours of the land. Buildings did show Chinese influence, however, constructed on earthen foundations, with large posts to support the roof placed on stone bases (McCune 1962:41). Roof tiles with inscriptions were found at the highest point of the hill, marking a "ceremonial hall" (McCune 1962:41) or "office building" (Kayamoto 1962:117). Other building sites were marked by cornerstones. Brick-paved streets edged with gutters and drains of stone and brick were also discovered. The cemeteries are outside the city. Over an area of about 8 × 4 km, 1,400 mounded tombs were mapped (Kayamoto 1962:106).

Other sites in Lelang territory have been excavated, but the reports are sketchy. For instance, the Chulmun site at Chitamni (see Fig. 4.1 for location) is within a mud wall ascribed to the Lelang age, with hand-fired gray stoneware in the upper layers.

Near modern Kaesong, yet another ruined city was found, Tang Tosong, surrounded by later brick tombs. This is thought to have been the capital of the Taebang commandery, formed in AD 204 when the southern area was retaken by the Kungsun family from the native Koreans (Pai 1989:59). Small earthen-walled fortresses are also found at Yonggangni and Oksongni. In the case of the former, nearby brick chamber tombs, as well as Han eave tiles, suggest this is a

Chinese settlement. The site measures 139 × 151 m. A monument raised in AD 85 and inscribed in Chinese characters with a dedication to a local mountain god was found in nearby Chinampo (Kayamoto 1962:107). Oksongni also has eave tiles and drainage bricks. Many burial styles are found, including urn burials. A great many villages in Korea are named Tosongni, meaning Earth Fortress Village, suggesting wide-spread walled villages, but of course the age of construction is unknown.

North central

The Huanren-Jian region, the heart of early Koguryo territory, contains at least 12,000 tombs. Many of them are "stone-piled" tombs (cairns), from which some bronze artifacts can be dated to the third century BC (Rhee 1989), as well as Chin and Han artifacts such as bronze jars, cooking vessels and axes. Both knife-shaped and spade-shaped coins are found as well, demonstrating that this region was well within China's Interaction Sphere. For example, a tomb at Wutuoling, west of Jian, included a slender bronze dagger, a fine-lined mirror, three bronze spears, five bronze axes, two ornamental bronzes and two iron arrowheads. Some of these items are closely connected to discoveries near Dandong at the mouth of the Yalu river (Rhee 1989).

Iron agricultural implements, other tools, and weapons are found in the graves with pyramidal mounds of cut stone. In this type of tomb, the burial chamber was neither underground nor at ground level, but near the top of the mound. The earliest were simple, but soon they acquired a stone base and became stepped pyramids (Lee Y.J. 1980).

Rhee (1989) mentions walled towns in Koguryo territory, especially Jian and Huanren (now part of China), in which earthen walls were found beneath the later stone walls. These earlier walls may date to the fourth or third century BC.

Even though Rhee (1989) argues for local development of Koguryo on the basis of archaeological discoveries in the Huanren-Jian region, he cannot gainsay the evidence of the Kwanggaeto stele itself (AD 414), which cites Chumong as the first ancestor. Rhee points to a lack of "massive migrations," but only a handful of new settlers are said to have come with Chumong, possibly providing leadership to the indigenous population. Koguryo was ultimately responsible for the rout of the Chinese from Lelang, and will be treated more fully in the next chapter as one of the Three Kingdoms.

Northeast

At Musan Pomuigusok on the Tumen river in North Korea, overlapping rectangular dwellings were discovered. Some contained central hearths and rows of post holes. The pottery includes some plain jars with lug handles, steamers, and bowls on pedestals. Several pig figurines were found, echoing the figurines common in Manchurian sites. Iron artifacts include axes, transverse two-holed (semi-lunar) knives, and fishhooks. Oracle bones made from scapulae, with burn holes but no writing, were also found at this level of the site, which was designated Layer 5. It is believed to date to the seventh to fifth centuries BC (Hwang K.D. 1975). Similarly treated shoulder blades were found in the Fuhe culture of Liaoxi dated much earlier (around 3000 BC), and much later in a South Korean shell mound, as well as the renowned Shang dynasty oracle bone. The relationships among these oracle bones are not at all clear.

Pit tombs are widespread in the Hamgyong provinces, as in the northwest. Graves in this region are characterized by many bronze artifacts and few of stone (Kim J.B. 1975a). Horse equipment and chariot fittings, however, are considerably less frequent than on the Taedong river (Kim J.B. 1978a). A group of pit tombs at Sorari, South Hamgyong, seem to have been associated with an earth-walled hill fort. Iron horse bits, bronze arrowheads and quiver lids were found in Tomb 8, along with iron axes, swords and knives.

Central

Susongni on the Han river has dwellings that differ from megalithic age houses in having hearths in a corner of the house rather than in the center (Kim W.Y. 1966a). There are at least eight sites of this type on the North Han and South Han branches.

The Jung Do site, on a sandy island in the North Han river, was occupied through several periods. In addition to the typical dolmens described in the previous chapter, house floors have been excavated at Sinmaeri. A square pit house with a stone-paved hearth was uncovered, with post holes on either side. Measuring 6 m on a side, the house contained a hardened clay floor. Associated sherds included hard-fired plain and Kimhae pottery. Millet seeds were found inside a jar. Iron tools included knives, arrowheads and sickles. The site is dated to the fourth century BC (National Museum of Korea 1981, Chi and Han 1982, Chi and Lee 1983, 1984, Kangwon National University Museum 1984, Im S.K. 1980, Yi K.M. *et al.* 1980).

Tunnaeri, between the two large branches of the Han river, has a semi-subterranean dwelling with a pebble hearth off-center, and pottery that places it in this time period. Also in central Korea, the Hachonni site, dated to the second century AD, contained a number of iron tools, including sickles and hoes. Tubular jade beads were also found, along with *wajil* pottery. A dwelling, 10.5 × 8.3 m, was constructed with vertical posts set around the periphery. A hearth containing two large flat stones in the middle was found near a wall (Yun 1984).

Majangni is a large site with numerous house pits. It was first discovered during the Korean War (during the digging of fox holes), and at that time only part of one dwelling could be excavated. The house was subrectangular, 5.2 × 6.5 m. A large circular hearth, about 1.3 m in diameter, occupied one corner

(MacCord 1958). This site has been investigated more extensively in recent years. Large vessels of both Kimhae pottery and Mumun have come to light, along with spindle whorls, pottery steamers and diamond-cross-section projectile points (Pak 1989).

Central Korean sites tend to have both Mumun and Kimhae pottery associated with iron, while further south the combination of Mumun pottery and iron is rare. This suggests that iron was introduced earlier on the Han river (Yoon D.S. 1984). A group of ten pottery kilns in Tokchong has been attributed to this time period. The kilns, about 5.4 m long and 1.5 m wide, were tunnel kilns, a type which can produce enough heat to produce stoneware.

Several forts and walled cities are known in the Seoul area on both banks of the Han river. These sites are described in the next chapter as early Paekche sites, but some of them may belong to the time of the Samhan. Chinese documents suggest that people from various conquered barbarian groups (Duyvendak 1928) as well as Chinese (Gardiner 1969a) escaped from uncongenial laws in China during the Chin and Han dynasties, and migrated to southern Korea. They could have brought advanced technologies from China.

The site of Pungnamni is particularly interesting in this regard, since it lies beside the river and is rectangular, in Chinese fashion, rather than being placed on a hill following the contours as most Korean walled fortresses are. Some of the pottery shows Chinese influences, strengthening the inference. In three pits where parts of dwelling floors were uncovered, roof tiles, a hearth, a burnt clay layer and iron clamps used in wooden architecture were found (Kim W.Y. 1967a). The wall is known to have been repaired in AD 285, and later Paekche occupation is noted as well.

At Karakdong, within the city of Seoul, earthen mounds were piled over typical pit tombs. One mound, designated Tomb 2, covered four pits. The ceramic pots left as grave offerings had the typical globular shape of Wonsamguk pottery in the region, and iron weapons and implements were found as well.

Four "early iron age" cairns were excavated at Kidong on the South Han river. Two iron arrowheads were found in the stones of the cairn, and pieces of Kimhae pottery lay on the clay floor of a burial chamber, which was 200 × 45 cm. The orientation of three of the graves is north–south, but Tomb No. 3 was aligned northeast–southwest instead (Hwang 1984a).

A stone tomb at Tohwari built in the form of a three-step pyramid probably dates to the second or third century. It contained Kimhae pottery and iron spears, chisels, axes, knives and sickles. This burial chamber is oriented east–west (Choi M.L., Lee H.J. and Pak Y.J. 1983).

Two other tombs reminiscent of Koguryo styles were found at Yangpyongni on the Nam Han river. No. 1 was 29 × 25 m at the base and 7.2 m high. The other, described as the largest piled stone tomb in Korea, was 9 m high at maximum, and 57 m in diameter. Iron spears and axes and a bronze horse were the only artifacts left after looting. Its date is estimated to be second to third century AD (Bae 1984). A C14 date of AD 115 comes from a burial in central Korea of a child of about ten years, flexed, with head to the east. The bones were partly burned, and a circle of cobbles surrounded the burial.

Southern pit tombs are widespread. In South Chungchong near Myongjiri, Tomb A has no traces of a wooden coffin, but otherwise contains an assemblage of artifacts similar to other pit graves, including an iron axe, hoe and knife hilt as well as a globular ceramic jar with a narrow neck (Kim J.B. 1978a:48). A more recent excavation at this site has uncovered a large area interpreted as a workshop for manufacturing polished stone daggers, arrowheads and net sinkers. Its age is estimated at 200–100 BC (Choi M.L. 1984b).

Southwest

A village on a hilltop in a bend above the river is currently being excavated at Naksuri in Sungju, South Cholla province, in connection with the construction of the Juam Dam. The village consists of rows of slightly subterranean houses, with several types of hard and soft-fired pottery (Fig. 6.13). It is believed to be connected with Mahan due to its location in the southwest and the time period of third to fourth century. Such a large village in this region was unexpected, as there is no reference to it in any of the contemporary Chinese documents. Of the fifteen houses excavated so far, the average size was 4–5 m × 3–4 m (Choi, Lee and Lee 1989). Drainage ditches were found at the sites, and the houses were more complex than earlier ones, some of them L-shaped, or with entrance porches, or having areas partitioned off with posts (Fig. 6.14). Iron implements, stone reaping knives, whet stones, spindle whorls, grinding stones, arrowheads and a clay paddle were among the artifacts found. Steamers and paddled pottery were made of relatively soft (*wajil*) pottery.

The Taegongni site was even larger, extending over 5,000 sq m directly on the river bank. The first report describes fifty-one pit houses (Choi, Kwon and Kim 1989), while the second includes seventy-five dwellings (Suh and Song 1989). These are divided into four time periods, but even so it is a large site.

The Kungongni shell mound is a complex site near the seashore in Cholla Nam Do, with fourteen layers in five time periods, from the third century BC to the fourth century AD. The site is on the edge of a hill above a plain. The report (Choi S.N. 1988b) includes the first oracle bones found in South Korea. These are animal scapulae with burn holes, but without writing (Fig. 6.15), similar to those from Musan in the northeast. The pottery ranges from Mumun steamers with knob handles to Paekche jars with paddled exteriors. Artifacts include net sinkers and spindle whorls of clay; digging sticks, netting needles, arrowheads, harpoons and knife handles of antler; and iron axes, knives and fishhooks. Some ornaments were found, most interestingly small *gokok*, jades and shell bracelets. Faceted beads and tally sticks also appeared. In the second season an oval house with several post holes was unearthed. Many shells, fish bones and animal bones

6.13 Houses at Naksuri, Cholla Nam Do. After Choi, Lee and Lee 1989.

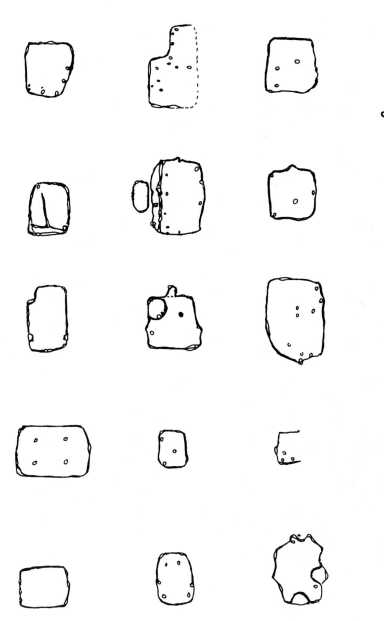

6.14 Floor plans of Naksuri dwellings. After Choi, Lee and Lee 1989.

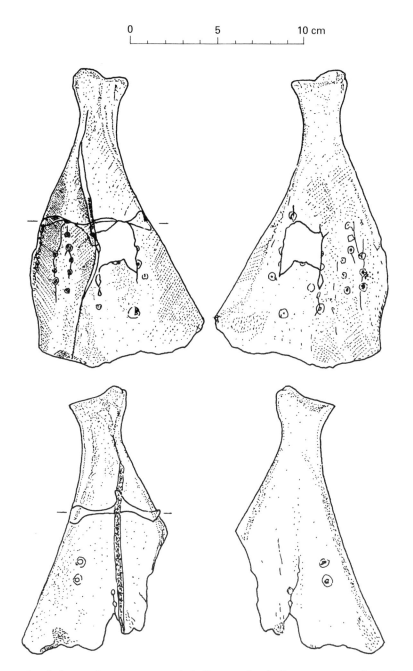

6.15 Oracle bones from Kungongni shell mound, Cholla Nam Do. After Choi S.N. 1988b.

were found, including a dog skull and pig bones (Choi S.N. 1988b). Charred wheat and rice grains were discovered in the third season, as well as a tunnel kiln, 6.3 × 1.1 m, for firing pottery (Choi S.N. 1989b).

Burials in the southwest consist of stone cists or jar burials, either of which may be covered by southern style dolmens. A stone cist grave at Hapsongni has the earliest glass discovered so far, in the second century BC. The tubular glass beads were accompanied by cast iron axes, as well as bronze bells, mirrors and swords (Puyo National Museum 1989). Bronze objects excavated from a deep stone-lined pit included the slender dagger, geometric mirrors and bells. These are accompanied by early *gokok*, small beads and horse trappings. The pottery – a roll-rimmed plain pot and a black long-necked jar – are local products (Anonymous 1969). In the Kobu area at least seven of the excavated mounds belong to this period, with iron spearheads, knives, pieces of gold ornaments and horse trappings (Rhee 1984:340).

The jar-coffin cemetery at Sinchangni produced fifty-three burials from the excavated area. One of these is in a single jar and one burial used three jars with the base broken out of the central jar; the rest are two-jar burials in various sizes of vessels placed mouth to mouth. Many of these jars have a pair of horn-shaped handles, and show no differences from pottery for daily use. No bones remained, but from the size of the jars most of the burials are assumed to be infants or children. A few small pots were placed beside the coffins as funerary gifts, but the only items found inside the jars were a piece of iron in one and a smooth flat pebble in another. A bronze pommel ornament, a stone axe, a polished stone arrowhead, a whetstone and two pieces of iron were found at the cemetery unassociated with any specific jar. This cemetery is dated to the "early iron age" (Kim W.Y. 1964).

At Wauri in the Yongsan river valley jar burials were excavated from mounds (Kwangju National Museum 1989b). Many of the mounds have several burials, like those of Kyushu in Japan. Artifacts found in the gray paddled jars include beads, iron objects and smaller globular jars.

Jar burials are much more common in the south than in the north, and are particularly prevalent in the southwest, in former Mahan territory (Fig. 6.16). Three jar-coffins found near Muyangcheng in Liaodong (Harada 1931) have been seen as corroboration of the movement of peoples from northeastern China to the south, the custom of jar burials being found in both places. Jar burials are not entirely unknown even in Siberia (Okladnikov 1964:87, 1965:157). Kaneko (1966) surveyed jar burials in Korea known up to that time, and compared them with Yayoi burials, finding important similarities.

Kim W.Y. (1986a) believes that most jar-coffins and stone-lined burial pits should be assigned to the early iron age in the southwest. By the second century BC a new burial form became prevalent, the wooden chamber tomb covered with a mound of earth, perhaps reflecting the arrival of King Chun, as mounded tombs are a northern style. However, jar-coffin burial, especially for children,

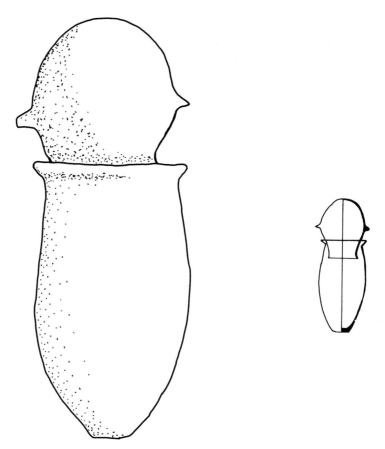

6.16 Typical jar burial arrangement.

continued in the southwest throughout the Paekche period. A plain pit burial containing iron agricultural implements was found at Sosan. A sword and simple jar were also present (Kim Y.B. and Han B.S. 1969).

Archaeological evidence has been found for large-scale irrigation by the end of the Sam Han period. A dam 3.24 km long in the alluvial plains near Kimje has produced C14 dates on reeds at its base ranging from AD 330 to 374 (Rhee 1984:230).

Southeast

Early pit graves in Choyangdong, Kyongju date from the first and second centuries AD. Small Chinese-style bronze mirrors from the Former Han dynasty, imported glass, and even a glass bead with a face on it from the western world suggest that a well-developed, complex society was in place (Choi J.G. 1981, 1982a). The pottery included reddish stoneware, jars with horn handles, and both black and white bowls (Chung Y.H. 1985). Footed gray ware was also found (National Museum Exhibit). First- to third-century burials in the area around Michu's tomb in Kyongju (Fig. 6.17) have unusual features such as horse burials and chimney-like constructions, which are difficult to interpret but also suggest complexity (Kim C.K. and Lee U.C. 1975). A gilt-bronze crown with three uprights was excavated from a tomb in Kyongsan-gun, North Kyongsang province. It is thought to belong to the ruler of a small state called Aptok in the early second century.

The Kujongdong tomb in Kyongju is a double tomb with both soft pottery (*Wajil*) and stoneware (*Kyongjil*). Built into a hill, the grave consisted of a square pit containing two wooden coffins. The north interment is 8 m long, but only 1.3 m wide. Military equipment, including iron spears, bronze swords with round pommel, iron axes and armor was abundant. The south coffin was 6 m long, with long spearheads laid out on the bottom. Bronze rattles were also found in the grave. These sites are believed to relate to the group called Chinhan.

Several shell mounds contained iron artifacts, including Kimhae, Yangsan, Puwondong, Cho Do, Songsan, Ungchon, Sugari and Nangmingdong (Yoon 1984). Associated artifacts include both weapons and tools made of iron. Five of these sites contained iron slag, and another (Sugari) had an actual iron furnace.

The interior of a hill fort at Songsan on the south coast of Korea east of Kimhae was partially excavated. The relatively flat top of the hill, covering about 200 sq m, contained dwellings surrounded by a stone wall. Evidence of iron smelting lies under heaps of shell and other living debris, including a *Wushu* coin issued in 61–58 BC. Thus the smelting is earlier than the deposition of the coin. A pottery imitation of a geometric bronze mirror was among the artifacts, suggesting that mirrors were important in the symbolic system (Choi M.L. 1976).

Similarly, on the top of Chaemisan hill, 215 m above sea level north of Ungchon, a large site produced over 40,000 artifacts. The pottery included both earthenware and stoneware, in shapes including steamers, lug handles and jars on cut-out stands. Engraved deer-horn pieces have been used for fortune telling, or for gaming. Iron implements include sickles, knives, arrowheads, spears and fishhooks. Tubular jasper beads and *gokok* shaped from animal bones and pottery were also found. Heaps of shell were found beneath half a meter of earth. The site was C14 dated to 1910 ± 150 BP (40 AD) (Kim J.H. 1967, Choi B.H. 1988).

Early graves at Yeanni are quite variable in size and grave goods, indicating ranking. One skull showed head flattening, a custom mentioned in the *Sanguo Ji*. The tomb, numbered 85, belonged to a middle-aged woman, and dates to the second century AD (Kim J.H. 1977, 1981).

Jar-coffins, in which the deceased were laid to rest in one, two or even three large jars, are assumed to have begun in the megalithic period in this region, since occasionally Mumun jars were used for the coffins. The most common form

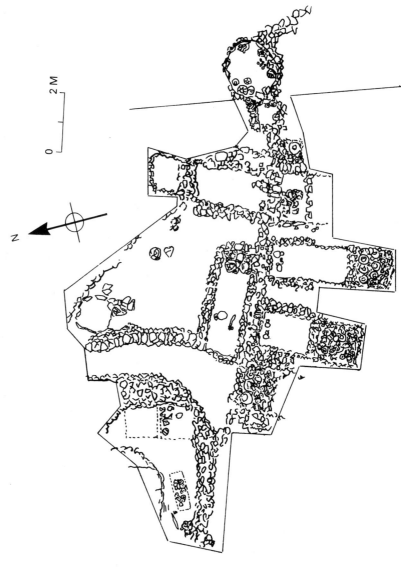

6.17 Excavations at Hwangnamdong, Kyongju. After Kang I.G. 1984.

consists of two jars placed mouth to mouth. At the Kimhae shell mound, for example, three burials in *Karak* type pottery were unearthed. Burials 1 and 3 contained bronze artifacts. Those of Burial 3 include eight bronze chisels, two bronze daggers and three dark green jade beads. Most jar burials, however, are in typical iron age jars. Jar burials are usually found in cemeteries, with or without southern style dolmens as markers (Kim W.Y. 1964). One jar burial at Chinaedong near Kimhae contained a Yayoi jar as a burial offering (Shim 1982a).

At a site in Nuk Do, Samchonpo, both dwellings and graves were discovered. The burials include pit graves, jar coffins and stone cists. The pottery includes triangular-rimmed large jars as well as necked jars without double rims, some ox-horn handles and crude bowls on pedestals. Yayoi pottery is also present, demonstrating trade with Japan. Implements include bone arrowheads, needles and awls, stone axes and semi-lunar knives and bronze knives and fishhooks. One well-preserved human skeleton was dated to the first century BC. An elderly woman had her canine teeth extracted (Pusan University Museum 1988), a custom which has also been noted in Japan (Harunari 1986).

The Yangdongni cemetery, also near Kimhae, has beads, iron tools and weapons, and hard-fired gray ware jars dated to the first to second centuries AD. The graves vary in size, but none is markedly larger or richer in contents than others (Han, Kim and Son 1989).

The Nopodong cemetery in Pusan included a combination of iron tools and weapons, glass beads and a crystal *gokok*, polished stone tools, and pottery with paddling marks. Pedestal vessels and iron swords were notable among the remains (Pusan City Museum 1988, Yoon B.Y. 1986, Kim W.Y. 1985:20).

Cho Do island is made up of two hills with a low-lying area between, where the present village is situated. Four areas were tested, all outside the village itself. At Area A, on a hill slope between 7 and 11 m in elevation, twelve subrectangular houses were exposed, some of them superimposed. The pottery was mostly triangular-rimmed plain vessels. A few horn-handled jars and pedestal bowls were found among the majority of tall wide-mouthed jars. Spindle whorls, awls, hoes, projectile points and antler tools were also found (Pusan University Museum 1989).

Important relics from the first century BC, attributed to early Kaya, have been found at Tahori near Musan, in Kyongsang Nam Do. The site, located beneath a rice paddy, has well-preserved lacquerware and other usually perishable items. Eleven burial pits contained wooden coffins, and two had jar coffins. The orientation of the graves is southeast–northwest. The tombs had been robbed, but underneath Tomb 1, which was waterlogged, a small pit contained a bamboo basket filled with important and unexpected items. For example, a lacquerware vessel with lid, a vessel on a stand still filled with persimmons (Fig. 6.18), a lacquerware sword stand, iron axes with wooden handles, writing brushes, and bows and arrows were found. A Han dynasty style bronze mirror, bronze daggers and various iron farm implements were also in the basket. *Wushu* coins

6.18 A lacquer stand filled with persimmons. From Tahori.

and glass beads suggest commercial exchanges. The coffins were unlike any found before in southern Korea, made of split and hollowed oak logs (Yi, Lee, Yun and Shin 1989). Very long cedar-log coffins have been excavated from later burials in Japan (Kondo 1986).

Several other cemetery areas have been excavated, including Toiraeri near Kimhae, where both beaten and plain pottery were excavated, some made with stands. The long, narrow pit graves also contained iron arrowheads and axes. Jar burials with no grave goods and stone-lined tombs containing iron and pottery were in the same cemetery. Kongpungni at Asan contained two tombs notable for their bronze, including *ge*-halberds, narrow swords, fine line mirrors, and axes (Yi K.M. 1989). Dated by the excavator to the first to third centuries AD, Samdongdong also contains a field of urn and stone-cist burials. Iron agricultural tools are particularly notable, along with many glass beads, crystal prismatic beads, *gokok* and Chinese style mirrors. The graves were oriented slightly east of true north (An C.B. 1984). Locally made copies of Han mirrors were found at Pyongnidong near Taegu (Yun Y.J. 1981), as well as Samdongdong (An C.B. 1984).

Summary

Discussions about when and where the state arose in Korea have been based on either the band-tribe-chiefdom-state evolutionary scheme, or on the documents, with archaeological evidence brought in to bolster the arguments. But the histories are considered suspect, and the evolutionary schemes tend to overlook the fact that states can fall as well as rise. The archaeological evidence indicates that polities formed and fell apart several times before a permanent state-based organization was reached.

It seems that a stratified state-level society was in place in the Lelang region well before the Han conquest. Attempts to play down the organization and complexity of the native state appear to me to be misplaced. It is easy to be misled by the fragmentary remains of archaeology. Choi Mong-lyong (1989) presents evidence of long-distance trade with China, especially the Yan coins, and argues on that basis that Wiman Choson was organized as a true state, although Pai (1989) feels the evidence is insufficient. Kayamoto (1962:100) asserts that Choson was considered "a big market" by Chinese traders. Accounts of the war of conquest (Gardiner 1969a) indicate that state-level societies of about equal power were engaged. Large armies fighting under generals express the ultimate control of a central state, with the power to punish. The tale of the conquest as we have it is told from the Chinese perspective, but it is evident that no unstructured barbarian horde was the enemy. Both Choi M.L. (1983a) and Kim J.B. (1977) assert that at least Wiman Choson (if not its predecessor, Ko-Choson) was a state-level society with coercive powers. It seems appropriate to consider it a tributary (Gailey and Patterson 1988), such as Patterson (1989) has proposed for southern Japan and Peru. This view is attractive because it does not demand continuous development, but acknowledges that states may fall as well as rise. It also accords well with the archaeological record. Wang (1982:1) has remarked regarding the Han civilization itself, "Seeing the remnants of its city walls and the scattered tiles there, one can hardly imagine the magnificent scale and the prosperity of Changan in the past." The city walls of Changan, according to Wang, took five years to build, with each section of the wall requiring about 145,000 laborers for one month (Wang 1982:2). Similar calculations could be made for the capital of Ko-Choson, smaller but still requiring extensive *corvée* or prisoner labor power.

Battles were fought under generals and armies were manipulated by state-level power. Although the areal extent of that state is neither described unambiguously in documents nor delineated by archaeological finds, by inference from the territory claimed at its defeat by Han China, its control was extensive. Ko-Choson must have reached at least as far south as the Han river, east to the sea of Japan, and as far north as the Tumen river. Whatever mechanisms may have been employed by Wiman and his successors to hold this territory together, or to extract tribute from this territory, the Chinese were relatively unsuccessful at emulating this feat and the area under Chinese rule shrank within a generation to the fertile plains in the northwest. The weight of the evidence, both documentary and archaeological, leans toward an interpretation of an organized, centralized bureaucracy with the power to mobilize both labor and armies, even in some of the peripheral areas, which may have been tributary to Ko-Choson even before Wiman arrived.

The tribes of the east, Ye-Maek and Ok-cho, seem to have been only loosely affiliated with Wiman Choson. The organization as described in the *Hou Han Shu* around AD 300 suggests ranked rather than stratified societies. Koguryo, however, coalesced as a state in the first century AD. In the south, there are traditions of settlement by Chinese and Sino-Korean refugees, including the former ruler of Choson, Ki Chun. Although archaeological interpretation is hampered by the paucity of finds that can be distinctly dated to this period, Kim Jong-bae (1975a, 1976) has boldly identified a cache of bronze and iron objects found near Iksan in North Cholla province as belonging to Ki Chun, and some recently discovered mirrors add more weight to the inference.

Locations of the six villages of Saro, the group that formed the Silla state, have been identified by Kim Won-yong (1976b), aiding in understanding the earliest stages in the formation of Silla. Groups of tombs and associated village areas which were at the edges of the hills bounding the Kyongju Plain rather than directly in Kyongju have been identified as the Saro sites. Each group had its separate cemetery, which suggests clan villages, and the locations suggest extensive agriculture. Hill forts near each cemetery probably protected the villages nearby.

Ranking is evident in the many cemeteries that have been excavated. The richness of the burial at Tahori, with its accidental preservation of lacquer cups and writing brushes, warns us that the burial furniture was often much richer than the remains usually divulge.

Chinese merchants had apparently been trading in Korea for some time, probably through the capital of Choson (Yu 1967:93) although the mechanism of trade is not known (Choi M.L. 1989). It is interesting to note that not only were many coins found in Lelang, but also molds for coins (Choi M.L. 1989), showing that they were locally minted. Coinage was forbidden to the provinces in 115 BC, but some coins were minted with dates of 136 BC, which of course is seven years before Lelang became a Han commandery (Kayamoto 1962:117). Yan knife-money was used: 5,000 pieces of it have been found in Choson territory, upon the upper reaches of the rivers rather than near the coasts, which suggests that the trade routes were over land and not by sea.

Internal trade in the south included ceramics and iron implements (Choi M.L. 1984b), and boat travel must have been the means of external trade. Iron tools and nails improved boat construction.

Iron was an important medium of exchange in the south, perhaps related to the fact that iron became a state monopoly in China. The iron mining and smelting of Chinhan may have been a response to that state monopoly – recall that there was a tradition of Chinese refugees into southeastern Korea, some of whom might have been traders seeking sources of iron, others perhaps blacksmiths.

Occasional Yayoi jars demonstrate connections with southern Japan. Some early rulers of Silla, the kingdom which arose in this region, belong to a blacksmith family according to tradition. A second-century gilt-bronze crown, with uprights like later Silla crowns, has been found in the territory of Aptok-guk, one of the Chinhan "states," suggesting more complexity than has generally been conceded for this period.

Artifacts from the western world found in Choyangdong point to long-distance trade. Such items have not been discovered in China, so it is possible that sea trade was carried on with groups farther to the south. In any case, the Korean peninsula was becoming increasingly tied to a much larger network, with China at its hub, beginning at the latest by 400 BC.

Trade aside, rice agriculture was the basis of the economy. The *Samguk Sagi* mentions regulations regarding agriculture, as well as the construction of reservoirs for irrigation. Early water control was confirmed in the southwest region.

Chinese documents relate that various ethnic groups including Han Chinese moved into the Korean peninsula. Some elements of Chinese cultures such as the funerary jade sets, mortuary figures and brick tombs suggest ethnic Chinese, and the Chinese language was inscribed on objects in tombs in the Lelang region. Pai (1989) discusses the process of acculturation to Chinese custom by native Koreans. In other regions, however, there is little that can be specifically attached to any named ethnic group. Indigenous pottery styles sprang up in various places, and developed along their own lines, along with mat-impressed gray ware obviously inspired by Chinese ceramics. Interfingered populations are the keynote of this period.

The states forming in the south had little power, and what they had did not extend far. The refugees were able to filter into the interstices between established groups, and for a few hundred years, remained free of the obligations imposed by expanding states. Eventually, however, they were all encompassed into one of the Three Kingdoms as will be seen in the next chapter.

CHAPTER 7

THREE KINGDOMS AD 300–668

Koguryo, Paekche and Silla were the Three Kingdoms (Samguk) which arose in the Korean peninsula. Another group of small polities, known collectively as Kaya, never became a true state, but existed alongside the Three Kingdoms (Fig. 7.1). Three Kingdoms archaeology consists largely of tombs and their contents, providing a one-sided, even if spectacular, view of the society. Little is known of the daily lives of ordinary people from settlements, although cemeteries with varying grave furniture allow some inferences of ranking. Excavated fortresses extend our knowledge of the organization and the material culture of the fourth to seventh centuries, and documentary evidence relating to this time period may also enlarge our framework of interpretation, when used with care.

The contrast between the large and labor-intensive tombs of the Samguk (Three Kingdoms) rulers and the smaller and simpler earlier burials bespeaks a notable difference in power and level of organization after AD 300. The ability to mobilize labor power to build great tumuli, the elaboration of craft specialists, the conspicuous consumption of goods made from precious materials, and the symbols of power and authority work together to indicate true states. The written documents confirm this view and amplify the archaeological evidence. The Korean histories, *Samguk Sagi* (History of the Three Kingdoms) by Kim Pusik and the *Samguk Yusa* (Memorabilia of the Three Kingdoms) by the monk Ilyon are useful, although not to be followed slavishly, for they were written many centuries after the events they record, and each has a point of view which guided the selection of topics to be included. Nevertheless these documents are thought to be based on histories of the Three Kingdoms which are now lost.

The Chinese state, frequently fragmented or divided between northern and southern dynasties after the Han dynasty, became reunited under the Tang dynasty (AD 618 to 907). Tending to its own wars and internal chaos in the period between the Han and Tang dynasties, China permitted the Korean states to develop along their own lines. The Korean polities developed linkages to various small Chinese states rather than any larger political entity on the continent. Meanwhile the various polities closer at hand had immediate impacts upon each other. Intermittent warfare and shifting alliances among the Samguk states, between them and various groups in the Japanese islands, and with various states in China characterize the Three Kingdoms period.

The fourth polity, variously called Kaya, Karak and Mimana (the Japanese name) was a confederation of related city-states which arose on the south coast and along the Naktong river in the region that was called Pyonhan in the early Chinese documents (see Chapter 6). In the *Nihon Shoki* and *Kojiki*, Mimana is linked to the early Japanese state, although the nature of this linkage has been inverted by Korean scholars (e.g. Hong 1988). Kaya was a phenomenon confined to the early centuries, for the cities were conquered piecemeal by Silla, and by AD 512 the entire Kaya territory was conquered and annexed, becoming part of Silla's expanding might. The Kaya region is now the focus of intensive archaeological exploration, and many new finds demand reassessment of Kaya's role in southern Korea. The Three Kingdoms are thus four. Koguryo, in the far north, was the first to organize itself effectively, so we begin there, and follow with Paekche, traditionally related to Koguryo. Kaya comes next because of its alliances with Paekche, and finally Silla. See Fig. 7.1 for the approximate locations of these polities, and the locations of the sites mentioned in the text.

The chapter is organized by region, rather than by chronology. In some cases a time factor is implicit in the region, for example with the shifting capitals of Koguryo and Paekche, but any definitive chronologies are within a region, rather than pan-Korean. Furthermore, a move of the capital did not necessarily mean an end to that region's importance. For example, both commoners and elites continued to live at Jian, and built stone tombs, long after the main city had moved to Pyongyang. Time differences will be noted within each section.

Koguryo

History

Koguryo's traditional founding date of 37 BC is later than the conquest of Wiman Choson by China and the foundation of the Chinese commanderies on the Korean peninsula, but as we have seen in the previous chapter, the region near Jian and Huanren (now in China) where Koguryo arose has been settled for a long time. When first noted in Chinese history, Koguryo consisted of a loose affiliation of five tribes, living in the mountainous region north of the Yalu river (Parker 1890:185). Although described as having little agricultural land, the archaeological sites imply successful farming (Rhee 1989). Some scholars (Osgood 1954:171, Hatada 1969:8, Choi 1971:21) echo the *Han Shu* in saying that the Koguryo had previously been a section of the Puyo polity, farming and herding villages on the Songhua river. On the other hand, Kim W.Y. (1986a:389) places the Koguryo antecedents in Liaoning, identified with bronze sites there, and Song-nai Rhee (1989) sees them as arising *in situ* north of the Yalu river. Wang M.H. (1990) suggests that the Wei-Mo (Korean Ye-Maek) were the Koguryo ancestors, having been noted in Chinese histories as far back as the Shang dynasty. Whichever is the case, Koguryo was pressed by the expanding Chinese empire and perhaps also the nomadic tribes on China's northern fron-

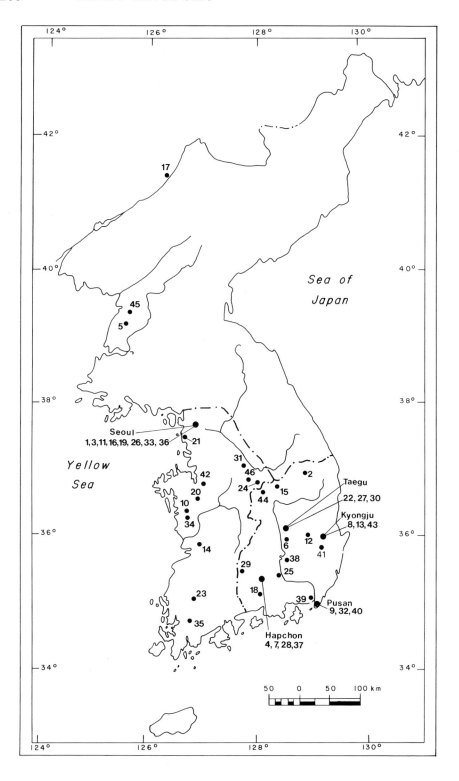

tier. In the process the Koguryo people became horse-riding warriors, posing intermittent threats to China's northeastern frontier.

By AD 12, when Koguryo revolted against Chinese control, their heartland was located along the middle and upper reaches of the Yalu river and its tributaries. Frequent battles and the fortunes of war are reflected in shifting boundaries. According to the *Wei Shu*, the Koguryo people conquered the east coast Korean tribes of Ok-cho and Ye-Maek, and extracted tribute from them. Gardiner (1969a) argues that in AD 233, Koguryo must have controlled the city of Xianbing (Hsienping), at the mouth of the Yalu, because Koguryo was able to send Wu officials home to China by sea.

According to the *Sanguo Ji*, Koguryo began as a confederation of five clans, each of which constituted a basic military unit. A council of the chief of each clan formed the ruling body of the group, with one chief elected as supreme commander. In the first century AD the chieftainship became hereditary (Joe 1972:22); Koguryo dated its origins from that point. A class system developed, in which the upper classes "do not work in the fields, there being some 10,000 of those who eat at raised seats and are supplied by the lower orders, who bring them rice, salt and fish from remote regions" (*Sanguo Ji* quoted in Gardiner 1969a:30). The classes included five ranks with the title *hyong*, meaning elder brother, followed by four with the word *saja* or messenger. The *saja* were minor officials, stationed in conquered lands to collect tribute.

Although Grayson (1976) believes the transmission of kinship to be strictly patrilineal, some recorded traditions are consistent with a matrilineal society, including matrilocality, in which the young husband went to live with his wife's family. The levirate, in which a widow marries her deceased husband's brother, was also practiced. An interesting example of the levirate occurred after the death of King Kogukchon (reign AD 179–97). His widow selected one of his brothers to be immediately elevated to the throne, for the queen declared that it was the will of her deceased husband. She then married the new king, retaining her position as royal consort for two successive reigns (Kim Y.C. 1977:31). At least one regency of a queen mother is recorded, in AD 53–63 during the minority of

---

7.1 Approximate locations of sites in Chapter 7.
1 Acha Sansong, 2 Andong, 3 Bangidong, 4 Bangyeje, 5 Chinpari, 6 Chisandong, 7 Chopori, 8 Choyangdong, 9 Hoechongdong, 10 Hwangsae, 11 Hwayang, 12 Imdangdong, 13 Inwangdong, 14 Ipchomni, 15 Ipsongni, 16 Isong Sansong, 17 Jian, 18 Kachoadong, 19 Karakdong, 20 Kongju, 21 Kosong, 22 Kuamdong, 23 Kumsong, 24 Kyesanni, 25 Kyodong, 26 Mongchon, 27 Naedongdong, 28 Okchon, 29 Paekchonni, 30 Pisandong, 31 Pobchonni, 32 Pokchondong, 33 Pungnamni, 34 Puso Sansong, 35 Shinchonni, 36 Sokchondong, 37 Songsanni, 38 Sunhungdong, 39 Taesongdong, 40 Tangkamdong, 41 Uisong, 42 Wanju, 43 Wolsongno, 44 Yangpyongdong, 45 Yonggangni, 46 Yonggongni.

King Taejo. During this time Koguryo was militant and expanding, but the queen's authority appears to have been unquestioned.

The tomb murals, showing husband and wife together, imply that women had considerable equality. A Chinese chronicle remarks, apparently with disapproval, on the fact that men and women danced and sang together until late at night. Marriages could be made at the will of the young couple, not arranged by the parents (Kim Y.C. 1977). The Koguryo people worshipped an ancestral goddess, who was both the daughter of the river god and the mother of Chumong, the legendary founder of Koguryo (Henthorn 1971:26). Clay and wooden images of this goddess were worshipped.

At least two social classes existed in Koguryo from the beginning; a noble class that lived well and an under class which may have been made up of conquered peoples (Joe 1972:40). The upper class were "fond of constructing palatial buildings" (Parker 1890), lived luxuriously with clothes of embroidered silk and gold and silver ornaments, and were buried in large and lavish tombs. Huge Koguryo palaces and tombs have been unearthed in both China and Korea.

Slaves were used for household duties and as middlemen in trade, not for production (Choi 1971:63). However they could be an item of export. War captives became slaves (if they were not ransomed or beheaded) and a person could be enslaved as a criminal penalty. A child could be sold into slavery by a poor family, and the children of slaves were themselves slaves. In the *Sanguo Ji*, Puyo chapter, there is reference to the burial of slaves with a tribal chieftain. Some archaeological evidence for such a practice does exist, although not in Puyo territory, but in Liaodong, and in the ninth and eighth centuries BC, much earlier than the Three Kingdoms period.

Tribute from conquered peoples was an important part of Koguryo's economy (*Shi Ji* Vol. 81: Dong I, Koguryo). The Ok-cho tribe, for instance, sent cloth, marine products including salted fish, and "beautiful women" for which they were famous. Between episodes of warfare, peaceful trade with China was carried on. Koguryo exported gold, silver, pearls, furs, ginseng, fabrics and slaves, and imported weapons, silk clothing, headdresses, books and stationery (Choi 1971:73). Mountain ponies were also a desirable export (Gardiner 1969a:34). Other than the fabrics, Koguryo's exports were raw materials and its imports were manufactured products.

A university was established in AD 372, to teach the Chinese language and the Confucian classics in order to train government officials on the Chinese model. The Chinese language and writing system were used for official purposes, and historical records were compiled in the Chinese fashion. The extant inscribed monuments demonstrate the literacy of the elite.

Buddhism was introduced from northern China, when two monks came to Koguryo, and each was allowed to erect a monastery. After Buddhism was officially recognized in AD 382, many temples sprang up, especially around Pyongyang (Henthorn 1971:55, and see the archaeology section).

The native shamanistic religion continued to coexist with Buddhism. The Koguryans "worshipped Heaven in the tenth moon at a great assembly, [and] ...made a pilgrimage to a great cave in the east, also in the tenth moon" (Parker 1890:186). Other divinities worshipped were the Puyo goddess and her son Chumong, the founding ancestor, as noted above. Sacrifices were also made to mountains and streams, and altars were erected to the spirits of earth and grain (Henthorn 1971:26). Shamans, probably mostly women, cured sickness, foretold the future, presided at national ceremonies and offered prayers for rain and blessings. Not only did early kings of Koguryo send for a shaman in times of illness, but as late as the seventh century AD a king appointed a woman shaman to help the country resist invaders (Kim Y.C. 1977:15). Thus, although Koguryo became somewhat Sinicized, it maintained native characteristics and traditions.

Koguryo expanded to the south in AD 313, defeating the Chinese Lelang colony. In spite of this southern conquest, Koguryo waited until AD 427 to create additional major cities as regional capitals – at Hwandosong on the Yalu, at Pyongyang, the former capital of the Nangnang colony, and at Hansong, north of the Han river. Several other towns and innumerable fortresses also came under Koguryo control.

The height of Koguryo's power came under King Kwanggaeto, who ruled from AD 391 to 413 (Fig. 7.2). His memorial stele still stands in Jian. The whole Liaodong peninsula as far as the Liao river became Koguryo territory. By the sixth century, Silla's expansion began encroaching upon Koguryo in the south. Silla finally defeated Koguryo with the help of Tang China in AD 668.

Jian and the Yalu river region

The earliest archaeological sites which can be attributed to Koguryo are near the present Chinese city of Jian on the north bank of the Yalu river. Remains of a great city, a protecting fortress and impressive mounded tombs can be seen in this region.

The ancient wall which surrounded the city of Jian is still in place on two sides. This wall, 8 km in circumference, was constructed of large shaped stones, with each level bantered in. Further fortification of exterior moats and dikes suggests that the town was prepared to defend itself against hostile raiding. The city wall is rectangular, following the pattern of Chinese cities, but the wall itself was constructed of stone, unlike the Chinese stamped-earth walls. Remains of a reservoir to insure the water supply have been located within the wall perimeter. Another fortified precinct only a few miles away still stands with a wall and gate. The site of a palace, with fancy decorated tiles, has been located (Kim W.Y. 1986a:266).

After the period of stone cairn tombs, described in the previous chapter, Koguryo tombs are distinguished by stone chambers which were often painted (Kim K.U. 1982, Kim W.Y. 1980d, 1983c). Enormous Koguryo tombs, con-

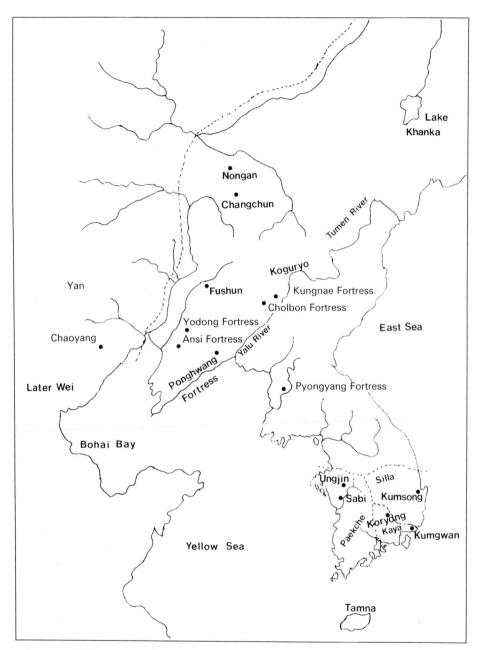

7.2 Koguryo at the height of its power. After Sohn, Kim and Hong 1970.

7.3 Dancing figures in the Tomb of the Dancers, Jian.

structed of cut stone and built on a square base in step-pyramid fashion, were an early type. The tombs were plundered in antiquity, and little remains except the architecture of the tombs themselves and wall murals painted in the interior rooms. The square-based burial mound continued to be a Koguryo tradition throughout the duration of the kingdom, although many other features of the tombs changed. While it is possible that the square-based tomb was an independent invention in the Jian region, it seems probable that it is related to square tombs in Liaoning, which date back at least as far as the Hongshan culture (Fang and Wei 1986). This new style of tomb appears as an elite style, quite suddenly and without antecedents in the Huanren Jian region.

The largest stone pyramid is known as the Tomb of the General, thought to be the burial place of King Kwanggaeto himself. It is almost 75 m long per side, which is about half the size of the Egyptian pyramids (McCune 1962:72). Monolithic stones, up to 3 × 5 m, are included in the lowest level. Four dolmen-like smaller tombs were placed in the four corners of the tomb precinct. The labor and organization that was needed to erect these massive tombs suggests the power of the Koguryo elite.

Later tombs consist of hemispherical earth mounds on a square base, oriented to points of the compass, covering an inner structure of stone. The countryside around Jian is dotted with these grave mounds, some of them large enough to dominate the landscape. Some variations in tomb style have been related to social status rather than chronology, for example differences in the burial chamber (stone-lined pit versus stone chamber) and square flat forms versus terraced pyramidal stone superstructures (Wei 1987).

Painted tombs reveal many details of elite lives, and also depict common people, as servants and entertainers. Clothing, architecture and activities depicted enrich the view of the Koguryo Kingdom. The Tomb of the Dancers, Tomb No. 1 at Jian, is one of the best known. A stone chamber lies beneath an earthen mound 50 m in diameter. The single chamber, plastered on the inside with lime, contained a round stone column. Paintings show dancers wearing long-sleeved jackets and trousers tied at the ankles (Fig. 7.3), similar to traditional Korean clothing. Armored soldiers on horseback are also depicted (Kim K.U. 1982). A few burial objects were missed by the ancient looters, including gold and gilt-bronze ornaments and glazed pottery. This tomb is dated to the fifth century (Rudolf 1978:332).

Tomb No. 4 was built of granite slabs and covered with an earthen mound 8 m high. Corbeled stone slabs formed a domed ceiling, covering three stone coffins and a stone altar in the central chamber. Paintings include Buddhist guardian figures with their hair in knots, wearing petal-like skirts and shoes with upturned toes. Tomb No. 5 is similar, but its paintings had been adorned with gold and precious stone inlays. These tombs are dated to the end of the sixth century.

Tomb No. 12 is a square earthen mound about 15 m across. On three sides, seven large rocks lean against the base. There are two interior chambers, each with an anteroom, and separate parallel passages with entrances on the west. The main chambers are square with corbeled ceilings (Fig. 7.4), and each is decorated with a painting of the noble and his wife seated together (Fig. 7.5). The southern chamber also depicts scenes from daily life: male and female servants using a mortar and pestle to pound grain, a stable, a granary and a large storage jar. A dancing scene and a procession of nobles are included, while a group of noble women in long pleated skirts stand behind a carriage. Two dogs, painted, guard the entrance, and the passageway contains paintings of a tiger hunt and a deer hunt. The north chamber contains similar scenes, and in addition a bear hunt is painted. A battle between groups of men in armor rages on another wall.

The latest tombs are those with strong Chinese influence. Tomb No. 17 is a square earthen mound, 50 m on each side, surrounded by a cobblestone pavement. On the front (south) side, where it survived intact, this pavement was 29 m wide and 30 cm thick. Some distance away a pair of stone pillars were placed in line with the tomb; they are thought to mark the beginning of a pathway leading up to it. The interior stone chamber was 3.55 × 4.4 m and 2 m high, roofed with corbeling, the passage 3 m long and 1.7 m wide. Vivid paintings still remain inside the chamber. These include a pair of guardians on either side of the entrance, one armed with bow and arrow and the other carrying a dagger. Animals of the four directions, one on each wall, are the major paintings (Kim W.Y. 1980d). Scenes from Chinese fairy tales show further influence from the Middle Kingdom. A ceiling painting of a white tiger and a blue dragon in combat was enhanced by gilt metal pieces, and jewels were used as eyes (Umehara 1952).

On the south bank of the Yalu river and along its tributaries, many other mounded tombs and settlements have been located. Dating to before the fourth century, the sites at Simguiri and Ronamni are particularly numerous. The tombs are found in various sizes (Chong 1975).

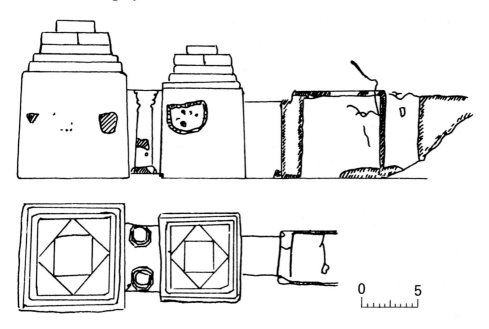

7.4 Corbeled ceiling in a Koguryo tomb, Pyongan Nam Do.

7.5 Painting of noble man and woman in a Koguryo tomb, Pyongan Nam Do.

Liaoning sites

In Liaoning, southeast of Fushun city, two areas of Koguryo burial mounds have been explored. Most of the nineteen tombs had semi-subterranean chambers of stone, covered with earthen mounds. Some have simple stone slab chambers, containing only one burial. Others have a larger chamber with corbeled ceiling, containing up to three burials, with heads to the south. Little grave furniture remains, although two pottery jars, a bronze bracelet and a gold-plated earring were found in one tomb (Rudolph 1978:335).

Ruins of a walled city lie nearby. The wall outlines, with a circumference about 2,300 m, follow the natural contours of the hills. Gates were located in the north, east and south sides. Bricks, tiles and bronze coins were unearthed along with many iron artifacts: plowshares, hoes, axes, horse and chariot fittings, spears, arrowheads, cooking pots and nails (Rudolph 1978:336).

To commemorate Koguryo victories in the Liaoning region, a monolith 6.34 m high, inscribed with 1,800 Chinese characters, was raised at Jian in AD 414. The military career of King Kwanggaeto (also known as Hotae Wang) is highlighted, including the defeat of sixty-four castles and 1,400 villages (Han W.K. 1970:47). This inscription has been a source of controversy since its rediscovery by the Japanese more than a century ago (Hatada 1979, Hong 1988, Hudson 1989), but the Koguryo accomplishments recorded on it are not disputed.

Central Korean sites

In AD 427 the primary Koguryo capital was relocated to the vicinity of Pyongyang. Archaeological remains of this period include both a fortress and a royal palace as well as extensive tombs. The palace, at the foot of the hill on which the fortress was built, was almost as large as the entire walled city of Lelang times – 622 m on a side. Buildings up to 80 × 30 m in size were lined up in rows along streets, and gardens included artificial hills and lotus ponds.

Beginning in AD 552, a new walled town with side streets was built, having a circumference of 15 km. On Taesongsan, "Great Fortress Mountain," a fortified wall 7 km long provided additional protection for the capital. There were twenty gates and towers in the wall, and wells, storehouses and armories within.

Three Buddhist temple sites from the fifth century have been excavated near Pyongyang. The most notable had a large central octagonal pagoda made of wood. Halls faced it on the north, east and west (Kim W.Y. 1986a:266).

Koguryo graves in the vicinity of Pyongyang are found in clusters. Like those farther north, they have been thoroughly plundered. The Twin Pillar Tomb in Yongganggun has two octagonal pillars between the main chamber and the anteroom, an uncommon architectural feature (McCune 1962:76). Many lively paintings decorated this tomb, including a group of noblewomen in pleated skirts, an armed warrior riding an armored horse, and an ox-drawn two-wheeled chariot with a canopy.

Near Chinpari, 20 km southeast of Pyongyang, a group of fifteen tombs has been explored. Legend ascribes the largest to Chumong, the legendary founder

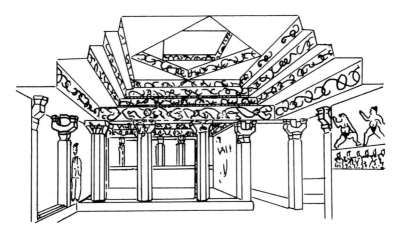

7.6 The interior of Anak Tomb No. 3.

of Koguryo; it has been well kept and tended on this account. The other mounds, of various sizes, have all been visibly plundered. These mounds have square bases, and entrances in the south. The stone passageways led to chambers with stone doors that moved on pivots. Tomb No. 4 had paintings of the animal symbols of the four directions (blue dragon of the east, red phoenix of the south, white tiger of the west, and black tortoise of the north). The ceiling glittered with stars made of gold foil (Umehara 1952).

Near the mouth of the Taedong river, in the Taebang district 16 km north of Sinchon, the discovery of a painted tomb with a long inscription has created some controversy. The Anak Tomb No. 3 is generally Koguryan in style, with a square base, 33 m on each side and 7 m high. The interior is laid out like a palace, with multiple stone chambers made of limestone slabs. Four rooms surround a central room with eighteen limestone columns (Fig. 7.6), although the plan is not quite symmetrical. The interior is 10 × 8 m at the widest point (Ch'hae 1959). The murals show the tomb inhabitant riding in a carriage, with hundreds of attendants including armed footsoldiers, bowmen, and knights on armored horses. The controversy that surrounds the tomb involves the interpretation of a long inscription. Although it names the tomb occupants as Tong Shou, the last Chinese ruler of the Taebang commandery, and his wife (Fig. 7.7), the date of AD 357 fixes the entombment *after* the historical date for the fall of the Chinese commanderies in 313. Gardiner (1969a:52–8) interprets the inscription as indicating the continuation of Chinese rule until the death of Tong Shou. The tomb would then be understood as a Lelang tomb rather than Koguryo. The pattern of grave features has many similarities with Koguryo practices, however, and Kim J.B. (1977), along with some North Koreans, attributes the tomb to a Koguryo king. However, the inscription surely speaks for itself.

7.7 Tong Shou's wife, from Anak Tomb No. 3.

Koguryo-style tombs have also been found on the upper reaches of the North Han river. They are likely to be burials of lesser officials during the era when Koguryo territory extended to this region. No burial goods remained in Tomb A at Kyesanni, but Koguryo-style potsherds were abundant. The basic structure of the tomb, a stone mound 9.5 m in diameter (Hwang 1984b), relates it to early Koguryo tombs rather than late ones. Tomb B was only 6 m in diameter, with a stone mound covering a rectangular burial chamber 3 × 2 m. The Yangpyong-dong A site is an example of a cairn (piled stone) tomb. Tomb No. 1 is 7.2 m high, and 29 × 25 m at the base (Choi and Im 1982). Tomb No. 2 is even larger, 60 × 57 m in plan and 9 m high (Bae 1984). At Sinmaeri on Jung Do Island a stone chamber tomb with a corbeled ceiling was excavated, while another Koguryo tomb near Yonggongni had been destroyed by plowing (Hwang 1984c), but seemed to be of the square-based type.

Baelz (1910) mentions Koguryo graves of quite large size in Wonsan, on the east coast. One granite step-pyramid is 25 × 20 m at the base, constructed of cut stones. River cobbles make a round mound at the top. A second similar tomb is on top of a hill nearby. The local people, according to Baelz, believe that Wiman and his son are buried here, but the style of these tombs is late, and the attribution is unlikely.

Kim Won-yong (1986a:390) postulates a change through time in the content of Koguryo wall paintings. The earliest style depicts only the deceased couple while later ones show them enjoying various entertainments, such as dancing and wrestling. Influence from China appears in early sixth-century tombs, with paintings of the deities of the four directions, temple guardians and flying spirits. Constellations depicted on tomb ceilings (Fig. 7.8) and on gameboards show the importance of the Great Bear, still revered by *mudang*s in Korea as *Chilsong*, the seven stars.

Few Koguryo artifacts have come to light. Some green-glazed pottery and gilt-bronze coffin ornaments, as well as remains of lacquered coffins, were recovered from tombs near the Yalu river. Near Pyongyang, a ceramic Buddhist figure and

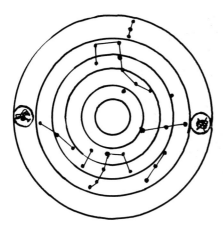

7.8 Constellation (Great Bear) painted on ceiling in Tomb of the Wrestlers.

a clay mold for such a figure, both made of fine porcelain clay, have been unearthed (McCune 1962:78). The National Museum of Korea exhibits a tripod with low feet, a white jar with stamped design, and a tall gray jar with painted checks as Koguryo pottery, but no specific provenience is given. An inscribed bronze bowl with lid, dating to AD 415 and including the name of King Kwang-gaeto, was found in a Silla tomb. One Koguryo gold earring was found when the railroad station in Pyongyang was built, and two Koguryo gilt-bronze crowns are exhibited, one in the Seoul National Museum and one in the museum in Shenyang, Liaoning, China.

A recently discovered monument at Ipsongni marks the southward pro-gression of Koguryo. A stone monolith with an inscription in Chinese charac-ters, the stele commemorates Koguryo victories in central Korea. Some controversy has arisen over the exact date of the monument, but scholars are agreed that it is mid-fifth-century AD (Kim W.Y. 1980a:5, Chung Y.H. 1979).

In AD 631, Koguryo protected its western flank with a wall stretching from modern Ning-an, now in Jilin province of China, to the Gulf of Bohai. This wall took sixteen years to build, requiring *corvée* labor of massive proportions. Although less substantial than China's Great Wall, it was effective, keeping out invaders until the combined forces of Tang China and Silla defeated Koguryo in 668 by simply bypassing the walls.

The archaeology of Koguryo indicates a stratified society with a well-provisioned and powerful elite able to mobilize considerable labor power to build elite tombs and public works. A diversified settlement system with capital cities, smaller walled towns (Fig. 7.9) and unprotected villages reflects the social stratification. Scenes from tomb murals depict servants, entertainers and war-riors as well as nobles. They demonstrate a continuity in dress and house styles from Koguryo to historic Korea, as well as indications that the Koguryo elite were literate in Chinese and participants in the Chinese Interaction Sphere.

7.9 Walled city depicted on a tomb at Yangsuri.

Paekche

History

The state of Paekche is known as the most refined and artistic of the Three Kingdoms. According to the *Samguk Sagi*, Paekche was founded in 18 BC when Onjo and his brother Piryu, sons of the same Chumong who is credited with founding Koguryo, moved south. A fort near Inchon on the central west coast has been attributed to Piryu's settlement (Bacon 1961), but the area proved to be unsuitable and the fort was soon abandoned. Onjo, who built his headquarters on the Han river near the present city of Kwangju, had better luck. Several forts from this period still exist.

Little is recorded of the early years. Rogers (1960) has pointed out discrepancies in the king lists, and believes that earlier history is fabricated for the sake of establishing early claims. Gardiner (1969b) is also skeptical regarding the early years, and believes that Paekche was not a kingdom until the mid-third century AD. The eighth king, Koi (reigned AD 234–85), is said to have had a complex administrative system with six ministries and sixteen administrative ranks (Joe 1972:27). The state of Paekche was in touch with polities in both western Japan and southern China. According to the *Qin Shu*, the Chinese emperor in 371 "sent an envoy to appoint King Yu-Ku of Paekche General of the East and Prefect of Lelang." Since the Lelang commandery had disappeared, this appears to have been more an effort to secure an ally than to continue Chinese claims on the Korean peninsula (Best 1982).

The government of Paekche is usually purported to have been imposed by northern invaders, whether the specific legend of Onjo is cited or not. However, the previous Mahan people were organized into a society which featured towns and some complexity (see Chapter 6). Documentary sources describe the territory of Paekche as divided into twenty-two administrative districts, each controlled by a member of the royal family (Choi H.C. 1971:51). The central government was managed by six ministers, tending respectively to the royal household, finance, education, security, internal affairs and defense (*Sui Shu* Vol. 81, Dong-I Chuan, Paekche). The ministers were replaced every three years, apparently in the hope of avoiding corruption. The rulers lived in fortified palaces and fortresses, in Chinese style, separated from the common people. Ranked officials had prescribed styles of clothing. For example, the highest six levels of officials were allowed to wear silver flower-shaped ornaments on their hats (*Pei Shu*, cited in Parker 1890:214), perhaps like the gold cut-out ornaments which were found in the grave of King Munyong and his queen.

The Paekche region is one of Korea's most productive rice-growing areas, and the economy was basically agrarian. Arts, handicrafts and industries were centralized and controlled by the state. In particular, the production of weapons, other metal products and fabrics such as silk and cotton were under the control of separate departments. According to the *Sui Shu* (Parker 1890:218), a vassal state called Tanmenlo, noted for its many deer, was tributary to Paekche. This region is thought to be Cheju Island, off the south coast of Korea, where metal artifacts do suggest connections with the peninsula.

The Paekche court was literate in Chinese in the fourth century, and possibly earlier. During the reign of King Kungwang (AD 375–83), a Paekche scholar was sent to the Yamato court in Japan to teach the Chinese classics. Buddhism was introduced to Paekche in 384, a mere dozen years after Koguryo accepted this new religion.

Interaction was friendly with the Yamato polity in Japan. Paekche exported Buddhism, literacy and many art forms to Japan. The crown prince of Paekche was sent to Japan in 393, cementing the relations (Hong 1988, Best 1979). In 405 two scholars were sent from Paekche to tutor the heir apparent (McCune 1962:66). Tombs with contents which have close stylistic ties with Paekche have been found in Japan, for example the recently excavated Fujinoki tomb near Nara.

Relations between Paekche and Koguryo were frequently antagonistic. King Kwanggaeto of Koguryo, conqueror of the north, attacked a number of Paekche fortresses along their common border near the Han river, capturing some of them. In 404 the Koguryo navy "defeated a Japanese fleet sent to aid Paekche" (Bacon 1961:7), and in 475 Koguryo conquered the Paekche capital and killed the king. The rest of the Paekche government fled south, setting up a new capital on the Kum river where the present city of Kongju lies. According to the *Sung Shu*, published in 488, Paekche developed as a seapower in the middle of the fifth century. Its troops attacked Koguryo in Hwanghae province, killing the king outside Pyongyang.

The Han river region continued to be a battleground. Silla and Paekche combined to attack and drive out Koguryo in 551. This was a Pyrrhic victory for Paekche, however, as Silla took sole control of the region two years later. This move gave Silla a much-needed port on the Yellow Sea. Paekche had simply exchanged Koguryo for Silla as her major enemy.

The Paekche capital was moved still farther south in 538, to a location near the present city of Puyo. The combined forces of Silla and Tang China defeated Paekche in 638. The Yamato fleet arrived too late to avert the defeat, and legend relates that the ladies of the court plunged into the river to their deaths from a rock above, to avoid capture by the foreign powers. A pavilion stands in commemoration on the Rock of Falling Flowers.

Archaeology

Paekche archaeology is hindered by the fact that little was left standing after the armies of Tang and Silla plundered and burned. Tombs were looted, cities burned and temples destroyed. Thus only a rare intact tomb and bits and pieces elsewhere remain of Paekche's civilization. Most surviving examples of Paekche art and architecture are to be found in Japan, some of them carefully preserved as sacred relics.

However, excavation of forts, temples and palaces in recent years have revealed new details about the elite, and some excavated cemeteries and villages allow glimpses of the life of the common people. The archaeological remains are best discussed by region, from north to south, which is roughly in chronological order since most of the remains belong to the elite and their capitals.

Han river sites

The remains of a walled town, perhaps Paekche's first capital, are found on the south bank of the Han river about 20 km east of Seoul. The village of Pungnamni now occupies the site, preventing a thorough excavation, but several trenches have revealed some of the old city. The remains of a rectangular earth wall, about 5 m high, surround the village on three sides only for the fourth side has been destroyed by the river. Present dimensions of the enclosure are 1,500 m north to south, and 300 m east to west. The original wall is estimated to have been about 4 km in circumference (Kim W.Y. 1967a). Test pits produced potsherds and iron clamps probably used in the architecture of wooden buildings. There was also evidence of hearths, and broken roof tiles. Five kinds of pottery were identified, one plain like Mumun, one with a coarse lattice pattern (Fig. 7.10), Kimhae pottery, Silla pottery and lustrous black ware (Fig. 7.11).

Not far from Pungnamni, Mongchon fortress was built near the south bank of the Han river. Recent C14 dates on wooden artifacts date the site to AD 230 (Kim W.Y., Im H.J. and Pak S.B. 1989b). Irregularly circular in shape, with walls 2,285 m long, the site covers 96 ha (Fig. 7.12). An earthen wall filled in

7.10 Lattice pattern vessel.

gaps in the hills that surround this natural bowl. Post holes indicate that a wooden fence strengthened the stamped-earth wall, and an outer moat further defended the fortress.

House floors are evidence of the ordinary family life which took place within the walls, rather than just an army garrison. *Ondol* floors have been found in some areas. The presence of many sherds of brown-glazed stoneware from the Chinese Western Jin dynasty (AD 265–316) suggests trade with the continent, although most of the pottery is locally made. Decorated roof tiles, indicating an area of elite housing, and Chinese celadon inkstones of the fourth century were found on a gentle slope (Jin 1989a). Subsistence activities are indicated by the remains of iron sickles, knives and fishhooks, as well as spindle whorls and weights (Barnes 1988:442).

A cylindrical pottery stand with horizontal ridges spaced along the cylinder and cut-out designs in the manner of Silla and Kaya has been interpreted as a forerunner of the *haniwa* cylinders placed around tombs in Japan from about 350–600 (Kim W.Y. 1986a:231). One would like to see more of these vessels to be convinced. Other pottery and stoneware shapes include tripods on short stubby legs, footed vessels and globular jars. The pottery has been divided into chronological types. The Mongchon type includes gray and blue-gray stoneware

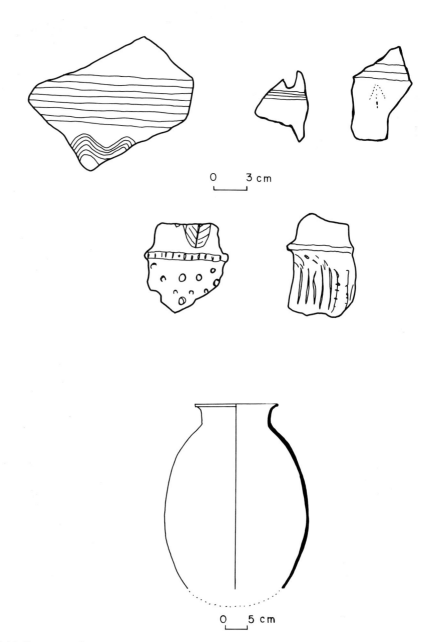

0   3 cm

0   5 cm

7.11 Pungnamni pottery.

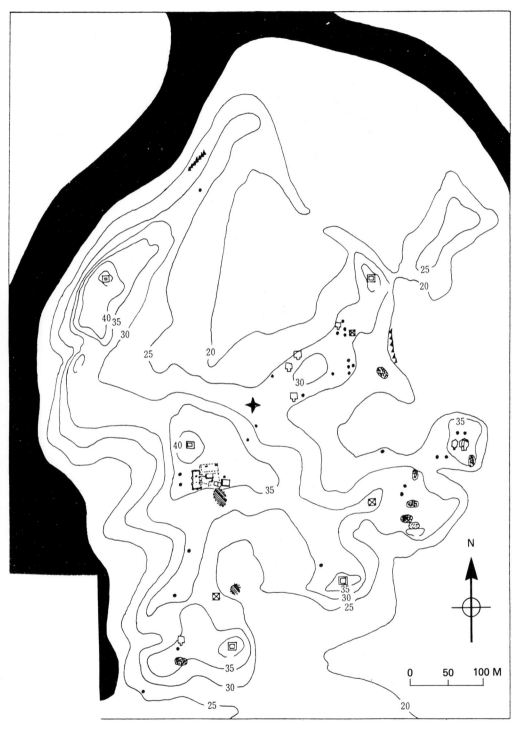

7.12 Mongchon fortress plan.

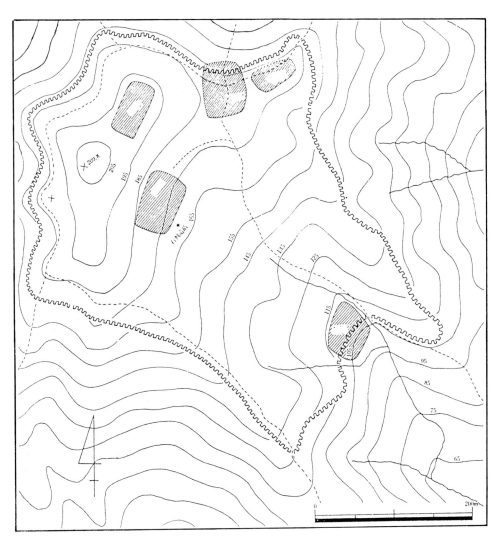

7.13 Isong Sansong.

dated AD 275–450. The Kuidong type is softer, dark gray to black or yellow-brown, and is ascribed to Koguryo after it conquered and occupied Mongchon fortress (Pak 1989b). These jars often have narrow necks and four strap handles. Tripod jars with lids are also associated with the Koguryo occupation. Pieces of two lacquer trays and a red bowl are the earliest lacquer found in this region (Kim W.Y., Im H.J. and Pak S.B. 1988). Metal artifacts include scissors, horse-bits, socketed hoes, spade tips, and nails and cramps.

Twenty-seven large storage pits contained gray Paekche globular jars covered with check-stamping, and pieces of horse armor made of ox-horn. A cache of iron arrowheads lay by one pit (Kim W.Y., Im H.J. and Lim Y.J. 1987).

Another area near the wall yielded swords and spears. The fortress-town was prepared for a long siege. Ultimately, however, it could not resist, and fell to Koguryo. The fortress was rebuilt by Koguryo, as later pottery styles attest.

On a high hill, 207 m in elevation, the fortress of Isong Sansong commands an excellent view of the valley sites previously discussed (Fig. 7.13). Removal of the vegetation has revealed an impressive stone wall, largely collapsed, which surrounded the fortress for 2 km. Two substantial buildings stand near what may have been the entrance, guarding a reservoir. Higher up the hill, stone footings for columns and large roof tiles identify the site of a palace. Forty-eight stone column bases are placed in four rows (Fig. 7.14). Nearby an unusual nine-sided building was located.

Clay and iron horse figurines, wearing saddles and bits, appear to be votive objects, and are thought to date to Silla times. United Silla pottery found among the foundation stones of the largest building shows that the hilltop was reoccupied with Silla's conquest of the region (Kim B.M. and Shim K.C. 1987). Across the Han river on the north lies the Acha fortress built by Koguryo, which has not yet been excavated.

Numerous other earth and stone fortresses are found in this region (Fig. 7.15). Some are known to have been used as late as the Yi dynasty (1392–1910), but they might have been established in earlier times. These forts were probably rebuilt many times according to the exigencies of the times, for the placement of forts to guard cities, passes and river crossings continues over the centuries. A few forts are still occupied or used as lookout posts by the Republic of Korea army. Bacon (1961) located sixteen forts in the vicinity of Seoul which might have been built (or at least used) by early Paekche. A fort known as Namsan Kosong is located on a hilltop southeast of the Yellow Sea port of Inchon. It is relatively small, and contains a shell midden. A local legend attributes this fortress to Piryu, brother of Onjo, first king of Paekche (Bacon 1961:35).

Several Paekche tombs near the Han river have been excavated. For example, an earthen mound, 1.8 m high and 14.8 m in diameter, covered a circular stone wall which enclosed a burned wooden structure at Kuidong, Seoul, on the top of a hill. The structure was not a typical burial chamber. It had an *ondol* floor, with an iron kettle at one end. A shaft 2.3 m deep and 2.7 m square was dug in the middle of the structure into the earth below. It bore no traces of coffin or skeleton, but was filled with burnt earth (Kim W.Y. 1978). Burial gifts included a pottery steamer with three holes drilled in the base, iron sickles, spearheads, an axe, cultivating forks, a plowshare and a tall brownish jar with lug handles (Fig. 7.16). This find may date to the Mahan, or pre-Paekche period, on the Han river, as the lug-handled jar would suggest. However, Kim Won-yong (1977a) proposes an alternative interpretation, that it could have been a mortuary house to keep a king's body in the years following death while a proper tomb was being prepared. It would be surprising, however, for a charnel house to be heated. Perhaps there was a dwelling which antedated the tomb.

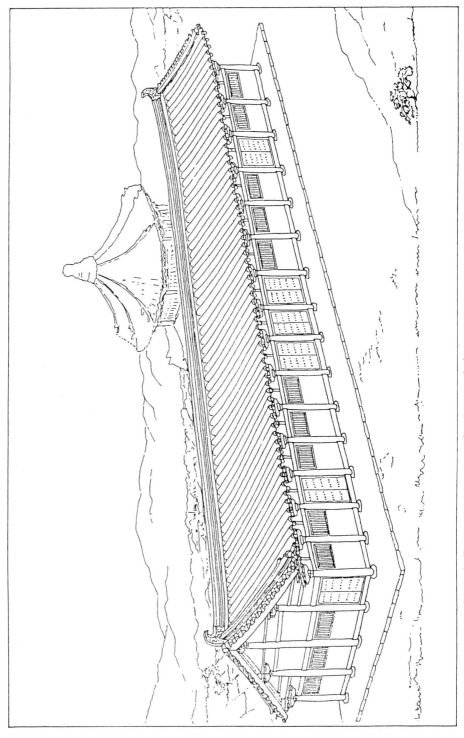

7.14 Reconstruction of long hall at Isong Sansong. After Kim and Shim 1987.

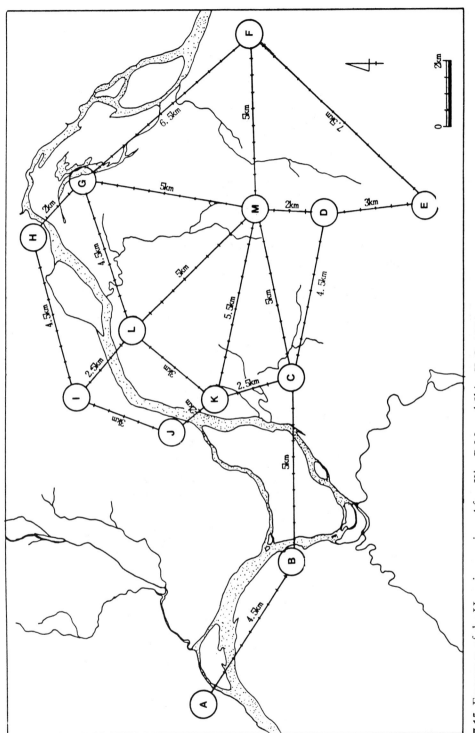

7.15 Fortresses of the Han river region. After Kim B.M. and Shim K.C. 1987.

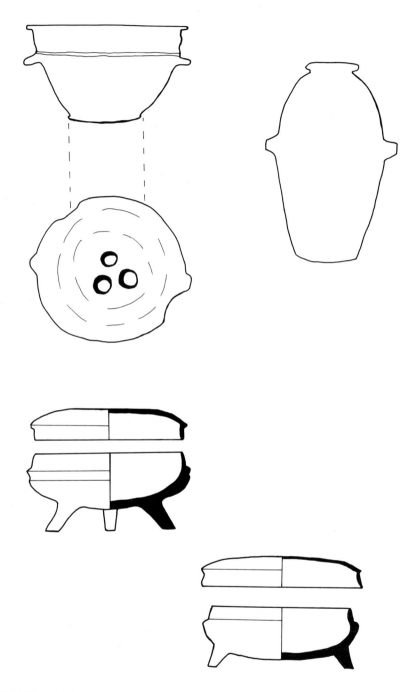

7.16 Vessels from Kuidong tomb.

Six stepped stone pyramid tombs of various sizes have been adduced as evidence of the connection between the ruling families of Paekche and Koguryo. Sokchondong Tomb No. 3 is 4.6 m high, 30 m in diameter, and has the plan and profile of a three-tiered step pyramid, like some Koguryo tombs found near the Yalu river (Seoul National University Museum 1975, Lim 1987). Two gold earrings and three gold ornaments (perhaps from a crown) were found in the tomb, although it had been looted. Celadon from the Eastern Jin (317–419) of the Six Dynasties period in China was also placed in the tomb.

Tomb No. 4 at Sokchondong is another pyramidal stone tomb 2.3 m high, while Tomb No. 1 contained two separate rectangular burials. A third stone tomb is found at Yangpyongdong (Kim W.Y. 1974a, Sokchondong Archaeological Team 1987). Jar and pit tombs were unearthed nearby. Several pit tombs were in a row oriented in the same direction. Each grave contained a pot or two, but nothing else, implying social differences rather than temporal ones. Another area has stone-lined pits with various orientations.

Near Bangidong, also in Seoul, a group of earthmound tombs was excavated (Chamshil Area Archaeological Team 1977). Tomb No. 5, a small stone-lined pit, may be the earliest. Tomb No. 6 has a rectangular stone chamber with a longitudinal partition, and Tomb No. 4 is a stone chamber tomb with an entrance passage (Kim B.M. 1977, An and Jeon 1981). Tomb No. 1 has been reconstructed in a park. It consists of a stone chamber with a vault-shaped ceiling, and an entry chamber. How these mounded tombs related to the stone pyramids is unclear.

In the Karakdong area of Seoul, two other early Paekche mounded tombs were excavated (Chamshil 1977). Traces of wooden coffins were found in the burial pits beneath, and one jar-coffin was found. Tomb No. 2 contained a burnished black pottery vessel (Yun 1974).

Possibly from the same time period, a small tomb in Pobchonni, contained a rectangular pit tomb lined with stone and covered with boards. Three gray pottery vessels accompanied the burial, but the most interesting item was a celadon sheep, a Chinese import. It is identical to a piece found in China near Nanjing, dated at around AD 350 (Kim W.Y. 1973:12). Tiger-shaped containers have appeared in two other Paekche tombs (Kim W.Y. 1979a:6).

Southern sites

As noted from the Seoul area discoveries, the burial customs within the Paekche kingdom were not uniform. Jar burials, cremations, stone tombs under mounds and brick tombs have all been found in southeastern Korea. It is difficult to sort out their meaning, but perhaps the burial styles belonged to different ethnic groups, for they coexist for a considerable length of time.

Several jar-coffin cemeteries have been found that are believed to date from Paekche times. Some of these consist of square or keyhole-shaped mounds, each of which has several jar burials in the top (Fig. 7.17). Most jar burials of this

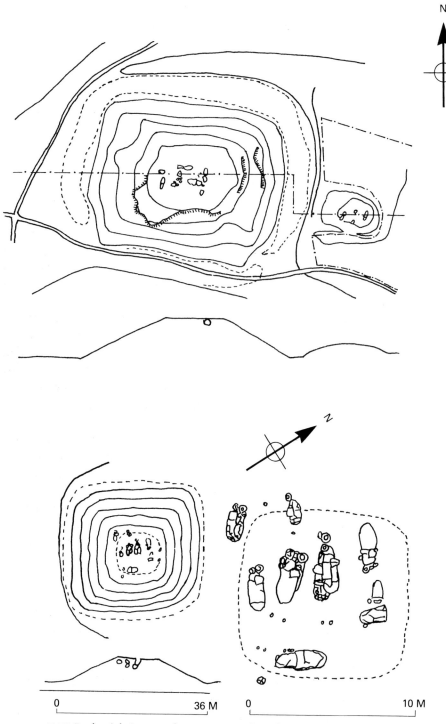

7.17 Jar burials in top of square mounds. After Kang I.G. 1984.

region appear to have contained the full body rather than ashes. Typically a large and small jar were placed mouth to mouth, but in some cases three jars were used. A major concentration of such coffins is found near Naju in the southwest (Kwangju National Museum 1988a). Burial gifts are rare in these jar-coffins, but a gilt-bronze earring was found in one jar (Kang 1973). A gilt-bronze crown accompanied by bronze shoes was discovered in a jar-coffin at Shinchonni, Naju (Fig. 7.18) (National Museum of Korea 1986), demonstrating that jar burials are not class-linked.

At Ipchomni in Iksan, a Paekche gilt-bronze crown and burial shoes remained in a partly plundered stone chamber tomb, along with harness fittings and stirrups (Kim W.Y. 1987a). The tomb dates to around AD 500. Other tombs were found nearby, including one containing a gold crown decorated with bird and lotus designs.

Nearly 200 tombs, most of which had been plundered, have been located near Wanju. A tomb made of cut granite blocks contained two bronze belt plaques with a dragon design in openwork. Similar pieces have been found in Japan (Kim W.Y. 1974a). The cut-stone tombs of Kongju are seen as deriving from China after AD 475 (Kim B.M. 1976).

When the long-hidden tomb of King Munyong was discovered in Kongju, some of the missing richness of the Paekche era was revealed. Inscribed tablets give King Munyong's death as AD 523, followed by his queen in 526. His brick tomb was built with a barrel vault, in the style of southern China. Burial gifts, placed within and around the lacquered wooden coffins in the entrance tunnel, were lavish. The items in the coffins were in local styles, while Chinese artifacts were found outside.

The king and queen each wore a gold crown and bronze shoes, and the royal heads were placed on elaborate pillows. The king was accompanied by a silver belt and a sword, while the queen was adorned with jewelry. Her silver bracelets are inscribed in Chinese characters with the name of the maker. Jade *gokok* (curved jewels) and gold earrings with leaf-shaped dangles bear close similarity to Silla jewelry of the time, but the golden crowns are single cut-out uprights in floral designs, presumably attached to a cap of some perishable material, quite unlike Silla crowns (Fig. 7.19).

Chinese white porcelain of the Liang dynasty was found at the entrance gate, and lamps of porcelain were placed in five wall niches. In the entrance passageway two bronze bowls, each with a gold spoon, were placed in front of the engraved tomb slabs, and a number of coins lay on top of the slabs. Behind the slabs a stone guardian animal crouched, and bronze cups were placed just before the coffins (National Museum of Korea 1971, Kim W.Y. and R. Pearson 1977).

Surprisingly little Buddhist imagery is present in this tomb. The lotus pattern on some of the bricks along with a small pendant worn by the queen which possibly represents a Buddha are the only reflection of the Buddhism that flourished in Paekche.

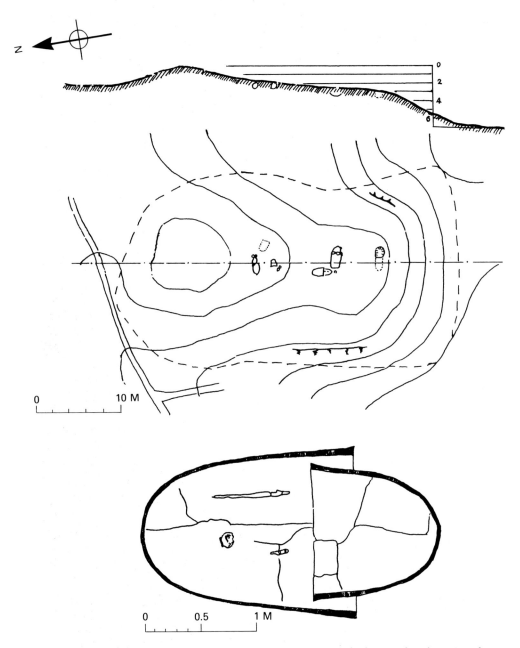

7.18 Jar burial containing gilt-bronze crown and shoes, Shinchonni. After
Kang I.G. 1984.

7.19 Crown from King Munyong's tomb.

Puyo is the site of the final capital of Paekche. A hillside near the city is covered with burial mounds from the last Paekche kings, queens and other elite (Kang 1977). Since they were constructed with stone-lined reentry passages, the tombs were easy to loot (An and Jeon 1981, Kim B.M. 1976, 1987). Traces of wall paintings, often too indistinct to identify the design, are all that is left of most tombs, although one retains paintings of the deities of the four directions on the stone walls of a simple rectangular chamber (Cho, Choi and Yoon 1989).

Two cremation urns from Puyo are assumed to be late, dated by a Tang dynasty coin which lay nearby. The practice of cremation is of Buddhist inspiration, but it did not become common in Korea until several centuries after Buddhism was accepted.

No Buddhist temples have survived from Paekche times, although a few stone pagodas and Miruks (standing Buddhas) still stand. Temple foundations near Puyo show that the layout was the same as early temples in Japan, duplicated there by Paekche architects. A rectangular wall enclosed an entrance gate. A large pagoda, the main hall and a lecture hall were all placed on a central axis. Excavation of the ruins of the Miruk-sa temple at Iksan, built in the early seventh century, reveals that three large halls, the largest 1,250 sq m, each had a pagoda before them. Fragments of wall paintings, roof tiles and a wooden door frame contribute to an understanding of the building's architectural details. Two skeletons, one male and one female, are unexpected (and unexplained) finds (Jin 1989b).

Several hill forts of Paekche age are located near the southern capitals and on the border with Silla. Most were constructed with irregular walls, following the contours of the hills, but a few are circular, simply surrounding a hilltop. One newly discovered fortress combines these two types into a complex shape (Yoon and Song 1977). Mount Chindang is the site of a Paekche fortress surrounded by a stone wall; Kumsong Fortress has an irregular wall around the top of a hill in Cholla Nam Do (Yi Y.M. 1989) with a rich grave, dated AD 350–450, nearby. Burial gifts in the stone-lined pit include a variety of iron artifacts: a double-edged dagger, three long swords, a spearhead, an axe, sickles and horse gear. Hard gray pottery jars also accompanied the burial (Rhee 1984:234).

Mount Puso near Puyo is the location of another ancient fortress site. Remains of a wooden palisade and a stack of roof tiles, some with lotus design, were among the discoveries. A dwelling with *ondol* heating system under the floor was uncovered (Jin 1989b) and another building was identified as a granary, because burned rice, barley and beans were found there (Yoon M.B. 1982). A walled settlement near Iksan has been investigated, and a palace site in Puyo has yielded roof tiles and square bases, both derived from Chinese architecture. An earlier palace in Kongju has post holes, but no stone bases. A stone-lined cistern was also excavated at this site. Hwangsae Fortress helped defend the capital from the west. It is a late fortress, one of several in this region (Song 1975).

Paekche kiln sites are among important recent finds. The tunnel kilns are angled up a hill, which allows high heat and produces hard-fired pottery (Kim *et al.* 1988). The whole question of pottery kilns and the capability of making stoneware is an important topic which has not yet been solved (Barnes 1989).

Paekche archaeology has produced fewer spectacular finds than the other two early kingdoms, but these recent discoveries demonstrate the possibility of uncovering yet more of this highly cultured society.

Kaya

History

A region at the mouth of the Naktong river and to the west of the river upstream for some distance was ruled by six polities (perhaps city-states) which collectively were known as Kaya. Of these, the two strongest groups were Ponkaya ("root" Kaya) in the area of present-day Kimhae at the mouth of the Naktong river, and Taekaya ("great" Kaya) in the Koryong region in northwestern Kyongsang province. The Kaya groups, although affiliated, never coalesced into a state. Kim J.H. (1982) argues that political and military parity among the smaller units prevented the development of a central state. The Kaya region was conquered by Silla in AD 532 and absorbed into the Silla state.

The basis of the economy was trade, especially trade in iron. Iron mines in this region were exploited, beginning in the third century BC, and iron was processed here into tools and weapons as well as ingots for exchange (see Chapter 6). Long-distance trade with the Japanese islands and China, as well as within the Korean peninsula, is known to have taken place, and some of the artifacts suggest relationships farther afield (Kim B.M. 1988). For example, a Scythian bronze jar has recently been excavated at Taesongdong, near Kimhae.

Many Japanese historians and archaeologists believe, based on the *Nihon Shoki*, that a region along the Korean south coast (called Mimana in Japanese) was conquered by the Yamato state and administered by it (Grayson 1977:67). This claim has been vigorously rejected by Korean historians and archaeologists as a revision to conceal the fact of Korean influence, and perhaps even conquest, of Kyushu and parts of Honshu (Hong 1988). A theory that "horse-riders" from "the continent" actually founded the Yamato state was propounded in Japan (Egami 1964), but the specifically Korean connection is often glossed over (e.g. Aikens and Higuchi 1982). Kim J.B. (1978a) disagrees with the horse-rider theory, on the grounds that neither literary nor archaeological evidence shows horse-riding to be prevalent in Korea. However, evidence for mounted warriors in southern Korea is piling up, especially in the Kaya region. In terms of documents, Silla sumptuary laws (Kim C.S. 1977) specify how many horses and what kinds of saddles the various "bone ranks" (see Silla section, below) were allowed, suggesting that all ranks and both sexes rode horses. Another Korean scholar has taken a different tack, suggesting that the tumulus builders in Japan (the supposed horse-riders) were actually Koreans coming from Kaya in the first wave and Paekche in the second (Kim K.U. 1974). A colorful presentation of this point of view can be found in Covell and Covell 1984. Considerable controversy also exists in Japan over the "horse-rider" theory, but those responses are outside the scope of this book.

Archaeology

Kaya archaeology of the fourth to sixth centuries AD consists almost exclusively of burials, although a few fortresses have been identified, with walls which encircle the tops of two hills with a high valley between. An Chun-bae (1982) summarized the archaeology of the region in a thorough study, listing all the known sites and their attributes, but considerable amounts of important data have emerged in the last decade.

With surveys for roads and dams in the Kaya region, several cemeteries of pit burials without mounds have been explored. Graves of various configurations have been unearthed in each cemetery. Im Hyo-taek (1978) summarized five areas of pit graves in the Kaya region. Generally, the graves are excavated into hillsides in rectangular or oval shapes. Most are oriented east–west, with the head to the east. No traces of coffins were found, but the pits suggest that the bodies were extended. Burial furniture is dominated by pottery (Fig. 7.20), with rarer items of iron and bone. Each grave has at least one large vessel with a stand, and a round-based jar. Mounted cups and wide-mouthed pots with mat or lattice pattern are often found.

Mounded tombs usually have long rectangular stone-lined pits, covered by a large stone cairn and a thin layer of earth. They are usually found on hill slopes. Lee Un-chang (1982a) has created a chronological ordering of Kaya graves in which larger rectangular stone-lined pits under mounds began around AD 300. These are followed by variations (extra pits for grave goods and their placement), and stone chamber tombs in the period 450–570. Kang's chronology seriates the burials at Yeanni (see Fig. 6.1 for location), and compares other sites with it. Thus, Samdongdong had two discontinuous units, one in the early fourth century and the other late fifth century. Tangkamdong burials fall between 450 and 500, while Chisandong ranges from 400 to 500 and Pisandong 450 to 550 (Kang 1989). This ordering is based on grave objects as well as the tombs themselves, and seems likely to stand the test of further excavations. Kim Se-ki (1985) has seriated "vertical entrance" tombs in the Kaya area, referring to graves in which the interment took place from above. Slab-stone cists and pit tombs have been treated in the previous chapter, as they are agreed to be early types. Stone chamber tombs begin in the fourth century. Between 450 and 550, many large chamber tombs with sacrificial burials have been found; Kim calls this the climax of the Kaya style. After the beginning of the sixth century the tombs were made with horizontal entrances. Each type could be accompanied by a separate chamber for burial gifts, which indicated higher status.

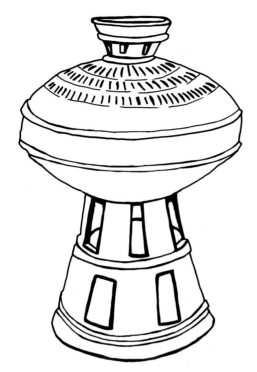

7.20 Kaya pottery vessel on a stand.

Artifacts found in stone-lined pit burials range from a few pieces of pottery to an extensive set of grave goods. The cemetery at Hoechongdong near Pusan includes only a pot or two and a few weapons in the narrow stone-lined graves (Chung J.W. 1983). Numerous examples of armor have recently been excavated from Kaya tombs. For example, Tomb 1 at Paekchonni included harness fittings, a quiver with iron arrows, pottery vessels, gilt-bronze earrings and belt, and other accouterments (Pusan University Museum 1986, Kim W.Y. 1987b). One tomb at Songsanni, west of the Naktong river, included iron armor, a gilt-bronze cap and gold earrings within the Three Kingdoms tradition of dangles on a chain, but unique in design – spiked balls with a medial rope-like ridge (Kim W.Y. 1986b). Tomb No. 1 contained a silver belt with dangling finials. Silver cap ornaments and belts were found at Kyodong Tomb No. 11. Kyodong No. 12 featured many gold earrings and a silver necklace, along with silver and gold bracelets. The finds at Pokchondong in Pusan begin around AD 300. Tomb No. 4 was particularly rich. Iron armor, including vests, helmets (Fig. 7.21), and horse masks, as well as iron weapons, bespeak a militaristic society. Iron ingots are found covering the floor at some burials. Horn-shaped cups were buried along with many other jars and bowls (Chung J.W. 1981, Chung J.W. and Shin K.C. 1983, Chinju National Museum 1988). Tomb 22 contained a quiver which has been reconstructed from its gilt-bronze elements. Horse-trappings are common in the more elaborate graves. Chung and Shin (1984) suggested that the long

7.21 Iron helmet from a Kaya site. After Soongsil Museum 1986.

armor represented in Koguryo wall paintings is appropriate for cavalry, while the short armor like that found at Pokchondong is intended for the infantry.

Swords with bird-shaped ornaments in the pommel, iron spearheads and arrowheads, and various horse bells and harness fittings of fine design attest to the warrior aristocracy. A bronze tripod vessel with spout and handle, and two metal vessels with handles (like historic ones used to iron cloth) were also found.

A recently discovered group of burials at Taesongdong, Kimhae, contains graves from the mid-fourth century to early fifth century. Of the thirty burials which have been excavated, twenty have wooden burial chambers, nine have wooden coffins, eight have burial chambers constructed of stone, and two are jar burials.

One tomb is thought to be a royal burial of the third century AD, to judge from the accompanying artifacts. The most unusual find was a Scythian bronze jar, 25 cm high. The pottery was arranged in rows by the head and foot – forty-eight vessels in eight rows above the head, and twelve vessels in three rows below the foot.

Tomb No. 18, ascribed to the mid-fourth century, had a hardened clay floor on which was placed a wooden coffin. Traces of red paint surrounded the spot where the body lay. Some pottery vessels contain fish bones or seeds. Two long swords lay beside the body.

A later tomb from the early fifth century, Tomb 39, was completely undisturbed. Stacks of earthenware were found, arranged in rows at the head and foot. Other artifacts uncovered at the site include two bronze mirrors of the Han period, sixteen suits of armor, quivers, swords, shields and horse gear, along with 241 ceramic vessels.

Near the ancient capital of Taekaya at Chisandong, Koryong ancient tombs are marked by earth mounds of various dimensions. Tomb 45 contains two main burial chambers and eleven pits under a mound 23 m in diameter and 3 m high. The larger of the two main chambers contained three skeletons, of which two were interpreted as those of slaves. Also in the chamber were a gilt-bronze crown, a piece of a bronze mirror, harness-trappings, and many pottery vessels, dating this grave to the fourth century AD.

Tomb 44 is later and larger, standing 7 m high and 32 m in diameter. In the center, three main burial chambers were constructed of stone: radiating around them under the mound are thirty-two smaller stone-lined pits (Kim C.C. 1981). In some of the pits, extended skeletons were preserved. The human remains included both males and females, with ages estimated from seven to fifty. One pit contained two subadolescent girls; another was occupied by the remains of a male of around thirty and an eight-year-old girl. The excavators interpret this configuration as human sacrifice to accompany the upper class to the world of the dead. It is dated around AD 450 (Kim W.Y. 1980a).

Excavation of four medium-sized tombs at Chisandong (Tombs 32–5) revealed a number of interesting features. Four major mounds seem to be in pairs, with one of each oriented to the north, the other to the northeast. These may be married couples, with different orientation according to gender. Two of these mounds join together with a child's burial between, strengthening the inference. Tomb 32 had a complete set of iron armor with helmet, and a gilt-bronze headdress.

The burial chambers themselves are recessed into the ground and lined with stones. Stone circles outline the edges of the mounds. Among the burial goods in these tombs was an unusual gilt-bronze crown with a very wide central upright reminiscent of a Paekche crown, as well as necklaces including round beads and *gokok*. One sword, although rusted, was seen to have a bird head in a pommel. Horse-trappings, including saddle parts, stirrups, buckles, bits and bells, were prominent. A suit of armor and a helmet along with iron swords and arrowheads underline once again the emphasis on warfare among the nobility. Food offerings of fish, bird and crab still remain. The pottery is elaborated with lids, handles and cut-out stands.

Another group of tombs with multiple burials occurs at Hapchon, in the territory of Taekaya. From two to ten burial pits may be found under a single mound. The Chopori Tomb B is of a slightly different type, with one central stone-lined grave in the middle of a mound encircled with stones. Grave goods including pottery, red tubular beads, prismatic beads, buckles, knives and axes were placed at each end of the grave (Park and Choo 1988). At Okchon four beautifully preserved silver sword pommels contain crossed heads of a dragon and a phoenix in the ring, as well as intertwined dragons decorating the hilt. The deceased was provided with armor for his horse as well as himself, gold earrings, bundles of iron arrowheads, many large jars and a whole deer. Tombs with a walk-in horizontal entrance in the style of Koguryo and Paekche tombs have also been discovered in the same region (Kim W.Y. 1983a, Shim 1982b).

Bangyeje earthen mound tombs were unearthed in the Hapchon area as well. Two large tombs and many smaller ones are found on each of three hills. The actual burial chambers are stone lined, piled over wth earthen mounds 16 to 18 m in diameter and about 3 m high. All the graves had iron objects, especially horse equipment and weapons. The highest tomb still contained gilt-silver earrings, a gilt-bronze cap very much like one found near Iksan, a long sword, an iron helmet and bronze bells. The pottery is late in style and ash-glazed. The burials may follow the Silla annexation (Chinju National Museum 1987).

Tomb 56 at Kuamdong consists of a stone cairn above two chambers made of stone slabs. The floor is entirely covered with stones as well. The grave had been robbed, leaving only pottery. It probably dates from the fourth century AD, and is considered to be related to northern cairn tombs (Kim T.K. and Lee U.C. 1978).

Some remarkable artifacts have been recovered from Kaya tombs. Two gilt-bronze crowns with upright tree and antler designs were found at Pisandong near Taegu. Several daggers with trefoil pommels have been found in graves of this region, and long swords with round pommels. Naedongdong produced iron saw knives, three-pronged pitchforks, large iron sickles and an iron stand for a lantern.

Not all cemeteries are brimming with high-status artifacts. At Tangkamdong, Pusan, the stone-lined pits contained pottery and iron, but little else (Pusan University Museum 1983a), while the Kachoadong stone-lined tombs in Chinju included beads with otherwise undistinguished sets of grave goods (Chinju National Museum 1989). Large tombs under mounds at Paekchonni have one long stone-lined chamber, with horse-trappings placed on one end of the body and pottery on the other. Extra stone-lined pits were filled with hard-fired jars. These might be thought of as middle-level tombs in terms of size and contents.

A tomb with mural painting was discovered in Sunhungdong, Koryong, the same general region as the Chisandong tombs. The tomb consisted of a mound covering a stone chamber with a low passage leading to it. The plastered walls are covered with paintings consisting of lotus flowers and cloud designs in red, green and brown (Kim W.Y. and Kim C.K. 1967). Radiocarbon dates of 1780 ± 90 BP (170 AD) and 1630 ± 70 BP (320 AD) (Lee Y.J. 1977, 1978) come from this site. These dates are unexpectedly early, according to the classification by Kim Se-ki (1985) described above. Kim Won-yong (1986a:398) suggests that the person buried in this tomb was a refugee from Koguryo. However, if the C14 dates bracket the correct time period, Koguryo tombs were covered with square mounds and did not yet have painted chambers. A Chinese settler from Lelang seems more likely. Influence from Paekche could explain this unusual painted tomb as well, except for the early date. It is interesting to note that a painted burial chamber of Takamatsuzuka in Japan seems to be closely related although it is several centuries later (Aikens and Higuchi 1982:285). Probably the Sun-hungdong tomb is mis-dated.

Silla

History

The kingdom of Silla arose from one of the Chinhan groups named Saro or Sorabol. According to the *Samguk Yusa*, in 37 BC the six villages of Saro, snuggled against hills surrounding the Kyongju plain (Kim W.Y. 1976b), held a council on the banks of a small stream. The *Samguk Yusa* records a specific account of this event, including the date and place, suggesting a cherished tradition. Members of the villages decided that "strong enemies nearby" required them to select a paramount chief. The first three leaders were all chosen from the Pak family, then Soks and Kims also ruled, until in the fourth century the kingship became hereditary in the Kim clan. The three clans of Pak, Sok and Kim made up the highest stratum in Silla society, called the *songgol*, or holy bone.

Silla was largely left to develop on its own, at a relatively safe distance from Chinese rivalries and influences. Protected from Paekche by the Sobaek range, and having little or no common border with Koguryo, Silla expanded by conquering its nearest neighbors, other small village confederations, and incorporating them into its expanding political structure. As the territory of Silla gradually increased, some skirmishes with more distant polities are recorded. During the reign of the second king, the people of Lelang invaded, and somewhat later "seven vassal states of Koguryo surrendered to the king" (*Samguk Sagi* Chapter 52). The third king "attacked and destroyed Isoguk," and in the same year Koguryo invaded Silla (*Samguk Sagi* Chapter 53).

In the third century Silla was invaded by a tribe subject to Koguryo that lived on the Upper Han river (Sohn, Kim and Hong 1970:40). However, by the fourth century Silla had established control over the area east of the Naktong river, and was beginning to prey on the Kaya states.

The titles of leadership changed as the size and strength of Silla grew. The earliest leader was called *kosogan*, which meant "big man," exactly as the Chinese translated the title of early Koguryo rulers. The next title, *chachaung*, held by only one leader, meant shaman or priest, and *nisagum*, which followed, simply meant a successor. In the fourth century AD the native Korean word *maripkan*, indicating a hereditary king, became the designation of Silla leaders (Joe 1972:38). Not until the sixth century did the kings take the Chinese title *wang*. These successive titles suggest indigenous development of leadership, rather than a model imposed from outside.

In the beginning, the leader did not have absolute power, but ruled by consensus and persuasion. Regular meetings were held in a special building in the capital city, and when particularly important issues were to be decided, representatives met at one of the "four holy places related to the native religion" (Sohn, Kim and Hong 1970:56).

According to the *Samguk Yusa*, an early Pak king, "changed the names of the six departments, creating new administrative districts, conferred family names on the six tribes, wrote songs, built ice cellars, and made ploughshares and carriages." This is an interesting list of achievements for a single ruler, covering administrative, economic and cultural activities. The six departments have been confirmed by a recently discovered stone inscription (discussed below).

As the government acquired more power, levels of social and political rank proliferated under the leader. Rather than thinking of genetic relationships in terms of "blood," in Silla the metaphor was "bone." Thus one's social standing and ability to hold political positions depended on one's *kolpum*, quality of bone (Kim C.S. 1965, 1977). The highest group were the *songgol*, holy bone, who were eligible to rule. The standard explanation is that the *songgol* were governed by a rule of hypodescent, so that a child took membership in the group from the lower-ranking parent. The next ranking group were the true bone, the *chingol*. Below the aristocracy were three lesser ranks, allowed to hold less important and less prestigious posts, and lower still were the commoners. Sumptuary laws regulated the size and splendor of houses, carriages, clothing, tableware and so forth (Kim C.S. 1977). In a multi-faceted study of social ranking based on burials, Pearson *et al.* (1986) have shown that these social distinctions are reflected in the Silla tombs. This caste hierarchy overrode any incipient gender hierarchy, making women eligible to be rulers, and in fact three queens appear in the kingly successions.

The base of Silla's economy was agrarian. A year of drought or flood could bring disaster, sometimes to the extent of families selling their children. But sources of wealth in addition to farming were present, including gold mines (Kim W.Y. 1982e), iron mines, and a complex handicraft industry orchestrated by the central government. Fourteen state-run departments produced: (1) pure silk fabrics for the royal families, (2) silk and cotton fabrics for lower level aristocrats and government officials, (3) fabrics of hemp and ramie, (4) wool blankets, (5) leather products, (6) leather shoes, (7) tables, (8) wooden containers, (9) willow and bamboo products, (10) ceramics and tiles, (11) clothes and embroideries, (12) tents, (13) lacquerware, and (14) metal weapons and tools (Choi 1971:66).

The capital at Kyongju became a large and splendid city, having a million inhabitants at its height. A new metropolitan market was opened in 490 (Choi 1971:69). In the smaller towns local markets were held, with pedlars who traveled from market to market. Rice and cloth were the media of exchange, rather than coinage, although coins minted in China have occasionally been found, and iron bars found in some Silla burials are regarded as currency.

Oxen and horses pulled carts for local transport, and people rode horses as well. Sumptuary laws regulated the saddles and trappings of men and women of all classes. A postal service was established in the fifth century, with relays of horses and riders (FLPH 1977:33).

International trade also flourished. Late in Silla's history, it is recorded that gold, silver, copper needles, fine cloth, horses, ginseng, dogs, pelts, ornaments and slaves were sent to Tang China. In return Silla received threads, silks, gold and silver ornaments, tea and books. A Silla envoy wearing a hat with wing-like projections is depicted in a wall painting in the tomb of Li Xian of the Chinese Tang dynasty, along with other foreign envoys (Kim W.Y. 1974b). This might be the same envoy who took with him two female musicians as gifts to the Tang court in 628 (Parker 1890:221). The girls were sent back, on the grounds that they would want to escape, like birds.

The early religion of Silla, in common with all the groups on the Korean peninsula, was shamanistic. The second king bore a title which means shaman, although the Korean tradition has leaned more toward women as shamans. The first queen's mother was worshipped as a goddess, residing on Mount Unji, near Kyongju. People prayed to her to send rain (*Samguk Yusa*: 51). Little else specific is known of Silla's early beliefs.

Silla was the last of the Three Kingdoms to accept Buddhism. The first Buddhist monk came to Silla in 424, but the doctrine was resisted and even persecuted for more than a century. By the beginning of United Silla, Buddhism had taken hold throughout Korea and many temples and monasteries were built. Statues of the Matreiya are particularly common in this period, and not a few Buddhist temples have survived in Silla territory.

Chinese thought and customs began to have influence in Silla a century before Buddhism was accepted. Confucian influence put an end to the custom of sacrifice and burial of retainers with the rulers in 503. Queen Sondok (632–54) introduced Chinese court dress to Silla, and presumably court customs as well. She established temples and schools, and sent students abroad to China to study. She erected the oldest astronomical observatory still standing in Asia.

Between 540 and 576, King Chinhung of Silla set up monuments, which still exist, to mark his new boundaries (Fig. 7.22). One monument was placed at Pukhan Sansong north of Seoul, others on ridges of Hwangchoryong and Maunnyong as far away as southern Hamgyong province (FLPH 1977:34), and a fourth in southwestern Kyongsang Nam Do. A fifth boundary stone has recently been discovered at Choksong mountain fortress in Tanyang in central Korea. All the steles have inscriptions in Chinese characters. King Chinhung also built Tanghang fortress near Inchon to guard his newly acquired port on the

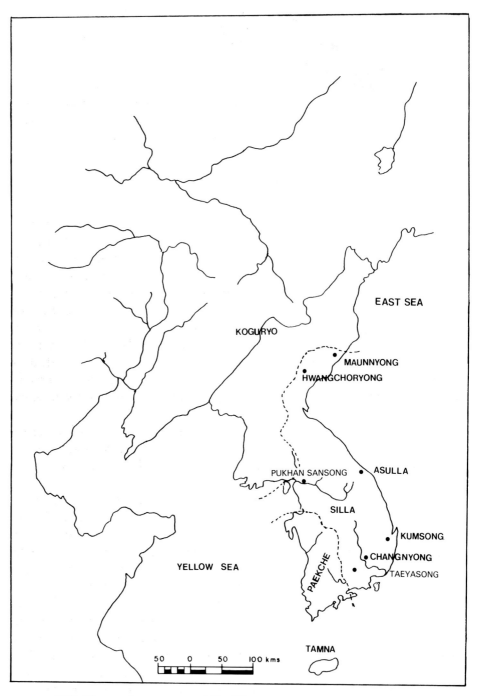

7.22 The maximum extent of Ko Silla.

Yellow Sea, as well as other outpost forts with garrisons (Joe 1972:57). Isong Sansong, the old Paekche fort on the south bank of the Han river, was reoccupied by Silla troops at this time.

The Kaya conquest was completed in 562, and battles with Paekche increased now that they shared a common border. Finally, allying with Tang China, Silla conquered the lower Han river basin, gaining a port on the Yellow Sea. Under Queen Chindok (reign 647–53), the Silla navy controlled the Yellow Sea (Joe 1972:62). Silla defeated Paekche in 660 and Koguryo in 668, becoming sole ruler of the peninsula as United Silla.

Archaeology

As in the other early Korean states, Silla is best known for its elite tombs. Rather than building tombs with passageways inviting robbers, however, Silla burials consisted of subterranean pits or wooden structures built on the ground, entirely surrounded by piles of large cobbles further covered with massive earthen mounds. This construction made looting all but impossible. Moreover, the region was never overrun by conquerors with opportunity and motive for plunder. Even when United Silla ultimately succumbed to Koryo in the tenth century, the turnover of government was peaceful. At least 155 Silla grave mounds have been counted in the city of Kyongju alone (Ito 1971), with their treasures largely intact until this century. Many large mounds remain, apparently untouched, even in the very heart of Kyongju city, the former Kumsong, capital of Silla.

Silla period grave mounds are found not only in Kyongju, although these are the most celebrated, but also in groups along the Naktong river and its tributaries, as well as on the Han river, the east coast, and on Ullung Island (Ito 1971).

In the previous chapter, burials from the early stages of Silla were described. They included the finds at Choyangdong containing glass beads imported from as far away as the Mediterranean, gold earrings, and other finery. Whole horse skeletons in round pits appear to represent sacrifices to accompany the elite to the afterworld. A complex society was already forming. Following the Choyangdong burials, wooden chamber tombs were dug into the top of a hill, using the hill as if it were an artificial mound. Kim Won-yong (1987b) identifies this time as the emergence of elite power, with visible glorifying of the nobility.

Silla tombs of the Three Kingdoms period take several forms. Many small mounds exist, although Silla is best known for the large royal tombs, identified by symbols of rulership: sheet-gold crowns with dangling *gokok* and golden belts with pendants. Tombs 19 and 20 at Inwangdong in Kyongju include up to ten burials under a single mound. They are interpreted as family tombs, unlike similar burials in the Kaya area which are proposed as evidence of human sacrifice. In the northern part of Silla territory, at Imdangdong, 130 large and

small tombs were unearthed. Four gilt-bronze crowns, belts with dangling ornaments, and gilt-bronze shoes are believed to date from the Apdok state, before
the Silla conquest of this area. A young person wearing a crown was buried near
the feet of an older woman. Royal graves of this independent state consisted of a
main chamber dug into bedrock accompanied by a wooden structure to contain
the grave goods. Each attached pit contained a sacrificial human on the bottom,
with stacks of pottery above (Chung Y.H. 1983b).

Jar-coffin burials are not common in the Silla territory, but they do occur. A
mound 6 m high near Andong covered two stone chambers containing small jar-
coffins (Kim W.Y. 1964). Some cremation burials are known from the period
after the introduction of Buddhism, but most cremations belong to the United
Silla period.

The chronological sequence of excavated Silla tombs is still in dispute. Sohn
asserts that the mounded tombs are not found before the second century, when
"a group of northern people distinguished by cairn construction moved into this
area, where they developed the basic form of Silla tomb structure, comprising a
cairn with wooden caskets inside" (Sohn, Kim and Hong 1970:40). In contrast to
this point of view, five mounds in Kyongju are associated by legend with the first
king, the first queen, and the second, third and fourth rulers (Adams 1979).
However, historical records relate that King Nulji (reign 417–58) added mounds
of earth to these tombs to "glorify his ancestors" (Kim W.Y. 1981:39).

Several sequences of Silla tombs have been proposed. Ito (1971) created a
chronology based on the tomb type and its contents, principally relying on
earring typology for seriation. According to his findings, the earliest Silla graves
were simple pits without mounds. The first earth-mound tombs were erected
over wooden burial chambers, the next had stone burial chambers, and finally,
with the increased importance of Buddhism, cremation urns without burial
goods became standard.

Several Japanese scholars have proposed seriations based on various other
artifacts (Pearson 1985). Because these are uni-dimensional, none of them is
satisfactory. The most convincing seriation of Silla tombs during the era of royal
tombs was made by Choi Byong-hyon (1981). Grave mounds of earth and stone,
he believes, were only permitted to the nobility. His chronology is in Table 7.1.

Tomb 98 in the Kim family burial ground in Kyongju is a double mound, with
a husband and wife each buried in one of the overlapping halves (Fig. 7.23). In
the south tomb, which was earlier, the male wore a gilt-bronze crown, "and
other personal ornaments of rather poor quality" (Kim W.Y. 1976a:6). He was
well endowed with military equipment, however. A separate pit contained a vast
quantity of iron weapons and many pottery vessels – more than 2,500 items all
together. Four imported western glass vessels were in his grave as well (Kim
W.Y. 1976a). A skeleton of a girl was found outside the chamber, tossed in as if
she were a last-minute sacrifice. Saddle and horse gear were found near the top of

Table 7.1. *Seriation of Silla tombs according to Choi B.H. (1981)*

Period	Date	Major tombs
1	1st half of fourth century (300–50)	Pits 3, 4, Tomb 109 Tomb 110 Pits 1, 2, Tomb 14
2	2nd half of fourth century (350–400)	South mound, Tomb 98 Pits 1, 2, Tomb 109 East pit, Tomb 82
3	1st half of fifth century (400–50)	North mound, Tomb 98 West pit, Tomb 82
4	Mid-fifth century (440–60)	Lucky Phoenix Tomb
5	2nd half of fifth century (450–500)	Heavenly Horse Tomb (155) Gold Crown Tomb Gold Bell Tomb
6	Early decades of sixth century (500–30)	The husband's Tomb, Pomunni Ho-u-chong Tomb

both mounds, perhaps substituting for the horse sacrifice of earlier burials. The north mound of Tomb 98 contained traces of a wooden structure. It is inferred to be the grave of the wife because a belt bears an inscription in Chinese, "belt for milady" (Kim C.K. and Lee V.C. 1975, Munhwajae 1985). The woman in Tomb 98 was probably a ruling queen, for she was interred with a magnificent gold crown and a gold belt with dangling pendants. No queen ruling in her own right is included in the king lists for the fourth century, however, which makes this queen an enigma. Elsewhere (Nelson 1992b) I have suggested that husband and wife pairs might have been co-rulers.

A small brown glazed bottle, manufactured in China around AD 300, is the earliest piece of Chinese pottery to be found in a Silla tomb. Trade from farther afield is demonstrated by a striped glass goblet "probably made in Alexandria around 300 AD" (Kim W.Y. 1975a:8), confirming Silla's place in the Eurasian trade network. According to Kim C.W. and Kim W.Y. (1966:13), Silla was referred to as the "gold-glittering nation" in a ninth-century Arabic work, and all of Korea was known in Arab lands as "el Sila" (McCune 1976:3). Silla may have had direct contact with the west by sea, as well as through the land-based silk road. Kim W.Y. (1982e:29) notes a Silla envoy who appears in a wall painting in Samarkand. Objects of this type do not appear in Chinese graves, suggesting direct Silla contact rather than "down-the-line" trade which is usually implied.

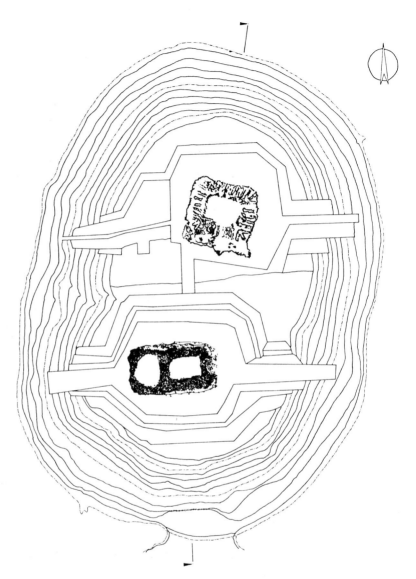

7.23 Plan of Tomb 98 (The Great Tomb at Hwangnamdong).

Tomb 155 (Fig. 7.24) was entirely intact, and proved to be extremely rich. Named the Heavenly Horse Tomb for a painted mud-guard depicting a galloping white horse, this was the first Silla tomb with a painted artifact. A wooden chamber with its main axis east–west was built on the ground surface, and covered with a mound of cobbles topped by a mound of earth. The tomb was 13 m high and 47 m in diameter. Inside the wooden chamber a wooden chest with burial gifts had been placed beside the coffin. The body was supine, head to the

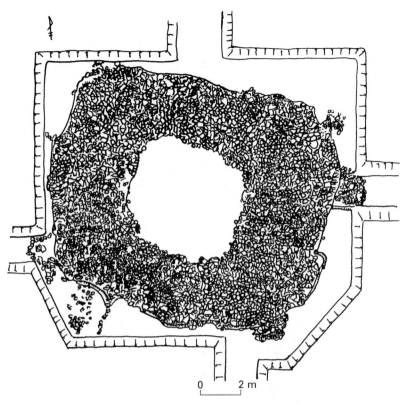

7.24 Plan of Tomb 155 (Heavenly Horse Tomb).

east. The ruler was buried wearing a gold crown, a golden belt with ceremonial pendants, gold bracelets, and a gold ring on every finger (Munhwajae 1974).

A chest for burial goods, measuring 1 × 1.8 m, stood at the head of the coffin, with the items arranged in three tiers. On the bottom, iron kettles and pottery vessels were arrayed, bronze vessels and decorated lacquerware were placed in the middle, four saddles and two sets of mud-guards made up the top band. The mud-guards were made of birch bark and lined with leather, decorated with polychrome paintings, as noted above. Painted birch bark hat brims were also among the burial gifts (Kim W.Y. and R. Pearson 1977).

Three golden crowns were found in tombs in the era of Japanese research in Korea. The first is known as the Gold Crown Tomb. When a cut was made for a railway, children were seen searching in the mound for beads, and ultimately more than 20,000 small glass beads were found. Although many of the artifacts were broken and scattered, gold objects with a total weight of 4.5 kg were removed from the tomb, along with some vessels of Roman glass (Umehara 1926:29). The personage buried wore a gold crown and a gold belt with rows of pendants, which have come to be identified as markers of sovereignty.

Further tombs to yield gold crowns were deliberately excavated. The Lucky Phoenix Tomb and the Gold Bell Tomb contained quantities of golden ornaments, as well as necklaces with beads of rock crystal and translucent green jade *gokok*. Two ceramic vessels in the form of mounted officials were also among the grave goods, with details of horse-trappings and clothing worn at the time (Umehara 1926:31).

Not far from the Gold Crown Tomb, a mound containing an inscribed Koguryo bronze vessel was excavated, and named Ho-u-chong, the Washing Vessel Tomb. The inscription dated the bronze to 415. In the same tomb a lacquered wooden mask with inset blue eyes ringed with gold was found, apparently pointing to Eurasian trade.

Two painted tombs have come to light in Silla territory. One is in Unmaeri, Yongju, near Silla's northern boundary. The form of the tomb with a side entrance and the lotus petal designs along with painted Buddhist style guardians suggest that the tomb may have been constructed for Koguryans. An inscription dates the tomb to 479 or 539 (Kim W.Y. 1986b). Another tomb was discovered on Mount Pibong. Designs of clouds, flowers and phoenixes are found on the north wall, while on the south wall a man holding a fish-shaped flag is depicted along with a two-line inscription in Chinese characters. A man holding a snake adorns the west wall. Several other stone burial mounds are nearby. Wide earrings and a glass bead necklace were found in one burial, while six short iron daggers and eleven ornaments were found in another.

Several Silla tombs have been excavated in the vicinity of Seoul on the Han river. These are late tombs, and must be graves of military commanders and lower aristocracy, for they are unremarkable in their content. Tomb No. 6 in Sokchondong, for example, is a stone chamber tomb which contained a late Silla mounted cup (Kim W.Y. 1977a:7).

Silla gold crowns, with their hints of shamanistic practices, are the best known of the Silla artifacts. Ten gold crowns have been found, each an individual creation but belonging to one tradition (Fig. 7.25). They are made of sheet gold, with a circlet from which spring several uprights in the shape of stylized trees and antlers, each ending in an aspen-leaf shape. Green *gokok* and gold spangles are profusely attached with gold wire to both the uprights and the circlets. The shimmering and tinkling effect must have bedazzled the populace. The crown from the Gold Crown Tomb had an inner golden cap as well, with intricate cut-out areas and wing-like projections. Kim Che-won and Kim Won-yong (1966) speculate on the possible association with bird feathers or wings, since the *Sanguo Ji*, Vol. 30, asserts that the predecessors of the Silla people included birds' wings in graves. The crown from the Lucky Phoenix Tomb ends in a phoenix-like finial, again a bird association, and the uprights are in the form of three "trees" and two antlers. A gilt-bronze crown from a tomb at Uisong about 70 km north of Kyongju has three uprights that are fringed and twisted, giving a feathery appearance (Kim W.Y. 1986a:352). Crowns found in Kaya are usually

7.25 Gold crown from Silla, Tomb 98, Kyongju, with the permission of the National Museum of Korea.

smaller, less elaborate, and made of gilt-bronze rather than pure gold, but they belong to the same tradition. Perhaps they symbolize leaders with lesser power. Connections have been suggested between the Silla crowns and those of Shibarghan in Afghanistan (Kang D.H. 1983).

Long golden belts with various pendant objects are always placed in royal tombs (Fig. 7.26). The belt from the Gold Crown Tomb is over 2 m long, and is made of thirty-nine plaques. Various objects pendant from the belt include a golden fish, an openwork container, and *gokok*. Each object very probably had a specific symbolic meaning, but no records which could guide an interpretation are extant. The design on one belt plaque is identical to that found on a belt in a fifth-century tomb near Nanjing, China, and a similar design was found in a Paekche tomb (Kim C.W. and Kim W.Y. 1966:186).

Bronze shoes with cut-out designs were provided for the royal feet. They would not have been practical to walk in, since gold pieces dangle from the soles. The shape of the shoes links them to Koguryo tomb paintings and traditional Korean footwear.

Gold earrings featuring dangles in leaf shape, sometimes with *gokok*, were a feature of all royal tombs. Lesser tombs contain earrings as well, often made of gilt-bronze instead of gold. Both sexes apparently wore these earrings. A style believed to be early (Ito 1971) is characterized by a thin solid gold ring while a later type of earring has a thick hollow ring. The most elegant earrings are decorated with fine gold granulations (Fig. 7.27). An example of the thick-ringed variety has been found in a Chinese-style tomb near Pyongyang, dated by inscribed tiles to AD 353 (McCune 1962). A few earrings appeared in Paekche tombs as well, suggesting that gold earrings were common throughout Korea in the Three Kingdoms period.

Gold bracelets are mostly plain, although some are molded into elaborate raised patterns. Silver and bronze bracelets also occur. A greenstone bracelet, apparently a trade item from Japan, has been discovered in Kyongju (Kim W.Y. 1986b), but this is not a local style. Gold finger rings are profuse, as many as twelve ornamented the same person (McCune 1962:85), and some royal personages were interred with rings on their toes.

Gilt-bronze saddle fittings and iron stirrups from various graves demonstrate the importance of horses. Isolated finds of bronze horse-bells and other horse-trappings are also known. The origin of the Korean stirrup is a matter of conjecture. Although chariots were important in the Shang dynasty, horse-riding does not seem to have appeared in China before the Warring States period in the fourth century BC, while stirrups in China can be dated only as early as the first or second centuries AD (Goodrich 1984:303). The stirrups presumably were adopted from the Steppe nomads, although that is not the only possible route. Toe stirrups may have been an independent invention in India. The *Samguk Yusa* tells of a boat appearing on the south coast bearing a princess from India. Kim B.M. (1987) has traced a group from India into China, and argues

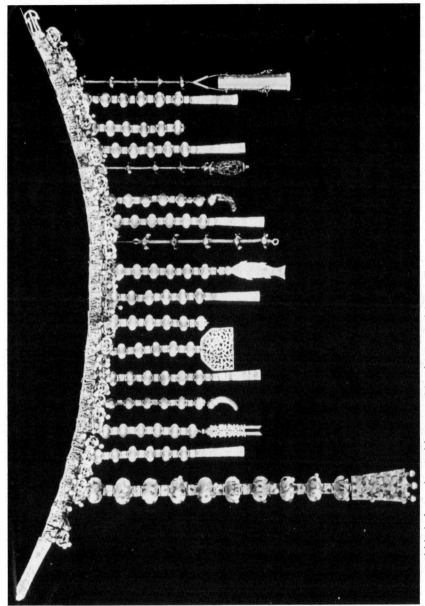

7.26 Gold belt from the Gold Crown Tomb, Kyongju.

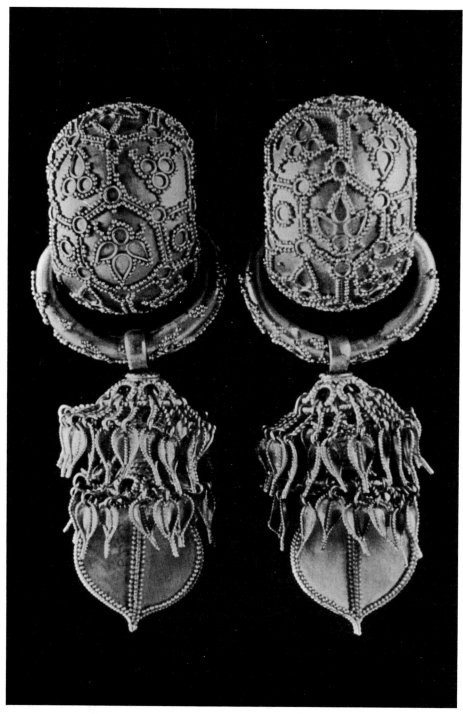

7.27 Gold earrings from Pomundong, Kyongju.

that they could have come to southern Korea, to provide both the legend of the Indian princess and the toe stirrups. However, most scholars decline to take the Indian princess literally. The earliest stirrups depicted in Silla are small, as in the ceramic warriors on horses from the Lucky Phoenix Tomb. However, actual stirrups in graves are large enough for the whole foot. Some tombs are dated by the stirrups on the supposition that stirrups in Korea must be later than those in China (Pearson 1985), but this may well be an erroneous assumption.

Gold and silver bowls and bronze kettles might also accompany the deceased. They were local and foreign made. A tripod bronze vessel with a pouring spout, found in the Gold Crown Tomb, is possibly a Chinese import. Even at this late date, ceramic tripods are virtually unknown in Silla, and metal ones are rare. A silver bowl of Persian style may be a gift from China, as described in the *Samguk Sagi*.

Iron weapons are found in some tombs in great profusion. Long swords, arrowheads, horse fittings, helmets and armor are included. Sword hilts often have elaborate pommels. Common designs include one which looks like a bird with spread wings or a fleur-de-lis, and another appears to represent a phoenix. A few pommel heads containing crossed twin dragons have also been found. Whether the iconography reflects rank, family or individual preference is not known.

Large quantities of pottery vessels accompanied the dead, possibly more for their contents than as offerings in themselves. For example Tomb 82 had 184 vessels, divided between the main chamber and a side chamber. Silla pottery is hard-fired gray ware, turned on a wheel. It is more elaborate than earlier pottery, made in a variety of shapes. Many vessels are attached to or rest in tall stands with decorative cutouts of rectangles or triangles (Fig. 7.28). Lids are common, often with small knobs. Loop or strap handles frequently have ceramic chains dangling from them, with leaf-shaped ceramic pieces at the bottom. Glazed pots are rare before United Silla, but a small jar with yellow lead glaze was found in a tomb at Wolsongno.

Some jars with representations of animals are of particular interest. One includes nine horses, one deer and an indeterminate creature that may be a tiger or a dog. The horses are drawn wearing antlers shaped like the antlers of the Silla crowns. A painted horse in a Koguryo tomb near Pyongyang also wears antlers. Some ancient shamanistic rite may be represented (Kim W.Y. 1966b). Another vessel has a three-dimensional pottery snake coiled around the lid in the process of devouring a frog. Kim Won-yong (1986a) relates this image to snake wine ingested for virility, considered especially potent if the snake was swallowing a frog! A larger jar has three-dimensional figures on the shoulder depicting a scene, including a lute player and a human copulating pair.

Although three-dimensional figures are rare in Silla except as ceramic vessels, at least two tombs have yielded figurines. An earlier tomb included humans dressed in the baggy trousers and skirts that constitute traditional Korean cloth-

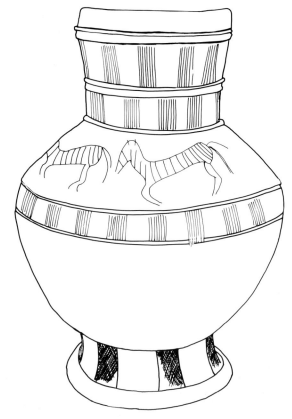

7.28 Jar on stand, with incised horses, from Kyongju, 5th–6th century.

ing. The human figures are engaged in various activities. One is even carrying something on his back in a *chige*, a characteristically Korean carrying device. Several kinds of animals were represented: rabbit, dog, cow, pig, tiger, tortoise, snake, duck and elephant. In a late tomb with human figures the influence from Tang China is clear, both in the style of the statuettes and the zodiac concept (Kim W.Y. 1987b).

More common than figurines are vessels representing various objects. Two mounted warriors in full regalia are replete with valuable information on horse-trappings and clothing. The riders wear body armor, and shoes with upturned toes. Their horses are a sturdy Mongolian variety. Some vessels depict manufactured items, including single-oared boats, still characteristic of Korean river craft, a cart, a sandal, a house and so forth. These allow glimpses into Silla life which are otherwise unavailable.

Architectural remains of Silla are numerous, including hill forts, shrines, pagodas, palaces and an astronomical observatory. The best known of the Silla fortresses is Panwolsong, Half Moon fortress, shaped something like a crescent moon. Located near the center of Kyongju, it enclosed the palace of the ruling family. The surrounding earth wall is 800 m in circumference, and large monolithic foundation stones are still visible. Tradition credits the fortress with eight gates in the wall and twenty-one buildings inside (Adams 1979:41). Recent excavations have revealed stone walls and storage areas outside the walls. A clay horse figurine resembles some figurines found in a cache at Isong Sansong in the Seoul area. It probably dates to the same era.

The Silla capital was not a walled city, but it was protected by fortresses on four sides in addition to Panwolsong. Traces of the hill forts are still visible around Kyongju. Fortresses some distance from the capital are each associated with burial grounds. Hill forts were constructed in the immediate neighborhood of mound cemeteries at a number of sites (Ito 1971:11). It seems likely that towns or villages supported both the forts and the nearby cemeteries.

The fortress of Pusan, which has stone walls and four remaining gates, guards a harbor, facing toward Japan. The remains of two Silla warehouses built in 663 were found above the fort. The larger warehouse was about 30 × 75 m, the smaller one only 12 × 30 m. The smaller one has thirty pillar foundation stones to reveal its construction. Kwisan, another late fortress, has been excavated at Chinhae. A stone wall and drainage ditches were found.

Stone monuments with Chinese inscriptions have been found in several locations, demonstrating that Silla was literate in the fifth century. The earliest yet found was located in Naengsuri, Kyongsang Do. It probably dates from 503 during the reign of King Chijung. The inscription lists titles of seven officials who came together to adjudicate a dispute relating to property. Another monument was found in Bongpyong, Uljin, dating to 524 from the reign of King Pobhung, formally annexing the east coast region. Ranking of Silla administrative officers is corroborated, as well as written laws.

Inscribed stones were erected by King Chinhung (reign 540–75) to mark his expanded borders. Four of these have long been known, two in the far north near Wonsan, one on the Han river and one in southwestern Kyongsang Nam Do. A newly discovered boundary stone in central Korea, at Choksong Fortress near Tanyang, seems to belong to this series as well. The flat side of a natural granite boulder carries 430 characters (Kim W.Y. 1979a:5).

Some Buddhist temples are still standing in the vicinity of Kyongju, in addition to isolated pagodas which mark the locations of former temples. The largest and most important of the Silla temples was Hwangyong-sa, erected in 553 and destroyed by the Mongols in 1238. The ground plan of this temple is now being uncovered. It covered 9,000 sq m, more than eight times as large as the famous Pulguk-sa, an architectural gem which remains intact. The ruins of a nine-story wooden pagoda erected in 645 by Queen Sondok were excavated at Hwangyong-sa. Artifacts include the first Tang dynasty porcelain ever found in a Silla ruin, as well as carved jade, bronze and copper jewelry, mirrors and 150 glass beads. More than 20,000 artifacts have been found, including many tiles (Kwangju

National Museum 1988b). One tile with a dragon in relief, and a gilt-bronze Buddha, are among the portable items (Kim B.M. 1981b:41).

The standing pagodas in Kyongju are made of either brick or stone. A truncated brick pagoda of only three stories resembles the Large Wild Goose Pagoda in Xian, China. Xian, at that time called Changan, was the capital of the Tang dynasty. Parts of Kyongju city were laid out in imitation of Changan, as was Nara, the approximately contemporaneous capital of Yamato, Japan. An astronomical observatory, built in the reign of Queen Sondok, is called Chomsongdae. The building is bottle-shaped, standing over 9 m high, and is 5 m in diameter at the base with an entrance high up one side. It is speculated that some superstructure must have been built on top for observing the stars and other heavenly bodies, although a variety of opinions have been expressed (Song 1983).

Summary

The Three Kingdoms of Koguryo, Paekche and Silla developed along parallel paths, with each of the contending kingdoms pursuing a policy of conquest. Intensive agriculture, long-distance trade, and craft specialization are present in each kingdom, and status differentiation, indicated in the historical sources, is underlined by the archaeology. Ranking is particularly well reflected in the tombs.

Koguryo, Paekche and Silla all began by absorbing their nearest neighbors, then gradually expanded by conquering more distant regions. Each new conquest brought more tribute, squeezed out of the farm families in the form of agricultural produce, woven cloth and *corvée* labor, and exhibited in the form of conspicuous consumption by the noble families. The result is very satisfactory for archaeologists who make and write about the spectacular discoveries, museums which exhibit them, and the populace who can claim the past glory for its own. One wonders, though, how glorious it was for the peasants of that era, caught in the lower end of a rigidly hierarchical system.

The only insight into ordinary lives is afforded by the sumptuary laws themselves, which prohibited the display of wealth beyond one's hereditary status, and a fragment of a census. The sumptuary laws are divided by *kolpum* (bone rank) and by sex. Vast differences of social status are evident, but gender stratification is absent. The women of each rank are treated equally with the men. Since the laws apply to many classes of materials, including saddles, we can deduce that everyone, men and women, rode horses freely, since various kinds of saddle embellishments are forbidden according to rank. Another indication of gender equality can be teased out of the census, which records more women than men at all ages, showing that boys were not preferred over girls. I have argued more extensively elsewhere that the Silla kingdom, which allowed ruling queens, is an unusual example of an early state in which male dominance played no part (Nelson 1992b). There is little to indicate whether or not Paekche shared Silla's gender equality. The Koguryo tomb paintings often depict a married pair, with no suggestion that the man is superior to the woman. This interesting characteristic of Korea's ancient past deserves further study.

Stylistically, the elite burials in Koguryo, Paekche and Silla are distinct. Koguryo's square-based stone mound tombs are quite different from any others and similar square tombs on the Han river lend weight to the tradition that Paekche was founded by half-brothers of an early Koguryo king. Later square mounded tombs in central Korea are less grand, but they demonstrate the extension of Koguryo power to that region in the mid-fourth century. Paekche tombs in the southern capitals owe much to southern China in construction, yet the tomb of King Munyong indicates a strongly Korean pattern in most of the artifacts. Silla and Kaya are much alike in pottery styles and artifacts and it is unlikely that they would be considered separate regions on the evidence of archaeology alone. Mounded earth and stone tombs, gold earrings, gold crowns, horse-riding and weaponry are characteristic of both regions.

The royal tombs of Kyongju are unique, but this is likely to be a status difference rather than a regional one. Koguryo artifacts are few, but the wall paintings demonstrate a number of traditional Korean traits in clothing, hair styles, housing and food preparation. In Silla, straw shoes depicted in clay, a basket carried on the back and a stringed instrument indicate continuities of items from daily life. Certainly the pattern of traditional Korean culture had antecedents in all the Three Kingdoms. When Silla unified the peninsula, it knit together groups which already shared a similar culture.

CHAPTER 8

ETHNICITY IN RETROSPECT

The population of the Korean peninsula is more homogeneous culturally, as well as physically and linguistically, than most large groups of people on earth. The formation of the Korean ethnicity, as it can be inferred from the archaeological record, is a central question in Korean archaeology. It is an interesting exercise to attempt to trace this cohesive Korean ethnicity back through time. Three elements of ethnicity will be addressed – tradition as it is maintained through time, synchronic boundaries marking territorial entities, and movement of ethnically distinct people (migration as distinct from diffusion). In this final chapter, I would like to follow each of these elements backward through time, to discover what each reveals separately.

Tradition

Tradition is represented by a continuation of style sets through time. Elements of tradition may be used as ethnic markers, although a danger lurks in this assumption. For example, the Buddhist style set, which appears in each of the Three Kingdoms, could be used (erroneously) to derive Korean ethnicity from China, or even from India. Tentatively let us set up three important criteria for assessing style sets as ethnic markers. One is a combination of time depth and spatial continuity. A second is to be found in contrast, notable differences between ethnic groups, marking and even flaunting ethnicity. Thirdly, the tradition should relate to basic elements of the culture, such as food, housing and clothing, rather than to "high culture" which reflects the tastes of the elite.

We have seen that a number of basic Korean traits can be traced to various parts of the peninsula during the Three Kingdoms period. Koguryo wall murals depict clothing, hair styles, dwellings and even kitchens that were little changed into this century. Straw sandals and the *chige*, a device for carrying loads on the back, are represented in Silla and Kaya pottery, along with shoes with upturned toes. It could be argued that the dangles found on many Silla artifacts, from earrings, crowns and belts to pottery, are still to be found in the repertoire of the *mudang*'s paraphernalia. Burials under different sizes of mound persist to this day. Royal burials continued to be made under the largest mounds through the end of the Yi dynasty. Continuous traditions since the Three Kingdoms period are quite clear.

Wonsamguk sites are less clearly part of the tradition, although there are some indications of continuity. For example the *ondol* floor goes back to that time, although it was not yet ubiquitous. A large town of semi-subterranean dwellings in Cholla Nam Do shows that houses built above the ground were not instantly adopted everywhere, and Chinese records (especially the *Wei Ji*) relate to this point as well. But traditions which might have been visible in perishable materials elude us in the iron age and before. If one can rely on stylistic details (a more tenuous procedure), a continuity in geometric styles, especially triangles and repeated short lines, can be traced backward in time. This trait may separate Koreanness from other contemporaneous ethnicities, such as Jomon in Japan and Yangshao in China, which preferred curvilinear and/or representative designs.

Bronzes from the megalithic period are decorated with fine line geometric designs. If symbolic meanings were attached to the rows of short slanted lines they have been lost in the mists of time, but it is interesting to note that the same pattern can also be found on pottery from Chulmun to Silla. Bowls on pedestals called *dou*, arguably important in ritual and ceremony, first appeared at this stage, and can still be seen on the *mudang*'s altar.

Early Villages used large storage vessels, which, as I have argued elsewhere (Nelson 1975a), may have been analogous to *kimchi* pots. There may be a continuity in basic cuisine that antedates even rice agriculture. Other traits have only tenuous connections with traditional Korea. By the time we reach back into the paleolithic, a Korean tradition is no longer visible at all.

Boundaries

When determining boundaries, the problem of scale, or level of contrast, must be addressed. Even if it is agreed that style may be "isochrestic" (Sackett 1986), so that there is no need to seek traits that might represent "pure" style, levels of contrast could be emphasized. How do we decide which level represents ethnicity? A good example from modern Korea is that of the *onggi*, large pottery jars made in local kilns (Sayers 1987). Several sizes and shapes of these jars are made, for serving, cooking and storage, especially for making *kimchi*, the vegetable pickle which is a basic part of the Korean diet. To discuss ethnicity with regard to this category of artifact, the pickling jars themselves are the significant artifact. The fact that there are some regional differences in surface decoration, shape and nuances of color (although the glaze always falls in the purple-brown range) is not relevant to any ethnic analysis. These minor differences could be used to determine the size of the market region or for other economic analysis, but they would not reflect ethnic divisions. Arguments regarding style as boundary marking thus need to be carefully made.

The conquest by Silla of most of the Korean peninsula in AD 668 surely effected cultural homogeneity to whatever extent it was not previously present. The Three Kingdoms had been mutual enemies and sometime allies, pursuing their separate policies of conquest and territorial expansion; but cultural and linguistic similarities, and a sense of being related peoples, are expressed in the extant histories. From an archaeological perspective, regional differences are most easily perceived in the tomb styles of the elite. Koguryo's rectangular tombs set themselves apart from the round mounded tombs of the south. Silla's tombs differ from Paekche's in not being possible to reenter. It is interesting to note that the early Paekche tombs in the Seoul region follow the Koguryo style of pyramidal stone tombs, lending weight to the tradition of the founding of Paekche by two brothers of a Koguryo king. The ruling elite of Paekche, moving its capital south and ceding the territory on the Han river to Koguryo, changed its burial style to cut stone tombs, clearly influenced by southern China (Kim B.M. 1976), and ended with brick tombs, also of Chinese design.

Silla featured tombs under large stone cairns covered in turn by earthen mounds. The Kaya states also made stone and earth mounds. In pottery styles, Silla and Kaya were close to each other, and both are related to the Sue ware of Japan. Koguryo and Paekche made utilitarian ware, apparently eschewing the lavish sculptural ceramic forms, high cut-out pedestals, chains and dangles of the southeast. However, since most Paekche and Koguryo tombs were robbed and have little left of their contents, we cannot be sure that the nobility of these polities did not also indulge in these fanciful forms of pottery.

Paekche and Koguryo were in closer contact with China than was Silla, judging more by the tombs themselves than by their little-known contents. Silla crowns all have tree-like uprights on a circlet, and are made of sheet gold or gilt-bronze. A central golden cap and wing-like attachments are often found as well. Even a second-century crown which is the earliest yet found has most of these attributes. Kaya crowns are similar, but have many deviations from the pattern. King Munyong of Paekche and his queen wore cut-out crowns of floral pattern, perhaps attached to a hat. No crowns are known from Koguryo. Wall paintings in the tombs depict hats with feathers, and even horse heads, but no crowns at all. The elite of the Three Kingdoms appear to have been stylistically distinct in headgear, at least.

The common people also displayed some regional differences. Jar burials continued in Paekche right up to United Silla. Although the lower classes are poorly represented in the archaeological record, in Silla and Kaya they continued to prepare stone-lined pits for their deceased family members, accompanied by simple pottery. Continuity in burial forms by region is clear in the Wonsamguk period as well as the Three Kingdoms – and of course the late iron age is the early Three Kingdoms period according to the Korean histories. From the archaeological record alone the separation of the Wonsamguk and the Three Kingdoms into three distinct regional ethnic groups is apparent.

The megalithic period suggests more homogeneity of style throughout the peninsula, although there are regional differences in pottery shapes. The similar dwellings, stone tool kits and general pottery shapes imply a population of rice farmers in nearly identical units. The chiefs, too, seem to share the same culture, with red painted vessels, polished stone knives, tubular jade and *gokok* beads placed in their interments in stone cists under dolmens. Locally made bronze weapons and mirrors are stylistically consistent throughout Korea. Regional pottery styles seem more analogous to the *onggi* example given earlier than to the stylistic differences of the preceding Chulmun. In other words, the styles tend to merge into each other and coexist in particular places, rather than displaying sharp distributional edges. There are "frontiers" between styles rather than "boundaries."

On the other hand, in the Early Villages period several design regions exist, showing more homogeneity within groups and sharper boundaries between groups than at any other time. It has been argued that these represent small tribes, an argument that need not be repeated here. In the paleolithic, differences in tool styles were found, but it is not possible to generalize about their spatial distribution. Whether there were territorial wandering bands is not within the evidence even to speculate.

Population movement

To distinguish migrations from diffusion, and either from evolutionary changes in place, is not an easy task. The simple fact of change demands attention to the problem of explaining how it came about. In the case of a movement of peoples, one would expect to find a whole complex of traits in a previous homeland reestablished in a new territory. Diffusion would produce new technology, and perhaps new styles attached to that technology, but no changes in other characteristics. Evolution would also affect one set of artifacts more than any others.

In the Three Kingdoms, development from the Wonsamguk seems clear. Each of the Three Kingdoms has roots in the preceding period, as we have seen. Influences from China arrived first in Paekche and Koguryo, and are visible archaeologically in tomb style, the painting style on tomb walls and, eventually, Buddhist symbols. Chinese writing is obviously imported, and tripods suggest some acceptance of ritual from China. However, there is no evidence of widespread ethnic population movement from China.

In the Wonsamguk period there are documents, and legends supplement the archaeological finds. Some of the Lelang tombs bespeak ethnic Han Chinese as one would expect, but many imply mixed cultures. Iron agricultural tools and weapons are very similar to those of China, and the technology must have been brought from there, in a clear case of diffusion of a useful technology. Some more widespread Chinese influence may be seen in the *dou*, but since tripods made no inroads, it is more likely that the influence was indirect, through the north.

Other new traits might have resulted from the introduction into the population of just a few people from other cultures. For example, the Kaya legend of a princess from India who arrived at Kimhae in a boat with a red sail, accompanied by rich marriage gifts and a retinue of servants and family, has possible archaeological corroboration. The legend relates that the princess, Yellow Jade, married King Suro and became the mother of all future kings of Kaya. To this day the Kim family of Kimhae cannot marry anyone named Ho – the family name of Yellow Jade. Symbols of a pair of pythons and a pair of carp facing each other are also associated with the princess, whose memory was kept alive with village festivals as well as the tending of her purported tomb (Kim B.M. 1987).

Additional events from legendary history also appear to be upheld by archaeological finds. Movement of a segment of the Koguryo ruling family to Paekche seems to be confirmed by the finding of large square stone-piled tombs on the south bank of the Han river. The earlier flight of King Chun from Ko Choson to Iksan also seems to be verified by archaeological finds of bronze weapons.

Other changes in burial styles are more difficult to interpret. The mounded tombs of Silla and Kaya, which appear to be imports, can be seen as only the addition of round stone and earth mounds to the cist tombs and pit tombs which were already found in the region. This may represent some Koreanized Chinese from the Lelang region, or disgruntled "barbarians" moving south and east to escape the burden of the Chinese commanderies, as the Silla folk memories suggest. Migrants from more "civilized" regions, perhaps with superior iron weapons, may have constituted themselves as an elite, but it is also possible that the elite developed locally but, needing visible signs of their growing power, borrowed the earth mound from the north.

The style of most fortifications is Korean from the very beginning and not Chinese, suggesting that the ruling class came from the native population and antedated the Chinese commanderies. Chinese built cities on the plain, laid out in grids with rectangular walls, while Koreans built hill forts with irregular walls following the contours of the hills. The site of Pungnamni on the Han river, and the city of Lelang in Pyongyang, conform to the Chinese pattern, but most of the fortifications are Korean. Indigenous styles of bronze objects also argue for Korean ethnicity at this time.

Interpreting the appearance of bronze, rice and megaliths as the invasion of Tungusic peoples from the north is a very popular interpretation in Korean archaeology, but careful attention to detail suggests rather that these traits arrived separately. Population movement is implied by the pottery, which is categorically different from the preceding Chulmun. However, the appearance of Mumun first in the south is a real stumbling block for the waves of Tungusic migrations theory.

If we turn to slab graves, which are clearly related to Manchuria, the case for movement from the north is much improved. However, no explanation of why these Tungusics might have left their previous territory has been offered. The area is not well enough studied to know what population pressure might have sent some of them on a migrating trek, or what attractions might have lain ahead. If we assume the congruence of burial styles and rice agriculture, we can speculate that the rice growers experienced a deteriorating climate and moved south, but there is no direct evidence, and indeed the Manchurian peoples grew millets as their basic crop. Bronze casters may have been seeking sources of tin, which was abundant in Korea. A good deal of research still needs to be done on this topic.

In the Early Villages period, new inhabitants seem to be indicated as well. It appears that the people who founded the villages came with their pottery techniques and fishing adaptation already in place. Given the site locations, it is likely that many of the newcomers came by boat. Although no boats have been found, it is not necessary to find a boat to know that they had to exist. Evidence of deep-sea fishing abounds. The paleolithic must have had many wandering groups, but the details are as yet hazy.

Summary

Many details of Korean archaeology tend to support the documentary evidence, much of which has been considered as simply fairy tales. Ethnicity through time has had varied content, with different sizes of self-identified social groups. Traditions that are ethnically Korean can be traced back in time as well. But the real message of archaeology is the complexity of the process. No simple answers will suffice. The Korean ethnicity was forged slowly, and made up of many strands.

BIBLIOGRAPHY

Ackerman, Robert E.
  1982 The Neolithic-Bronze Age Cultures of Asia and the Norton Phase of Alaskan
    Prehistory. *Arctic Anthropology* 19(2):11–38.
Adams, Edward B.
  1979 *Kyongju Guide: Cultural Spirit of Silla in Korea*. Seoul: International Tourist.
Aigner, Jean S.
  1972 Relative Dating of North Chinese Faunal and Cultural Complexes. *Arctic
    Anthropology* 9(2):36–79.
  1978 Important Archaeological Remains from North China. In *Early Paleolithic in
    South and East Asia*. F. Ikawa-Smith, ed., pp. 163–232. The Hague: Mouton.
  1984 The Asiatic-New World Continuum in Late Pleistocene Times. In *The
    Evolution of the East Asian Environment*, Vol. 2: *Paleobotany, Paleozoology, and
    Paleoanthropology*. Robert Orr Whyte, ed., pp. 915–37. Hong Kong: Centre of
    Asian Studies, University of Hong Kong.
Aikens, C. Melvin and Takayasu Higuchi
  1982 *Prehistory of Japan*. New York: Academic Press.
Akazawa, Takeru
  1986 Regional Variation in Procurement Systems of Jomon Hunter-Gatherers. In
    Prehistoric Hunter-Gatherers in Japan. Takeru Akazawa and C. Melvin Aikens,
    eds., pp. 73–89. Tokyo: University of Tokyo Press.
Allen, Chizuko T.
  1990 Northeast Asia Centered Around Korea: Ch'oe Namson's View of History.
    Journal of Asian Studies 49(4):787–806.
An Byong-chan
  1983 A Study of Bronze Swords in Early Northwestern Korea. *Kogo Minsok*
    1983:58–98. (In Korean)
An Chun-bae
  1977 Study of the Prehistoric Culture on the Upper Reaches of the Namgang River.
    Paeksan Hakbo 1977(12):17–62. (In Korean)
  1982 A Study of Culture Changes of the Prehistoric Age in the "Kaya" Area.
    Hanguk Kogo Hakbo 12:101–56. (In Korean)
  1984 *Changwon Samdongdong Jar Burials*. Pusan Women's University Museum. (In
    Korean)
  1989 On the Neolithic Layer at Imbulli. *Hanguk Kogo Hakbo* 23:233–8. (In
    Korean)
An Ho-sang
  1974 *The Ancient History of the Korean Dong-I Race*. Seoul: Institute of Baedal
    (Korean) Culture.
An Jiayao
  1984 Early Glass Vessels of China. *Kaogu Xuebao* 1984:413–48. (In Chinese)

An Sung-joo and Jeon Young-rae
  1981 A Study of Chamber Tombs of the Paekche Dynasty. *Hanguk Kogo Hakbo*
    10/11:109–36. (In Korean)
An Sung-mo
  1988 Neolithic. *Hanguk Kogo Hakbo* 21:35–62. (In Korean)
An Sung-mo, Cho Hyun-jong and Yoon Kwang-jin
  1987 *Songgungni Site III*. Report of the Research of Antiquities of The National
    Museum of Korea, Vol. 19. National Museum of Korea. (In Korean)
An Zhi-min
  1955 Stone Knives of Ancient China. *Kaogu Xuebao* 10:27–51. (In Chinese)
  1980 The Neolithic Archaeology of China: A Brief Survey of the Last Thirty Years.
    K.C. Chang, trans. *Early China* 1979/80(5):35–45. Berkeley: Institute of East
    Asian Studies, University of California.
Anderson, Atholl
  1987 Recent Developments in Japanese Prehistory: A Review. *Antiquity* 61:270–81.
Anonymous
  1969 Bronze Objects Excavated from Taejon. *Kogohak* 2:78–104. (In Korean)
Arimitsu Kyoichi
  1962 *The Comb Pattern Pottery of Korea*. Department of Archaeology Publication,
    Vol. 3. Kyoto University. (In Japanese with English summary)
Ayres, William S. and Song Nai Rhee
  1984 The Acheulean in Asia? A Review of Research on Korean Palaeolithic Culture.
    Proceedings of the Prehistoric Society 50:35–48.
Bacon, Wilbur D.
  1961 Fortresses of Kyongi-Do. *Transactions of the Royal Asiatic Society* 37:1–64.
Bae Ki-dong 1984 Report on the Yangpyongni Stone Tomb. In *Chungju Dam
    Submergence Area Cultural Resource Report*, Vol. 1: *Archaeology*, pp. 615–92.
    Chungbuk University Museum. (In Korean)
  1987a On the Date of the Chongongni Industry on the Basis of the Geological
    Process of the Hant'an River Basin. In *Papers in Honor of the Retirement of
    Professor Kim Won-yong*, Vol. 1. Im Hyo-jai, ed., pp. 783–97. Seoul National
    University.
  1987b L'Industrie lithique du site paléolithique ancien de Chongokni, Corée.
    L'Anthropologie 91(3):787–96.
  1989a The Development of the Hantan River Basin, Korea and the Age of the
    Sediment on the Top of the Chongok Basalt. *Abstracts* of the *Korean Journal of
    Quaternary Research*. Seoul, Korea, December 1989.
  1989b The Significance of the Chongokni Stone Industry in the Tradition of the
    Paleolithic Culture in East Asia. PhD Dissertation, University of California,
    Berkeley.
Baelz, E.
  1910 Dolmen und alte Königsgräber in Korea. *Zeitschrift für Ethnologie*
    42:776–81.
Banwol Area Excavation Team
  1979 Report of the Excavation of Sites in the Banwol Area. *Hanguk Kogo Hakbo*
    7:1–130. (In Korean)
Barnard, Noel
  1983 Further Evidence to Support the Hypothesis of Indigenous Origins of
    Metallurgy in Ancient China. In *The Origins of Chinese Civilization*. David N.
    Keightley, ed., pp. 237–77. Berkeley: University of California Press.

Barnes, Gina L.
  1983 State Formation in the Southern Korean Peninsula. *Archaeology in Korea* 10:40–51.
  1988 Walled Sites in Three Kingdoms Settlement Patterns. *Academy of Korean Studies No. 5*, Vol. 1: *Prehistory*, pp. 436–64.
  1989 The Protohistoric Socio-Economic Development of the Southern Korean Coast. Paper presented at the Circum-Pacific Prehistory Conference, Seattle.
  1990 Early Korean States: A Review of Historical Interpretation. In *Hoabhinian, Jomon, Yayoi, Early Korean States*. Oxford: Oxbows Books.
Bartz, Patricia M.
  1972 *South Korea: A Descriptive Geography*. Oxford: Oxford University Press.
Bergman, Sten
  1938 *In Korean Wilds and Villages*. F. Whyte, trans. London: Travel Book Club.
Best, Jonathan W.
  1979 Notes and Questions Concerning the *Samguk Sagi*'s Chronology of Paekche's Kings Chanji, Kuisin and Piyu. *Korean Studies* 3:125–34.
  1982 Diplomatic and Cultural Contacts Between Paekche and China. *Harvard Journal of Asiatic Studies* 42(2):443–501.
Binford, Lewis R.
  1968 Archaeological Theory and Method. In *New Perspectives in Archeology*. Sally R. Binford and Lewis R. Binford, eds., pp. 1–32. Chicago: Aldine Publishing Company.
  1972 Contemporary Model Building: Paradigms and the Current State of Palaeolithic Research. In *Models in Archaeology*. David L. Clark, ed., pp. 109–66. London: Methuen.
Bishop, Isabella
  1905 *Korea and Her Neighbours*. London: John Murray.
Boas, Franz
  1940 *Race, Language and Culture*. New York: The Free Press.
Bowen, Greg
  1979 Report on Stone Tools from Chongongni. *Chintan Hakpo* 46/47:48–55.
Chamshil Area Archaeological Team
  1977 Archaeological Report of Chamshil Area, Seoul. *Hanguk Kogo Hakbo* 3:17–80. (In Korean)
  1978 Archaeological Report of the Chamshil Area, Seoul. *Hanguk Kogo Hakbo* 4:7–52. (In Korean)
Chang, Kwang-chich
  1977 *The Archaeology of Ancient China*, 3rd edn. New Haven: Yale University Press.
  1980a The Chinese Bronze Age: A Modern Synthesis. In *The Great Bronze Age of China*. Wen Fong, ed., pp. 35–45. New York: Alfred A. Knopf.
  1980b *Shang Civilization*. New Haven: Yale University Press.
  1986 *The Archaeology of Ancient China*, 4th edn. New Haven: Yale University Press.
Chang Nam-kee
  1983 Biological Environment of the Chon'gongni Paleolithic Site. In *Chon'gongni*. Kim W.Y. and Bae K.D., eds., pp. 563–76. Seoul: Munhwajae Kwalliguk. (In Korean)
Chard, Chester S.
  1960 Neolithic Archaeology in North Korea. *Asian Perspectives* 4:151–5.
  1974 *Northeast Asia in Prehistory*. Madison: The University of Wisconsin Press.

Chase, David
  1960 A Limited Archaeological Survey of the Han River Valley in Central Korea.
    Asian Perspectives 4:141–9.
Chen Cheng-hui, Lu Yen-chou and Shen Cheng-teh
  1978 Development of Natural Environment in the Southern Part of Liaoning
    Province During the Last 10,000 Years. *Scientia Sinica* 21(4):516–32.
Chen Chun
  1984 The Microlithic in China. *Journal of Anthropological Archaeology* 3(2):79–115.
Chen Dawei
  1989 The Gaogouli Remains within Liaoning. *Liaohai Wenwu Xuagan* 1989(1):136–41.
Chen Xiang-wei
  1965 Three Neolithic Sites at Jian, in the Middle Reaches of the Hun River, Jilin
    Province. *Kaogu* 1965(1):42–3. (In Chinese)
Ch'hae Pyong-so
  1959 Notes on the Excavation of the Ancient Tombs with Wall Paintings near Anak
    in North Korea. *Asia Yon'gu* 2(2):109–30. (In Korean)
Chi Kon-gil
  1977a Excavation of Dolmens at Naedongni, Taedok. *Paekche Yongu* 8:107–28.
  1977b A Stone-Lined Tomb and its Burial Goods from Inwang-dong, Kyongju.
    Hanguk Kogo Hakbo 2:41–58. (In Korean)
  1982 A Study of Dolmen Distribution in Northeastern Asia. *Hanguk Kogo Hakbo*
    12:245–61. (In Korean)
Chi Kon-gil and An Sung-mo
  1984 *Report of a Survey of West Coast Islands. Appendix I, Jung Do V.* National
    Museum of Korea, pp. 81–111. (In Korean)
Chi Kon-gil, An Sung-mo and Song Ui-jung.
  1986 *Songgungni Site II.* Report of the Research of Antiquities, Vol. 28. National
    Museum of Korea. (In Korean)
Chi Kon-gil and Cho Hyun-jong.
  1989 *Song Do Site I.* Report on the Research of Antiquities, Vol. 19. Kwangju
    National Museum. (In Korean)
Chi Kon-gil and Han Yong-hee
  1982 *Jung Do Site III.* Report of the Research of Antiquities, Vol. 14. National
    Museum of Korea. (In Korean)
Chi Kon-gil and Lee Kon-mu
  1988a *Shinamni Site I.* Report of the Research of Antiquities, Vol. 20. National
    Museum of Korea. (In Korean)
  1988b *Songgungni Site Pottery Analysis.* Report of the Research of Antiquities, Vol.
    20:107–48. National Museum of Korea. (In Korean)
Chi Kon-gil and Lee Yong-hun
  1983 *Jung Do Site IV – Dolmens on the Han River.* Report of the Research of
    Antiquities, Vol. 15. National Museum of Korea. (In Korean)
  1984 *Archaeological Investigation of Jung Do Island in Chunchon, Progress Report
    V.* Report of the Research of Antiquities, Vol. 16. National Museum of Korea.
    (In Korean)
Chin Hongsup
  1960 Report of the Excavation of a Silla Tomb at Hwangori, Kyongju. *Misul
    Charyo* 2:7–13. (In Korean)
Chinju National Museum
  1987 *Hapchon Bangyeje Tombs.* Research Report No. 2, Chinju National Museum.
    (In Korean)

1988 *Chinju National Museum Catalog.* (In Korean)

1989 *Yokchi Do.* Research Report No. 3, Chinju National Museum. (In Korean)

Cho Yu-chon

1987 Study of Prehistoric Culture in the Nam River Basin (I). *Hanguk Kogo Hakbo* 20(12):23–58. (In Korean)

Cho Yu-chon, Choi Mang-sik and Yoon Kun-il

1989 *Iksan Ipchonni Ancient Tomb Research Report.* Seoul: Munhwajae Kwalliguk. (In Korean)

Choe Chong-pil

1982 The Diffusion Route and Chronology of Korean Plant Domestication. *Journal of Asian Studies* 41(3):519–29.

1986 Subsistence Patterns of the Chulmun Period: A Reconsideration of the Development of Agriculture in Korea. PhD Dissertation, University of Pittsburgh.

1991 A Critical Review of Research on the Origin of Koreans and Their Culture. *Hanguk Sangkosa Hakbo* 8:7–43.

Choi, Byong-hyon

1981 The Evolution and Chronology of the Wooden-Chamber Tombs of the Old Silla Period. *Hanguk Kogo Hakbo* 10/11:137–228. (In Korean)

1988 Korean Archaeology Since 1945: Retrospect and Prospect. Early Silla. *Hanguk Kogo Hakbo* 21:119–38. (In Korean)

Choi Chong-Kyu

1982 The Dawn of the Emergence of Stoneware Pottery. *Hanguk Kogo Hakbo* 12:213–24.

Choi Chong-Kyu and An Jai-pai

1983 *Shinchonni Tombs Site.* Appendix 2 in Report of the Research of the Antiquities of the National Museum of Korea, Vol. 15. (In Korean)

Choi Hochin

1971 *The Economic History of Korea.* Seoul: The Freedom Library.

Choi, Jong-gyu

1981 Report on Pit Burials in Choyangdong, Kyongju. *Hanguk Kogo Hakbo* 9:35–9. (In Korean)

1982a Report of the Fourth Season at Choyangdong, Kyongju. *Archaeology in Korea* 9:35–9. (In Korean)

1982b The Previous Stage of the Earthen Ware's Formation and its Progress. *Hanguk Kogo Hakbo* 12:213–44. (In Korean)

Choi Mong-lyong

1976 *An Excavation Report on the Southwestern Part of Songsan Shellmound.* Seoul: Munhwajae Kwalliguk.

1978 Archaeological Report of Songamdong House Site Excavation, Kwangju. *Hanguk Kogo Hakbo* 4:53–74. (In Korean)

1980 Scientific Analysis of Plain Coarse Pottery Sherds from Cholla Namdo, Southwest Korea. *Hanguk Kogo Hakbo* 9:79–83.

1981 Analyses of Plain Coarse Pottery from Cholla Province. *Hanguk Kogo Hakbo* 10/11:261–9.

1983a The Trade System of the Wiman State. *Asian Pacific Quarterly* 15(3).

1983b Proto-Three Kingdoms Period. *Archaeology in Korea* 10:98–104. (In Korean)

1984a Bronze Age in Korea. *Korea Journal* 24:23–33.

1984b *A Study of the Yongsan River Valley Culture: The Rise of Chiefdom Society and State in Ancient Korea.* Seoul: Dong Song Sa.

1989 The Trade System of the Wiman State in Ancient Korea. Paper presented to the Circum-Pacific Prehistory Conference, Seattle.

Choi Mong-lyong and Im Yong-jin
  1984 Excavation Report on Yangpyongni B Site of Chewon. In *Chungju Dam Submergence Area Cultural Resources Report*, Vol. 1: *Archaeology*, pp. 293–335. Chungbuk National University Museum. (In Korean)
  1986 Yangpyongni Prehistoric Settlement. In *Hunamni Prehistoric Studies*, pp. 123–50. (In Korean)
Choi Mong-lyong, Kwon O-yong and Kim Sung-ok.
  1989 A Report on the Excavation of Taegongni Settlement Sites (I). *Juam Dam Report* 6:145–394. (In Korean)
Choi Mong-lyong, Lee Song-ju and Lee Kun-ok
  1989 A Report on the Excavation of Naksuri Settlement. *Juam Dam Report* 6:21–144. (In Korean)
Choi Mong-lyong, Yi Hui-jung and Pak Yang-jin
  1983 Summary Report on Excavations of Sites at Paehwa-ri Site of Chewon. In *Chungju Dam Submergence Area Cultural Resources Report*, Vol. 1: *Archaeology*, pp. 315–28. Chungbuk National University Museum. (In Korean)
  1986 Excavation Report on the Tohwari Stone Tomb. In *Hunamni Prehistoric Studies*, pp. 169–200. (In Korean)
Choi Mou-chang
  1982 Report of the Third Excavation. In *Chon'gongni Palaeolithic Site*. Konguk University. (In Korean)
  1983a Konguk University Report. In *Chon'gongni*, pp. 453–513. Seoul: Munhwajae Kwalliguk. (In Korean)
  1983b The Plain Pottery of the Han River Reaches. *Hanguk Kogo Hakbo* 14/15:61–76. (In Korean)
  1984 Summary Report of Excavation of Sites in Myongori B Site, Chewon. In *Chungju Dam Submergence Area Cultural Resources Report*, Vol. 1: *Archaeology*, pp. 31–44. Chungbuk National University Museum. (In Korean)
  1986 Environment of Paleolithic Korea. *Hanguk Kogo Hakbo* 19:5–18. (In Korean)
  1987 Le Paléolithique de Corée. *L'Anthropologie* 3:755–86.
Choi Sung-nak
  1982a A Study of Some Problems Related to Radiocarbon Dates in Korea. *Hanguk Kogo Hakbo* 13:61–95. (In Korean)
  1982b A Study on the Polished Stone Arrowhead of Korea. *Hanguk Kogo Hakbo* 12:263–320. (In Korean)
  1984 A Study on the Typological Method in Korea. *Hanguk Kogo Hakbo* 16:1–24. (In Korean)
  1987 *Report on the Excavation of Kumgongni Shell Mound I*. Research Report No. 8, Mokpo National University. (In Korean)
  1988a Proto-Three Kingdoms Pottery. *Yongnam Archaeological Review* 5:1–17. (In Korean)
  1988b *Report on the Excavation of the Kumgongni Shell Mound II*. Research Report No. 11, Mokpo National University. (In Korean)
  1989a Chronology in Korean Archaeology. *Hanguk Kogo Hakbo* 23:5–20. (In Korean)
  1989b *Report of the Excavation of Kumgongni Shellmound III*. Research Report No. 15, Mokpo National University. (In Korean)
Chon Young-nae
  1976 On the Chinese-Type Bronze Dagger from Sangnimni, Wanju. *Chonbuk Yujok Chosa Pogo* 6:3–25. (In Korean)

1983 Korean Bronze Age Culture Research. *Mahan-Paekche Culture Document* 6:77–126. (In Korean)

1984 *Report on the Asan Dam Area Archaeological Project*. Chunchon City Museum. (In Korean with English summary)

1989a Introduction of Rice Agriculture into Korea and Japan from the Perspective of Polished Stone Implements. Paper presented at the Circum-Pacific Prehistory Conference, Seattle.

1989b Chonju Yoidong Prehistoric Remains. *Hanguk Kogo Hakbo* 23:256–65. (In Korean)

Chong Chan-young

1975 A Study of Koguryo Burials up to the Fourth Century AD. *Kogominsok* 1975:1–74. (In Korean)

Chonnam University Museum

1987 *Juam Dam Report I*. (In Korean)

Choo Youn-sik 1991 Cylindrical Net Sinkers and Bottom Set Gill Nets: The Use of Relational Analogy in Archaeological Reasoning. Paper presented at British Association for Korean Studies 1991 Conference, Cambridge.

Chung Jing-won 1980 A Study of Neolithic Pottery on the Southern Coast. *Pusan History* 4:191–210. (In Korean)

1981 Summary Report of the Pusan, Pokchondong Site. *Archaeology in Korea* 8:16–18. (In Korean)

1982a Bronze Age Sites and Artifacts in the Kyongnam Region. *Hanguk Kogo Hakbo* 12:321–42. (In Korean)

1982b *South Seacoast Area Chulmun Pottery Research (1)*. History Department, Pusan University. (In Korean)

1983 Pusan Hoejungdong Old Tombs. In *Pusan City Museum Annual Report* 6:28–45. (In Korean)

1985 South Sea Coast Area Yungkimun Pottery Research. *Pusan University History Journal* 9:9–56. (In Korean)

1986 Sandal Do Shell Mound Excavation, Chulmun Pottery. *Yongnam Archaeology*, Occasional Papers No. 1:133–49. (In Korean)

1989 *Shinamni Site II*. Report of the Research of Antiquities, Vol. 21. National Museum of Korea. (In Korean)

Chung Jing-won and Shin Kyong-chol

1983 Ancient Tombs at Pokchondong in Tongnae. *Pusan University Report* 5. (In Korean)

1984 Profiles of Ancient Korean Armor. In *Papers in Commemoration of Dr Yoon Mubyong's Sixtieth Birthday*, pp. 273–98. Chungnam National University. (In Korean)

1987 The Last Period Style of the Plain Coarse Pottery. *Hanguk Kogo Hakbo* 20:113–31. (In Korean)

Chung Jing-won, Shin Kyong-chol and Im Hyo-taek

1981 *Kimhae Sugari Shellmound*. Pusan University Museum. (In Korean)

Chung Yong-ho, ed.

1979 Papers on the Koguryo Stone Monument at Chungson. *Sahak Chi* 13:1–150. (In Korean)

Chung Yong-ho, Han Chang-kyun, Sin Suk-chong and Yang Hyon-gu

1988 *The Bronze Age Tomb at Sogungni*. Tanguk University Museum Report No. 11. (In Korean)

Chung Yong-hwa

1983a Yongnam University Report. In *Chon'gongni*. Kim W.Y. and Bae K.D., eds., pp. 175–331. Seoul: Munhwajae Kwalliguk. (In Korean)

1983b Report on Ancient Tombs at Imdangdong. *Archaeology in Korea* 10:23–6. (In Korean)

1984a *Chon'gongni Site Progress Report*. Taegu: Yongnam University Museum. (In Korean)

1984b Acheulean Handaxe Culture of Chon'gongni in Korea. In *The Evolution of the East Asian Environment*, Vol. 2: *Paleobotany, Paleozoology, and Paleoanthropology*. Robert Orr Whyte, ed., pp. 894–913. Hong Kong.

1985 *Report of Excavation of Choyangdong Site*. Publication No. 6, Yongnam University Museum. (In Korean)

1986a *Kyongsan Region Investigation Report*. Publication No. 7, Yongnam University Museum. (In Korean)

1986b Korean Paleolithic Stone Tools. *Hanguk Kogo Hakbo* 19:63–104. (In Korean)

Chungbuk University Museum

1983 *A Research Report on the Woraksan Area*. Publication No. 3, Chungbuk National University Museum. (In Korean)

Clare, Kenneth G., Gerald J. Foster, Robert C. Hannus, William Hrabko, Carolyn Knapp, Kyung Lee, Robert T. Mott and Yung Park

1969 *Area Handbook for the Republic of Korea*. DA Pam 55–0410. Washington, DC: Superintendent of Documents, US Government Printing Office.

Clark, J. Desmond

1983 Report on a Visit to Palaeolithic Sites in Korea. In *Chon'gongni*. Kim W.Y. and Bae K.D., eds., pp. 594–8. Seoul: Munhwajae Kwalliguk.

Covell, Jon Carter and Alan Covell

1984 Japan's Hidden History – Korean Impact on Japanese Culture. Seoul: Hollym.

Crawford, Gary W. and Hiroto Takamiya

1990 The Origins and Implications of Late Prehistoric Plant Husbandry in Northern Japan. *Antiquity* 64:889–911.

Dallet, Charles

1954 *Traditional Korea*. New Haven: Human Relations Area Files.

deJesus, Prentiss S.

1977 Considerations on the Occurrence and Exploitation of Tin Sources in the Ancient Near East. In *The Search for Ancient Tin*. A.D. Franklin, J.S. Olin and T.A. Wertime, eds., pp. 33–42. Washington, DC: Smithsonian Institution.

Derevianko, A.P.

1978 The Problem of the Lower Paleolithic in the South of the Soviet Far East. In *Early Paleolithic in South and East Asia*. F. Ikawa-Smith, ed., pp. 303–15. The Hague: Mouton.

Dong Xue-zeng

1964 Excavations of Stone Cist Tombs at Xituanshan, Jilin. *Kaogu Xuebao* 1964(1):29–49. (In Chinese)

1983 Some Preliminary Remarks on the Xituanshan Culture of the Jilin Region. *Kaogu Xuebao* 1983(4):407–26. (In Chinese)

Dong-A University Museum

1984 *Sangnodaedo*. Research Report No. 8, Dong-A University Museum, Pusan. (In Korean)

Duyvendak, J.J.L.

1928 *The Book of Lord Shang*. Chicago: University of Chicago Press.

Egami Namio

1964 The Formation of the People and the Origin of the State in Japan. *Memoirs of the Toyo Bunko* 23:35–70. (In Japanese)

Engle, Anita
    1976 *Readings in Glass History No. 6/7.* Jerusalem: Phoenix Publications.
Esaka, Teruya
    1986 The Origins and Characteristics of Jomon Ceramic Culture: A Brief
        Introduction. In *Windows on the Japanese Past.* R. Pearson, ed., pp. 223–8.
        Center for Japanese Studies, University of Michigan.
Eyre, S.R.
    1968 *Vegetation and Soils: A World Picture,* 2nd edn. Chicago: Aldine.
Falkenhausen, Lothar von
    1987 *Probleme der Koreanischen Frühgeschichte.* OAG Aktell No. 29. Tokyo.
Fang Dien-chen and Wei Fan
    1986 Brief Report of the Excavation of the Goddess Temple and Stone Graves of
        the Hongshan Culture at Niuheliang in Liaoning Province. *Liaohai Wenwu
        Xuegan* 1986(8):1–17. (In Chinese)
Flenniken, J. Jeffrey
    1987 The Paleolithic Dyuktai Pressure Blade Technique of Siberia. *Arctic
        Anthropology* 24:117–32.
FLPH (Foreign Language Publishing House)
    1977 *The Outline of Korean History (Until August 1945).* Pyongyang, Korea.
Francis, Peter Jr
    1985 *A Survey of Beads in Korea.* Occasional Paper No. 1, Center for Bead
        Research. Lake Placid, NY: Lapis Route Books.
    1986 *Chinese Glass Beads: A Review of the Evidence.* Occasional Paper No. 2,
        Center for Bead Research. Lake Placid, NY: Lapis Route Books.
Frenzel, Burkhard
    1968 The Pleistocene Vegetation of Northern Eurasia. *Science* 161(3842):637–49.
Fried, Morton
    1975 *The Notion of Tribe.* Menlo Park, CA: Cummings Publishing Company.
Fujihara Koji
    1976 The Transition from Jomon to Yayoi As Seen Through Plant Opals. *History
        Journal* (1):63–70. (In Japanese)
Fujita Ryosaku
    1930 Excavation of the Neolithic Site at Songpyongdong, Unggi. *Seikya Gakuso*
        2:179–80. (In Japanese)
    1933 Historical Sketch of the Archaeology of Korea. *Dolmen* 4:13–17. (In Japanese)
Gailey, Christine W. and Thomas C. Patterson
    1988 State Formation and Uneven Development. In *State and Society: The
        Emergence and Development of Social Hierarchy and Political Centralization.* J.
        Gledhill, B. Bender and M.T. Larsen, eds., pp. 77–90. London: Unwin Hyman.
Gale, Esson M.
    1931 *Discourses on Salt and Iron: A Debate on State Control of Commerce and
        Industry in Ancient China.* Sinica Leidensis, Vol. 2. Leiden: E.J. Brill.
Gardiner, Kenneth Herbert James
    1969a *The Early History of Korea.* Honolulu: University of Hawaii Press.
    1969b Some Problems Concerning the Founding of Paekche. *Archiv Orientalni*
        37(4):562–88.
    1969c Hou-Han-Shu as a Source for the Early Expansion of Koguryo. *Monumenta
        Serica* 28:148–87.
Goodrich, Chauncey S.
    1984 Riding Astride and the Saddle in Ancient China. *Harvard Journal of Asiatic
        Studies* 44(2):279–306.

Grayson, James H.
  1976 Some Structural Patterns of the Royal Family of Ancient Korea. *Korea Journal*
    6(6):27–32.
  1977 Mimana: A Problem in Korean Historiography. *Korea Journal* 7(8):65–8.
Guilcher, André 1976 Les Côtes à rias de Corée et leur évolution morphologique.
  Annales de Géographie 472:641–71.
Hamada Kosaku
  1936 *On the Painting of the Han Period*. Memoirs of the Research Department.
    Tokyo: Toyo Bunko. (In Japanese with English summary)
Hamada Kosaku and Koisumi Akio
  1934 *The Tomb of the Painted Basket of Lo-lang*. Archaeological Research, Vol. 1.
    Seoul: The Society for the Study of Korean Antiquity. (In Japanese with English
    summary)
Han Byong-sam
  1968 On the Objects of Early Metal Age Found at Yonghung-ni, Kaech'on, North
    Korea. *Kogohak* 1:61–76. (In Korean)
  1970 *Si Do Shell Mound*. Seoul: National Museum of Korea. (In Korean)
  1974 Neolithic Culture of Korea. *Korea Journal* 14(4):12–17.
  1976 The Origin of the Comma-Shaped Jade. *Kogo Misul* 129/30:222–8. (In Korean)
  1977 Important Prehistoric Sites. *Korea Journal* 17(4):14–17.
  1984 A Group of Wajil Pottery from Songju. In *Papers in Commemoration of Dr
    Yoon Mubyong's Sixtieth Birthday*, pp. 169–82. Chungnam National University.
    (In Korean)
Han Woo-keun
  1970 *The History of Korea*. Lee Kyung-shik, trans. Seoul: Eul-yoo.
Han Yong-hee
  1978 The Neolithic Culture of Central-Western Korea. *Hanguk Kogo Hakbo*
    5:17–108. (In Korean)
  1982 Majangni Site Excavation Report. In *Jung Do III*. National Museum of Korea.
    (In Korean)
  1983 A Study on Horn-Shaped Pottery. *Hanguk Kogo Hakbo* 14/15:77–132. (In
    Korean)
  1984 Sosan, Taerori Dwelling Site Remains. Appendix 2 in *Jung Do V*. National
    Museum of Korea.
Han Yong-hee, Kim Hong-wan and Son Myong-jo
  1989 *Kimhae Yangdongni Ancient Tomb Research Report*. Cultural Research
    Society. Seoul: Kye-mun Sa Publisher. (In Korean)
Han Yong-hwa and An Sung-mo
  1983 *Survey of the West Coast Islands (I)*. Report of the Research of Antiquities,
    Vol. 15. National Museum of Korea. (In Korean)
Harada Yoshito
  1931 Mu-yang-ch'eng, Han and Pre-Han Sites at the Foot of Mount Lao-T'ieh in
    South Manchuria. In *Archaeologia Orientalis*. Vol. 2. Tokyo: Toyo Bunko. (In
    Japanese with English Summary)
Harunari Hideji
  1986 Rules of Residence in the Jomon Period, based on the Analysis of Tooth
    Extraction. In *Windows on the Japanese Past*. R.J. Pearson, ed., pp. 293–312.
    Center for Japanese Studies, University of Michigan.
Hatada Takashi
  1969 *A History of Korea*. Warren W. Smith, Jr and Benjamin H. Hazard, eds.,
    trans. Santa Barbara: Clio Press.

1979 An Interpretation of the King Kwanggaet'o Inscription. *Korean Studies* 3(9):1–17.

Henderson, Gregory
1959 Korea through the Fall of the Lolang Colony. *Koreana Quarterly* 131:147–68.

Henthorn, William E.
1966 Recent Archaeological Activity in North Korea (I): The Cave at Misongni. *Asian Perspectives* 9:73–8.
1968 Recent Archaeological Activity in North Korea (II): The Shellmound at Sopohang. *Asian Perspectives* 11:1–18.
1971 *A History of Korea*. New York: The Free Press.

Hewes, Gordon
1947 *Archaeology of Korea: A Selected Bibliography*. Research Monographs on Korea, Series F, No. 1. Ann Arbor, Michigan.

Hirth, Frederick
1908 *The Ancient History of China to the End of the Chou Dynasty*. New York: Columbia University Press.

Ho Ping-ti
1975 *The Cradle of the East*. Chicago: The University of Chicago Press.

Hole, Frank, Kent V. Flannery and James A. Neely
1969 *Prehistory and Human Ecology of the Deh Luran Plain*. Memoirs No. 1 of the Museum of Anthropology, University of Michigan.

Holt, James
1948 Some Points of Interest from Han Sung Su's *Studies on Megalithic Cultures of Korea*. *American Anthropologist* 50: 573–4.

Hong Pin-ki and Sun Sung-hun
1981 Puyo Chongamni Ancient Graves. In *Jung Do II*. National Museum of Korea, Appendix. (In Korean)

Hong, Wontack
1988 *Relationship Between Korea and Japan in Early Period: Paekche and Yamato Wa*. Seoul: Ilsimsa Publisher.

Huang, Jinsen
1984 Changes of Sea-Level since the Late Pleistocene in China. In *The Evolution of the East Asian Environment*, Vol. 1: *Geology and Paleoclimatology*. Robert Orr Whyte, ed., pp. 309–19. Hong Kong: Centre of Asian Studies, University of Hong Kong.

Hudson, Mark J.
1989 Ethnicity in East Asia: Approaches to the Wa. *Archaeological Review From Cambridge* 8(1):51–63.

Hutterer, Karl L.
1977 Reinterpreting the Southeast Asia Paleolithic. In *Sunda and Sahul*. J. Allen, J. Golson and R. Jones, eds., pp. 31–71. New York: Academic Press.

Hwang Ki-dok
1960 Interim Report of Excavation of Hogok Prehistoric Site in Musan. *Munhwa Yusan* (1):52–76. Pyongyang. (In Korean)
1965 A Study of Social Relationships and the Burial System in the Korean Bronze Age. *Kogo Minsok* 1965(4):2–23. (In Korean)
1975 Report on the Musan Pomuigusok Remains. *Kogo Minsok* 1975(6):124–226. (In Korean)

Hwang, Pae-gang
1967 A Study on the Tangun Myth. *Paeksan Hakbo* 3:111–31. (In Korean)

Hwang Yong-hun
  1974 A Study of Prehistoric Cup-Marks in Korea. *The Journal of Regional Development* 5:21–40. (In Korean)
  1975 Typology and Techniques of Prehistoric Rock Drawings in Korea. *Kogo Misul* 127. (In Korean)
  1979 Brief Survey of Newly Discovered Jon'gok Hand-axe Culture. *Korea Journal* 19:35–40.
  1981 The General Aspect of Megalithic Culture of Korea. In *Megalithic Cultures in Asia*. B.M. Kim, ed., pp. 41–64. Seoul: Hanyang University Press.
  1983 Kyung-hee University Report. In *Chon'gongni*. Kim W.Y. and Bae K.D., eds., pp. 333–451. Seoul: Munhwajae Kwalliguk. (In Korean)
  1984a Excavation Report on the Kidong-ni A Site. In *Chungju Dam Submergence Area Cultural Relics Report*, Vol. 2: *Archaeology and History*, pp. 477–525. Chungbuk University Museum. (In Korean)
  1984b Excavation Report on the Kyesanni A Stone Mounded Tomb. In *Chungju Dam Submergence Area Cultural Relics Report*, Vol. 1: *Archaeology*, pp. 337–52. Chungbuk University Museum. (In Korean).
  1984c Excavation Report on Yonggongni Tomb Site. In *Chungju Dam Submergence Area Cultural Relics Report*, Vol. 1: *Archaeology*, pp. 601–14. Chungbuk University Museum. (In Korean)
  1984d *Chungju Dam Submergence Area Cultural Relics Report*, Vol. 1: *Archaeology*, pp. 581–600. Chungbuk University Museum. (In Korean)
  1987 *Northeast Asian Rock Art*. Seoul: Min-um-sa Publisher. (In Korean)
  n.d. A Study of the Palaeolithic Cultures of the Korean Peninsula. (Manuscript, files of the author)
Ikawa-Smith, Fumiko
  1976 On Ceramic Technology in East Asia. *Current Anthropology* 17(3):513–15.
  1978 The History of Early Paleolithic Research in Japan. In *Early Paleolithic in South and East Asia*. F. Ikawa-Smith, ed., pp. 247–86. The Hague: Mouton.
  1986 Late Pleistocene and Early Holocene Technologies. In *Windows on the Japanese Past: Studies in Archaeology and Prehistory*. Richard J. Pearson, ed., pp. 199–216. Center for Japanese Studies. Ann Arbor: University of Michigan.
Ikeuchi, Hiroshi
  1929 The Chinese Expeditions to Manchuria under the Wei Dynasty. *Memoirs of the Toyo Bunko* 4:71–119. (In Japanese with English summary)
  1930 A Study of Lo-lang and Tai-fung, Ancient Chinese Prefectures in the Korean Peninsula. *Memoirs of the Toyo Bunko* 5:79–95. (In Japanese with English summary)
Ilyon
  1972 *Samguk Yusa: Legends and History of the Three Kingdoms of Ancient Korea*. Tae-Hung Ha and Grafton K. Mintz, trans. Seoul: Yonsei University Press.
Im Hyo-jai
  1966 Dolmens in Kicha Island. *Hanguk Kogo* 1:5–18. (In Korean)
  1967 Dolmens in Sunch'on Area. *Hanguk Kogo* 2:21–8. (In Korean)
  1968 The Pottery with Raised Decoration Found from Sosaeng-myon, Tongnae, near Pusan. *Kogohak* 1:115–25. (In Korean)
  1977 Similarities and Differences among Neolithic Cultures of Central Korea. *Hanguk Kogo Hakbo* 2:19–39. (In Korean)
  1981 Misari Summary Report. *Archaeology in Korea* 8:10–13. (In Korean)
  1982a *Amsadong Remains Emergency Excavation Report*. Seoul: Seoul National University. (In Korean)

1982b Fouilles du site de Osan-ni. *Revue de Corée* 14(2):3–20.
1982c Osanni Summary Report. *Archaeology in Korea* 9:26–33. (In Korean)
1983 The Comb Pattern Pottery Culture of the West Coast of Korea with an Emphasis on its Chronology. *Hanguk Kogo Hakbo* 14/15:1–18. (In Korean)
1984a The Neolithic of Korea: A Consideration on Chronology and Morphological Transition of Ceramics. *Papers in Commemoration of Dr Yoon Mubyong's Sixtieth Birthday*, pp. 533–48. Ch'ungnam National University. (In Korean)
1984b Korean Neolithic Chronology: A Tentative Model. *Korea Journal* 24:11–22. (In Korean)
1985a *Amsadong*. Archaeological and Anthropological Papers, Vol. 11, Seoul National University. (In Korean)
1985b North Korean Sites, Artifacts and Excavations, and the North/South Korean Academic Exchange Plan. *Tong-A Munhwa* 23:183–99. (In Korean)
1986 A Study on Korean and Japanese Neolithic Cultures. *Korea Historical Essay* 16:1–29. (In Korean)
1987 Neolithic Korea and China, Direction of Influence and Cultural Characteristics. *Academy of Korean Studies, Archaeological Publication* 1:3–22. (In Korean)
1988 Prehistoric Agriculture in Korea. *Papers of the 5th International Congress of Korean Studies*, pp. 384–93. Songan: Academy of Korean Studies. (In Korean)
1989 Prehistoric Agriculture in Korea. Paper presented at the Circum-Pacific Prehistory Conference, Seattle.
Im Hyo-jai and Kwon Hak-su
1984 *Osanni Site: A Neolithic Village Site on the East Coast*. Archaeological and Anthropological Papers, Vol. 9, Seoul National University. (In Korean)
Im Hyo-jai and Lee Chun-jeong
1988 *Osanni Site III*. Archaeological and Anthropological Papers, Vol. 13, Seoul National University. (In Korean)
Im Hyo-jai and Sarah M. Nelson
1976 Implications of the Sizes of Comb-Pattern Vessels in Han River Sites in Korea. *Hanguk Kogo Hakbo* 1:117–21.
Im Hyo-jai and Pak Soon-bal
1988 *Oi Do Shell Mound*. Seoul University Museum. (In Korean)
Im Hyo-taek
1978 A Study on the Pit Grave of Kaya on the Lower Nakdong River. *Hanguk Kogo Hakbo* 4:75–120. (In Korean)
Im Se-kwon
1980 On the Prehistoric Site at Jung Do Island, Chunchon. *Hanguk Kogo Hakbo* 9:45–69. (In Korean)
Ito Akio
1971 *Zur Chronologie der frühsillazeitlichen Gräber in Südkorea*. Munich: Bayerische Akademie der Wissenschaften, Philosophische-Historische Klasse. (In German with English summary)
Jeon Sang-woon
1974 *Science and Technology in Korea*. Cambridge, MA: MIT Press.
1976 Chemical Technology in Ancient Korea. *Korea Journal* 16(11):34–40.
Jettmar, Karl
1983 The Origins of Chinese Civilization: Soviet Views. In *The Origins of Chinese Civilization*. David N. Keightley, ed., pp. 217–36. Berkeley: University of California Press.

Jia Lanpo and Huang Weiwen
 1986 On the Recognition of China's Palaeolithic Cultural Traditions. In
 *Palaeoanthropology and Palaeolithic Archaeology in the People's Republic of
 China*. Wu Rukang and John W. Olsen, eds., pp. 259–65. Orlando: Academic
 Press.
Jin Fengyi
 1983 Studies of the Cultural Remains with Curve-Edged Bronze Daggers in
 Northeast China (Part 2). *Kaogu Xuebao* 1983(1):39–54. (In Chinese)
 1987 The Upper Xiajiadian Culture and its Ethnic Attribution. *Kaogu Xuebao*
 1987(2):177–208. (In Chinese)
Jin Hyun-ok
 1989a Mongch'onT'osong, the Capital of Ancient Paekche. *Seoul Magazine*, pp.
 7–14. Seoul.
 1989b Pusosansong: Legendary Fortress of the Ancient Paekche Kingdom. *Seoul
 Magazine*, pp. 14–19. Seoul.
 1989c A Drained Lake Bed Yields Paleolithic Bonanza. *Seoul Magazine*, pp. 12–17.
 Seoul.
Joe, Wanne J.
 1972 *Traditional Korea: A Cultural History*. Seoul: Chung'ang University Press.
Kaneko, Erika
 1966 A Review of Yayoi Period Burial Customs. *Asian Perspectives* 9:1–26.
Kang Bong-won
 1984 Research on Kaya and the Adjacent Area in the Formative Period. Kyunghee
 University Thesis Collection No. 12, pp. 7–33.
 1990 A Megalithic Tomb Society in Korea: A Social Reconstruction. MA Thesis,
 Arizona State University.
Kang Chang-kwang
 1975 On the Chronology of Neolithic Lightning Pattern Vessels. *Kogo Minsok*
 1975(6):31–58. (In Korean)
Kang Duk-hee
 1983 Gold Crowns of Shibarghan in Afghanistan and of the Three Kingdoms Period
 of Korea. *Korea Journal* 23(6):35–8.
Kang Hyon-suk
 1989 A Preliminary Study on the Structure of Kaya Stone Cists. *Hanguk Kogo
 Hakbo* 23:59–84. (In Korean)
Kang In-gu
 1973 An Aspect of Jar-Coffins of the Paekche Dynasty. *Paekche Munhwa*
 6:101–21. (In Korean)
 1976 On the Jar-Coffin from Yongchangni in Puyo. *Misul Charyo* 19:25–8. (In
 Korean)
 1977 *Studies on Paekche Tombs*. Seoul: Ilchisa Publisher. (In Korean)
 1984 *Research on Three Kingdoms Age Mounded Tombs*. Taegu: Yongnam
 University Press. (In Korean)
Kang In-gu, Yi Kon-mu, Han Yong-hee, and Yi Kang-sung 1979 *Songgungni I*.
 Seoul: National Museum. (In Korean)
Kang Man-gil
 1990 How History is Viewed in the North and the South: Convergence and
 Divergence. *Korea Journal* 30(2):4–19.
Kangwon National University Museum
 1984 *Survey Report of the Jung Do Site in Chunchon City*. Report No. 3. (In
 Korean)

Kayamoto Kamejiro
  1961 On the Excavation of the Tomb of Wangkeng, Lelang. *Misul Charyo* 4:17–30.
    (In Korean)
Kayamoto Tojin
  1962 *Han Tombs of Lo-lang: Their Studies by Japanese Scholars.* Tokyo: Memoirs
    of the Toyo Bunko No. 21. (In Japanese with English summary)
Kent, Kate P. and Sarah M. Nelson
  1976 Net Sinkers or Weft Weights? *Current Anthropology* 17(1):152.
Kim Byong-mo
  1976 The Origin of the Cut Stone Tomb in China and Its Influence in Korea.
    Hanguk Kogo Hakbo 11:1–25. (In Korean)
  1977 Ancient Tombs at Bang-i-dong, Seoul. *Kogohak* 4:1–35. (In Korean)
  1978 A Study of Paekche Tombs. *Hanguk Kogo Hakbo* 6:124–6. (In Korean)
  1981a A New Interpretation of Megalithic Monuments in Korea. In *Megalithic
    Cultures in Asia.* B.M. Kim, ed., pp. 164–89. Seoul: Hanyang University Press.
  1981b Excavations Uncover New Evidence. *Korean Culture* 2(2):40–1.
  1981c A Study on the Origin of Korean Megalithic Culture. *Hanguk Kogo Hakbo*
    10/11:55–78. (In Korean)
  1983 Investigation of the Prehistoric Cultures of the West Coast – Anmyon Do and
    the Islets and Coastal Regions of the Southwest. *Hanguk Kogo Hakbo*
    14/15:19–60. (In Korean)
  1987 Regarding Ho Hwang-ok. *Papers in Honor of the Retirement of Professor Kim
    Won-yong*, Vol. 1. Im Hyo-jai, ed., pp. 673–81. Seoul National University. (In
    Korean)
  1988 Cultural Exchange Between Ancient Korea and West Asia. *Korea History*
    1:471–91. (In Korean)
Kim Byong-mo and Shim Kwang-chu
  1987 *Isong Fortress Excavation Report.* Hanyang University Museum Research
    Series No. 5. (In Korean)
Kim Chae-kuei and Lee Un-chang
  1975 *A Report on the Excavation of Tombs at Hwangnamdong, Kyongju.* Yongnam
    University Museum Monograph No. 1. (In Korean with English summary)
  1978 *A Report on the Excavation of Tombs in Kuamdong, Chilgok.* Yongnam
    University Museum Monograph No. 2. (In Korean with English summary)
Kim Che-won
  1949 Han Dynasty Mythology and the Korean Legend of Tangun. *Archives of the
    Chinese Art Society of America* 3:43–8.
Kim Che-won and Kim Won-yong
  1966 *Treasures of Korean Art: 2000 Years of Ceramics, Sculpture and Jeweled Arts.*
    New York: Harry N. Abrams.
Kim Che-won and Yun Mu-byong
  1967 *Studies of Dolmens in Korea.* National Museum of Korea, Vol. 6. (In
    Korean)
Kim Chong-chol
  1966 The Comb Pattern Pottery Site at Misari. *Korean Archaeology* 1:19–27. (In
    Korean)
  1981 *Ancient Tombs at Chisandong, Koryong.* Keimyong University Museum. (In
    Korean)
Kim Chong-ki
  1968 Study on the Dwelling Sites in Prehistoric Korea. *Kogohak* 1:31–60. (In
    Korean)

1976 Dwelling Sites from the Geometric Period, Korea. *Asian Perspectives*
18(2):185–203.
Kim Chong-sun
1965 The Emergence of Multi-Centered Despotism in the Silla Kingdom: A Study
of Factional Struggles in Korea. PhD dissertation, University of Washington.
1969 Sources of Cohesion and Fragmentation in the Silla Kingdom. *Journal of
Korean Studies* 1(1):41–72.
1977 The Kolpum System: Basis for Sillan Social Stratification. *Journal of Korean
Studies* 1(2):43–69.
Kim Chong-won
1989 *The Chodo Site*. Pusan University Museum.
Kim Chong-won, Kwon Sang-yol and Im Hak-Jong
1990 *Kosong Yuldaeri, Tomb No. 2*. Chinju National Museum.
Kim Dong-ho
1984 *Sangnodaedo*. Pusan: Dong-A University Museum. (In Korean)
Kim Jong-bae
1975a Bronze Artifacts in Korea and their Cultural Historical Significance. In *The
Traditional Culture and Society of Korea: Prehistory*. R.J. Pearson, ed., pp.
130–91. Honolulu: The Center for Korean Studies, University of Hawaii.
1975b Formation of the Korean People. *Korea Journal* 15(12):12–16.
1976 Several Problems Regarding King Chun. *Hanguk Sa Yon'gu* 13:3–28. (In
Korean)
1977 The Character of the State of Wiman Choson. *Sachong* 21/2:57–73. (In Korean)
1978a The Question of Horse-Riding People in Korea (I). *Korea Journal*
18(9):39–50. (In Korean)
1978b The Question of Horse-Riding People in Korea (II). *Korea Journal*
18(11):41–52.
1979 A Study on the Origin of Korean Bronze Culture. *Ko Munhwa* 17:2–22. (In
Korean)
1983 *The Origin of the Korean Ethnic Group and Its Culture*. Koryo University
Publication No. 2.
1987 Formation of Ethnic Korean Nation and Coming of Its Ancient Kingdom
States. *Korea Journal* 27:33–9.
Kim Jong-hak
1967 A Study of Korea's Non-Decorated Pottery Culture. *Paek-San Hakbo*
4:1–100. (In Korean with English summary, pp. 244–9)
1968 A Study of Geometric Pattern Pottery Culture in Korea. *Paek-San Hakbo*
4:1–100. (In Korean with English summary, pp. 244–9)
1977 The Excavation Report on Yeanni Tombs. *Hanguk Kogo Hakbo* 2:2–18. (In
Korean)
1978a The Chronology of Bronze Culture in Korea. *Hanguk Kogo Hakbo* 5:1–16.
(In Korean)
1978b *The Prehistory of Korea*. R. and K. Pearson, trans. Honolulu: The
University of Hawaii Press.
1982 The Development of Ancient State "Kaya." *Hanguk Kogo Hakbo* 12:1–20. (In
Korean)
1983 Kimhae Naedong Stone Tomb. Appendix in *Pusan Dang Kamdong Old
Tombs*. Pusan University Museum. (In Korean)
Kim Jong-hak and Chung Jing-won
1980 *Kumgokdong Rock Shelter and Shell Mound*. Pusan University Museum. (In
Korean)

Kim Ki-ung
  1974 North Korea During the Bronze Age. *Puk-han* 3–5:303–12. (In Korean)
  1982 *Tomb Paintings in Korea*. Seoul: Dong-ho. (In Korean)
Kim Kwang-su
  1970 Amsadong Riverbank Site Excavation Report. *Yoksa Kyoyuk* 13:85–107. (In Korean)
Kim Kyo-kyong
  1979 Tokchon Songnisan Site Report. *Kogo Minsok* 1979(7):2–9.
Kim Se-ki
  1985 A Study on Vertical Entrance Style Tombs in Kaya Area. *Hanguk Kogo Hakbo* 17/18:41–90. (In Korean)
Kim Seong-jin
  1978 *A Handbook of Korea*. Seoul: Korean Overseas Information Service, Ministry of Culture and Information.
Kim Shin-kyu
  1966 A Study of Prehistoric Mammals in Korea. *Kogo Minsok* 1966(2):4–7. (In Korean)
Kim Song-ok, Shin Kwang-sop, Kim Chong-man and Kang Hee-chon
  1988 *Research Report on the Excavation of Kiln Sites of the Paekche Dynasty in Puyo*. Report of the Research of Antiquities, Vol. 2, Puyo National Museum.
Kim Tae-gon
  1983 A Study on the Rite of Changsung, Korea's Totem Pole. *Korea Journal* 23:4–19.
Kim Taek-kyu and Lee Un-chang
  1978 *Report of the Excavation of the Tombs in Kuamdong, Chilgok*. Yongnam University Museum. (In Korean)
Kim Won-yong
  1961 Comb Pattern Pottery Site at Misari, Kwang-ju. *Yoksa Hakbo* 14:133–45. (In Korean)
  1962 Stone Implements and Pottery from the Amsari Site. *Yoksa Hakbo* 18:355–83. (In Korean)
  1964 *A Jar-Coffin Cemetery at Shinchangni, Southwestern Korea*. Archaeological and Anthropological Papers, Vol. 1, Seoul National University. (In Korean)
  1966a Excavation of a Prehistoric Dwelling Site at Susongni near Seoul. *Misul Charyo* 11:1–16. (In Korean)
  1966b Wall Paintings of Koguryo Tombs. *Korea Journal* 6(4):21–3.
  1967a *Excavation of the Deposit Layers of Pungnamni, Seoul*. Archaeological and Anthropological Papers, Vol. 3, Seoul National University. (In Korean with English summary)
  1967b A Black Pottery Pot from Susongni. *Hanguk Kogohak* 1:1–4. (In Korean)
  1967c The Comb Pattern Pottery Culture Along the Reaches of the Yalu River. *Paeksan Hakpo* 3:99–108. (In Korean with English summary)
  1968a Prehistoric Objects from Cave Site at Kyodong, Chunchon City, Central Korea. *Kogohak* 1:129–40. (In Korean)
  1968b A Proposed Grouping of the Plain Coarse Pottery of Prehistoric Korea. *Kogohak* 1:1–30. (In Korean)
  1969 Carbon Dates in Korean Archaeology. *Kogohak* 2:1–16. (In Korean)
  1973 A Silla Pottery Jar with Incised Drawing of Animals in the Collection of the Kyongju Museum. *Kogo Misul* 118:4–9. (In Korean)
  1974a *Archaeology in Korea 1973*. Seoul National University Museum, Vol. 1. (In Korean with English summary)
  1974b On the Possible Silla Envoy Depicted on the Wall Painting of the Tomb of Li Hsien, Tang Dynasty. *Kogo Misul* 123/4:17–25. (In Korean)

1975a *Archaeology in Korea 1974*. Seoul National University Museum, Vol. 2. (In Korean with English summary)

1975b The Neolithic Culture of Korea. In *The Traditional Culture and Society of Korea: Prehistory*. R.J. Pearson, ed., pp. 61–111. Honolulu: The Center for Korean Studies, The University of Hawaii Press.

1976a *Archaeology in Korea 1975*. Seoul National University Museum, Vol. 3. (In Korean with English summary)

1976b The Six Villages of Saro and Kyongju Tombs. *Yoksa Hakbo* 70:1–14. (In Korean)

1977a *Archaeology in Korea 1976*. Seoul National University Museum, Vol. 4. (In Korean with English summary)

1977b Prehistoric Art. *Korea Journal* 17(4):7–13.

1978 *Archaeology in Korea 1977*. Seoul National University Museum, Vol. 5. (In Korean with English summary)

1979a *Archaeology in Korea 1978*. Seoul National University Museum, Vol. 6. (In Korean with English summary)

1979b Chojiri Shell Mound Excavation Report. *Hanguk Kogo Hakbo* 7:1–48. (In Korean)

1980a *Archaeology in Korea 1979*. Seoul National University Museum, Vol. 7. (In Korean with English summary)

1980b Prehistoric Rock Art at Bangudai, Ulchu, SE Korea. *Hanguk Kogo Hakbo* 9:5–22. (In Korean)

1980c Reconsideration of the Stone Engravings of the Wu Tomb and the Tangun Legend. *Kogo Misul* 145/7:10–15. (In Korean)

1980d *Murals in Old Korean Tombs*. Seoul: Ilchisa. (In Korean)

1981 Korean Archaeology Today. *Korea Journal* 21(9):22–43.

1982a Discoveries of Rice in Prehistoric Sites in Korea. *Journal of Asian Studies* 41(3):513–18.

1982b *Archaeology in Korea 1981*. Seoul National University Museum, Vol. 9. (In Korean with English summary)

1982c Proposal for "Puwondong" Period. *Hanguk Kogo Hakbo* 12:21–38. (In Korean)

1982d Development of Korean Archaeology I, Paleolithic and Neolithic Studies. *Dong-A Munhwa* 20:1–26. (In Korean)

1982e Kyongju: The Homeland of Korean Culture. *Korea Journal* 22(9):25–32.

1983a *Recent Archaeological Discoveries in the Republic of Korea*. Tokyo: The Centre for East Asian Studies, UNESCO.

1983b *Archaeology in Korea 1982*. Seoul National University Museum, Vol. 10. (In Korean with English summary)

1983c *Ancient Korean Painted Tombs*. Korean Cultural Publication, No. 1. (In Korean)

1985 *Archaeology in Korea 1984*. Seoul National University Museum, Vol. 12. (In Korean with English summary)

1986a *Art and Archaeology of Ancient Korea*. Seoul: The Taekwang Publishing Company.

1986b *Archaeology in Korea 1985*. Seoul National University Museum, Vol. 13. (In Korean with English summary)

1987a *Archaeology in Korea 1986*. Seoul National University Museum, Vol. 14. (In Korean with English summary)

1987b Evolution of Silla Burials in Kyongju. Address to the Pacific Science Congress, printed in the *Korea Herald* 29 August 1987, p. 4.

1988 Korean Archaeology Since 1945 – Retrospect and Prospect. Introduction. *Hanguk Kogo Hakbo* 21:5–24. (In Korean)

Kim Won-yong and Bae Ki-dong
    1983 Seoul National University Report. In *Chon'gongni*. Kim W.Y. and Bae K.D.,
        eds., pp. 5–173. Seoul: Munhwajae Kwalliguk. (In Korean)
Kim Won-yong and Chung Young-hwa
    1979 Note préliminaire sur l'industrie acheulienne de Chongokni en Corée. *Chintan
        Hakbo* 46/7:25–47.
Kim Won-yong and Im Hyo-jai
    1968 *Reconnaissance in the Southern Islands, Korea*. Seoul: Seoul National
        University. (In Korean with English summary)
Kim Won-yong, Im Hyo-jai, Choi Mong-Iyong, Yo Jung-chool and Kwak Sung-hun
    1973 *The Hunamni Site – A Prehistoric Village Site on the Han River: Progress
        Reports 1972–73*. Archaeological and Anthropological Papers of Seoul National
        University, Vol. 4. (In Korean with English summary)
    1974 *The Hunamni Site – A Prehistoric Village Site on the Han River: Progress
        Reports 1974*. Archaeological and Anthropological Papers of Seoul National
        University, Vol. 5. (In Korean with English summary)
    1976 *The Hunamni Site – A Prehistoric Village Site on the Han River: Progress
        Reports 1975*. Archaeological and Anthropological Papers of Seoul National
        University, Vol. 7. (In Korean with English summary)
    1978 *The Hunamni Site – A Prehistoric Village Site on the Han River: Progress
        Reports 1976, 1977*. Archaeological and Anthropological Papers of Seoul National
        University, Vol. 8. (In Korean with English summary)
Kim Won-yong, Im Hyo-jai and Kwon Hak-su
    1985 *Osanni Site Report II*. Archaeological and Anthropological Papers of Seoul
        National University Museum. Vol. 10. (In Korean with English summary)
Kim Won-yong, Im Hyo-jai and Lim Yong-gin
    1987 *Mongchon Fortress*. Seoul National University Museum. (In Korean)
Kim Won-yong, Im Hyo-jai and Pak Soon-bal
    1987 *Mongchon Tosong Report*. Seoul City Publication. (In Korean)
    1988 *Mongchon Tosong Report*. Seoul National University Museum. (In Korean)
Kim Won-yong and Kim Chong-ki
    1967 Report on a Tomb with Mural Painting in Koryong. *Hanguk Kogo* 2:1–20. (In
        Korean)
Kim Won-yong and Richard Pearson
    1977 Three Royal Tombs: New Discoveries in Korean Archaeology. *Archaeology*
        30(5):302–13.
Kim Yang-ok
    1981 A Study on the Designs of Bronze Artifacts in Korea. *Hanguk Kogo Hakbo*
        10/11:23–54. (In Korean)
Kim Yang-sun and Lim Byung-tae
    1968 Yoksamdong Dwelling Site Excavation Report. *Hanguk Sa Yongu* 20:1–51. (In
        Korean with English summary, pp. 443–4)
Kim Yong-bae
    1965 A Paekche Tomb in Kongju. *Misul Charyo* 10:22–3. (In Korean)
Kim Yong-bae and Han Byong-sam
    1969 Report on the Excavation of the Paekche Tombs at Taesan-myon, Sosan.
        Kogohak 2:49–76. (In Korean)
Kim Yong-gan
    1964 *Kumtalli Prehistoric Site Report*. Yujok Palgul Pogo, No. 10. Pyongyang:
        Society for the Study of History and Archaeology. (In Korean)
    1979 Evolutionary Characteristics of Korean Neolithic Transitional Clay Vessels.
        Kogo Minsok 1979(7):45–108. (In Korean)

Kim Yong-gan and So Guk-tae
   1972 Sopohang Prehistoric Remains Report. *Kogo Minsok* 4:31–145. (In Korean)
Kim Yong-gan and Suk Kwang-jun
   1984 *Namgyong Site Research*. Pyongyang: Kwahak Paek Kwa Sachon Chulgwansa.
      (In Korean)
Kim Yong-ki
   1965 *Excavation and Investigation of the Shell Mound Located at Nongsori*. Pusan
      National University Museum. (In Korean)
   1971 Tadaepo Shell Mound Excavation Report. *Pusan History* 2:113–31. (In
      Korean)
Kim Yong-ki and Chung Jing-won
   1965 The Songsan Shell Mound. *Paeksan Hakpo* 1:133–53. (In Korean)
Kim Yung-chung
   1977 *Women of Korea: A History from Ancient Times to 1945*. Seoul: Ewha
      Women's University Press.
Kondo Yoshiro
   1986 The Keyhole Tumulus and Its Relationship to Earlier Forms of Burial. In
      Windows on the Japanese Past. R. Pearson, ed., pp. 335–48. Center for Japanese
      Studies, The University of Michigan.
Kwangju National Museum
   1988a *Investigation Report of Ancient Tombs at Bannammyon in Naju County*. (In
      Korean)
   1988b *Hwangnyong Temple Excavation 1988*. (In Korean)
   1989 *Excavation Report of Jar-Coffin Tombs at Wauri in Yongam County*. (In
      Korean)
Kwon, Byung-rin
   1991 The Kaya Tombs: Unearthing a Trace of the Lost Kingdom. *Seoul Magazine*,
      March: 30–7.
Kwon Tae-won
   1988 A Study on the Yemaek, Choson and its Boundary. In *Papers of the 5th
      International Conference on Korean Studies*, Part I: *Archaeology and Prehistory*,
      pp. 299–315. (In Korean)
Kwon Yi-gu
   1986 A Physical Anthropological Study on Ancient Skeletal Remains from Korea.
      Hanguk Kogo Hakbo 19:105–28. (In Korean)
   1990 The Population of Ancient Korea in Physical Anthropological Perspective.
      Korea Journal 30(10):4–12.
Larichev, V.E. and B.G. Grigorenko
   1969 The Discovery of the Paleolithic in Korea (The Coulpo Culture). *Arctic
      Anthropology* 6(1):128–33.
Lee Chong-kyu
   1982 The Typology of the Korean Bronze Slim Dagger and its Temporal
      Transformation. *Hanguk Kogo Hakbo* 13:1–38. (In Korean)
   1985 The Nature of Early Iron Age Implements and the Development of Plain
      Coarse Pottery Culture on Cheju Do Island. *Hanguk Kogo Hakbo* 17/18:13–40.
      (In Korean)
   1987 *Taegwangni Juam Dam Report I*. Chonnam University Museum. (In Korean)
   1988a Bronze Age. *Hanguk Kogo Hakbo* 2:63–84. (In Korean)
   1988b *Pokchonni Rockshelter*. Cheju University Research Report 4.
Lee Hee-jun
   1983 Seriation and its Application to Korean Archaeological Data. *Hanguk Kogo
      Hakbo* 14/15:133–64. (In Korean)

1984 A Critique on the Chronological Studies of Korean Archaeology. *Hanguk Kogo Hakbo* 16:25–42. (In Korean)

Lee Hyong-ku

1988 The Origin of Stone Tomb Cultures of Northeast Asia. *Academy of Korean Studies, Part I*, pp. 395–432. (In Korean)

Lee In-suk

1987 Report Concerning Korean Prehistoric Gokok. *Papers in Honor of the Retirement of Professor Kim Won-yong*, Vol. 1. Im Hyo-jai, ed., pp. 357–69. Seoul National University. (In Korean)

1989 A Study of Korean Ancient Glass. *Komunhwa* 34(6):79–95. (In Korean)

Lee, J.W.

1978 The Formation and Growth of Paekche. *Korea Journal* 18(10):35–40.

Lee Kang-sung

1979 A Study on Bronze Culture in Liaoning: Bronze-Dagger Culture and the Xiajiadian Upper Culture through Bronze Artifacts. *Hanguk Kogo Hakbo* 6:1–95. (In Korean)

Lee Ki-moon

1977 *Geschichte der Koreanischen Sprache*. Wiesbaden: Dr Ludwig Reichert Verlag.

Lee Nan-yong

1983 *Bronze Mirrors of Korea*. Academy of Korean Studies. (In Korean)

Lee Sang-man

1983 Geological Setting and Environment. In *Chon'gongni*. Kim W.Y. and Bae K.D., eds., pp. 531–61. Seoul: Munhwajae Kwalliguk. (In Korean)

Lee Soon-jin

1983 A Study of Wood Coffins in Northwestern Korea. *Kogo Minsok* 15:99–158. (In Korean)

Lee Un-chang

1961 Some Examples of Menhirs in Chungchong Nam Do. *Misul Charyo* 3:13–15. (In Korean)

1962 Menhirs in Chungchong Nam Do. *Misul Charyo* 5:15–18. (In Korean)

1982a The Chronological Study on Tombs of "Kaya." *Hanguk Kogo Hakbo* 12:157–212. (In Korean)

1982b *Kiln Sites of Silla and Kaya Pottery*. Hosang Women's University. (In Korean)

Lee Yung-jo

1977 A New Interpretation of the Prehistoric Chronology of Korea: The Application of MASCA Theory. *Hanguk Sa Yongu* 15:3–43. (In Korean)

1978 A New Interpretation of the Prehistoric and Historic Chronology of Korean Archaeology. *Korea Journal* 18(6):33–8.

1980 Korean Dolmen Society and Ritual. *Dongbang Hakji* 23/4:287–307. Yonsei University. (In Korean)

1982 Paleolithic and Mesolithic Cultures in Korea: An Overview. *Korea Journal* 22(3):39–46.

1983 *Turobong Paleolithic Culture Report*. Chungbuk National University Report No. 4. (In Korean)

1984a Excavation Report on the Suyanggae Paleolithic Site. *Chungju Dam Submergence Area Cultural Relics Report*, Vol. 1: *Archaeology*, pp. 101–86. Chungbuk University Museum. (In Korean)

1984b 1982–3 Excavation of Archaeological Sites in the Submergence Area of Ch'ungju Dam Construction. *Korea Journal* 24(11):4–26.

1984c Excavation Report of the Hwangsongni B Site. *Chungju Dam Submergence*

Area Cultural Relics Report, Vol. 1: *Archaeology*, pp. 391–464. Chungbuk University Museum. (In Korean)

1986a Paleolithic Culture in Korea – Especially the Turubong and Suyanggae Sites. *Special Exhibition of Korean Paleolithic Culture*, pp. 96–101. Chungbuk National University Museum. (In Korean)

1986b On the Faunal Remains from the Paleolithic Sites in Korea. *Hanguk Kogo Hakbo* 19:19–62. (In Korean)

1988a Report on Usanni Kogchon Dolmens. *Juam Dam Report II*, pp. 23–122. Chonnam University Museum. (In Korean)

1988b *Progress Report on the Upper Paleolithic Culture at Suyanggae in Tanyang Korea*. Academy of Korean Studies. (In Korean)

1989 *A Study on the Boat-Shaped Tools of the Upper Paleolithic*. Komunhwa: Korean Association of University Museums. (In Korean)

1990 Paleontological and Archaeological Remains from Turubong Cave Complex in Korea. 14th Congress of the IPPA, *Abstracts*. Indo-Pacific Prehistory Association.

Lee Yung-jo, Ha Moon-sik and Choi Sang-ki

1988 Sasuri Taejon Dolmens. *Juam Dam Report II*. Chonnam University. (In Korean)

Lee Yung-jo, Lee Young-mon, Dong Mun-sok and Woo Jong-yoon

1988 *Dolmens at Usanni, Gokchon*. Chonnam University Museum. (In Korean)

Lee Yung-jo, Woo Jong-yoon and Ha Moon-sik

1988 *Juam Dam Submerged Area – Research Report on Excavations No. 5*. Chonnam University Museum. (In Korean)

Leroi-Gourhan, André

1946 Archéologie du Pacific nord. *Travaux et Mémoires de l'Institut d'Ethnologie, Université de Paris*, pp. 1–553.

Li Hui-lin

1983 The Domestication of Plants in China: Ecogeographical Considerations. In *The Origins of Chinese Civilization*. D.N. Keightley, ed., pp. 21–64. Berkeley: University of California Press.

Li Ki-baek

1984 *A New History of Korea*. Edward W. Wagner and Edward J. Shultz, trans. Cambridge, MA: Harvard University Press.

LICRA (Liaoning Institute of Cultural Relics and Archaeology)

1986 A Brief Report on Exploratory Excavation of Neolithic Ruins in Fuxin, Cha-hai, Liaohai. *Wenwu Xuegan* 1986(8):1–17. (In Chinese)

Lim Byung-tae

1968 The Chronology of Mumun Pottery in the Han River Region. *Hanguk Sa Yongu* 547–67. (In Korean)

Lim Young-jin

1985 Classification and Transition in Pit Houses. *Hanguk Kogo Hakbo* 17/18:107–62. (In Korean)

1987 Report on Sokchondong Stone Coffins and Earth Mounds. In *Papers in Honor of the Retirement of Professor Kim Won-yong*, Vol. 1. Im Hyo-jai, ed., pp. 475–500. Seoul National University. (In Korean)

1988 Koguryo and Paekche. *Hanguk Kogo Hakbo* 21:85–118. (In Korean)

Lin Yun

1985 The Tuanjie Culture. *Beifang Wenwu* 1985(1):8–22. (In Chinese)

1986 A Reexamination of the Relationship between Bronzes of the Shang Culture and of the Northern Zone. In *Studies of Shang Archaeology*, K.C. Chang, ed., pp. 237–73. New Haven: Yale University Press.

Liu, Zhenhua
  1982 On Late Xituanshan Culture of Jilin. *Dongbei Kogo Yu Lishi* 1982(1):80–4. (In Chinese)
MacCord, Howard A.
  1958 The Able Site, Kapyong, Korea. *Asian Perspectives* 2(1):128–38.
McCune, Evelyn
  1962 *The Arts of Korea: An Illustrated History*. Rutland, VT: Charles E. Tuttle Company.
McCune, Shannon
  1956 *Korea's Heritage: A Regional and Social Geography*. Tokyo: Charles E. Tuttle Company.
  1976 Geographical Observations on Korea. *Bulletin of the Korean Research Center, Journal of Social Sciences and Humanities* 44:1–19.
Meacham, William
  1983 Origins and Development of the Yüen Coastal Neolithic: A Microcosm of Culture Change on the Mainland of East Asia. In *The Origins of Chinese Civilization*. David N. Keightley, ed., pp. 147–75. Berkeley: University of California Press.
Michael, Henry L.
  1984 Absolute Chronologies of Late Pleistocene and Early Holocene Cultures of Northern Asia. *Arctic Anthropology* 21(2):1–68.
Mikami Tsugio
  1961 *The Dolmens and Stone Cists in Manchuria and Korea*. Tokyo: Yoshikawa Kobunkan. (In Japanese with English summary)
Miller, Roy Andrew
  1980 *Origins of the Japanese Language*. Seattle: University of Washington Press.
  1986 Linguistic Evidence and Japanese Prehistory. In *Windows on the Japanese Past: Studies in Archaeology and Prehistory*. Richard J. Pearson, ed., pp. 101–20. Ann Arbor: Center for Japanese Studies, University of Michigan.
Miyamoto Kazuo
  1985 Chronological and Areal Differences in the Prehistoric Pottery of Northeast China and Contiguous Areas. *Shirin* 69(2):167–217.
  1990 Research on the Shangmashi Upper Layer Culture. Circum-Bohai Archaeological Conference, Dalian, PRC.
Mokpo University Museum
  1984 *Dolmens in Chongnyongni and Changchonni in Yongamgun*. Mokpo University Museum Monographs. (In Korean)
  1986 *A Dwelling Site at Changchonni in Yongam*. (In Korean)
Mongait, A.L.
  1969 Archaeological Cultures and Ethnic Units. *Soviet Anthropology and Archaeology* 7(1):3–25.
Movius, Hallam
  1948 The Lower Paleolithic Cultures of Southern and Eastern Asia. *Transactions of the American Philosophical Society* 38(4):329–420.
Mun Myong-dae
  1973 Prehistoric Rock Art at Ulssan. *Munhwajae* 7:33–40. (In Korean)
Munhwajae Kwalliguk
  1974 *Chonmachong*. Institute of Cultural Properties. (In Korean)
  1985 *Hwangnamdong Great Tomb, North Mound*. Institute of Cultural Properties. (In Korean)
  1987 *Kimhae Yangdongni Old Tombs*. Institute of Cultural Properties. (In Korean)

Nagamine Mitsukazu
   1986 Clay Figurines and Jomon Society. In *Windows on the Japanese Past: Studies in Archaeology and Prehistory*. R. Pearson, ed., pp. 255–66. Ann Arbor: Center for Japanese Studies, University of Michigan.
National Museum of Korea
   1968 *Selected Bronze Objects of the Early Metal Period in Korea.*
   1971 *Treasures from the Tomb of King Munyong (r. 501–523) of the Paekche Dynasty.* (In Korean)
   1977 *A Stone Cist at Namsongni.* Research Publication, Vol. 10. (In Korean)
   1979 *Songgungni Site I.* (In Korean)
   1981 *Jung Do Island Progress Report II (Second Year).* Research Publication, Vol. 13. (In Korean)
   1986 *Catalog, National Museum of Korea, Seoul.*
   1988 *Yongingun Relics.* Research Publication, Vol. 20. (In Korean)
Needham, Joseph
   1958 *The Development of Iron and Steel Technology in China.* London: Newcomen Society, The Science Museum.
Nelson, Sarah M.
   1973 Chulmun Period Villages on the Han River in Korea, Subsistence and Settlement. PhD Dissertation, University of Michigan.
   1975a The Subsistence Base of Middle Han Sites of the Chulmun Period. *Asian Perspectives* 18(1):5–14.
   1975b *Han River Chulmuntogi.* Program in East Asian Studies, Occasional Paper No. 9. Western Washington State College.
   1982 The Origins of Rice Agriculture in Korea, A Symposium. Introduction, pp. 511–12. The Effects of Rice Agriculture in Prehistoric Korea, pp. 531–43. Comments on Kim and Choi, pp. 547–8. *Journal of Asian Studies* 41(3):511–48.
   1983 The Past Decade in Korean Archaeology. *Hanguk Kogo Hakbo* 10:52–6.
   1987 Tribes in the Chulmun Period. In *Papers in Honor of the Retirement of Professor Kim Won-yong*, Vol. 1. Im Hyo-jai, ed., pp. 805–13. Seoul National University.
   1990 The Neolithic of Northeastern China and Korea. *Antiquity* 64(243):234–48.
   1991a Mumumtogi and Megalithic Monuments: A Reconsideration of The Dating. *Papers of the British Association of Korean Studies*, Vol. 3:183–94.
   1991b The Statuses of Women in Ko-Silla: Evidence from Archaeology and Historic Documents. *Korea Journal* 31(2):101–7.
   1992a Korean Archaeological Sequences from the First Ceramics to the Introduction of Iron. In *Chronologies in Old World Archaeology*, 3rd edn. R.W. Ehrich, ed. Vol. 1, pp. 430–8; Vol. 2, pp. 417–24. Chicago: University of Chicago Press.
   1992b Gender Hierarchy and the Queens of Silla. In *Sex and Gender Hierarchies*. B.D. Miller, ed. Cambridge: Cambridge University Press.
Nishida, Masaki
   1983 The Emergence of Food Production in Neolithic Japan. *Journal of Anthropological Archaeology* 2(4):305–22.
OAPSPM (Office for the Preservation of Antiquities and Shenyang Palace Museum)
   1985 The Second Excavation of the Neolithic Site at Xinle in Shenyang. *Kaogu Xuebao* 1985(2):209–22. (In Chinese)
Oh Chi-young
   1971 A Pollen Analysis in the Peat Sediments from Pyungtaek County in Korea. *Korean Journal of Botany* 14:3. (In Korean)

Ohno Susumu
  1970 *The Origin of the Japanese Language*. Tokyo: Japan Cultural Society.
Ohyi, Harva
  1978 Some Comments on the Early Paleolithic of Japan. In *Early Paleolithic in South and East Asia*. F. Ikawa-Smith, ed., pp. 299–310. The Hague: Mouton.
Okladnikov, A.P.
  1964 Ancient Population of Siberia and its Culture. In *The Peoples of Siberia*. M.G. Levine and L.P. Potapov, eds., S. Dunn, trans., pp. 13–98. Chicago: University of Chicago Press.
  1965 *The Soviet Far East in Antiquity: An Archaeological and Historical Study of the Maritime Regions of the USSR*. Arctic Institute of North America, Anthropology of the North: Translations from Russian Sources, No. 6. Toronto: University of Toronto Press.
  1978 The Paleolithic of Mongolia. In *Early Paleolithic in South and East Asia*. F. Ikawa-Smith, ed., pp. 317–25. The Hague: Mouton.
Olsen, Stanley J.
  1984 The Early Domestication of the Horse in North China. *Archaeology* 62–62, 77.
Osgood, Cornelius
  1954 *The Koreans and Their Culture*. Tokyo: Charles E. Tuttle Company.
Paekche Culture Research
  1988 *Nonsan Taegongni Paekche Tombs*. (In Korean)
Pai, Hyung-il
  1989a Lelang and the "Interaction Sphere": An Alternative Approach to Korean State Formation. *Archaeological Review From Cambridge* 8(1):64–75.
  1989b Lelang and the Interaction Sphere in Korean Prehistory. PhD Dissertation, Harvard.
Pak Chan-kirl and Yang Kyung-rin
  1974 KAERI Radiocarbon Measurements III. *Radiocarbon* 16(2):192–7.
Pak Dong-won
  1983 Paleo-Environment of the Paleolithic Sites at Chon'gongni. In *Chon'gongni*, Kim W.Y. and Bae K.D., eds., pp. 515–30. Seoul: Munhwajae Kwalliguk. (In Korean)
Pak Hi-hyun
  1984 Report on the Upper Paleolithic Culture of Changnae at Chewon, Korea. In *Chungju Dam Submergence Area Cultural Resource Report*, Vol. 1: *Archaeology*, pp. 187–270. Chungbuk University Museum. (In Korean)
  1990 The Upper Palaeolithic Habitation Site at Ch'angnae, Korea. In 14th Congress of the IPPA, *Abstracts*. Indo-Pacific Prehistory Association.
Pak Son-hung and Li Won-kun
  1965 Interim Report of Excavations of a Prehistoric Site at Soktalli. *Kogo Minsok* 3:28–35. (In Korean)
Pak Soon-bal
  1989a On the Proto-Three Kingdoms Period Pottery in the Han River Valley. *Hanguk Kogo Hakbo* 23:21–58. (In Korean)
  1989b Mongchon Tosong Excavation Research Report. *Hanguk Kogo Hakbo* 23:266–81. (In Korean)
Pak Yong-an
  1977 Submergence of the Yellow Sea Coast of Korea and Stratigraphy of the Sinpyeongcheon Marsh, Kimje, Korea. *Hanguk Kogo Hakbo* 3:81–91. (In Korean)

Pak Young-sook
   1988 The Origins of Silla Metal Work. *Orientations* September:44–53.
Park Dong-baek and Choo Youn-sik
   1988 *Hapchon Chopori B Tomb*. Changwon University Museum Research Report
      No. 2.
Park Kwan-sup
   1987 A Historical and Geographical Study of Manchuria and Chientao, Lost Land
      of Korea. *Korean Observer* 18(1):1–28.
Park Sun-joo
   1990 Upper Pleistocene Child's Skeleton from Hungsu Cave, Ch'ongwon, Korea.
      *Abstracts of the International Symposium on the Quaternary Natures, with Special
      Reference to the Quaternary Natures of East Asia*. Seoul: Seoul National
      University.
Park Young-chol
   1976 The Prehistoric Natural Environment of Korea. *Hanguk Sa Yongu* 14:16–18.
      (In Korean)
Parker, E.H.
   1890 On Race Struggles in Korea. *Transactions of the Asiatic Society of Japan*
      23:137–228.
Patterson, Thomas C.
   1989 Combined and Uneven Development: Alternate Routes to the Formation of
      Tributary States in Peru and the Far East. Paper presented at the Circum-Pacific
      Prehistory Conference, Seattle.
Pearson, Richard J.
   1974 Pollen Counts in North China. *Antiquity* 68(191):226–8.
   1976 Japan, Korea and China: The Problems of Defining Continuities. *Asian
      Perspectives* 19:176–89.
   1977 Paleoenvironment and Human Settlement in Japan and Korea. *Science*
      197(4310):1239–46.
   1978 Lolang and the Rise of Korean States and Chiefdoms. *Journal of the Hong
      Kong Archaeological Society* 7(1976–8):77–90.
   1980 Archaeology. In *Studies on Korea, a Scholars' Guide*. Kim Han-kyo, ed., pp.
      13–26. Honolulu: University of Hawaii Press.
   1985 Some Recent Studies in the Chronology and Social Development of Old Silla.
      In *Essays in Honor of Professor Dr Tsugio Mikami on his 77th Birthday –
      Archaeology*. Tokyo: Heibonsha.
Pearson, Richard J. and Im Hyo-jai
   1968 Preliminary Archaeological Research on Cheju Island, Korea. *Proceedings of
      the VIII International Congress of Anthropological and Ethnological Sciences*
      3:199–204.
Pearson, Richard J., Jong-wook Lee, Wonyoung Koh and Anne Underhill
   1986 Social Ranking in the Kingdom of Old Silla, Korea: Analysis of Burials.
      Journal of Anthropological Archaeology 8:1–50.
Pirazzoli-t'serstevens, Michele
   1982 *The Han Dynasty*. J. Seligman, trans. New York: Rizzoli.
Pope, Geoffrey
   1990 Replacement Versus Regionally Continuous Models: The Fossil Evidence from
      East Asia. Paper presented at the 14th Congress of the Indo-Pacific Prehistory
      Association, Yogyakarta, Indonesia.
Pusan City Museum
   1983 *Pusan Tokchondong Tomb*. Research Report No. 1. (In Korean)

1988 *Pusan Nopodong*. Research Report No. 2. (In Korean)

Pusan University Museum

1983a *A Group of Tombs from Pokchandong, Tongnae, Pusan*. Research Report No. 5. (In Korean)

1983b *Ulchu Hwasanni Remains*. Research Report No. 6. (In Korean)

1983c *Pusan Tangkamdong Old Tombs*. Research Report No. 7. (In Korean)

1986 *Hamyang Paekchonni 1 Tomb I*. Research Report No. 10. (In Korean)

1988 *Catalog*, Silla and Kaya Exhibit.

1989 *Nuk-do Residential Area*. Research Report No. 13. (In Korean)

Puyo National Museum

1988 *Puyo Chongamni 1*. (In Korean)

1989 *Hapsongni Stone Cist*. Hanguk Kogo Misul Yenjusuo 1. (In Korean)

Qiu Zhonglang

1985 The Middle Palaeolithic of China. In *Palaeoanthropology and Palaeolithic Archaeology in the People's Republic of China*. Rukang Wu and John W. Olsen, eds., pp. 187–210. Orlando: Academic Press.

Rawson, Jessica and Emma Bunker

1990 *Ancient Chinese and Ordos Bronzes*. Exhibition Catalog. Hong Kong Museum of Art.

Renfrew, Colin

1973 *Before Civilization: The Radiocarbon Revolution and Prehistoric Europe*. New York: Alfred A. Knopf.

1978 Space, Time and Polity. In *Evolution of Social Systems*. J. Friedman and M.J. Rowlands, eds., pp. 89–112. Pittsburgh: University of Pittsburgh Press.

Rhee Song Nai

1984 Emerging Complex Society in Prehistoric Southwest Korea. PhD Dissertation, University of Oregon.

1989 Secondary State Formation: The Case of Early Korea. Paper presented to the Circum-Pacific Prehistory Conference, Seattle.

Rhi Chong-sun 1976 A Study of Stone Cists in Korea. *Hanguk Kogo Hakbo* 1:29–86. (In Korean with English summary)

Rindos, David

1984 *The Origins of Agriculture: An Evolutionary Perspective*. Orlando: Academic Press.

Riotto, Maurizio

1989 *The Bronze Age in Korea. A Historical Archaeological Outline*. Italian School of East Asian Studies Occasional Papers No. 1. Kyoto.

Ro Hyuk-jin

1986 English summaries. In *Prehistory of Kangwondo Province, Korea*. Seoul: Hallym University Publisher.

Rogers, Michael C.

1960 The Thanatochronology of Some Kings of Silla. *Monumenta Serica* 19:335–48.

Rostoker, William

1982–3 Cast Iron in the Han Dynasty: A Study in Mass-Production (abstract). *Early China* 8:177.

Rouse, Irving

1986 *Migrations in Prehistory: Inferring Population Movement from Cultural Remains*. New Haven: Yale University Press.

Rowlands, Michael

1987 Centre and Periphery: A Review of a Concept. In *Centre and Periphery in the Ancient World*. Rowlands, Larsen and Kristiansen, eds., pp. 1–11. Cambridge: Cambridge University Press.

Rudolf, Richard C., ed.
  1978 *Chinese Archaeological Abstracts*. Monumenta Archaeologica 6. Los Angeles:
    The Institute of Archaeology, University of California.
Sackett, James R.
  Isochrestism and Style: A Clarification. *Journal of Anthropological Archaeology*
    5:266–77.
Sahlins, Marshall
  1968 *Tribesmen*. Englewood Cliffs, NJ: Prentice-Hall.
Sample, L.L.
  1967 Culture, History and Chronology in South Korea's Neolithic. PhD
    Dissertation, University of Wisconsin.
  1974 Tongsamdong: A Contribution to Korean Neolithic Culture History. *Arctic
    Anthropology* 11(2):1–125.
  1978 Prehistoric Cultural Relations between Western Japan and Southeastern Korea.
    Asian Perspectives 19(1):172–5.
  1989 Impact of Metal Technology on State Formation in Ancient Korea. Paper
    presented at the Circum-Pacific Prehistory Conference, Seattle.
Sample, L.L. and Albert Mohr
  1964 Progress Report on Archaeological Research in the Republic of Korea. *Arctic
    Anthropology* 2:99–104.
Sarton, George
  1936 Chinese Glass at the Beginning of the Confucian Age. *Isis* 25:73–9.
Sayers, Robert with Ralph Rinzler
  1987 *The Korean Onggi Potter*. Smithsonian Folklife Studies No. 5. Washington,
    DC: Smithsonian Institution Press.
Seoul National University Museum
  1975 *Stone-Mounded Tombs at Sokchondong, Seoul*. Archaeological and
    Anthropological Papers of Seoul National University Museum, Vol. 6.
  1984 *Archaeological Atlas of Korea*. Seoul National University.
Serizawa, Chosuke
  1978 The Early Paleolithic in Japan. In *Early Paleolithic in South and East Asia*. F.
    Ikawa-Smith, ed., pp. 287–97. The Hague: Mouton.
  1986 The Paleolithic Age of Japan in the Context of East Asia: A Brief
    Introduction. In *Windows on the Japanese Past*. R. Pearson, ed., pp. 191–7.
    Center for Japanese Studies, Michigan.
Service, Elman
  1962 *Cultural Evolution*. New York: Holt, Rinehart and Winston.
  1966 *Origins of the State and Civilization*. New York: Random House.
Shao Zongzheng
  1990 A Preliminary Analysis of Hebei Ancient Xia and Shang Cultures. Paper
    presented to the International Circum-Bohai Archaeological Conference, Dalian,
    China.
Shim Bong-kun
  1981 Relationship between the Dolmens of Korea and Japan. *Hanguk Kogo Hakbo*
    10/11:79–108. (In Korean)
  1982a Jar Burial at Kimhae Jinaedong. *Hanguk Kogo Hakbo* 12:89–100. (In Korean)
  1982b *Ancient Tombs in Sanma Area of Hapchon*. Report of the Research of
    Antiquities No. 6, Tong-A University Museum. (In Korean)
  1984 *Kimhae Kwisan*. Report of the Research of Antiquities No. 9, Tong-A
    University Museum. (In Korean)
Shin Kyong-chol
  1982 A Study on the Soft Grayish Potteries of 1st–3rd Century AD, Discovered in

Pusan and Kyongnam Province. *Hanguk Kogo Hakbo* 12:39–88. (In Korean)

So, Kuk-tae
  1964 Top-shaped Pottery at Sinhungdong Dwelling Site. *Kogo Minsok*
    1964(3):35–45. (In Korean)

Sohn Pow-key
  1972 Lower and Middle Paleolithic Industries of the Stratified Sokchangni Cultures.
    Hanguk Sa Yongu 7:1–58. (In Korean)
  1973 The Upper Paleolithic Habitation, Sokchangni, Korea. *Hanguk Sa Yongu*
    9:15–57. (In Korean)
  1974 Paleolithic Culture of Korea. *Korea Journal* 14(4):4–11.
  1975 Chommal Cave. *Hanguk Sa Yongu* 11:9–53. (In Korean)
  1978a The Early Paleolithic Industries of Sokchang-ni, Korea. *Early Paleolithic in
    South and East Asia*. F. Ikawa-Smith, ed., pp. 233–45. The Hague: Mouton.
  1978b Korean Paleolithic Research: Investigations at Chommal Cave, Chejon.
    Hanguk Sa Yongu 19:1–18. (In Korean)
  1982 *Early Man at Sangnodae Do*. Seoul: Soo Su Won Publishing. (In Korean)
  1983 *Early Man at Turubong Cave No. 9 near Ch'ongju, Korea*. Seoul: Museum of
    Yonsei University. (In Korean)
  1984a Early Man in Prehistoric Korea – Lower Paleolithic to Bronze Age Culture:
    The Case of Kumgul Cave Site at Todamni, Maepo-up, Tanyang-gun,
    Chungdong Puk Do. *Chungju Dam Submergence Area Cultural Relics Report*,
    Vol. 1: *Archaeology*, pp. 15–99. Chungbuk University Museum. (In Korean)
  1984b The Paleoenvironment of Middle and Upper Pleistocene Korea. In *The
    Evolution of The East Asian Environment*, Vol. 2: *Paleobotany, Paleozoology and
    Paleoanthropology*. Robert Orr Whyte, ed., pp. 877–93. Hong Kong.
  1985 Homo Sapiens Sangsiensis. *L'Anthropologie* 89(1):47–150.
  1988 *Korean Paleolithic Study Guide 1988*. Seoul: Yonsei University Press. (In
    Korean)
  1990 A Summary Report on Pleistocene Research in Korea. Paper presented to the
    14th Congress of the Indo-Pacific Prehistory Association, Jakarta,
    Indonesia.

Sohn Pow-key, Kim Chol-choon and Hong Yi-sup
  1970 *The History of Korea*. Seoul: Korean National Commission for UNESCO.

Sohn Pow-key and Park Young-chol
  1980 *Report of the Excavation at Yonggul Cave at Chommal: The Palaeoecology*.
    Yonsei University Museum. (In Korean)

Sohn Pow-key, Park Young-chul and Han Chang-gyun
  1990 Yonggul Cave: Paleontological Evidence and Cultural Behavior. Paper
    presented to the Indo-Pacific Prehistory Conference, Jakarta, Indonesia.

Sohn Pow-key, Pyon T'ae-sop, Han Yong-u, Yi Ki-dong and Im Hyo-jai
  1987 Reflections on Studies in Ancient Korean History, Colloquium of Five
    Historians. *Korea Journal* 27(12):4–22.

Sohn Pow-key and Shin Sook-chung
  1990 Recent Study on Excavation of the Shell-Midden at Sangnodae Do. Paper
    presented at the Indo-Pacific Prehistory Conference. Jakarta, Indonesia.

Sok Kwang-jun
  1979 Research on Dolmens in Northwestern Korea. *Kogo Minsok* 1979(7):109–82.
    (In Korean)

Sokchondong Archaeological Team
  1987 *Report on the Stone Mounded Tombs at Sokchondong*. Seoul: Seoul City. (In
    Korean)

Son Byong-hon
    1982 Artifact Classification in Archaeology. *Hanguk Kogo Hakbo* 13:135–43. (In
        Korean)
    1985 People Buried in Lo-Lang Tombs. *Hanguk Kogo Hakbo* 17/18:1–12. (In
        Korean)
Song Ju-taek
    1975 A Study of Paekche Forts. *Studies of Paekche* 6:71–104. (In Korean)
Song Sang-yong
    1983 A Brief History of the Study of the Chomsongdae in Kyongju. *Korea Journal*
        23(8):16–21.
Soongsil Museum
    1986 *Catalog of Korean Christian University Museum.*
Spaulding, Albert
    1982 Structure in Archaeological Data: Nominal Variables. In *Essays on
        Archaeological Typology.* Robert Whallon and James A. Brown, eds., pp. 1–20.
        Evanston, IL: Center for American Archeology.
SSI (Social Science Institute)
    1986 *Neolithic Culture of North Korea.* Pyongyang: Social Science Institute. (In
        Korean)
Suh Sung-hun and Shin Kwang-sop
    1984 Pyojongni Paekche Ruins. Appendix 3 of *Jung Do V.* National Museum of
        Korea.
Suh Sung-hun and Song Nak-jun
    1989 *Second Report on the Excavation of Taegongni Dwelling Site.* Juam Dam
        Report No. 6. Chonnam University.
Sun, E-tu Zen and John de Francis
    1966 *Chinese Social History.* New York: Octagon Books.
Taylor, Sarah
    1989 The Introduction and Development of Iron Production in Korea: A Survey.
        World Archaeology 20(3):422–33.
To Yu-ho
    1964 Problems of the Kulpo Palaeolithic Culture in Korea. *Kogo Minsok* 2:3–7. (In
        Korean)
To Yu-ho and Hwang Ki-dok
    1957 Preliminary Report on the Chitamni Site. *Munhwa Yusan* 5:20–37. (In
        Korean)
Tong Enzheng
    1982 Slate Cist Graves and Megalithic Chamber Tombs in Southwest China:
        Archaeological, Historical and Ethnographical Approaches to the Identification of
        Early Ethnic Groups. *Journal of Anthropological Archaeology* 1:266–74.
Tong Zhuchen
    1979 On Microlithic Cultures in North and Northeast China. *Kaogu Xuebao*
        1979(4):403–22. (In Chinese)
Torii, Riuzo
    1926 *Les Dolmens de la Corée.* Memoirs of the Research Department of the Toyo
        Bunko. Tokyo: Toyo Bunko.
    1930 *Les Dolmens du Chan-toung.* Memoirs of the Research Department of the
        Toyo Bunko. Tokyo: Toyo Bunko.
Townsend, Alexander H.
    1975 Cultural Evolution During the Neolithic Period in West Central Korea. PhD
        Dissertation, University of Hawaii.

Umehara Sueji
  1926 Deux grandes découvertes archéologiques en Corée. *Revue des Arts Asiatiques*
      3:24–33.
  1952 Newly Discovered Tombs with Wall Paintings of the Kao-kou-li Dynasty.
      Archives of the Chinese Art Society of America 6:8–9.
Vreeland, Nera and Rinn-sup Shinn
  1976 *Area Handbook for North Korea*. Washington, DC: Superintendent of
      Documents.
Waltham, Clae
  1971 *Shu Ching: Book of History*. Chicago: Henry Regnery.
Wang Chengsheng
  1990 An Introduction of the Bronze Daggers Unearthed in Liaoning Province in
      Recent Years and Their Ages. Paper presented to the Circum-Bohai
      Archaeological Conference, Dalian, PRC.
Wang Chi-wu
  1961 *The Forests of China*. Maria Moors Cabot Foundation Publication No. 5.
      Cambridge, MA: Harvard University Press.
Wang Mianhou
  1990 "Liang Mo" and "Mo Cheng" in the Han Dynasty and Earlier. Paper
      presented to the Circum-Bohai Archaeology Conference, Dalian,
      PRC.
Wang Yong-buo
  1987 Ancient Wooden Boat Found on the Liaodong Peninsula. *Wenwu*
      1987(5):29–31. (In Chinese)
Wang Zhongshu 1982 *Han Civilization*. K.C. Chang *et al.*, trans. New Haven: Yale
      University Press.
Watanabe Hitoshi
  1985 The Chopper-Chopping Tool Complex of Eastern Asia: An
      Ethnoarchaeological-Ecological Reexamination. *Journal of Anthropological
      Archaeology* 4(1):1–18.
  1986 Community Habitation and Food Gathering in Prehistoric Japan. In *Windows
      on the Japanese Past*. R. Pearson, ed., pp. 229–54. Ann Arbor: Center for
      Japanese Studies, University of Michigan.
Watson, Burton
  1961 *Records of the Grand Historian of China*, Vol. 2. New York: Columbia
      University Press.
Watson, William
  1971 *Cultural Frontiers in Ancient East Asia*. Edinburgh: University Press.
Wei Cuncheng
  1987 Types and Evolution of the Gaoguli [Koguryo] Stone Barrow Tombs. *Kaogu
      Xuebao* 3:321–38. (In Chinese)
Wheatley, Paul and Thomas See
  1978 *From Court to Capital*. Chicago: University of Chicago Press.
Wu En
  1985 The Bronzes of Northern China from the Late Shang Dynasty to the Early
      Western Zhou Dynasty. *Kaogu Xuebao* 2:135–56. (In Chinese)
Wu Rukang and Dong Xingren
  1985 *Homo erectus* in China. In *Paleoanthropology and Paleolithic Archaeology in
      the People's Republic of China*. R. Wu and J.W. Olsen, eds., pp. 79–90.
      Orlando: Academic Press.

Xu Yulin
  1989a A Highlight of Bronze Culture during the Shang and Zhou Dynasties.
    Liaohai Wenwu Xuehan 1989(2):63–70.
  1989b An Outline of the Neolithic Age Culture in Northeast Asia. *Liaohai Wenwu*
    Xuehan 1989(1):57–87.
Yan Wenming
  1990 China's Earliest Rice Agriculture Remains. Paper represented at the 14th
    Congress of the Indo-Pacific Prehistory Association, Yogyakarta, Indonesia.
Yang Kyung-rin
  1970 Atomic Energy Research Institute of Korea: Radiocarbon Measurements I.
    Radiocarbon 12(2):350–2.
  1972 Atomic Energy Research Institute of Korea: Radiocarbon Measurements II.
    Radiocarbon 14(2):273–9.
Yang Lien-sheng
  1952 *Money and Credit in China: A Short History*. Cambridge, MA: Harvard
    University Press.
Yasuda Yoshinori and Kim Jun-min
  1980 *History of Ecological Changes in Korea*. Tokyo.
Yi Chong-hang
  1977 On the True Nature of "Wae" in Samguk Sagi. *Korea Journal* 17(11):51–9.
Yi Kon-mu
  1989 Asan Kongpyongni Excavation. *Kogo Hakchi* 1:175–85. (In Korean)
Yi Kon-mu, Choi Jong-kyu, Pak Pang-nyong and Kim Sang-myon
  1985 Field Survey in Wolsonggun and Yongilgun. *National Museum of Korea*
    Archaeological Report 17:101–57. (In Korean)
Yi Kon-mu, Lee Yong-hun, Yun Kwang-jin and Shin Dae-gon
  1989 Excavation of the Proto-Three Kingdoms Site at Tahori, Uichang-gun. *Kogo*
    Hakchi 1:5–174. (In Korean)
Yi Kon-mu, Yi Kang-sung, Han Yong-hee, Yi Paek-kyu and Kim Chae-yol
  1980 *Jung Do I*. Report of the Research of Antiquities No. 12, National Museum
    of Korea. (In Korean)
  1981 *Jung Do II*. Report of the Research of Antiquities No. 13, National Museum
    of Korea. (In Korean)
Yi Nam-kyu
  1982 A Study of Early Iron Age Culture in South Korea. *Hanguk Kogo Hakbo*
    13:39–60. (In Korean)
  1987 Classification and Origin of the Pit Tombs in the North-Western Part of the
    Korean Peninsula. *Hanguk Kogo Hakbo* 20:59–78. (In Korean)
Yi Seon-bok
  1983 Geoarchaeology of Chon'gongni, Korea. In *Chon'gongni*. Kim W.Y. and Bae
    K.D., eds., pp. 577–85. Seoul: Munhwajae Kwalliguk. (In Korean)
  1984 Geoarchaeological Observation of Chongokni, Korea. *Korea Journal*
    24(9):4–10.
  1986 Lower and Middle Paleolithic of Northeast Asia: A Geoarchaeological Review.
    PhD Dissertation. Arizona State University, Tempe.
  1988 Korean Archaeology Since 1945 – Paleolithic. *Hanguk Kogo Hakbo* 21:25–34.
    (In Korean)
Yi Seon-bok and G.A. Clark
  1983 Observations on the Lower Palaeolithic of Northeast Asia. *Current*
    Anthropology 24(2):181–202.

1985 The "Dyuktai Culture" and New World Origins. *Current Anthropology* 26(1):1–20.

Yi Seon-bok, Lee Kyodong and Shin Jong-won
1989 Bibliography of North Korean Archaeology. *Hanguk Kogo Hakbo* 23:93–217. (In Korean)

Yi Young-mun
1987 Distribution and Style of the Dolmens in Chollanamdo Province. *Hanguk Kogo Hakbo* 20:79–112. (In Korean)
1989 *Kumsong Sansong*. Chonnam University Museum. (In Korean)

Yim Yang-jai
1977 Distribution of Forest Vegetation and Climate in the Korean Peninsula, IV. Zonal Distribution of Forest Vegetation in Relation to Thermal Climate. *Japanese Journal of Ecology* 27(4):269–78.

Yokoyama Shozaburo
1933 Report on the Tongsamdong Shell Mound, Yongdo, Pusan. *Shizengaku Zasshi* 5(4):1–49. (In Japanese)

Yongnam University Museum
1986 Silla Culture Exhibit Catalog.

Yoon Byung-yong
1986 Excavation Report on Tombs at Nopodong in Pusan. *Hanguk Kogo Hakbo* 19:129–35. (In Korean)

Yoon Dong-suk
1984 *Metallurgical Study of the Early Iron Age Artifacts Found in Korea*. Pohang Iron and Steel Co Ltd.
1986 Early Iron Metallurgy in Korea. *Bulletin of the Metals Museum* 11 (special issue):68–75. (In Korean)
1989 Early Iron Metallurgy in Korea. *Archaeological Review from Cambridge* 8(1):92–9.

Yoon Dong-suk and Lee Nam-kyu
1985a An Investigation into Some Aspects of Paekche Iron-Making Methods. In *History and Archaeology* (Proceedings of the 28th National Meeting of Korean Historians), pp. 261–7. Seoul: National History Association.
1985b A Study on Korean Ancient Iron Artifacts by CMA and EPMA. *Hanguk Kogo Hakbo* 17/18:91–106. (In Korean)

Yoon Dong-suk and Shin Kyung-hwan
1982 Metallurgical Considerations regarding the Early Iron Age Artifacts Excavated from Pit Graves throughout the Korean Peninsula. *Hanguk Kogo Hakbo* 13:97–134.

Yoon Duk-hyang
1988 A Report on the Excavation of the Dukchieri Dolmens. In *Juam Dam Report III*, pp. 75–170. Chonnam University Museum. (In Korean)

Yoon Mu-byong
1978 The Namsongni Site. *Hanguk Kogo Hakbo* 6:122–3. (In Korean)
1982 Report on the Excavation of the Walls of Paekche Fortress at Pusosan. *Hanguk Kogo Hakbo* 13:145–52. (In Korean)
1987 *A Study of Korean Bronze Age Culture*. Seoul: Ichyong Press. (In Korean)

Yoon Mu-byong and Song Ju-taik
1977 A New Type of Paekche Mountain Fortress. *Paekche Yongu* 8:9–32. (In Korean)

Yoon Nae-hyun
   1986 *Ancient Korean History: A Reinterpretation.* Seoul: Ilchisa. (In Korean)
   1987 True Understanding of Old Choson. *Korea Journal* 27(12):23–40.
Yu, Ying-shih
   1967 *Trade and Expansion in Han China.* Berkeley: University of California Press.
Yun, Mu-byong, Han Yong-hee and Jung Joon-Ki
   1990 *Hyamni Site.* Report of the Research of Antiquities of the National Museum of Korea, Vol. 22. National Museum of Korea.
Yun Se-young
   1974 Preliminary Report of the Excavations of Paekche Tombs 1 and 2 at Karakdong, Seoul. *Kogohak* 3:131–46. (In Korean)
   1980 On the Study of Old Korean Crowns and Hats – Mainly the Crowns and Hats of Three Kingdoms Period. *Hanguk Kogo Hakbo* 9:23–44. (In Korean)
Yun Yong-jin
   1981 A Study on the Korean Bronze Culture with Reference to the Artifacts Discovered at Pyongnidong, Taegu. *Hanguk Kogo Hakbo* 10/11:1–22. (In Korean)
   1984 Summary Report on Excavation of Site at Hachonni F Site, Chewon. In *Summary Report on Excavation of Cultural Sites in Submergence Area of Chungju Dam in 1983*, pp. 385–476. Chungbuk National University. (In Korean)
Zaichikov, V.T.
   1952 *Geography of Korea.* New York: International Secretariat, Institute of Pacific Relations.
Zhang, Senshui
   1985 The Early Palaeolithic of China. In *Palaeoanthropology and Palaeolithic Archaeology in the People's Republic of China.* R. Wu and J.W. Olsen, eds., pp. 147–86. Orlando: Academic Press.
Zozayong, Emille Museum
   1972 *Spirit of The Korean Tiger.* Korean Art Series, Vol. 2. Seoul.

INDEX